AMERICAN ARCHIVAL ANALYSIS:

The Recent Development of the Archival Profession in the United States

by

RICHARD J. COX

The Scarecrow Press, Inc.
Metuchen, N.J., & London
1990

The author gratefully acknowledges permission to reprint the following material:

"Professionalism and Archivists in the United States" and "American Archival Literature: Expanding Horizons and Continuing Needs, 1901-1987." Copyright ©1986, 1987, <u>American Archivist</u>. Not to be reprinted without permission.

"A Reappraisal of Municipal Records in the United States" and "Archivists and Public Historians in the United States." Copyright © 1981, 1986 by the Regents of the University of California. Reprinted from <u>Public Historian</u>, Vol. 3 (Winter), pp. 49-63, and Vol. 8 (Summer), pp. 25-41, by permission.

"Educating Archivists: Speculating on the Past, Present, and Future." <u>Journal of the American Society for Information Science</u>. Copyright ©1988 by John Wiley & Sons, Inc. Reprinted by permission of John Wiley & Sons, Inc.

British Library Cataloguing-in-Publication data available

Library of Congress Cataloguing-in-Publication Data

Cox, Richard J.
    American archival analysis : the recent development of the archival profession in the United States / by Richard J. Cox.
        p.   cm.
    Includes bibliographical references.
    ISBN 0-8108-2338-1
    1, Archivists--United States.   2. Archives--United States.
3. Archives--Study and teaching--United States.   4. United States--Archival resources.   5. Archives--Research--United States.   I. Title.
CD3021.C68   1990
020'.973--dc20   90-36213

To
Lynn and Emma,
who put up with a lot

CONTENTS

Preface   The Origins and Themes of this Book; or,   vii
             the Personal Odyssey of an Archivist

One   Our Disappearing Past: The Precarious   1
             Condition of America's Historical Records
             and the Archival Profession in the 1980s

Two   Professionalism and Archivists in the   22
             United States

Three   Laying a Foundation for Archival   53
             Leadership: The SAA Goals and Priorities
             Task Force Report

Four   Failed Opportunities: Archival Leadership   69
             and Local Government Records

Five   Archival Education in the United States: 98
             Old Concerns, But New Future?

Six   A Research Agenda for Archival   113
             Education in the United States

Seven   Archival Research and Writing: 164
             Expanding Horizons and Continuing
             Needs, 1901-1987

Eight   On the Value of Archival History in the   182
             United States

Nine   Archivists and Public Historians in the   201
             United States

Ten   Government Publications as Archives: 221
             Building A Case for Cooperation
             Between Archivists and Librarians

Eleven   Contending with the Hydra-Headed   243
             Monster: Preservation Selection of
             Enduring Information

Twelve   Analytical Bibliography and the Modern   261
             Archivist: A Commentary on Similarities,
             Differences, and Prospects for Cooperation

Thirteen   Archivists Confront a Changing World: 291
             Documentation Strategies, the

Reformulation of Archival Appraisal,
and the Possibilities of
Multi-Disciplinary Cooperation

Fourteen   Archivists and Information Policy in the   304
               United States: Looking Toward the 1990s

Fifteen   Bibliographical Essay: Essential Writings   328
               on the Archival Profession in the United
               States in the 1980s

Index   339

PREFACE THE ORIGINS AND THEMES OF
THIS BOOK; OR, THE PERSONAL
ODYSSEY OF AN ARCHIVIST

Introduction

Carl Sagan introduces Stephen Hawkings' *A Brief History of Time* with a rather unnerving statement: "We go about our daily lives understanding almost nothing of the world."[1] Prior to the 1980s, it seemed indeed that many archivists viewed things strictly from their individual and diverse repositories, limiting their potential for comprehending their own universe. They were like Ptolemy, struggling to understand the universe by placing the earth at the center, surrounding it with the spheres of the moon, the sun, the stars, and the planets, and knowing little about what was beyond that last sphere. Standing on the roof of their repository may hardly be the best place for archivists to be in order to understand their profession, professional mission, and how to meet that mission.

I believe I know something about this because I stood exactly in that position for a number of years. When I first started work as an archivist in the early 1970s I had little appreciation of that work, and viewed myself more as a local historian defined by the historical society in which I happened to commence my career (although, honestly, I didn't even look at it much as a career then). As I will recount below, my conception both of myself as an archivist and the archival community changed over time. The essays in this book have been part of my effort to understand more about the fundamental nature of the archival profession, its roles in the information professions and society, and where that profession needs to be going in order to meet its important and unique mission of documenting society. The essays in this book are also semi-autobiographical, in that they are not an effort to present a comprehensive portrait of the archival profession in the 1980s, but rather one archivist's view of his profession in recent times and his hopes for that profession for the future.

Personal Notes

The derivation of my interest in archives rests with my own

---

[1](New York: Bantam Books, 1988), ix.

development of curiosity about the past. This historical curiosity was first awakened when I travelled with my family to Williamsburg, Virginia in 1957 and, for whatever reason, became interested in knowing more about the past. For the remainder of my adolescence I read historical studies and also became fascinated with the Civil War as this nation celebrated its centennial in the first half of the 1960s. When I entered college in 1968 it was a foregone conclusion that I would declare myself to be a history major.

None of this explains, however, how I happened to start work as an archivist. There were no career brochures describing the glories of such an occupation (there still aren't), recruiters coming to campus, or even faculty knowledgeable about such vocations. In fact, I remember vividly my first meeting with my history department advisor. He asked me if I was concerned about employment after graduation. When I said of course that I was, he somewhat acidly remarked that I should consider another major field of study. I stuck with my interest, resigned that I probably would develop a keener sense of historical research and writing to prepare me for a lifetime avocation, while I labored in a bank or department store.

All of this changed within the first year after graduation. I had entered a master's of theological studies program in order to prepare for later graduate study in American religious history, a topic that I became interested in as an undergraduate. I soon felt uncomfortable in the seminary, however, and packed up my bags and headed back home to Baltimore. I wrote to the wife of one of my undergraduate history professors who worked as a manuscripts curator in a local historical society inquiring about any history-related positions in her organization or in the Baltimore area. This was, as I remember, a long-shot, and I had already resolved myself to be doing something completely unrelated to my interests, while I prepared myself to apply to graduate history programs for the next year. To my surprise, a position in preparing a microfilm edition of a manuscript collection at the Maryland Historical Society had just opened unexpectedly due to a premature resignation. Because the society was in a lurch, and I was something of a known quantity, a match was made. Several days after Christmas 1972 I started work, considering myself as probably the most ignorant and inexperienced archivist in North America. Years later, I discovered that many of my peers had started their careers in a very similar fashion.

The position that I took in 1972 was to last only a year, a circumstance that bothered me not in the least since my plans were clearly to be heading back into graduate historical study. But two developments changed this. First, an opportunity occurred a year later, because of two staff resignations, to take over the position of curator of manuscripts at the historical society. Second, I found myself becoming more interested in the nature of archival work. This early interest was mainly propelled by a fascination with how manuscripts were acquired and used for research, a concern that derived from the first project I worked on and that led to my first published professional article.[2] Despite all this, however, I still perceived myself to be a local historian working as a manuscripts curator and even had a notion that I might be in this or a similar position for a lifetime.

I have no intention of describing in great detail all the subsequent changes that my attitude toward the archival field went through, but I do need to summarize them to some extent because these attitudinal changes represent a primary part of the genesis of the essays in this volume.

As I have already mentioned, for the initial part of my career I was mainly aware of myself as an historian. This gradually changed as I attended professional archival meetings and as I systematically read the archival literature. During this phase, I also completed a master's in history at the University of Maryland which surprisingly contributed to this re-focusing of my notion of archival work because of a relationship with the late Walter Rundell; Rundell ably wore many hats, including those of a historian of the American West, an officer and later President of the Society of American Archivists, and a policy maker for federal historical activities. By the time I finished my master's in 1978 I had a better grounding in historical method and archival practice, although I must candidly admit that I lacked a sense of the *changing* nature of the archival community.

Several events in my life led me to become more perceptive of the present nature of the American archival profession. Starting in 1978 I began attending regularly the annual meetings of the Society of American Archivists. This not only introduced me to many of the leaders, thinkers, and activists in that organization, but made me more aware of the primary issues, controversies, and topics of discussion that had captivated archivists. Basic concepts and practices were being challenged, and issues of professional competence and image were emerging as vital concerns. The year 1978 was also a

---

[2]"A History of the Calvert Papers, MS. 174," *Maryland Historical Magazine* 68 (Fall 1973), 309-22.

turning point for me because I changed positions, moving from the calmer, more placid environment of the historical society to the political, bureaucratic challenges of administering both a municipal archives and current records management program. This career move, in combination with an increased involvement in the archival profession, stretched my own conception of what an archivist does and the limitations, weaknesses, strengths, and future prospects of archival work in this country.

These changes are readily obvious to me, not only because of the benefit of a 20-20 hindsight, but because of the changes in my writings that I can look back on. Prior to 1979, my writings were equally divided between local history, archival history, and genealogical and local history guides. In 1979, I was moved to write my first article that addressed some national concerns, even though it focused on Baltimore.[3] Within a couple of years, the majority of my writing came to focus on such broader issues, buttressed by my evaluation in 1983 of the first round of state historical records assessment and reporting projects sponsored by the National Historical Publications and Records Commission, service on one of the working committees of the Society of American Archivists' Goals and Priorities Task Force, service on SAA's Committee on Education and Professional Development, direction of the state historical records assessment and reporting project in Alabama, and, finally but not least, election to a three-year term on SAA's governing council. By 1985, when I applied for and received one of the Bentley Historical Library's fellowships for research on modern documentation and the archival profession, I had become firmly convinced of the need to study the archival profession and to advocate for change in certain basic assumptions, principles, and practices that archivists held about themselves and their work. The essays in this volume represent ten years of thinking about the archival profession in the United States, that thinking modified by discussions with many archivists and other professionals. Still, I consider this only a preliminary volume; I have already commenced work on another set of essays that re-examine archivists' basic consensus and understanding about the nature of archival institutions and education.[4]

---

[3]"The Plight of American Municipal Archives: Baltimore, 1729-1979," *American Archivist* 42 (July 1979), 281-92.

[4]For an idea of my focus, refer to "What Are the Goals for the Archival Profession? Views of a Former Council Member," Society of American Archivists *Newsletter*, November 1989, 16-18.

The Essays

A valued colleague once said to me after reading a draft of one of my essays on an archival topic that I was "stuck in a rut." Another said to me that every time he read one of my essays he felt that there were really about four essays trying to break out of the one. Some individuals may discover such feelings as they read this volume. They do represent a rut in the sense that I believe that archivists must work much harder to strengthen their profession through individual certification, institutional accreditation, accreditation of graduate education programs, and more precise standards, to name a few of the more essential and noteworthy potential activities. These essays also are somewhat repetitive because they concern a core group of basic themes - the archival mission, the archival community as profession, a basic core of knowledge, relationships with the information and historical professions, and an agenda for change. The nature of these essays is also partly dictated by the result of the majority of them being written for specific occasions and over a period of time; some key changes have been made to transform these essays into a book about the recent development of the archival profession, all of them somehow linked by Bruce Dearstyne's timely and lucid depiction of the 1980s as the "Age of Archival Analysis."[5] For me, as well, these essays represent a body of thought that I hope to build on for additional research about the archival profession and its work, but which I also hope is worth sharing with the archival profession and historical and information professions.

The first essay in this volume, "Our Disappearing Past," is an expanded version of an essay that was originally written for the Organization of American Historians' *Newsletter*. It was composed for this vehicle because of that organization's growing interest in archival administration, especially through the more recent public history movement which seeks to encompass archival work. "Our Disappearing Past" was included first in this volume because it introduces many of the themes and recommendations that are explored in greater detail in the essays that follow it.

---

[5]The phrase comes from his introduction to the special Summer 1986 issue of *The Public Historian* on archives and public history. Dearstyne wrote that "this is a time of change and excitement in archives . . . . This new feeling is perhaps most apparent in the earnest interest, amounting almost to a preoccupation, in self-study. Indeed, the past few years may someday be known as the Age of Archival Analysis" (pp. 6-7).

The second essay, "Professionalism and Archivists in the United States," was originally published in the *American Archivist* and is the initial article of seven in this book that focus on fundamental aspects of the archival community as profession. It was written as part of my 1985 summer fellowship at the Bentley Historical Library, and it is an effort primarily to identify key aspects, drawing on sociological and historical notions of professions, of the archival profession that need re-structuring or strengthening. It is an essay that I continually refer back to when meditating on the archival community as profession. Many of the ideas discussed in this volume are threads running out of this single essay.

"Laying a Foundation for Archival Leadership" was an advocacy piece written to provoke serious consideration of SAA's report from its Goals and Priorities Task Force. It has been updated to include actions and accomplishments that have occurred during the past years, and is included to make a point about the continued need for national archival planning. It was originally published in *Provenance*, the journal of the Society of Georgia Archivists.

Chapter four on local government records is a composite essay drawn from three previously published essays in the *Public Historian*, *Documenting America: Assessing the Condition of Historical Records in the States*, edited by Lisa B. Weber and published in 1984, and the *Midwestern Archivist*, the journal of the Midwest Archives Conference. This essay is a case study of the need for more energetic archival leadership, standards, and other actions. It also represents an area of personal interest and experience, as well as an aspect of important documentation that archivists have had a difficult time contending with throughout this century.

The two essays on archival education concern an aspect of archival administration that is crucial to the well-being of the archival profession's future, and an area that is undergoing rapid change. The first of these two essays, summarizing past trends and predicting future directions for archival education, was written for a special issue of the *Journal of the American Society for Information Science* on education for the information professions, later expanded for presentation at the 1988 annual meeting of the Association des archivistes du Québec, and subsequently published in that association's journal, *Archives*. The other essay on a research agenda has been unpublished until now, and represents my new duties as a faculty member in a library and information science school and work on a doctorate in library science. It tries to identify an agenda of empirical research needed to develop the kinds of graduate, continuing, and in-service archival education programs required by the profession. This essay uses the research that ha's been done on library science education as a starting point for identifying similar kinds of potential research in the archival profession.

The next essay on "Archival Research and Writing" was originally presented at the 50th anniversary meeting of the Society of American Archivists and published in its journal, *The American Archivist.* This article concerns the need for developing a sound archival knowledge that can guide the profession's work and help it succeed in its mission. Its historical emphasis represents the theme of the milestone SAA meeting.

The following essay also relates to improvement in archival research by attempting to make a case for the validity of conducting research into the profession's past. This essay, first published in the journal *Libraries & Culture,* reflects personal interests and strives to show that archivists' concern for documenting society for society's benefit even extends to their own institutions and profession.

The next group of chapters, nine through thirteen, concern archivists' relationships to other professionals. Chapter nine on the relationship between archivists and public historians was written for a special issue of *The Public Historian,* and tries to present the issues, benefits, and caveats for archivists about the emergence of public historians as a part of the larger historical profession. "Government Publications as Archives," "Contending with the Hydra-Headed Monster," and "Analytical Bibliography and the Modern Archivist" are all efforts to demonstrate how archivists fit, or don't fit, into the information professions. The essay on government publications was first published in the *Journal of Library Administration.* The essay on the implications of archival appraisal for library preservation selection was co-authored by my wife, Lynn, and initially appeared in *Re-Thinking the Library in the Information Age: Issues in Library Research; Proposals for the 1990s* (Washington, D.C., 1988). The final essay in this group is a new piece written in an effort to connect the tracks of rare books librarianship and archival administration being developed in the School of Library and Information Science at the University of Pittsburgh.

"Archivists Confront a Changing World" is an effort to show how the archival profession needs to work with, as well as use the principles of, other professionals that are concerned with selecting information sources for continuing use. This essay, previously unpublished and presented at the 1989 meeting of the Rare Books and Manuscripts Section of the American Library Association, also demonstrates the needed multidisciplinary nature of archival practice and principles.

Chapter fourteen, "Archivists and Information Policy in the United States," is an effort to summarize many of the themes, issues, recommendations, and opinions expressed throughout the book by stressing the need to develop a coherent agenda that is aggressively promoted by the archival community in Washington, D. C., the state capitals, and wherever else such advocacy is needed. I had, at one point, contemplated writing an essay that predicts what the archival profession and archival institutions might look like in the future, but abandoned that as the topic for another book *and* because I sense that the archival profession's future lies wherever it wants it to be.

Acknowledgments

Many people have had an influence on the contents of this book or have provided encouragement to me through the years in my writings. The bibliographical essay that concludes the book mentions many of these individual's own writings. But I would like to list some of the key individuals, in alphabetical order, that have had some influence on my work: David Bearman, Ed Bridges, Paul Conway, Bruce Dearstyne, Tim Ericson, Larry Hackman, Avra Michelson,   James O'Toole, Helen W. Samuels, and Julia Marks Young. Some of these essays have also been influenced more recently by my new colleagues at the School of Library and Information Science, University of Pittsburgh: R. Stephen Almagno, Toni Carbo Bearman, Ellen Gay Detlefsen, and Margaret Mary Kimmel. A special thanks goes to my wife, Lynn, who not only put up with all this but who co-authored one of the essays contained in this book, and to the administrative staff of the Department of Library Science (Christine Bishop, Grace Duncan, Marcy Livingston, and Corinne Sanford) who all had a hand in helping to get this book published.   None of these people deserve any of the blame for what is in this book, but have certainly influenced its better parts.

Thanks is also extended to the many publishers who first printed these essays and granted permission for reprinting: John Wiley & Sons, Inc. for use of the essay in the *Journal of the American Society for Information Science*; Haworth Press, Inc. for use of the article in the *Journal of Library Administration*; the Society of Georgia Archivists for use of the *Provenance* essay; University of Texas Press for use of the essay originally featured in *Libraries and Culture*; Society of American Archivists for the articles in the *American Archivist*; University of California Press for the article in the *Public*

Historian; and the Midwest Archives Conference for the article in the *Midwestern Archivist*.

Richard J. Cox
School of Library and Information Science
University of Pittsburgh
December 1989

ONE   OUR DISAPPEARING PAST: THE PRECARIOUS CONDITION OF AMERICA'S HISTORICAL RECORDS AND THE ARCHIVAL PROFESSION IN THE 1980s[1]

History, Humanity, and Historical Records

Knowledge of the past is important to any society and its inhabitants. Many reasons have been given for knowing about individual and collective history. It helps people understand the present and guides them into the future. It satisfies a basic human need to comprehend something of a person's origins and to be able to place oneself in the universe. It is a means of gaining access to a greater wealth of experience than any single human being could gain on his or her own. It can help a person grapple with the present immense societal changes popularized in best-selling publications like Alvin Toffler's *The Third Wave* and John Naisbitt's *Megatrends*. If nothing else, however, historical knowledge makes us more human. Eminent historian Henry Steele Commager once brushed aside the practical purposes of historical study and concluded that it is really useful "in the sense that art and music, poetry and flowers, religion and philosophy are useful. Without it - as without these - life would be poorer and meaner; without it we should be denied some of those intellectual and moral experiences which give meaning and richness to life."[2] More recently Gerda Lerner, in her presidential address to the Organization of American Historians, sought to capture the same "essentiality" and "humanness of history." "The desire of men and women to survive their own death has been the single most important force compelling them to preserve and record the past." She continued that "history is the means whereby we assert the continuity of human life - its creation is one of the earliest humanizing activities of *homo sapiens*."[3]

---

[1]This is an expanded version of an essay originally published in the Organization of American Historians' *Newsletter* 15 (February 1987), 8-9.

[2]*The Nature and the Study of History* (New York: Charles E. Merrill Books, Inc., 1965), 73.

[3]"The Necessity of History and the Professional Historian," *Journal of American History* 69 (June 1982), 9-10.

An understanding of history is not just important to the quality of life but possesses numerous practical, even if sometimes mundane, uses for individuals, communities, and nations. Historical records, the means by which we study the past, are often essential protection of legal rights, crucial to the understanding of past trends and prediction of future developments, valuable for educational purposes, necessary for the resolution of such present issues as the protection of the environment and health care, and significant as illustrations of the impact of public policy decisions. In an important evaluation of the condition of historical records in the Empire State, the New York State Historical Records Advisory Board succinctly summed up the significance of historical records: "They provide the basis for understanding where we have been, they orient us to our present, and they provide guidance for our progress into the future."[4] If history is important to a society, then historical records are equally as significant.

Without historical records - whether written, printed, or computer-generated - there is, of course, little chance for comprehending the past because there is little way of knowing it. Oral tradition or historical artifacts are valuable but incomplete means to get into the past without accompanying documentary evidence; the reverse is true as well, that historical records are often insufficient means to comprehend fully the development of our society.[5] But should Americans be worried about such a problem? The United States is steeped in tradition, supporting a landscape covered with museums, historical societies, monuments, libraries, historic houses and sites, and historical records repositories. There is a seemingly endless variety of institutions and individuals in this country dedicated to the preservation of cultural collections, including historical records. Yet, America faces the specter of a disappearing past because it is failing, and doing so badly, to care for its historical records. The millions of documents from the colonial period and the nineteenth century housed in repositories are deteriorating. The essential records of the twentieth century, especially after the Second World War, are being lost in the gigantic mass of contemporary documents and in the elusive maze of modern information technology. If a

---

[4]*Toward A Usable Past: Historical Records in the Empire State* ([Albany]: New York State Historical Records Advisory Board, January 1984), 19.

[5]See chapter thirteen in this volume for additional views on this important matter.

knowledge of the past is important to a society, America is on the brink of a national tragedy. Its past is disappearing, its memory is fading. How has this happened in the United States in the 1980s?

Americans were not the first to be concerned with records possessing enduring value. It seems that mankind has nearly always exhibited a desire to preserve some information captured in records whether for reasons of governmental operation, an interest in what transpired before, or a desire to perpetuate societal traditions. In the ancient world important clay tablets were enclosed in clay envelopes for additional protection, a practice that is described in Jeremiah 32 in the Bible.[6] Even hundreds of years before Christ, many ancient societies had established official repositories for the safe keeping of essential government records.[7] In late medieval Europe, when paper was first being introduced, many royal decrees were issued that forbade its use out of fear that paper was not a permanent medium for the recording of important and vital information. During the Renaissance, when many monastic orders ceased or were threatened, a number of individuals endeavored to collect the irreplaceable manuscripts of the scriptoriums or petitioned for the creation of national libraries to achieve this purpose.[8] Even when the first European settlers in America struggled for their very survival, a few fashioned time to write down their experiences, compose histories, and preserve their papers. Nearly always among the earliest legislative acts of the colonial assemblies or decrees by colonial proprietors and royal governors were regulations governing the preservation of records.[9] It is almost as if it

---

[6]"Take these deeds, both this sealed deed of purchase and this open deed, and put them in an earthenware vessel, that they may last for a long time." Jeremiah 32:14 (RSV).

[7]Ernst Posner, *Archives in the Ancient World* (Cambridge: Harvard University Press, 1972).

[8]A good introduction to such activities is Lucien Febvre and Henri-Jean Martin, *The Coming of the Book: The Impact of Printing 1450-1800* (London: Verso Editions, 1976).

[9]Prime examples of early settlers endeavoring to preserve their papers and history are William Bradford and John Winthrop; see Alan B. Howard, "Art and History in Bradford's *Of Plymouth Plantation*," *William and Mary Quarterly*, 3rd series, 28 (April 1971), 237-66 and Richard S. Dunn, "John Winthrop Writes His Journal," *ibid.*, 3rd series, 41 (April 1984), 185-212. For example of legislated efforts to manage early public records see H. G. Jones, *For History's Sake: The Preservation and Publication of North*

were a part of mankind's psyche, transcending culture and era, to desire to preserve something of the past and protect information important to the present and future well-being of society. Unfortunately, the desire does not always result in effective actions to ensure the maintenance of mankind's documentary heritage.

Assessing the Condition of Historical Records in the United States

If it is true that man's inner self yearns to know the past, then something is definitely amiss in modern America. Over the last few years professional archivists and allied colleagues such as historians have engaged in an extensive and intensive series of evaluations of their own work in preserving historical records. Starting in 1982 and extending into the late 1980s, with funding from the National Historical Publications and Records Commission (NHPRC), a granting arm of the National Archives, over forty states assessed the condition of historical records programs and proposed plans for the better management and preservation of historical documents. These projects, the most in-depth analysis of historical records programs ever undertaken in this country, were coordinated by historical records advisory boards in every state consisting of archivists, librarians, and researchers. Nearly every board concluded that the care of historical records is abysmal and growing worse. Supplementing this important national survey, partly summarized in a 1984 publication of the NHPRC and the National Association of State Archives and Records Administrators (NASARA),[10] are three other reports released in the 1980s. The Society of American Archivists (SAA) published a report by its Goals and Priorities Task Force that laid out an agenda for change and improvement in the archival profession's ability to identify and preserve historical records. Also issued was the report by the Committee on the Records of Government, supported by the American Council of Learned Societies, the Social Science Research Council, and the Council on Library Resources with funds from the Andrew Mellon Foundation, that evaluated the condition of American public records. The final study, issued in two parts, was the

Carolina History 1663-1903 (Chapel Hill: University of North Carolina Press, 1966), chapters one and two, and Richard J. Cox, "Public Records in Colonial Maryland," *American Archivist* 37 (April 1974): 263-75.

[10]This organization subsequently changed its name to the National Association of Government Archives and Records Administrators (NAGARA).

American Association for State and Local History's (AASLH) profile of the "state and local history field," a major part of which is responsible for the administration of this country's historical records. All of these reports provided convincing proof that modern America is not caring as well as it could for its documentary heritage.

A fitting place to begin a review of the present condition of America's historical records is the 1984 report, *Documenting America: Assessing the Condition of Historical Records in the States*, issued jointly by the NASARA and the NHPRC.[11] This brief volume of slightly more than seventy pages contains four essays on the major elements of America's historical records programs. Each essay was marked by pessimism and considerable concern, attitudes reflected by the various state reports themselves even after careful study and evaluation of the historical records and the programs that care for them. Organizations responsible for the administration and preservation of state government records are pictured as weakened by inadequate legislative support and resources that are less than meager. These state archives, long in the forefront of the development of the archival profession in the United States, are seen as "trapped in the cycle of poverty"; "the picture of public records programs is one of inadequate resources which prevent state archives from mounting effective programs, while the lack of effective programs renders the archives vulnerable to disregard by departmental administrators and state budget officials."[12] The historical records of the local governments are in even greater disarray, with few of the political subdivisions even interested in the care of what are among the most important documents, containing invaluable information on families, neighborhoods, communities, towns, counties, and cities. One can find little improvement in the private historical institutions, caught in a "prevailing pattern . . . in which the majority of historical records repositories are barely capable of providing even the most rudimentary and

---

[11]Lisa B. Weber, ed., *Documenting America: Assessing the Condition of Historical Records in the States* ([Albany]: National Association of State Archives and Records Administrators and the National Historical Publications and Records Commission, [1984]). This is the publication of the proceedings of a conference held in Atlanta, Georgia on June 24-25, 1983. Four consultants summarized and evaluated the state reports in the areas of state government records (Edwin C. Bridges), local government records (Richard J. Cox), historical records repositories (William L. Joyce), and statewide functions and services (Margaret Child).

[12]Bridges, *Documenting America*, 8.

basic maintenance of their holdings." Again there is the image of a cycle of poverty:

> In a culture often described as ahistorical and rootless, there is a limited public appreciation of history and the usefulness of historical records. Lack of public understanding and regard leads to under-funding of historical records repositories and under-utilization of their holdings. This process has a circular effect in that low use perpetuates low funding which prevents repositories from upgrading the management of their collections which might in turn increase their use.[13]

The essayists in *Documenting America* were not pessimistic archival doomsayers, although they have been characterized that way by some of their colleagues. The evidence is on the side of these essayists that our documentary heritage is, indeed, in very serious trouble. To reveal this, it is possible to step slightly away from archival institutions for a broader view. Close to the same time as publication of *Documenting America*, the AASLH issued two detailed surveys on the state of American historical agencies and museums that included public and private archival institutions.[14] Again the image of poverty abounded through the pages of these reports despite the remarkable growth in the quantity of such historical programs (a doubling just since 1962). Surely such growth must mean some public support, but consider some of the conclusions by the AASLH:

> Ours is a poverty-ridden field supporting a growing number of professionals.
>
> Historical agencies and museums are trying to preserve history on a shoestring, and "professionalism" sounds to them expensive . . . .
>
> For 20 years, AASLH and other organizations have preached professionalism to those who would collect, preserve, and interpret our country's history. Now a

---

[13]Joyce, *Documenting America*, 39.

[14]Charles Phillips and Patricia Hogan, *The Wages of History: The AASLH Employment Trends and Salary Survey* (Nashville: AASLH, 1984) and *A Culture at Risk: Who Cares for America's Heritage?* (Nashville: AASLH, 1984).

full-fledged, young profession is in place. The question is, can we afford it?[15]

It is these institutions that are responsible for this country's historical records and, given their resources, the condition of America's documentary heritage can only be described as precarious.

The report of the Committee on the Records of Government also highlighted the poor legacy of the care of America's historical records. Not only did this committee consider the views and opinions of leading archivists and historians but those of prominent public policy-makers such as Philip W. Buchen, Joseph A. Califano, and Elliot Richardson. Their conclusions echoed those reports already cited. Despite the fact that the "creation and preservation of government records is important for everyone," the report provided a litany of failures in the mission supporting this important fact. Professional archivists and records managers are not properly placed within government to administer records. The rapid growth of government has made its functions much more complex and difficult to document. The use of electronic technology for records creation has outstripped our present capacity to preserve the essential information in such systems. Traditional paper records are "haphazardly" stored in governments at all levels, costing over a third of a billion dollars annually. If it is true, as this report contends, that government archives "contribute to a sense of community, a national consciousness and understanding of our society and culture," then all Americans have considerable reason for alarm.[16]

After reading to this point one might wonder what archivists, those professionals charged with preserving America's historical records, have been doing for the past half-century since the formation of their national association? As *Planning for the Archival Profession: A Report of the Society of American Archivists Task Force on Goals and Priorities* revealed, archivists are very aware of and anxious about the immense problems challenging the preservation of our historical

[15]*The Wages of History*, 9, 26, 76.

[16]*Committee on the Records of Government: Report* (Washington, D.C.: The Committee, March 1985).

records.[17] The main recommendation of this report was for the
creation of a planning group, established in 1986 by the SAA,
that provides a steady national focus on the issue of the
preservation and management of America's documentary
heritage as well as creating an agenda of priorities for action.
Some of the primary assumptions of this task force reveal the
reasons for the poor condition of our nation's historical sources:
insufficient public support for archival work; a legacy of failure
by archivists to plan better use of their very limited resources;
and the tendency of archival institutions to labor in isolation.
These assumptions - plus a lengthy assemblage of objectives,
strategies, and activities in the identification of historical
records, archival administration, and access to documents -
tend to overwhelm anyone with the sense of the immense work
lying *ahead*. Although for years archivists have been prone to
write optimistic and rosy assessments of their work, there has
been a growing consensus in the past decade that the most
important efforts are yet to be made.   This is a distinct
characteristic of the American archival profession of the 1980s.

Why America's Historical Records Are in Jeopardy

Knowing that America's historical records are endangered is
only half the battle. In order to improve the preservation and
management of the documentary heritage there must be better
understanding of why these records have been allowed to get
in this condition. Although there have been many *descriptions*
of the condition of our historical records, there have been few
serious *analyses* and *explanations* for this condition.   What
follows is only a recapitulation of a few themes that have
consistently surfaced in the recent reports on historical records
in the United States, but even this might provide a framework
for further study and discussion.   The subsequent essays in
this volume attempt to grapple with some of the more
prominent issues raised by the reports of the 1980s regarding
the management of America's documentary heritage.
The most difficult aspect to understand about the
preservation of historical records in the United States is that
there is a continuous threat to their protection *despite* a rapid
growth of historical organizations dedicated to this cause. The
sanguine statement by Gerald George, former Executive
Director of the AASLH, regarding the quantitative growth of
historical associations that this shows "there is at least

---

[17](Chicago: SAA, 1986). For my fuller views on this report see chapter
three of this volume.

something to the cliche-encrusted argument that people in a society characterized by rapid change and various forms of dislocation feel the need of roots, of group pride, of social identity,"[18] is, in fact, only half the story. What George has missed is the essential paradoxical nature of American society first best described by Michael Kammen in *People of Paradox: An Inquiry Concerning the Origins of American Civilization*[19] and since captured in other more recent studies such as David E. Shi, *The Simple Life: Plain Living and High Thinking in American Culture.*[20] Kammen noted that "Americans have managed to be both puritanical and hedonistic, idealistic and materialistic, conformist and individualist, consensus-minded and conflict-prone."[21] To this one could easily add "history-minded and present-minded." Indeed, a recent president of the Society of American Archivists, grasped precisely this paradox. David B. Gracy, former Texas State Archivist, lamented that "the most perplexing paradox must be the fact that the public values records but not keepers of records." Speaking of the contradiction surrounding archivists' work in America, Gracy went on to say that

> We [archivists] work to save, in an age that prizes disposability and impermanence. We build research collections that the patron uses by reading, in an age that prizes information presented in video form. We work for, or at least are identified with, history, in a fast-paced age focused on the present and the future.[22]

It is no wonder that archivists and others endeavoring to preserve the remnants of the past have such insufficient resources or that some of these professionals view the proliferation of additional programs and institutions as a strain on limited resources already stretched too thin. Archivists, historians, and others dedicated to the preservation of historical documents are swimming against a very strong tide of sentiment that does not support this work.

---

[18]American Historical Association *Perspectives* 23 (March 1985), 9.

[19](New York: Alfred A. Knopf, 1973).

[20](New York: Oxford University Press, 1985).

[21]*People of Paradox*, 290.

[22]"Our Future is Now," *American Archivist* 48 (Winter 1985), 15-16.

The poverty of the archival profession has been, of course, a major cause of the failure to preserve and manage adequately America's documentary heritage. David Gracy, focusing on the societal image of the archivist, ended crest-fallen with the notion that "archival service to society . . . has fallen to its saddest condition since modern archival institutions took root in this country fifty years ago with the founding of our National Archives."[23]   Although there are some who might argue with such a conclusion, it is incontrovertible that this profession is incapable of preserving all of the nation's historical records and is now overmatched in its efforts to document adequately a fast-paced and ever changing modern environment, unless the archival profession transforms some of its basic practices. And this is not just an impoverished state brought on by inadequate funding but the result of weak professional standards, a lack of stringent educational criteria, and poor research and development capabilities. Even though there are notable improvements in recent years in all of these areas, the continuing weaknesses strike at the very heart of the elements that constitute a profession. Although in the remaining pages of this essay I go somewhat beyond this issue, the essays that follow in this volume all focus on the archivist as professional.   There are additional topics that could be explored in greater detail, some of which are mentioned below, but the nature and condition of archival professionalism is paramount in importance for the successful safeguarding of the documentary heritage.

On the surface the American archival profession seems to be thriving.   The membership of the SAA, the main professional archival association, has more than doubled over the past decade, and there seems to be, unlike academic historians and other scholars, a fairly steady employment demand for archivists in a wide variety of institutions and organizations. Added to this apparent sign of vitality is the remarkable recent growth of archival publications on standards and practices. A brief bibliography of basic works on archival administration published in 1980, had over ninety percent of its total   citations   products   of   1970   and   after;   a   similar bibliography compiled in 1989 had a very large portion of its publications released since 1980.[24]   But a closer look at the

---

[23]"Our Future is Now," 13.

[24]Richard J. Cox, *An Annotated Bibliography of Basic Readings on Archives and Manuscripts* (Nashville: American Association for State and Local History, 1980); Cox, *An Annotated Bibliography of Basic Readings on*

majority of this literature reveals it is more a result of describing archival practice rather than promulgating archival theory.[25] Although there is increasing acceptance of basic archival practices, a trend that many archivists see as a tremendous advancement, there has been less emphasis placed upon developing theory that supports such basic archival work and the development of new methods of dealing with the preservation and management of historical records. Indicative of this is that a recent major work on American archival theory could concentrate only upon the arranging and describing (cataloging) of historical records, lamenting that the ability to determine what constitutes a record having historical value had been virtually ignored by the professional literature.[26] Archivists have made great strides in being able to describe historical records, an easy goal to reach in comparison to some of the other challenges before them.

Such problems facing the archival profession are the result of improper educational standards and a nearly complete lack of research and development resources.[27] The archival profession gradually emerged from the historical profession between 1900 and 1940, but has maintained an extremely close alliance with its historian colleagues. There are many individuals working in archival positions that consider themselves historians, and this identity crisis is reflected in and perpetuated by the educational system for the training of archivists. There is no single graduate program in the United States in archival administration. Archivists come from traditional history programs, library schools, and the newer applied or public history programs receiving a wide variety of instruction. In fact, most archivists laboring in the United States probably know what they know from on-the-job experience. No wonder Frank Burke, former Executive Director

---

Archives and Manuscripts Administration (Nashville: American Association for State and Local History, 1989).

[25]See chapter seven in this volume for a fuller presentation of my views on archival literature.

[26]Richard C. Berner, *Archival Theory and Practice in the United States: A Historical Analysis* (Seattle: University of Washington Press, 1983). However, increasing attention has been devoted to this issue in the last few years; see the chapters eleven and thirteen in this volume for a discussion of these developments.

[27]See chapters five and six in this volume for discussion of the nature and role of education to the archival profession.

of NHPRC, has worried that archival education programs are "producing a large corps of parish priests when no has bothered to devise a theology under whose standard they can act,"[28] and Richard Berner, a prolific archival writer, has complained that "too few [archivists] have raised themselves above narrow mastery of mere technique borrowed from myriad institutional settings."[29] Advancements in the theory of archival administration must move at a snail's pace under such circumstances.

The weakness of archival education programs also has severely handicapped this profession's ability to conduct research in problematic and challenging areas and to develop new and improved solutions. Most archivists work in institutions in which they are so harried with pressing daily responsibilities of cataloguing and servicing collections for their various publics as to have very little time left to think through broader issues. Some archivists even think so little time has been spent on the more wide-ranging matters that they have dug themselves too deeply into a trap of limited resources and too much work to ever be able to escape. Because the existing educational programs are so tied to such practical labor, there has been only spotty development in more theoretical issues like archival cooperation, records appraisal, and similar concerns that would help archivists break out of this dilemma. Archivists have even displayed a kind of desperate pride in their predicament by referring to these single person programs as "lone-arrangers" while librarians, with more stringent professional standards, have moved to emphasize a distinction between professional duties such as planning and management and "para-professional" work such as cataloguing and other tasks. Indeed, one librarian, in evaluating the recent state assessment projects mentioned earlier, was concerned by the basic "tunnel vision" of archivists to "not only . . . go it alone but to reinvent the wheel wherever and whenever possible." "At times," this individual went on, "the American archival profession seems to resemble nothing so much as Sisyphus endlessly rolling his rock up the mountainside."[30] Unfortunately, the immense challenges of preserving and managing the documentary heritage require tremendous

[28]"The Future Course of Archival Theory in the United States," *American Archivist* 44 (Winter 1981), 45.

[29]*Archival Theory and Practice*, 5, 119.

[30]Child, *Documenting America*, 47, 52.

innovation and creativity that archivists may not have (or at least think they don't) the time for. This has to change.

Although there have been some recent breakthroughs in archivists' capacity to support better research and development that is essential to their work, most notably the Bentley Historical Library's Research Fellowship Program for the Study of Modern Archives supported by the Andrew W. Mellon Foundation and other funding sources, such positive strides forward have been somewhat checked by the lack of coordination and cooperation between the various professions most interested in the improved management of historical records. Anna Nelson, an historian and one of the chief architects of the report of the Committee on the Records of Government, has written elsewhere that the divisions within the community interested in the preservation of historical sources -- in her categorization the academics, amateurs, and archivists -- has weakened the possibilities of achieving an important goal, "to seek national support from the society and government whose documents we so carefully preserve, whose history we record and analyze, whose culture we proudly exhibit."[31]   Nelson's   conclusion   is   a   masterpiece   of understatement. Everywhere one goes the various segments of this historical community grapple for the few crusts of bread that America has seen fit to throw its way. Records managers and archivists see themselves as separate professions despite the fact that if they do not work together the chances of identifying and preserving historical documents are considerably lessened. One Canadian archivist's conclusion that the "ethos of the [archivist and records manager] are antithetical: the records manager seeks to destroy, the archivist to preserve" is abysmally inaccurate but is an opinion widely shared.[32] Archivists also have been critical of the recent emergence of applied or public historians, missing the potential value of that discipline in achieving the better management of the documentary heritage. Characterizing applied or public history as a "fad" or as only a "cynical" effort to combat the "declining fortunes of academe," as some have done,[33] is simply wrong.

[31]"In Support of History," American Historical Association *Perspectives* 22 (March 1984), 15.

[32]George Bolotenko, "Archivists and Historians: Keepers of the Well," *Archivaria* 16 (Summer 1983), 21.

[33]David A. Clary, "Trouble is My Business: A Private View of 'Public' History," *American Archivist* 44 (Spring 1981), 106.   For the potential value of the public history perspective, see chapter nine in this volume.

Public historians, because of a strong commitment to the value of history for the public and in policy-making, bring a wide range of interests and skills that archivists share or could use. Many archivists and academic historians distort the differences between their professions to be insurmountable or indecipherable, minimizing the possibilities of necessary cooperation. Even the relationship between archivists and autograph collectors at times has deteriorated to that of feuding siblings. The private collector's rich legacy of assisting in documentary publications and the establishment of historical societies and public archives has been forgotten in the wake of replevin actions or threats by public archivists to regain every stray public document regardless of value.[34] Such a scattered and disorganized historical community will not help preserve the historical records in this country.

Even if the public strongly sustained the care of this nation's historical records, the archival profession was in better shape, and the historical community unified and strong, America's historical documents would still remain in a precarious condition because of the self-destructing nature of all recording media. Every material on which information can be captured contains in its manufacture the seeds of its own destruction. Machine-made paper, for example, generally includes the use of chemicals that weaken it over time. The same is true, of course, for photographic records. Other media, such as computer tapes, were never designed to be maintained for long periods of time; the rapidly improving technology and the easy reusability of such electronic records encourages the destruction of any information that appears to have lost its immediate value.

Some of the above threats to archival materials can be resolved by current preservation practices, but only at huge monetary outlays. Almost a decade ago it was estimated that the National Archives held over four billion pieces of paper. Proper preservation of such a volume ranges from hundreds of dollars and more for each document such as a manuscript map or architectural drawing to a few cents each for routine files of

---

[34]For the most important recent controversy over replevin, see William S. Price, Jr., "Toward a Definition of Public Records: North Carolina's Replevin Action," *Carolina Comments* 25 (November 1977), 127-31; Price, "N.C. v. B.C. West, Jr.," *American Archivist* 41 (January 1978), 21-24; P.W. Filby, "On Replevin," *Manuscripts* 30 (Winter 1978), 30-33; James E. O'Neill, "Replevin: A Public Archivist's Perspective," *College & Research Libraries* 40 (January 1979), 26-30; "Replevin Committee Draft Statement," SAA *Newsletter*, September 1979, 8-9; and Thornton W. Mitchell, "Another View of the West Case," *Carolina Comments* 29 (November 1981), 126-31.

government offices that require only exposure to some system of mass-deacidification or microfilming. It has also been recently estimated that America's major research libraries hold 305 million books, with at least twenty-five percent of those in very fragile condition;[35] the quantity of archival materials is much greater and the percentage of seriously deteriorating documents probably much higher. The problem should be readily obvious, then. If our historical records repositories lack adequate funding for staff, proper storage facilities and suitable records containers -- which they do, it is inevitable that proper preservation methods will remain simply unobtainable. A consistent pattern among America's archival repositories is claiming that preservation is a top priority while it ranks among the bottom of actual expenditures. At a 1977 conference on historical records priorities, one leading conservator issued the following jeremiad-like warning:

> The great majority of the written records of our heritage, after having been gathered in historical societies, offices of town and county clerks, court record repositories, state archives, and private collections, have been deteriorating at an ever increasing rate. We have reached the point at which if some positive steps are not taken, much of the information in these records will be lost.[36]

Little has changed in the past decade to soften the urgency of this statement. In 1986 an analysis of the condition of state government records having historical value concluded that these records "created during the past century cannot withstand the rigors of use and time without significant loss in image quality, physical strength, and chemical stability," while "no state archives approaches the goal of providing total preservation care for its permanently valuable records."[37]

---

[35]*Chronicle of Higher Education* (30 April 1985), 5.

[36]George M. Cunha, "The Conservation and Preservation of Historical Records," *American Archivist* 40 (July 1977), 321.

[37]*Preservation Needs in State Archives* (Albany: National Association of Government Archives and Records Administrators, 1986), 7. For broader views on the preservation of the historic remains of our country, see Jane Sennet Long, ed., *Invest in the American Collection: A Regional Forum on the Conservation of Cultural Property* ([Chicago]: National Committee to Save America's Cultural Collections, [1987]).

Moving Forward to Preserve America's Documentary Heritage

The present condition of America's historical records
provides a gloomy portrait for anyone interested in this nation's
rich heritage, even with some significant progress in improving
the care of these documents over the past decade. The
numerous efforts within just the last few years by archivists,
librarians, historians, and others to study seriously this issue
is testimony to a reawakened concern that matters are not as
good as they could or should be. The willingness of
professionals to criticize their own failures is a positive move
to draw the public's attention to the seriousness of the
condition of historical records in the United States. Moreover,
since the early 1970s, there has been an increasing
professionalism among archivists and others charged with
protecting our documentary heritage. There are greater
numbers of individuals working full-time to manage the
historical records, and these people are generally better trained
and have easier accessibility to better defined professional
standards and practices. There are also new opportunities for
archivists and colleagues to remove themselves from the hectic
pace of the office in order to investigate important notions of
how to identify and preserve those sources possessing historical
value. Archivists have also been working in the 1980s to
define more precisely the nature of their work, reopening
discussion on archival certification and accreditation of
educational programs. There has even been some reunification
of the various segments of the historical community in the
1980s. The successful movement of archivists, academic
historians, applied historians, and researchers to gain
independence of the National Archives from the General
Services Administration in order to make this national
repository a more effective leader in the preservation of
America's historical records may be just the beginning of a
sustained crusade in behalf of the documentary heritage. Such
a crusade is essential since most of the fundamental work lies
ahead. No matter what progress has been made, however, no
one should delude themselves in thinking that the battle for
the preservation of the country's historical records has been
won.

It is sometimes easier to depict the grave circumstances of
America's historical records than it is to suggest ways for their
improvement. After reading the above, any individual, whether
professional archivist or amateur genealogist, probably could
recommend steps to follow in bettering the management of the
documentary heritage. What follows is, then, only a bare-bones
list that is addressed equally to records creators, records users,

and records custodians. It is not a new or especially innovative catalog of suggestions but flows naturally from the various reports and studies cited earlier in this essay, and these suggestions are further elaborated on in the essays making up the remainder of this volume.

The general public must be better informed of the value and relevancy of knowledge of the past AND why historical records are essential for this to occur. Those who reside in the historical community generally have firm notions of the reasons for devoting themselves to their vocations, but few have articulated extremely well these convictions to the public. The reports by former NEH director William Bennett and his successor, Lynne V. Cheney, on the humanities show how our present society has lost sight of its past by the dissolution of the humanities as a core element of the educational system in this country.[38] Not only have archivists *just* recently discovered the importance of educating the public why they must preserve historical records, but very few archival institutions have made any serious commitment to such public outreach. Professional historians are even further removed from the general public; popular histories by scholars such as Samuel Eliot Morison and Daniel Boorstin remain rare exceptions rather than the rule and many academics remain suspicious of devoting time to public rather than scholarly ventures.

There must be greater resources for improving the preservation and management of historical records. Without a greater number of trained conservators and a stronger commitment by our historical records repositories, a large percentage of the documents presently in the archival repositories will be lost within many of our lifetimes. Here money is the preeminent issue. The establishment of a new Office of Preservation within the National Endowment for the Humanities seems to be a step in the right direction, but even its increasing millions of dollars seem paltry in comparison to the immensity of the preservation task. Moreover, the Reagan and Bush administrations have threatened the cutting of funding for such federal-aid programs as the NEH and NHPRC, organizations that have provided the greatest amount of money for records preservation. The federal government should take the lead in this area and promote corresponding efforts by private foundations and other levels of government. The recent effort to establish a "Trust for Our Documentary

---

[38]Bennett, *To Reclaim a Legacy* (Washington, D.C., 1984); Cheney, *American Memory: A Report on the Humanities in the Nation's Public Schools* (Washington, D.C., 1987).

Heritage," modelled after the historic preservation trust with the aim of marshalling both private and public funds, was a step in the right direction, although the Trust never gathered the support it needed from the various allied professional associations and public officials.

The historical community must be united in order to become an effective advocate for the proper management of our documentary heritage. Although there will remain professional distinctions between archivists, historians, librarians, and others, it is necessary that these groups rally behind the key issues affecting the preservation of historical records in the United States. The lessons learned from the movement to gain independence for the National Archives must include that such national efforts continue on related matters.[39] The National Coordinating Committee for the Promotion of History, under the aegis of the American Historical Association -- one of the principal leaders in the fight to restore the National Archives to independence -- should receive greater support from other professional associations and should be a model for the type of energetic and persistent lobbying needed to be adopted by these additional associations. Most important, the SAA Committee on Goals and Priorities should help the SAA evolve into an organization capable of issuing periodic reports to the public on the condition of this nation's records that can serve as a focus for increased public and professional involvement.[40] One prominent archival leader has also recently challenged his profession to work for a "national records policy" because without it "we lack a guide for sound decisions on a vital public good - historical records" and "we also deny our posterity a clear criteria to hold us accountable for the treatment of one of their most important resources - their documentary heritage."[41]

The archival profession must strengthen itself to improve the management of America's historical records. Most archivists agree with the need for improved educational standards,

[39]See Page Putnam Miller, "Archival Issues and Problems: The Central Role of Advocacy," *Public Historian* 8 (Summer 1986), 60-73.

[40]For a model of the kind of annual statement that is needed, see Andrew Decker, "The State of Museums: Cautious Optimism Prevails," *Museum News* 66 (March/April 1988), 23-33.

[41]Larry J. Hackman, "The United States Needs a National Historical Records Policy!" *History News* 43 (March/April 1988), 32. For additional thoughts on archivists and information policies see chapter fifteen in this volume.

ensuring that the profession maintains its fundamental ethos through the entry of well-trained individuals. But the need is much greater than merely education. Archivists must continue to develop their newly-adopted individual certification program and, at the same time, strengthen their image and the view of their mission by the general public. The archival profession also requires the acquisition of greater support for basic research and development. Improvements in the identification, preservation, and management of historical records will not appear without serious study and testing of archival practices and standards. The archival profession also needs, of course, more resources in general just to meet basic responsibilities. The preservation of a state's, or nation's, historical records will not occur when there are only a handful of archivists, poor storage facilities, and little time or opportunity for cooperation between repositories.

Records creators must be convinced of their basic responsibility to preserve and manage, for the good of their own organizations and the public, their records possessing historical value. For many years most archivists worked on the premise that they were responsible for identifying and bringing into their institutions all of the historical records of our culture. An increasing number of archivists now realize that this is an unobtainable goal. Without records creators themselves aware of their responsibility, many of our nation's historical records will not be saved. Even now few local governments, business corporations, civic organizations, and professional associations have adequate records programs despite significant efforts in all of these areas. Archivists and the wider historical community must take the lead in this important mission.

The growth of archival repositories must be better planned in light of the severely limited resources available for the management of the American documentary heritage. For too long the historical community has applauded the growth of programs without evaluating their success in preserving historical records. As long as the American public is content to provide the level of support that it has, archivists cannot willy-nilly propagate such programs. The preservation of our documentary heritage is not only expensive but in jeopardy if attempted by institutions lacking the means to meet existing professional standards. The management of historical records cannot be achieved through ill-informed and under-funded archival operations. One archivist recently urged the following change in the orientation of his profession: "For those archives that cannot afford an archivist, or any of the elements that would constitute a program, professional accountability requires all of us to urge that institution either to improve its care of its records or to deposit them in a repository that can appropriately manage them."[42] Although this may seem harsh, it is an absolute and basic requirement for this profession's successful pursuit of its mission.

Archivists must abandon their institutional parochialism and work on cooperative records projects such as state and regional documentation strategies. One of the great traditions of the archival profession has been independent collecting; for many archivists the most enjoyable aspect of their work has been in the thrill of the chase after historical documents, including keen competition with other repositories and private collectors. Over the past decade there has been an increasing number of essays on the importance of cooperative and planned collecting, although such efforts have been minimally practiced. Because of this characteristic, not only have archivists failed to document adequately historic events, which by nature transcend single actors or institutions, but as one archivist stated, it has encouraged the "growth of poor collections of marginal value."[43] The final report of the Joint Committee on the Archives of Science and Technology has clearly shown, for example, that even single developments within this realm involve a multiplicity of individual scientists and engineers, private industry, educational institutions, and the federal government.[44] Documentation strategies - plans "formulated to assure the documentation of an ongoing issue, activity or area" and "carried out through the mutual efforts of many institutions and individuals influencing both the creation of the records and the archival retention of some of them" - or their equivalent must become a normal mode of operation within the historical records community.[45]

The analysis that has been lavished upon America's historical records in the past few years is unlikely ever to be

[42]Joyce, *Documenting America*, 44.   There have been similar statements made by individuals in allied professions; see Dennis K. McDaniel, "In My Opinion: Stop Museum Proliferation!" *History News* 39 (March 1984), 31-32.

[43]Faye Phillips, "Developing Collecting Policies for Manuscript Collections," *American Archivist* 47 (Winter 1984), 31.

[44]Clark A. Elliott, ed., *Understanding Progress as Process: Documentation of the History of Post-War Science and Technology in the United States* (n.p., 1983).

[45]Refer to chapter thirteen in this volume for more information about this.

undertaken again, at least in the foreseeable future. There is more now known about the condition of these documents and what needs to be done about them than ever before. This is a distinct legacy of the archival profession of the 1980s. If this decade has been an "Age of Archival Analysis," as someone has already called it,[46] the 1990s must be a time of archival action, learning from and building upon the recent efforts. The historical community, especially the archival profession, must energetically lobby for the improved care of this country's documentary heritage. More important, all Americans must realize the seriousness of the care of their historical records and take actions to better preserve and manage them. James Reston, in one of his columns, quoted then Secretary of Education William J. Bennett, on the decline of history in American schools. "To be ignorant of history is to be," Bennett stated, "intellectually defenseless, unable to understand the workings either of our own society or of other societies."[47] If something is not done to ensure better the preservation of America's documentary heritage, most of us may live to see if Bennett's warning is, indeed, accurate.

---

[46]Bruce W. Dearstyne, "Archives and Public History: Issues, Problems, and Prospects - An Introduction," *Public Historian* 8 (Summer 1986), 7.

[47]*New York Times*, 5 May 1985, 27.

TWO PROFESSIONALISM AND ARCHIVISTS IN THE UNITED STATES[1]

Archivists' Continuing Concern with Professionalism

Despite the immense task facing the archival profession in its quest to stop America's past from disappearing, American archivists can still be pleased with their progress since they organized as a profession in 1936, the year the Society of American Archivists (SAA) was established. Archivists have made significant strides toward accomplishing many of their founders' dreams and, as a result, they are in a better position to preserve and manage America's documentary heritage. At the first Conference of Archivists in 1909, the SAA's precursor under the aegis of the American Historical Association, Waldo G. Leland charted a course in which the archivist would emerge as an independent professional with standard methodologies and specialized education.[2] At the final Conference of Archivists in 1935, Theodore C. Blegen called for an autonomous professional association, noting that the recent founding of the National Archives "heralds a new era" for the archival community.[3] And at the first assemblage of the SAA a year later, A. R. Newsome stated that one of the three main objectives of the new organization was the "development of a genuine archival profession in the United States."[4] The archivist's concern with professionalism is by no means new. Since the founding of the first major archival program in 1901, professionalism has been a consistent theme.

Leland, Blegen, and Newsome would be especially proud of the achievements archivists have made just in the past decade. There is now an excellent descriptive literature on archival practice; archival education is much stronger; national standards exist for some archival practices and are developing

---

[1]This essay was originally published in the *American Archivist* 49 (Summer 1986), 229-47.

[2]"American Archival Problems," American Historical Association *Annual Report 1909* (Washington, D.C.: Government Printing Office, 1911), 342-48.

[3]"Problems of American Archivists," *Bulletin of the National Archives*, no. 2 (November 1936), 3-4.

[4]"Objectives of the Society of American Archivists," *Society of American Archivists Proceedings, Providence, R.I. December 29-30, 1936 and Washington, D.C., June 18-19, 1937* (Urbana, Illinois: [Society of American Archivists, 1937]), 64.

in others; national leadership is more evident and improving
yearly; and archivists are much more aware of their
occupation's condition after the recent years of intensive self-
analysis on institutional, state, regional, and national levels.
Still, improvements are needed in all of these, and other, areas.

At least two major concerns of American archivists
concerning their profession have emanated from these recent
efforts. The first is the better articulation and adoption of a
mission for the archival profession, culminating in the SAA's
Goals and Priorities Task Force report. The report succinctly
described the mission of archivists to be "to ensure the
identification, preservation, and use of records of enduring
value" and presented a variety of goals necessary to accomplish
such a mission.[5] The increasing realization and acceptance of
the problems archivists face in accomplishing their mission is
the second trend of recent years. The archival community is
extremely weak in resources - staff, facilities, and funds -
needed to work toward its mission with any realistic hope for
success. Compounding this problem, archivists lack the
authority, public recognition, and influence to pursue
successfully the necessary resources. In addition, the
documentation of modern society presents a myriad of
challenges - such as an increasingly complex information
technology, the voluminous nature of modern records, and the
intricate relationship of contemporary documentation creators -
that stretch the barely adequate existing archival resources
even thinner, forcing archivists to devise creative ways to use
their assets.[6]

The reasons for the difficulties impeding the archival
mission are both internal and external. The external cause of
this dilemma is the manner in which society appreciates - or
fails to appreciate - archival records. David Gracy, in a series
of interesting essays, has clearly shown that the public has a
weak image of archivists, the nature of their work, and the

---

[5]*Planning for the Archival Profession: A Report of the Society of
American Archivists Task Force on Goals and Priorities* (Chicago: SAA,
1986); see also F. Gerald Ham, "Planning for the Archival Profession,"
American Archivist 48 (Winter 1985), 26-30 and chapter three in this
volume.

[6]For a convenient summary of these problems, see Bruce W. Dearstyne,
"The Records Wasteland," *History News* 40 (June 1985), 18-22.

importance of their occupation.[7]   The subject requires
considerably more study and corrective action. The internal
factors are inherent in the structure of the archival community.
Are there problems that weaken its quest? Apparently there
are, as this essay will suggest.

This essay is an examination of the nature of the archival
profession to determine to what extent internal conditions are
responsible for the kind of poor management of America's
documentary heritage sketched out in the first chapter in this
volume. What follows, then, is not a comprehensive picture of
the challenges archivists face in striving to accomplish their
mission. As a gauge for evaluating the internal weaknesses of
the archival profession, sociological models of professionalism
are employed. The essay is not designed to argue whether or
not archivists constitute a true profession.   Rather, the
sociological models are intended to portray a framework for the
discussion about how to strengthen the archival profession,
continuing a process that started with the state assessment
reports, the SAA Goals and Priorities Task Force report, and
the various statements of the SAA Archives and Society Task
Force. It is hoped that this essay (and the others in this
volume) will stimulate further evaluation of archival issues of
the 1980s, such as individual certification and institutional
accreditation, that are important to the future success of the
archival profession.   Over a decade ago, in 1973, an SAA
President lamented that archivists "are still not sure what a
professional archivist is or what makes him so, or how he is
distinct from a non-professional or unprofessional archivist."[8]
The problem is that time is growing short and archivists need
to decide about such basic concerns. Archivists are literally at
a crossroads, having recently celebrated in this decade the
golden anniversary of their professional association while also
facing a new world of information technology and its related
challenges.

---

[7]David B. Gracy II, "What's Your Totem? Archival Images in the Public
Mind," *Midwestern Archivist* 10, no. 1 (1985), 17-23 and "Our Future is
Now," *American Archivist* 48 (Winter 1985), 12-21.

[8]Wilfred I. Smith, "Broad Horizons: Opportunities for Archivists,"
American Archivist 37 (January 1974), 11.

Sociologists and Professions

Despite a vast literature on the subject of professions, sociologists have readily acknowledged difficulties in defining what a profession is or enumerating its characteristics. Identifying the elements of professions is difficult because they are fluid; "professionalism is a matter of degree."[9] Because professions claim social standing and recognition, many sociologists have been hesitant to identify occupations as professions and to help them acquire the accompanying social benefits, especially since the late 1960s, a period marked by anti-credentialism and similar sentiments.[10] Many sociologists have also found it difficult to measure empirically the characteristics of a profession because professional status is mostly the result of image: "a professional is a person whom other people . . . are willing to treat as a professional."[11] Nevertheless, two major models of professionalism are useful for studying the nature of occupations.

The oldest, and still very important, sociological model of professionalism is the taxonomic paradigm that dates back to Abraham Flexner and 1915.[12] The model remained ascendant at least through the 1960s. Although the model only determines the "ideal" characteristics of a profession, it remains useful because it distinguishes phenomena of occupations often

[9]Bernard Barber, "Some Problems in the Sociology of the Professions," *The Professions in America*, ed. Kenneth S. Lynn (Boston: Houghton Mifflin, 1965), 17.

[10]Julius A. Roth, "Professionalism: The Sociologist's Decoy," *Sociology of Work and Occupations* 1 (February 1974), 6-23; Douglas Kelgon, "The Sociology of Professions: An Emerging Perspective," *Sociology of Work and Occupations* 5 (August 1978), 259-83; and Eliot Freidson, "Are Professions Necessary?" in *The Authority of Experts: Studies in History and Theory*, ed. Thomas L. Haskell (Bloomington: Indiana University Press, 1984), 3-27.

[11]Adam Yarmolinsky, "What Future for the Professional in American Society?" *Daedalus* 107 (Winter 1978), 159; and Mike Saks, "Removing the Blinkers? A Critique of Recent Contributions to the Sociology of Professions," *Sociological Review*, n. s., 31 (February 1983), 1-21.

[12]"Is Social Work a Profession?" *School and Society* 1 (June 26, 1915), 901-11.

viewed as professions.[13]   The lists of such characteristics usually included at least five attributes, briefly described as follows:

Specialized knowledge or systematic theory.   A profession has a body of knowledge that is the foundation of its work.   Usually such knowledge is intellectual rather than based upon purely practical experience; such knowledge constitutes theory, and an understanding of this theory is a requisite for entry into the profession.   The profession's specialized knowledge is developed through systematic research, the primary source of which is the location of professional schools within the university.

Community sanction.   A profession has been sanctioned by the public to the extent that it controls its own educational   system   through   accreditation,   governs practitioners admitted into its ranks, and possesses some degree of independence from the public's judgment on technical issues.   A profession has far more exacting standards for itself than the public has for it.   Implicit in the community's sanction is its recognition of the profession, usually including as well acknowledgment from clients, other professions, employers, government regulatory agencies, and educational institutions.

Professional cohesion or organization.   A profession displays cohesion via the existence of a professional association in which most of its practitioners hold membership and participate.   Professional associations reinforce the mutual identification of distinctly occupational interests, provide social support for individuals, sponsor continued education, and work to enforce standards of professional competence.   Such organizations are the key to general professional improvement and growth and, as a result, often provide the main forums for the resolution of intra-professional conflicts necessary to the continued growth of the profession.

[13]Recent efforts to measure empirically such elements are by John B. Cullen, *The Structure of Professionalism: A Quantitative Examination* (New York: PBI, 1978) and "An Occupational Taxonomy by Professional Characteristics: Implications for Research," *Journal of Vocational Behavior* 22 (June 1983), 257-67.

Professional culture. The difference between an occupation and a profession has often been said to be that the latter possesses values, norms, and symbols that transform work to a calling. A profession is not only full-time work, distinguishing it from the efforts of amateurs, it is a calling that attracts individuals to pursue it actively. One of the signs of a fully-developed profession is the duration and stability of a professional association and its membership. There is a "community," a sense of identity, shared values, and common language supported by the continuity of practitioners.

Institutionalized altruism. Built into a profession is a structural system that promotes behavior of its practitioners beneficial to others. This type of service orientation includes concerns for staying abreast of developments in a field so that clients are not harmed and standards are maintained to protect clients. This altruism is founded on the responsibility mandated by the profession's monopoly of knowledge and control of its use.[14]

Such a list of attributes characterizing a profession should be an extremely helpful standard for evaluating an occupation's ability to accomplish its mission.

The other predominant professionalism model is one that analyzes the process of professionalization. Proponents of this approach point to what they perceive as the main weakness of the taxonomic paradigm, that it cannot be empirically tested. The professionalization model uses a historical view to examine an occupation's ability to gain authority from society over a

---

[14]These five elements are based on the following studies: Ernest Greenwood, "The Elements of Professionalization," in *Professionalization*, eds. Howard M. Vollmer and Donald L. Mills (Englewood Cliffs, New Jersey: Prentice Hall, Inc., 1966), 9-19; Cullen, *Structure of Professionalism*; J. A. Jackson, ed., *Professions and Professionalism*, Sociological Studies, no. 3 (Cambridge: Cambridge University Press, 1970), 3-15; Barber, "Some Problems"; Wilbert E. Moore with Gerald W. Rosenblum, *The Professions: Roles and Rules* (New York: Russell Sage Foundation, 1970); William J. Goode, "Community Within A Community: The Professions," *American Sociological Review* 22 (April 1957), 194-200; Ronald L. Akers, "Framework for the Comparative Study of Group Cohesion: The Professions," *Pacific Sociological Review* 13 (Spring 1970), 73-85; Robert K. Merton, *Social Research and the Practicing Professions*, ed. Aaron Rosenblatt and Thomas F. Gieryn (Cambridge: Abt Books, 1982), 109-34, 199-209; and Philip Elliott, *The Sociology of the Professions* (London: Macmillan, 1972).

period of time. The earliest models of professionalization were efforts to arrange the characteristics from the taxonomic model into some logical set of chronological phases. Such a sequence might run from the formation of an occupation, to the development of training schools and professional associations, to a period of political agitation for legal recognition, establishment of entry standards and a code of ethics, and finally to the full emergence of a profession.[15] More recent models have seen the essence of professionalization as a "power-orientation" or abiding concern with "ideology."[16] One of the newest and most useful schemes for professionalization posits that the professional power held by an occupation is the main element of its success: the "most professional occupations are those having members who exhibit high levels of autonomy [in his or her area of competency] from clients and autonomy from employing organizations." According to this model, an occupation's potential for claiming professional status lies in the characteristics of its service (whether it is essential, exclusive, or a complex service requiring special status) and in its ability to build a suitable image. The level of an occupation's professionalism is determined by the degree of autonomy society grants it.[17]

The Sociological Models and the Classic Professions

Very early in American history three occupations - divinity, law, and medicine - began to acquire significant power and influence in American society. Sociologists have studied these occupations as the epitome of professionalism. Although all three vocations exerted significant influence in the nineteenth century, strongly held democratic beliefs conflicted with the idea of divinity, law, and medicine gaining authority and power greater than that of individuals or families. During the Progressive period from 1890 to 1920, the increasing complexity of an urban-industrial society assigned a new value to

---

[15]For example, see Harold L. Wilensky, "The Professionalization of Everyone?" *American Journal of Sociology* 70 (September 1964), 137-58.

[16]The most detailed description of this is Magali Sarfatti Larson, *The Rise of Professionalism: A Sociological Analysis* (Berkeley: University of California Press, 1977).

[17]Patrick B. Forsyth and Thomas J. Danisiewicz, "Toward a Theory of Professionalization," *Work and Occupations* 12 (February 1985), 59-76.

expertise, social control, and economy and efficiency.[18] Law and medicine especially solidified their strength during this era, clearing the ground for their remarkable growth since 1920.

It is evident that law and medicine are the quintessential professions as defined by the taxonomic model. Society has fostered their growth by highly valuing their missions; medicine is, as one sociologist declared, the result of "a vital and universal need" and justice is the hallmark of every advanced society. Both occupations have developed considerable bodies of specialized knowledge, strong and energetic professional associations, strict control over professional entry through licensing and control of their knowledge, excellent educational standards, and immense political influence. Finally, both the legal and medical professions can claim essential roles in society, even retaining levels of respect beyond the limits of their own realms of expertise; the extent of such success has enabled both professions to survive scandals, controversies, and other challenges.[19]

Both law and medicine are also classic examples of the sociological models of professionalization, having gained significant power and autonomy from clients, regulatory agencies, and society at large. Prior to the end of the nineteenth century, medicine had little control over standards of practice within its discipline; well-trained doctors often competed equally with quacks and drummers of patent medicines and elixirs. The growth of urban areas, however, led to the spread of modern hospitals, which in turn became centers of education, specialization, and research and development. These changes were supported by the growth of self-regulating medical societies, which gradually tightened standards and control over the market for physician care and the training necessary to administer it. The development and

[18]Robert H. Wiebe, *The Search for Order,* 1877-1920 (New York: Hill and Wang, 1967); and Robert M. Crunden, *Ministers of Reform: The Progressives' Achievement in American Civilization 1889-1920* (New York: Basic Books, Inc., 1982).

[19]For studies of the two professions, see Eliot Freidson, *Profession of Medicine: A Study of the Sociology of Applied Knowledge* (New York: Harper and Row, 1970); Paul Starr, *The Social Transformation of American Medicine* (New York: Basic Books, 1982); Larson, *Rise of Professionalism,* 159-77; Douglas Alan Klegon, "Lawyers and the Social Structure: An Historical Analysis of the Role of Professionalization Among Lawyers in the United States" (Ph. D. dissertation., University of Wisconsin-Madison, 1975); and Maxwell Bloomfield, *American Lawyers in a Changing Society, 1776-1876* (Cambridge: Harvard University Press, 1976).

adoption of the germ theory of disease coupled with a wider interest in public hygiene, successes in surgery and antiseptics, stunning victories over diseases like tuberculosis and polio, and the increased membership and visibility of the American Medical Association (its membership grew from 8,000 to 70,000 between 1900 and 1910 alone) earned a greater trust from American society.   Such trust was very evident after the Second World War when medicine essentially received public endorsement of its self-regulation and the release of immense quantities of research monies.

The legal profession has shown a similar pattern of development.   Throughout most of the nineteenth century, it lacked power over admission to practice in the courts and had no educational standards.   During the latter years of the nineteenth century, however, large legal firms supporting the new and larger American business corporations were formed. These firms led to the creation of the American Bar Association and the establishment of a more scientific body of knowledge. Lawyers led the political reform efforts of the Progressive era, acquiring a greater public image in the United States. Throughout the twentieth century the notion of law has remained a prevalent concern of many citizens, and that concern has been largely entrusted to a powerful legal profession.

American   Archivists   and   the   Sociological   Models   of Professionalism

According to the criteria outlined above, the archival community has a number of fault lines that impede progress in its management of America's documentary heritage.   The taxonomic model of professionalism reveals that the archival community is very weak in at least three of the five attributes. The professionalization paradigm shows that archivists have not moved much farther beyond the initial stage of establishing a "potential" for professional status.   In contrast with the successful cases of medicine and law, the archival community's flaws are even more apparent.   A comparison to the more closely allied occupation of librarianship also shows the difficulties   impeding   archivists'   progress   toward   their occupational goals.

One attribute of a profession is a body of specialized knowledge or theory, an area briefly touched upon in the first chapter of this volume but deserving mention again.   Archival theory, however, is only partially developed.   Although over the past decade a stronger archival literature has developed, its orientation has been toward the description of practices rather than the fostering and sustenance of theory.[20] Archivists have learned better how to arrange and describe, exhibit, and care for historical records, but they have still not satisfactorily figured out how to identify what constitutes a historical record[21] or how to deal with the complexities of a modern society awash in information.[22] A major reason for the lack of theoretical orientation may be that since the early 1970s archivists have mainly emphasized building a strong professional association - a commendable goal that has, unfortunately, focused too much of the energies of SAA on assistance to novice or inexperienced professionals.[23] Archivists have few opportunities for pure or sophisticated applied research,[24] and virtually no control over or even influence on archival education, except for institutes or apprenticeships. There are only minor distinctions between the training of archivists and the training of historians or librarians, and there is no evidence of any internal hierarchy in archives administration that distinguishes professional from para-professional or technical work.[25] Archivists have recently

---

[20]See the separate essay on archival literature in this volume for a fuller explanation of this topic.

[21]See the comments on appraisal in Richard C. Berner, *Archival Theory and Practice in the United States: A Historical Analysis* (Seattle: University of Washington Press, 1983).

[22]See, for example, two strong arguments in this direction by Hugh Taylor, "Information Ecology and Archives of the 1980s," *Archivaria* 18 (Summer 1984), 25-37; and Richard M. Kesner, "Automated Information Management: Is There a Role for the Archivist in the Office of the Future?" *Archivaria* 19 (Winter 1984/85), 162-72.

[23]The most influential aspect of the SAA probably continues to be its annual meetings, which provide the main focus for the discussion of professional issues and account for the origins of a significant portion of published archival literature.

[24]The main exception to this is the recent research fellowship program for study of modern archives sponsored by the Bentley Historical Library of the University of Michigan, with funding primarily from the Andrew W. Mellon Foundation, NHPRC, and the National Endowment for the Humanities (NEH).

[25]For some of the most critical comments on this matter, see Lawrence J. McCrank, "Public Historians in the Information Profession: Problems in Education and Credentials," *Public Historian* 7 (Summer 1985), 7-22 and the essay in this volume.

heard much about their "cycle of poverty" in resources; there also seems to be a similar cycle of poverty in archival theory. A lack of standards on professional education perpetuates a system of poor education and training, which in turn weakens the development of archival theory and the establishment of stronger professional standards. Other professions have faced similar difficulties. Reform efforts in both law and medicine were led by a few universities, which influenced the adoption of strong educational platforms by their professional associations.[26]

Community sanction of the archival occupation is probably the weakest element of archival professionalism. This weakness is closely related to the difficulties faced by archivists in education and theory. Archivists do not, in any substantive way, control entry to their ranks. It seems that virtually anyone can become a "professional" archivist by simply declaring to be one. Furthermore, because of the apparent greater concern of the professional archival associations about strength in numbers rather than standards, these groups are often quick to embrace such self-anointed practitioners of archival administration.[27] It is small wonder, then, that the public has such a poor or incomplete understanding of the work of the archivist. The until recent, but still uncertain, lack of certification of individual archivists and the continuing absence of accreditation of archival education programs -- or the installation of some other system to strengthen and enforce standards of archival work -- only suggests that such problems will continue to haunt archivists. Indeed, archivists need to face the fact that such problems have existed for a very long time. Over a decade ago, a survey of the archival profession concluded that it was "still in the formative stage . . . . [its] bounds . . . still remain undefined, and the professional

[26]Paul Starr noted that once a single institution, Harvard University, risked reform in medical education, other medical schools began to follow suit. After the Johns Hopkins University medical school introduced very radical changes in 1893, its innovations became the common standards of the American Medical Association in only two decades. See Starr, *Social Transformation*, 115-120.

[27]This is not to dismiss the value of such services by these professional bodies, but only to suggest that the predilection of the associations has been too long with providing assistance to entry-level and young professionals, without comparative opportunities for mid-career archivists. This is especially important because the profession is aging and gaining experience and responsibility. See David Bearman, "1982 Survey of the Archival Profession," *American Archivist* 46 (Spring 1983), 233-39.

identity of the members is still uncertain."[28] If many archivists remain confused about whether they are historians, public historians, librarians, information specialists, records managers, or just archivists,[29] how will the public know what to sanction about archivists?

Professional cohesion is one of the strengths of the archival occupation, although even it leaves much to be improved. For many years archivists were proud of the relative youth of their vocation. Now, however, a certain maturation has settled in as the National Archives - the catalyst for many professional developments - and the SAA have both attained their half-century marks. While the National Archives has been somewhat shaken in recent years with the protracted debate about its administrative independence, the SAA has jelled into the dominant professional archival association with large and well-attended annual meetings, a quarterly journal that remains the main outlet for professional publication, a lengthy list of special publications, and a growing budget and professional staff. But questions remain about how cohesive archivists are. Is SAA's membership anywhere close to comprehensive in scope of the archival community?[30] What are the legitimate roles of the regional and state associations?[31] Is national professional leadership too divided among SAA and other associations such as the Association of Records Managers and Administrators (ARMA), the American Association for State and Local History (AASLH), and the National Association for Government Archives and Records Administrators (NAGARA)? Does the allegiance of many archivists to other professionals - for example, historians, records managers, and librarians - also

[28]Frank B. Evans and Robert B. Warner, "American Archivists and Their Society: A Composite View," *American Archivist* 34 (April 1971), 172.

[29]This is especially evident in the debate about the relationship between history and archives as displayed in recent issues of *Archivaria*. See 16 (Summer 1983), 5-25; 17 (Winter 1983-84), 286-308; 18 (Summer 1984), 241-47; 19 (Winter 1984-85), 185-95; 20 (Summer 1985), 149-57.

[30]Any quick scanning of a recent SAA membership directory reveals severe gaps among the personnel of the National Archives and state archives, the very groups that have shared (and continue to have) a tremendous responsibility for professional leadership.

[31]Patrick M. Quinn, "Regional Archival Organizations and the Society of American Archivists," *American Archivist* 46 (Fall 1983), 433-40.

weaken the professional archival community?[32]   Are the
resources of any of these professional associations really
sufficient for the kind of advocacy necessary in the later 1980s
and beyond?   These issues are very important because
archivists are "terribly isolated" in their work environments.[33]
The tremendous social influence of groups like the American
Medical Association and American Bar Association testify to the
necessity of great cohesion in the strengthening of other
professions.

Closely related to professional cohesion is the notion of
professional culture, an attribute growing stronger among
archivists. At one time individuals viewed work in archives as
an alternative career for historians or librarians. Although this
attitude is still evident in many circles,[34] an increasing number
of people seem to become archivists as a first choice. The idea
of what composes a professional culture is certainly subjective,
but there is the concept of an archival calling and strong
commitment to the mission of managing America's documentary
heritage. Most archivists become archivists because they are
somehow convinced the past is relevant to understanding the
present and is a vital aspect of our lives, whether in a
utilitarian way or simply for enjoyment.   The only real
impediment to the development of a professional archival
culture has been the reluctance of archivists to define or
describe the nature of their work. Now, however, there are at
least some descriptions of what archivists do, their purpose,
and an increasing degree of common language and technique.[35]
Considering the relative youth and small size of the

[32]Such obstacles can be overcome, as seen in the development of the
American engineering profession; Robert Perrucci and Joel E. Gerstl,
Profession Without Community: Engineers in American Society, Studies in
Occupations and Professions (New York: Random House, 1969).

[33]Bearman, "1982 Survey," 237.

[34]The development of public history during the past decade is the prime
example. This movement grew out of the employment crisis of historians.
Archival administration was co-opted because of its non-academic
employment possibilities and the relative weaknesses of archivists' own
definitions and control over their field. For a more complete exploration of
this subject, see the essay on this topic in this volume.

[35]Cf., "Final Report of Task Force on Standard Reporting Practice," SAA
Newsletter, November 1983, 13-16; "Archivist: A Definition," SAA *Newsletter*,
January 1984, 4-5; "Archives: What They Are, Why They Matter," SAA
Newsletter, May 1984, 6-7.

community, it has done as well in this area as the older and larger professions such as medicine and law.

Like the idea of professional culture, institutionalized altruism is difficult, at best, to measure within the archival community (or within any occupation for that matter). The strongest evidence of the altruistic motivations of archivists has been their long desire to make historical records accessible to the public. The tradition of articles on reference and arrangement and description and the development of a genre on archival materials in exhibitions, audio-visual programs, and public relations efforts[36] reveal the extent of an ingrained archival altruism. Efforts by associations such as the SAA and NAGARA to develop codes of ethics and statements of basic operating principles in key areas also reflect this urge.[37] As in many of the areas already discussed, however, the archival profession seems intent to rely upon persuasion rather than enforceable standards. The SAA's completely voluntary institutional self-evaluation is but one example of this attitude.[38] While excellent in content, this program's future impact on the profession is debatable unless it is viewed as but the first step toward accreditation of archival institutions. Although there are rewards for altruistic behavior,[39] there are no penalties for activities that are not. The same attitude can be seen in the recent AASLH survey of the historical field: much of the great talk on increased professionalism has been rejected because of the perception of a lack of necessary resources and the inability of the ubiquitous "lone-arranger" to

---

[36]Gail Farr Casterline, *Archives & Manuscripts: Exhibits*, Basic Manual Series (Chicago: Society of American Archivists, 1980); and Ann E. Pederson and Gail Farr Casterline, *Archives & Manuscripts: Public Programs*, Basic Manual Series (Chicago: Society of American Archivists, 1982).

[37]"A Code of Ethics for Archivists," *SAA Newsletter*, July 1979, 11-15; and the NAGARA brochures, *Policy Statement Regarding the Preservation and Disposition of the Official Records of Governors* (1981) and *Principles for Management of Local Government Records* (1982).

[38]Task Force on Institutional Evaluation, *Evaluation of Archival Institutions: Services, Principles, and Guide to Self-Study* (Chicago: Society of American Archivists, 1982).

[39]The SAA and regional archival associations provide a number of awards for leadership and achievements in the archival profession.

participate in or gain anything from professionalism.[40] Meanwhile, other professions, like medicine and law, rigorously patrol and discipline their practitioners.

Turning to the professionalization paradigm that uses "autonomy" as its linchpin, it becomes further evident that archivists have not realized their full potential as a profession or succeeded in the necessary image building. Although the American archival profession originated in the same Progressive climate as many other professions, it remained closely tied to the historical profession and larger local history field of historical societies, historic houses and sites, and museums.[41] Historical societies perpetuated the traditions of collecting and antiquarianism.[42] The relationship between archivists and historians, despite many positive benefits,[43] restricted archivists in developing a unique body of theory, educational criteria, and their own professional identity. In the 1960s and 1970s as the writings of academic historians became increasingly monographic, indistinguishable from those of social scientists and indecipherable to the public, the public image of archivists suffered by association. The general public and even employers of archivists now seem to lack any real comprehension of the nature or importance of archival work.[44] At best it can be said that the reemergence of the issues of archival certification and accreditation and an increased concern for more productive archival advocacy are evidence of the laying of a better

[40]Charles Phillips and Patricia Hogan, *A Culture At Risk: Who Cares for America's Heritage?* and *The Wages of History: The AASLH Employment Trends and Salary Survey* (Nashville: AASLH, 1984).

[41]The Progressive origins of archival administration needs further investigation, but for some suggestive comments see William S. Price. Jr., "Plowing Virgin Fields: State Support for Southern Archives, Particularly North Carolina," *Carolina Comments* 29 (March 1981), 41-47.

[42]The best account remains Leslie W. Dunlap, *American Historical Societies 1790-1860* (Madison, Wisconsin: Privately printed, 1944), chapter 6.

[43]Mattie U. Russell, "The Influence of Historians on the Archival Profession in the United States," *American Archivist* 46 (Summer 1983), 277-85.

[44]See Sidney J. Levy, "The Status of Virtue: Resource Allocators' Perceptions of Archives," *SAA Newsletter*, August 1985, 5-7.

groundwork for archival professionalism. Still, these concerns are only beginning to be important to the archival community.

As a result of all these circumstances, archivists possess little autonomy from most clients or employing organizations. A sociologist endeavoring to classify the archival occupation would probably characterize it as a "semi-profession" or "mimic profession." Amitai Etzioni described semi-professions as follows: "Their training is shorter, their status is less legitimated, their right to privileged communication less established, there is less of a specialized body of knowledge, and they have less autonomy from supervision or societal control than 'the' professions."[45] Forsyth and Danisiewicz have more recently coined the term mimic professions to cover occupations that lack autonomy: "The mimicry concept is borrowed from evolutionary theory that holds that principles of natural selection may explain the evolution of one animal species to *look* like another species having some vital advantage. Analogously, mimic professions may have a code of ethics and other trappings of professions, but they have no power. They have taken on the coloration but not the substance of profession."[46]

The importance of such professional issues for archivists becomes clearer in an examination of their librarian colleagues. Sociologists consider that the library community represents a semi-profession,[47] and librarians, in a remarkable array of self-reflective studies, have generally agreed.[48] Most importantly,

[45]*The Semi-Professions and Their Organization: Teachers, Nurses, Social Workers* (New York: Free Press, 1969), v.

[46]"Toward a Theory of Professionalization," 64-65.

[47]Cf., William J. Goode, "The Librarian: From Occupation to Profession?" *Library Quarterly* 31 (October 1961), 306-20; and William Joseph Reeves, *Librarians as Professionals: The Occupation's Impact on Library Work Arrangements* (Lexington, Massachusetts: Lexington Books, 1980). There have been some critiques of Goode's ideas, such as Michael F. Winter, *The Professionalization of Librarianship*, Occasional Papers, University of Illinois Graduate School of Library and Information Science, no. 160 (July 1983).

[48]Among the more important essays are the following: Thomas Gwinup, "The Failure of Librarians to Attain Profession: The Causes, the Consequences, and the Prospect," *Wilson Library Bulletin* 48 (February 1974), 482-90; Lester Asheim, "Librarians as Professionals," *Library Trends* 27 (Winter 1979), 225-57; Mary Lee Bundy and Paul Wasserman, "Professionalism Reconsidered," *College & Research Libraries* 29 (January

librarianship seems to lack a truly systematic body of knowledge, and its education is largely job-oriented. A full study of this subject concluded that over the past four decades,

> education for library science, while marked by quantitative growth, has been characterized by intellectual confusion... This confusion exhibits itself in the inability of library science educators to identify those unique problems which would create an independent scientific profession of library science. This confusion has sent the profession off in all directions, looking to other more established fields such as history, management science, sociology, education or psychology.[49]

The public does not really understand library work. A continuing criticism by librarians is that the public believes in libraries but not librarians. Many librarians think this results from the advocacy methods of library associations and attitudes among librarians themselves. Librarianship is completely subordinate to the clients' needs, fostering a clerical or routine work orientation at the expense of developing either a theoretical basis for practice or better management skills. Librarianship lacks the authority it needs to enforce job standards, license practitioners, and distinguish between professional, para-professional, or technical work.[50] In 1972 Christian Boissonnas wrote that "librarians are facing an identity crisis."[51] The crisis seems to have continued, unresolved.

1968), 3-26; and Ralph M. Edwards, "The Management of Libraries and the Professional Functions of Librarians," *Library Quarterly* 45 (April 1975), 150-60. Not surprisingly, there have also been objections to these views; see William F. Birdsall, "Librarians and Professionalism: Status Measured by Outmoded Models," *Canadian Library Journal* 37 (June 1980), 145-48; and Gardner Hanks and C. James Schmidt, "An Alternative Model of a Profession for Librarians," *College & Research Libraries* 36 (May 1975), 175-87.

[49]L. Houser and Alvin M. Schrader, *The Search for a Scientific Profession: Library Science Education in the U.S. and Canada* (Metuchen, New Jersey: Scarecrow Press, 1978), 144, 146.

[50]For discussion of such concerns, see a special issue on library certification of *Library Journal* 102 (September 1977), 1715-29.

[51]"ALA and Professionalism," *American Libraries* 3 (October 1972), 972.

Despite these admitted weaknesses, librarians possess a number of significant advantages, further revealing the impoverished condition of the archival profession. Despite whatever problems might beset the librarians' educational standards, there is the notion of a core curriculum, bolstered by an accreditation process for library school programs. Moreover, most librarians are aware of the need to strengthen significantly their educational foundations, as reflected in such efforts as the Conant Report.[52] Related to this is the fact that the M.L.S. has become the accepted ticket into the profession, although again many librarians acknowledge its weaknesses and needs for significant revisions. An impressive array of journals and specialized publishers offers ample opportunities for the publication of theory and description of practice.[53] Librarians possess strong professional associations, most notably the American Library Association, experienced and adept at lobbying and in pushing its goals into the public forum; the American Library Association supports a branch office in Washington, D.C., putting librarians considerably beyond archivists in the public eye. When National Library Week rolls around, America's citizens are literally bombarded by posters, the media, and other promotional efforts. Many of these achievements have been realized because librarians have been striving for professional standards twice as long as archivists. This older legacy has also enabled the establishment and acceptance of many basic technical standards in library administration that increasingly form the basis of distinctions between professional, para-professional, and technical support staff.[54]

[52]Ralph W. Conant, *The Conant Report: A Study of the Education of Librarians* (Cambridge: MIT Press, 1980).

[53]Consider the range available in library journals. There are general journals (e.g., the *Library Quarterly* and *Library Journal*), those catering to the needs of specific types of libraries (e.g., *Behavioral & Social Sciences Librarian, College & Research Libraries, Journal of Academic Librarianship, Medical Reference Services Quarterly, Online,* and *Special Libraries*), and those focusing on specific functions of librarians (e.g., *Cataloging & Classification Quarterly, Collection Management, Information Technology and Libraries, Journal of Library Administration, Library & Information Science Research, Library Resources & Technical Services,* and *RQ*).

[54]Allen B. Veaner, "Librarians: The Next Generation," *Library Journal* 109 (April 1984), 623-25.

The Archival Community as Profession: Why Does It Matter?

Archivists have long been concerned about professionalism whether they recognize it as such or not. Discussions about improved training, greater resources, and the validity of standardized practices all relate to what it means to be a profession and have sufficient power to accomplish a profession's goals. Unfortunately, many archivists have reacted to the negative connotations of professionalism. In one of the few essays on archival professionalism, historian Howard Zinn characterized "professionalism" as a "powerful form of social control" and warned that archivists' attention to their improved status supported such a perverse society.[55] Equally unfortunate, however, has been the tendency by archivists to undervalue professionalism as simply a variety of activities that individual archivists can pursue in order to become better archivists. Somehow to be more professional means only being better trained, able to acquire meaningful work experience and to participate in professional associations, and competent to contribute to scholarship.[56]

For a number of important reasons, archivists need to think more systematically about the issue of professionalism. First, the archival community lacks resources and authority partly because it fails to assert itself effectively as a profession with an essential role in modern society.

Second, the threats (and opportunities) of the advancing information age and the complexity of modern society have prompted some archivists either to argue for the redefinition of historical records as information sources and archivists as information specialists or to call for a stronger cultural role for archivists.[57] Regardless of one's predilections, archival work

---

[55]"Secrecy, Archives, and the Public Interest," *Midwestern Archivist* 2, no. 2, (1977), 15.

[56]Cf., Harold T. Pinkett, "Professional Development of an Archivist: Some Ways and Means," *Georgia Archive* 3 (Summer 1975), 107-15. A remarkable exception to this is Samuel S. Silsby, Jr., *Archives Standards and Professionalism*, Information Bulletin no. 3 (Augusta: Maine State Archives, [1976]), which deserves broader reading and notice than it has received.

[57]For more on the growth of the information industry, see Anthony Debons, Donald W. King, Una Mansfield, and Donald L. Shirey, *The Information Professional: Survey of an Emerging Field*, Books in Library and Information Science, vol. 38, ed. Allen Kent (New York: Marcel Dekker,

must make substantial accommodations to modern society just to maintain its role of documentation. Information scientists, although still attempting to define their own field, are quite willing to assume a larger role that either encompasses archives or forgets about the need to care for historical records.[58] One archivist has characterized his community as a "colorful mosaic of archivists, records managers, manuscript curators, librarians, historians, and information specialists" unable to agree on stronger standards of self-regulation and definition.[59] Many of these groups are, in fact, actively working on stronger standards, whether archivists are or not.[60]

Third, because of our increasingly complex society, buttressed by information technology, archivists' ability to document that society requires extraordinary efforts unlike those commonly employed in the past. Archivists can no longer afford to collect the records of individuals and institutions as if they represented isolated, autonomous agents. Our post World War II society is characterized by a myriad of "complex relationships between institutions and individuals" plus new forms of record-keeping, which require new definitions, new

1980). For various reactions by archivists, see Hugh Taylor, "Information Ecology and the Archives of the 1980s," *Archivaria* 18 (Summer 1984), 25-37 and "The Collective Memory: Archives and Libraries as Heritage," *ibid.* 15 (Winter 1982-83), 118-30; Richard M. Kesner, "Automated Information Management: Is There a Role for the Archivist in the Office of the Future?" *ibid.* 19 (Winter 1984/85), 162-72; F. Gerald Ham, "Archival Strategies for the Post-Custodial Era," *American Archivist* 44 (Summer 1981), 207-16; Terry Cook, "From Information to Knowledge: An Intellectual Paradigm for Archives," *Archivaria* 19 (Winter 1984-85), 28-49, and "Clio: The Archivist's Muse?" *ibid.* 5 (Winter 1977-78), 198-203; Wilcomb Washburn, "The Archivist's Two-Way Stretch," *ibid.* 7 (Winter 1978), 137-43; and George Bolentenko, "Archivists and Historians: Keepers of the Well," *ibid.* 16 (Summer 1983), 5-25.

[58]See, for example, Elaine Svenonius and Rutherford Witthus, "Information Science as a Profession," *Annual Review of Information Science and Technology* 16 (1981), 291-316.

[59]Peter J. Wosh, "Creating a SemiProfessional Profession: Archivists View Themselves," *Georgia Archive* 10 (Fall 1982), 5-6.

[60]Records managers are a good case. See J. Michael Pemberton, "Library and Information Science: The Educational Base for Professional Records Management," *Records Management Quarterly* 15 (April 1981), 48-50, 52-53. There have even been rumblings among historical editors; see Thomas E. Jeffrey, "The Education of Editors: Current Status and Future Prospects," *Documentary Editing* 7 (March 1985), 12-16.

partnerships, and new methods from archivists.[61]   It is reasonable to assume that stronger archival credentials will be important assets; the credibility of the archivist is equally as important as the social utility of archives.

Fourth, and finally, modern society and information technology have brought an increased concern with deprofessionalization, "a loss to professional occupations of their unique qualities, particularly their monopoly over knowledge, public belief in their service ethos, and expectations of work autonomy and authority over the client."[62] In American society the ascendancy of professions has been challenged, according to a number of critics, by the proliferation of knowledge (again, especially information technology), the growth of bureaucratic institutions, and the spread of democratic ideas and ideals.[63] At the same time, a number of professions have seen the societal changes as opportunities for strengthening their ability to accomplish their missions.[64] If archivists are going to ensure the preservation and use of America's documentary heritage, they must guarantee that their mission is kept before the American public. This requires clarifying the definition of an archivist and strengthening the archivist's occupation.

Thus the position of archival administration as an occupation and the changes in modern society mandate that

[61]Helen Samuels, "Who Controls the Past," *American Archivist* 49 (Spring 1986), 109-24; Joan K. Haas, Samuels, Barbara Trippel Simmons, *Appraising the Records of Modern Science and Technology: A Guide* (Cambridge: Massachusetts Institute of Technology, 1985); and Larry J. Hackman, "Historical Documentation in the United States: Archivists - and Historians?" *OAH Newsletter* 13 (August 1985), 17-18.

[62]Marie R. Haug, "Deprofessionalization: An Alternate Hypothesis for the Future," in *Professionalization and Social Change*, The Sociological Review Monograph 20, ed. Paul Halmos (December 1973), 197. See also Nina Toren, "Deprofessionalization and Its Sources," *Sociology of Work and Occupations* 2 (November 1975), 323-37 and Haug, "The Deprofessionalization of Everyone?" in *Libraries in Post-Industrial Society*, ed. Leigh Estabrook (Phoenix: Oryx Press, 1977), 67-84.

[63]Yarmolinsky, "What Future for the Professional in American Society?"; and Marie R. Haug, "Computer Technology and the Obsolescence of the Concept of Profession," in *Work and Technology*, ed. Marie R. Haug and Jacque Dofny, SAGE Studies in International Sociology, no. 10 (Beverly Hills: SAGE Publications, 1977), 216-24.

[64]Cf., Brian Nelson, "Online Bibliographic Searching and the Deprofessionalization of Librarianship," *Online Review* 4 (September 1980), 215-24.

archivists seriously consider their status as a profession. Specifically, archivists must consider and resolve issues like those described below:

Archivists need to define and promote the social utility of historical records, regardless of format. In the introductory essay to this volume, it was stressed that the general public must become better informed of the value and relevancy of historical records.[65] Archivists bear the responsibility of making this happen. Without society's acceptance of the value of archives, archivists will never acquire the resources or the means to accomplish their mission on behalf of society. Archivists must demonstrate that the preservation of historical records contributes positively to society, as does the practice of law or medicine. If no documentation enabled research on contemporary problems and issues, guaranteed administrative continuity or protection of citizens' rights, allowed the study of the past, or educated or entertained the public about its history, what would society be like? Archivists need to continue to build upon the efforts of such bodies as SAA's Archives and Society Task Force, as well as to promote the study and discussion of this important subject in both professional and public circles.

In promoting the social utility of archives, archivists and others must be careful to stress the importance of individual archivists in accomplishing the archival mission. Archivists need to avoid the problems of gaining increased public recognition of archives but little appreciation for the necessity of archivists. As noted earlier, many librarians have complained about their own promotional efforts having a similar result. If archivists expect to establish and maintain professional standards for individuals, such a problem cannot be allowed to occur. Employers of archivists especially must be able to distinguish between qualified archivists and those seeking archival positions who lack proper education and experience.

Archivists need to develop a much stronger national voice for archival issues and concerns. At present such a strong, unified voice seems impractical because of the variety of

[65]See pp. 22-23.

national associations - SAA, NAGARA, ARMA, and AASLH - concerned with records and the generally limited resources of each association. These groups working together under national leadership could bring public attention to the deteriorating documentary heritage of the United States.[66] There are many examples of what has been and needs to be done in this regard. The National Archives' success in gaining political independence exemplifies the kind of national effort required, a linking of concerned professional associations and individuals in the political process.[67] Archivists know more about their profession than ever before. They need to build upon the various NHPRC-sponsored state assessment reports.[68] They need to issue regular national reports on the management of America's archives. To facilitate this, archivists need to develop better means of disseminating information throughout their community and to the public.[69] The increased and improved profile of the newly-independent National Archives is essential to ensuring that this happens.[70] Perhaps not just a national voice but a national platform for archival administration is needed. As one commentator on the archival profession stated, "there is no national archival program . . . But without some kind of larger plan, can any

[66]Anna K. Nelson, "In Support of History," AHA *Perspectives* 22 (March 1984), 14-16, and the essay on leadership and local government records in this volume.

[67]Charlene N. Bickford, *The Coalition to Save Our Documentary Heritage: An Important Lesson in Archival Advocacy*, MARAC Occasional Publication, no. 3 (n.p.: Mid-Atlantic Regional Archives Conference, 1983), and Page Putnam Miller, "Archival Issues and Problems: The Central Role of Advocacy," *Public Historian* 8 (Summer 1986), 60-73.

[68]Cf., Edie Hedlin, "Archival Programs in the Southeast: A Preliminary Assessment," *Provenance* 11 (Spring 1984), 1-15; and Virginia Stewart, "Archives in the Midwest: Assessments and Prospects," *Midwestern Archivist* 10, no. 1 (1985), 5-16.

[69]A conclusion of the NAGARA study on the feasibility of establishing an archival clearinghouse was the fact that the profession did not need more information, but needs to organize and manage the information more effectively. Victoria Irons Walch, *Information Resources for Archivists and Records Administrators: A Report and Recommendations* (Albany: National Association of Government Archives and Records Administrators, 1987).

[70]See Robert M. Warner, "The National Archives at Fifty," *Midwestern Archivist* 10, no. 1 (1985), 25-32.

of us be fully satisfied that we are really working effectively?"[71]

Archivists should strengthen their educational foundation, theory, and public profile by forming full masters-level archival administration programs. American archivists need to deemphasize their heavy reliance upon apprenticeship in the education of professionals. Apprenticeship is most useful for only a limited range of archival activities that do not reflect the full variety of responsibilities an archivist encounters. Apprenticeship also "perpetuates the standards, and even more, the outlook of the dominant old hands,"[72] limiting severely the opportunity to learn about new theories and methods. Beyond the training of new professionals, archival education must also be a forum for the discussion and creation of archival theory that encourages practicing archivists to ask *why* and not just how they administer historical materials. Critics of archival education have noted that the present system perpetuates the scenario of busy archivists with little time to consider the theory underlying their work.[73] This pattern could best be broken by an independent masters' program. Terry Eastwood, director of the only such offering in North America at the University of British Columbia, has stated that the "first purpose of professional education . . . is to inculcate a body of general principles, a theoretical framework . . . which supports and guides the actual practice of the profession."[74] Without such a visible educational standard, archivists may never be in a suitable bargaining position for more resources or influence and may be unable to deal with the challenges of the modern information era. In an interesting commentary on the state of archival education, recent

[71]Jeffrey Field, "The Impact of Federal Funding on Archival Management in the United States," *Midwestern Archivist* 7, no. 2 (1982), 81-82.

[72]Michael Cook, "Professional Training: International Perspectives," *Archivaria* 7 (Winter 1978), 28.

[73]Edwin Welch, "Archival Education," *Archivaria* 4 (Summer 1977), 49-59; Frank G. Burke, "The Future Course of Archival Theory in the United States," *American Archivist* 44 (Winter 1981), 40-46.

[74]"The Origins and Aims of the Master of Archival Studies Programme at the University of British Columbia," *Archivaria* 16 (Summer 1983), 40.

graduates of American archival educational programs noted exactly such difficulties. Because of the fuzzy identity of archival programs, one student worried that "no one out there [is] promoting the archival profession and recruiting promising students into established programs." Another, criticizing the joint masters programs in history and library science, concluded, "we were pursuing neither careers in historical research nor careers in librarianship. We were caught in a no man's land, a void, between the two professions."[75]

Archivists should develop systems for individual certification and institutional accreditation in order to support their education and broader mission in society. During the debate about archival certification in the late 1970s, Trudy Peterson argued that archivists have "two fundamental responsibilities": "to protect the general public from incompetent or unscrupulous practitioners" and "to assist members of the profession in securing employment commensurate with professional status." She concluded that a "program of institutional and personal archival certification is the logical first step" toward meeting these responsibilities.[76] It is surprising that archivists did not move more deliberately in this direction until the late 1980s. Without certification and accreditation, the public identity of archivists will remain unclear, distinctions between professionals and non-professionals will always be uncertain at best, and the continued establishment of inadequate archival programs will continue, threatening the preservation of our documentary heritage.[77] Moreover,

---

[75]Virginia Cain, ed., "Archives By Degree: Personal Perspectives on Academic Preparation for the Archival Profession," *Provenance* 2 (Fall 1984), 44, 47.

[76]Peterson, Patrick M. Quinn, and Hugh A. Taylor, "Professional Archival Training," *American Archivist* 40 (July 1977), 315. Individual certification was finally adopted by the SAA Council in January 1987. The impact of that decision will be understood only after the program is fully operative in the early 1990s.

[77]On the latter matter, both archives and historical agencies face similar problems. See Dennis K. McDaniel, "In My Opinion: Stop Museum Proliferation!" *History News* 39 (March 1984), 31-32; and William L. Joyce, "Historical Records Repositories," in *Documenting America: Assessing the Condition of Historical Records in the States,* ed. Lisa B. Weber ([Albany]: National Association of State Archives and Records Administrators and the

related disciplines are actively working in these areas.[78] The specter of archivists absorbed into another profession or severely weakened in the competition for resources is a very real possibility. Fears of limiting the size of an already small profession or further weakening poor institutions and programs must be weighed against the chances for strengthening the identity of archivists and their work in modern society.

Archivists should not limit their quest for increased professionalism by dwelling on their small numbers, but should concentrate instead on their potential for employment. They should realize that their efforts to improve professional standards can open up additional avenues for societal influences. Nothing in the literature suggests that the degree of an occupation's professionalism has anything to do with the number of its practitioners. Rather, it is the importance of the occupation's mission and its ability to convince society of its importance that determines professional status and the successful pursuit of mission. Opportunities are great for archivists to seek influence and create employment, only one example being that of local governments. If only a small portion of America's political subdivisions employed a professional archivist, the size of the archival community would expand significantly.[79] But archivists are not now in a position even to urge such proselytizing efforts. Without stronger standards that distinguish archivists, local governments will have little ability to hire the right individuals. Without more and stronger archival education programs, local governments will not have a qualified pool of applicants from which to recruit. The future of the archival profession really rests with archivists themselves.

National Historical Publications and Records Commission, 1984), 44.

[78]Debora Shaw, "Accreditation and Information Science," *ASIS Bulletin* 11 (April-May 1985), 13-14; Susan M. Bronder, "Gaining Professional Status: The Leadership Role of the Institute of Certified Records Managers," *Records Management Quarterly* 18 (January 1984), 20-22, 24-26, 32; and Evelyn H. Daniel, "Accreditation," *Library Journal* (1 April 1985), 49-53.

[79]There are an estimated eighty thousand political subdivisions; H. G. Jones, *Local Government Records: An Introduction to Their Management, Preservation, and Use* (Nashville: American Association for State and Local History, 1980), x.

With this agenda archivists will *make* the opportunities needed to strengthen their position in modern society and enable them to fulfill their mission of documenting it.

The Individual Archivist and Concept of the Profession

Whether what archivists do constitute a profession or not is extremely important not just for the occupation, but for the individual archivist's well-being. It is difficult to function as a professional in any field in the late twentieth century. As one recent management volume declared, "the management of creative workers has become the most critical area faced by management in both the private and public sectors."[80] This is an area critical enough that a whole host of new writings and research about the management of professionals has emerged.

Public administration theorists have recently begun to draw on developmental psychology for its insights into life patterns that can aid both individuals and institutions in which they work. Developmental psychologists see that the adult psyche is continually changing and that this development has definable stages. The later concept has been conveniently summarized into stages of an early adulthood - a time of personal search for establishment, middle adulthood - a turbulent period in which adults attempt to deal with many conflicting changes and choices, and late adulthood - the preparation stage for retirement and retirement itself.[81]

It is not hard to imagine how such insights could be useful for institutional managers responsible for administering complex programs and teams of diverse people, common to what many archivists experience. One public affairs professor has recently argued for greater uses of such studies: "Managers need to be aware that life stage development is a major influence on the psychological 'set' which individuals bring to superior-subordinate relations and on the capacity of the organization to motivate and harness the creative energies of its employees." He goes on to state that the quality of management may

[80]Albert Shapero, *Managing Professional People: Understanding Creative Performance* (New York: Free Press, 1985), ix.

[81]For a convenient summary of these ideas, see Richard L. Schott, "The Psychological Development of Adults: Implications for Public Administration," *Public Administration Review* 46 (November/December 1986), 657-67.

depend "on the extent to which they [good managers] have successfully traversed the various developmental tasks of adult life" and their "capacity for empathy and the ability to divine where an individual is 'at' in terms of his or her needs and motivations."[82]

Some of the ideas of developmental psychologists and others in related fields have been popularized and through this popularization it is even easier to discern some of the potential implications for archival administrators and individual archivists. Judith Bardwick's *Plateauing Trap* applies many of the ideas concerning the middle adulthood period to common crises faced in a person's professional life. She says that we have become conditioned to thinking of professional, even personal, goals in terms of only promotions and chronicles the crises that set in when "plateauing" - the stabilization of promotions and opportunities for promotions - occurs. Perceptively, Bardwick shows how when this occurs, the organization, manager, *and* individual have responsibilities and points the way to the role of professionalism:

> In an enlightened corporate culture, we must help people reach a point where their professionalism is the essential source of their pride, their sense of growth, their feeling of achievement. They have to perceive 'success' as using their abilities, meeting challenges, continuing to learn, and making a contribution. Then they can feel fulfilled in the present and anticipate the future as exciting.[83]

Dual ladder promotional schemes, sabbaticals, retraining, and reassignment all take on a much more important role than ever before, along with the individual archivist's perception of his or her own profession.

Two other management consultants have looked at this issue from a very different angle, but nevertheless mirror some of the same traits, problems, and concerns that intrigue the developmental psychologists. Terrence Deal and Allen Kennedy wrote in the early 1980s a book exploring the notion of "corporate culture," the "system [where it adequately exists] of informal rules that spells out how people are to behave most

---

[82]Schott, "Psychological Development," 662-65.

[83]*The Plateauing Trap: How to Avoid It in Your Career . . . and Your Life* (New York: Amacom, 1986), 46.

of the time."[84]   Although these authors give many reasons why they believe strong corporate cultures are important, one of the main arguments relates to how employees now approach their jobs:

> Unlike workers ten or twenty years ago, employees today are confused . . . . they feel cheated by their jobs; they allow special interests to take up their time; their life values are uncertain; they are blameful and cynical; they confuse morality with ethics.   Uncertainty is at the core of it all.   Yet strong culture companies remove a great degree of that uncertainty because they provide structure and standards and a value system in which to operate.[85]

It can be argued that a stronger sense of professional identity, which this essay has built a case in behalf of, may be the most important element necessary for dealing with the uncertainty that Deal and Kennedy wrote about.

If individuals working as archivists have a strong perception of their profession and their part in it, then some of the problems they face as professionals may be resolved or, at least, lessened.   Focusing on the significance of the archival mission for society, what we can term our professional culture, can provide a safety valve when individual crises occur, as they inevitably will.   Keeping attuned to resolving obstacles to achieving the archival mission - like those in the first two essays of this volume - can also counter-balance individual archivists' problems.   And a greater sensitivity by the supervisors of archivists to their needs to participate in, feel a part of, and work to strengthen their own profession can instill a greater sense of meaning to how these archivists view and approach their own individual jobs.   A stronger archival profession will help lead to more competent archival practitioners, stronger archival repositories, and a better managed documentary heritage.

[84]*Corporate Cultures: The Rites and Rituals of Corporate Life* (Reading, Massachusetts: Addison-Wesley Publishing Co., 1982), 15.

[85]*Corporate Cultures*, 16.

Final Thoughts: Archivists and Power

The essence of professionalism is having power within society, but a power that benefits society. Discussion of such power usually brings up various negative connotations, but it is nevertheless the means by which any professional mission will be achieved. Archivists finally seem to be grasping that reality. Virginia Stewart has reminded her colleagues that to gain control over records, archivists need to recognize that success depends on more than just definitions of responsibilities and functions: "It is a power issue, involving both formal authority and informal mechanisms of implementation. Archivists may consider themselves most qualified to control records, but this claim is not widely shared."[86] A few years earlier, Frank Burke had similar thoughts: "The [archival] profession has been too lax too long in not protecting its own territory and fighting for its principles. We should be out on the ramparts struggling for recognition of our important role in society . . . ."[87] Instead, "archivists enjoy the status of virtue, not the status of power," according to the recent study by SAA on the attitudes of resource allocators toward archives and archivists.[88] If this continues archivists will remain in basements, will acquire funding only when it is surplus from other more essential functions, and can only hope for a chance to document modern society rather than energetically pursuing that goal. Professionalism is one route by which archivists can break away from such situations.

Two logical arguments can be expected in opposition to the recommendations of this essay. One is that somehow, despite whatever problems exist, archivists have managed to do a fairly respectable job gathering the materials needed for understanding the past. To this the answer is obvious. The changes in documentation of the late twentieth century demand that archivists fulfill new roles and develop new strategies. Documenting an event of 1975 is exceedingly more complex than documenting an event of 1800. The second argument contends that the very changes of modern society, primarily its reliance on technology, are making professions as such

[86]"Archives in the Midwest," 10.

[87]"Archival Cooperation," *American Archivist* 46 (Summer 1983), 303.

[88]Levy, "The Status of Virtue: Resource Allocators' Perceptions of Archives," 7.

obsolete.[89] Why, then, should archivists, or members of any occupation, waste their time trying to achieve professional attributes belonging to an outmoded system? This argument is not as easily refuted. The best response is to say that such discarding of professions is not guaranteed. Warren I. Susman cautioned against "technological determinism": "the acceptance of any technological innovation obviously depends on the nature of the culture into which any proposed innovation is introduced. Even more significantly, the *form* such innovation takes is culturally shaped."[90] Archivists cannot afford to gamble on predictions, but should instead grasp the best means available for accomplishing their mission. That means is professionalism.

[89]Alvin Toffler, *The Third Wave* (New York: Bantam, 1981) is an example of such projections.

[90]*Culture As History: The Transformation of American Society in the Twentieth Century* (New York: Pantheon Books, 1984), 253. For examples of fuller comments of such concern, see Peter N. Stearns, "Forecasting the Future: Historical Analogies and Technological Determinism," *Public Historian* 5 (Summer 1983), 31-54; and "The Idea of Postindustrial Society: Some Problems," *Journal of Social History* 17 (Summer 1984), 685-93.

THREE   **LAYING A FOUNDATION FOR ARCHIVAL LEADERSHIP: THE SAA GOALS AND PRIORITIES TASK FORCE REPORT[1]**

Planning and the Archival Profession

Archivists have long recognized that theirs is a profession with a broad mandate handicapped by far too limited resources. In the past few years, through a series of major investigations and reports, archivists have learned the extent of the threat to historical records in the United States caused by their profession's own weaknesses, especially their lack of leadership in preparing broad plans, and acting on those plans, for strengthening the care of this nation's documentary heritage.[2] Some archivists will bristle at that last sentence and argue correctly that numerous other reasons exist for the poor condition of this nation's historical records. However, the *major* responsibility for the care of America's documentary heritage is one that archivists can not deny belongs to them. Given their profession's general poverty and its tremendous obligations, archivists must learn, among other things, to plan carefully for the more judicious use of resources and for programs that will enable them to gain greater resources for use in new areas and in new ways. The report of the Society of American Archivists' (SAA) Goals and Priorities (GAP) Task Force is the archival profession's most recent and best opportunity to begin to do just that. This report is also the major part of the foundation for renewed national archival leadership.

The archival profession has been involved in planning in one way or another for over thirty years. Ernst Posner's *American State Archives*[3] is a typical result of 1960s planning, as well as a classic of archival literature. The SAA Committee for the Seventies led to the hiring of the association's first executive director and laid the foundation for a stronger, more vibrant

---

[1]This essay was originally published in *Provenance* 3 (Fall 1985), 22-37.

[2]See the first essay in this volume for a summary of these reports.

[3](Chicago: University of Chicago Press, 1964). For a more complete description of the legacy of archival planning see F. Gerald Ham's introduction to *Planning for the Archival Profession: A Report of the SAA Task Force on Goals and Priorities* (Chicago: Society of American Archivists, 1986), 1-5 and "Planning for the Archival Profession," *American Archivist* 48 (Winter 1985), 26-30.

profession.[4]   This committee's report reflected the archivists' notion of planning in the 1970s. The concise report envisioned, among other things, an extensive set of writings on the basics of professional practices and standards, a goal that has been partly achieved,[5] and focused on the profession's major association, SAA.

Planning in the 1980s has been different, although only results in the 1990s will indicate how effective it has been. Some archivists talk about planning as if it was something new, and it seems to be. Most now realize that previous efforts at planning have been generally unsuccessful. The first SAA committee on planning produced a single paragraph report; the next committee only searched (unsuccessfully) for their predecessor's records.   Posner's excellent report was treated as a reference book or history of the profession and not the agenda for change that it really was and asked to be.[6] The Committee for the Seventies, while perhaps the most successful planning effort, largely restricted itself to the internal organization of the SAA and did not touch upon many broader professional issues. More typical, unfortunately, is the legacy of the already forgotten 1977 Conference on Setting Priorities for Historical Records which issued a report, raised some issues, and hoped things would work out; there was no commitment to monitoring progress on meeting these priorities.[7] Even many of the state assessment and reporting projects reports, completed in the first half of the 1980s, seem forgotten and unused in some of the states. The apparent difference with planning in the late 1980s is that is was done in an environment of urgency that did not accept the luxury of failure. A small but growing group of archivists have staked on national and state planning the means to resist the rapidly deteriorating condition of America's documentary heritage. These individuals argue that one way of combating the poor condition of America's historical records is through planning for

[4]Philip P. Mason, "Archives in the Seventies: Promises and Fulfillment," *American Archivist* 44 (Summer 1981), 199-206.

[5]Terry Abraham, "Publishing for the Archival Profession," *Scholarly Publishing* 15 (April 1984), 265-71 and the essay on archival literature in this volume.

[6]H.G. Jones, "The Pink Elephant Revisited," *American Archivist* 43 (Fall 1980), 473-83.

[7]Mary Lynn McCree and Timothy Walch, eds., "Setting Priorities for Historical Records: A Conference Report," *American Archivist* 40 (July 1977), 291-347.

the transformation of the archival profession into a more vibrant and vital player in modern society. In a sense, this entire volume is a document resulting from recent archival planning efforts.

The 1980s represented a much more complex world than could be known or dreamt of by the archival forebears. Although the profession has grown significantly in numbers, it still must appoint a task force to grapple with the issue of why it is misunderstood, not only by the general populace, but by its administrators.[8] This is the "information age," yet many archivists question their own ability to deliver information. There is an ever increasing use of technology to capture and control information, but many archivists not only remain more comfortable with paper records, but treat them as revered artifacts. Perhaps most disheartening, archivists call themselves a profession, yet must admit that their standards are lax; they continually welcome into their fellowship persons who, with little or no training, are declared to be archivists and given the responsibilities of such, voiding one of the preeminent characteristics of any profession.[9] It was in this climate that the SAA Goals and Priorities (GAP) Task Force originated, issued its report for consideration by the archival profession, and evolved into a standing committee of the association.

The GAP Task Force and Its Report

The GAP Task Force only dates back to the early 1980s, developing in the same time as the National Historical Publications and Records Commission (NHPRC)-sponsored state assessment and reporting projects and out of the 1982 SAA meeting's theme of "Planning in an Archival Environment." The task force was appointed in September 1982 and for two years - beefed up by the addition of several working groups and the support of NHPRC funds - worked on preparing *Planning for the Archival Profession: A Report of the SAA Task Force on Goals and Priorities*, the most extensive agenda ever set for the American archival profession. This report was not the end of the task force's work; the report was an action document requiring further discussion and refinement,

[8]David B. Gracy, "Archives and Society: The First Archival Revolution," *American Archivist* 47 (Winter 1984), 7-10. See also Edward Weldon, "Archives and the Challenge of Change," *ibid.* 46 (Spring 1983), 125-34.

[9]See chapter two in this volume for more information about the nature of a profession and how the archival community compares to a profession.

suggesting that archival planning is a continuous process. SAA's governing body, its Council, adopted priorities for the association based on the report and transformed the task force into a standing committee, charged with the monumental task of charting progress on the report's original goals and refining priorities as necessary.

While the report is not easily summarized, it is important to review the assumptions of the group responsible for the report, look at the report's content and structure, and examine the accomplishments and implications of the ongoing committee on archival planning for the future of the archival profession.

The task force report rested on five assumptions. First, support for archival work is insufficient to identify and preserve America's documentary heritage. Second, the archival profession must more aggressively encourage and carry out planning, cooperation, research and development, and advocacy and public information programs if it expects to make efficient use of its limited resources. Third, the responsibilities of the archivist and his or her repository must extend beyond any single individual or institution if the profession is to achieve what must be its preeminent goal of preserving the historical record. Fourth, records and information management are integral components of the archival profession; without them, its ability to preserve the historical record is seriously restricted. Fifth, and finally, the archival community is considered to encompass all individuals, institutions, and associations involved in the labor of preserving historical records.[10]

The report itself was built around a brief mission statement for the archival profession - "to ensure the identification, preservation, and use of records of enduring value to society" - and included one section devoted to each major goal of that statement. The codification of the archival mission into such a concise, and powerful, statement is a noteworthy accomplishment in its own right. Each goal was also broken down to more specific objectives, strategies, and activities that constitute an agenda for action, at least as far as could be perceived in the late 1980s. The main criticism of the report in the late 1980s was not directed to its content but to its breadth of concern, causing some to see it as little more than an elaborate - and largely unattainable - "wish list" for the archival profession. It is precisely for this reason that the primary focus of continuing deliberation about the report should be equally divided between analyzing its recommendations and

---

[10]*Planning for the Archival Profession*, 4.

acting on them and considering the need for supporting the work of an ongoing planning committee that provides a broad, national focus on planning and development.[11]

A standing committee on archival planning was a necessity for any success in accomplishing the goals stated in the task force report. As presently constituted, the committee consists of members appointed by the SAA[12] and has a threefold mission:

1. To carry out an active and open process to establish, refine, update, and promulgate statements of mission, goals, objectives, strategies, and activities and to recommend priority activities for the archival community;

2. To foster the activities recommended through this process, especially the activities of high priority; and

3. To promote planning by archival organizations and associations.

As such, the committee is an effort to create a climate that encourages and coordinates efforts like the Bentley fellowships, National Information Systems Task Force (NISTF), the Joint Committee on the Archives of Science and Technology (JCAST), and the Coalition for the Preservation of Architectural Records (COPAR), and to provide a long-needed mechanism for encouraging cooperation with other related professions as well as records users and creators. If the archival profession is honest with itself, it must admit that the task force report is only a proposed agenda and the resultant planning committee only one means for beginning to meet that agenda. What was really proposed in the report was some very fundamental changes to the profession that encourage greater sustained research, development, and action. The SAA Council has already taken the first step in such a change by establishing and supporting the ongoing Committee on Goals and Priorities

[11]This committee is discussed in *Planning for the Archival Profession*, 36-38.

[12]As originally proposed the committee was also to consist of individuals from regional and state archival associations and related professions such as history and library science.

and adopting goals and priorities for itself that clarify its role in continued planning for the archival profession.[13]

Certainly the creation of the SAA planning committee has been one of the most important and fundamental changes for the archival profession in the 1980s. For the first time it gives the potential for an interdisciplinary national focus to the needs and goals of the archival profession and its mission. It potentially equips the national associations, like the SAA and the National Association of Government Archives and Records Administrators (NAGARA), to do what they have not been able to do very successfully - to move beyond organizational needs and goals to plan for the *entire* profession. Such a committee has begun to knit together, if only on paper at this time, such national efforts as the local government records committee sponsored by the American Association for State and Local History (AASLH), the industry action committees of the Association of Records Managers and Administrators (ARMA), the various sections of the SAA, the Committee on the Records of Government, and NAGARA into a more coherent national agenda for America's documentary heritage. Despite how diverse the archival profession might seem to be, with a wide variety of specialties, institutions, and constituencies, its primary mission to preserve and manage historical records is one that begs for a national plan.[14] The planning committee is not, of course, the answer to all of the archival profession's problems and needs. For the committee's agenda to have any reasonable chance of success there must be important changes in archival education and training programs, state historical records advisory boards, regional archival associations, archival institutions, to name a few components of the profession. The remainder of this essay (and this entire volume) touches upon

---

[13]See Anne R. Kenney, "SAA Council Priorities Modified," *SAA Newsletter*, September 1987, 7; Richard J. Cox, "Council Revises Its Priorities," *ibid*, September 1988, 4-5.

[14]CGAP has been partly engaged, in its brief history, in "consensus building," that is, attempting to gain support "both within the profession and from other allies and constituencies to carry out planning activities"; *Planning for the Archival Profession*, 36. One effort was cooperating on the development of a national trust for the preservation and management of this country's historical records. Despite such work, most of CGAP's early efforts have been on defining its role *within* SAA, its relationship to SAA's governing body, and monitoring and encouraging initiatives in the profession (still generally focused on SAA) on priority needs. For the still remaining need to move toward a more coherent national historical records policies, see the last chapter in this volume.

these aspects of the archival community in the context of national planning for America's documentary heritage.

Implications of the GAP Report

Of all of the above elements of the archival profession there has been more written about education than any other, and with good reasons. Educational standards are an important aspect of the foundation of every profession,[15] yet archivists lack control over this important area. The formulation of archival theory has been slowed because of a poor footing in the university and a continuing orientation to practical rather than theoretical issues.[16] The GAP report suggests changes in the profession's attitude toward and practice of archival education, but without some basic, remedial changes in archival education the profession will be unable to support adequately efforts to strengthen the education of archivists. Specifically, archival education - whether tied to history department, library school, or public or applied history program[17] - must be as attentive to theory as practice. For example, some ground breaking historical studies evolve out of the graduate school thesis or dissertation; the same could occur for the archival profession. More importantly, in most professions new ideas, studies, and proposals for applications in the field come from the full time university faculty educating aspiring practitioners in that discipline. Many archival education programs do not encourage, however, the study and writing of theses on archival subjects or the writing of theses at all, since most programs consist of only a few courses and emphasize practice. The GAP Task Force report could be used as one agenda for such

---

[15]See chapter two of this volume for a fuller explanation of the role that education plays in professions.

[16]These problems are clearly reflected in the historical development of archival education in this country; see Richard C. Berner, *Archival Theory and Practice in the United States: A Historical Analysis* (Seattle: University of Washington Press, 1983), chapter 7; Jacqueline Goggin, "'That We Shall Truly Deserve the Title of Profession': The Training and Education of Archivists, 1930-1960," *American Archivist* 47 (Summer 1984), 243-54; and the chapters on archival education in this volume.

[17]There is an extensive literature on archival education that focuses on such matters. For a discussion of this literature, and my own views on archival training, see the essay on this topic in this volume.

research and writing.[18]   Some archivists examining the task force report have even suggested that it could be used to introduce individuals, studying to be archivists, to the nature of the modern archival profession (or, at least, the manner in which the archival profession views itself at the end of the 1980s).

Much of the discussion about archival theory in recent years has lamented an individual's lack of free time from administrative responsibilities as a reason for the profession's difficulties in developing an adequate theory.[19]   While this argument is persuasive, it is certainly not comprehensive and, in fact, neglects the strengths of doing research and developing or testing archival theory in the heated atmosphere of the archival repository.   "Research . . . is defining what is unknown and finding answers by asking questions. This . . . explanation [of research] is offered to demonstrate that the everyday work of archivists involves the research process."[20]   Although it would be difficult to state that ignoring the research and theory building responsibilities has not had a generally negative influence upon the development of archival theory, there have been bright spots in the past. All through his career, for example, Theodore R. Schellenberg was devoted to the "development, systematization, and standardization of archival principles and techniques."   In each phase of his career, Schellenberg's experiences sharpened his archival writings.   At the National Archives as director of archival management, he prepared a series of Staff Information Circulars, building the foundation for his Australian lecture

[18]See the three research agenda papers on appraisal, management, and reference in the Winter/Spring 1989 issue of the *American Archivist* as examples of what the report can stimulate. The original versions of these essays were presented at the 1987 annual meeting of SAA and officially sponsored by the SAA CGAP.

[19]Frank G. Burke, "The Future Course of Archival Theory in the United States," *American Archivist* 44 (Winter 1981), 40-46, and Richard C. Berner, "Toward National Archival Priorities: A Suggested Basis for Discussion," *ibid.* 45 (Spring 1982), 172.   There have also been more extreme views presented, arguing that there are *no* theoretical underpinnings to archival methodology; see John W. Roberts, "Archival Theory: Much Ado About Shelving," *ibid.* 50 (Winter 1987), 66-74.

[20]Richard J. Cox and Helen W. Samuels, "The Archivist's First Responsibility: A Research Agenda to Improve the Identification and Retention of Records of Enduring Value," *American Archivist* 51 (Winter/Spring 1988), 28-42.

tour and subsequent publication, *Modern Archives*.[21]   This volume did more to begin standardization of the archivists' practice than any other single publication. Until the 1970s, it was the standard textbook for archival education courses. Schellenberg, for all practical purposes, was the "National Archives theoretician-in-charge,"[22] and, as such, he had tremendous influence on that institution and the profession.

What would happen if the archival profession could formally establish a number of positions, similar to what Schellenberg held during the 1950s? Creation of institutional research and development units could free individuals to study archival matters, prepare published studies, exchange ideas of practice between repositories, foster inter-institutional cooperation, and prepare case-study and other materials that are needed in graduate and continuing education programs. The duties of such units could consist of fostering long-range goals and priorities; conducting research projects required by the repository and also identified as needs by the profession; publishing research; overseeing the continued professional development of the institution's staff through internal seminars, coordination of guest speakers, and inter-institutional exchange of professional staff; and identifying and acquiring funding sources for special or more complex projects. Since many of the identified goals of the task force report concern or relate to archival institutions, especially state archives and other large research repositories, the creation of such units is a logical step for the benefit of these programs and the profession. Research and development units do not necessarily have to be large divisions but can consist of single individuals freed from administrative duties that normally hinder the profession's ability to produce such work. If business corporations only relied upon universities and colleges to develop technology necessary for the creation of new products, they would not remain competitive for very long.[23] Why should the archival profession similarly rely only on such formal education programs and not make a broader commitment to developing archival theory and to planning for its development? In one

[21]T. R. Schellenberg, *Modern Archives: Principles and Techniques* (Chicago: University of Chicago Press, 1956).

[22]Jane F. Smith, "Theodore R. Schellenberg: Americanizer and Popularizer," *American Archivist* 44 (Fall 1981), 313-26.

[23]See, for example, Thomas J. Peters and Robert H. Waterman, Jr., *In Search of Excellence: Lessons from America's Best-Run Companies* (New York: Warner Books, 1982).

sense, the Committee on Goals and Priorities could serve as a national archival research and development body.[24]

One of the groups that has received the greatest attention recently, in regards to planning, has been the State Historical Records Advisory Board created to support the funding program of the NHPRC. Although the NHPRC has hoped for these boards to be much more than they have been,[25] prior to the state assessment and reporting projects they were little more than grant reviewers and, in many cases, most have remained tied to that function. Since the early 1980s, however, their role has been significantly expanded to one of statewide planning and coordination because of the state assessment and reporting projects. These boards, or other statewide bodies, can encourage information gathering on historical records and the programs that care for them, plan for and report on progress in the strengthening of these programs, advocate for increased support for these programs, educate repository staffs and provide information that these staffs require, foster cooperation between programs that ensures the effective use of resources, push for and develop standards and guidelines governing the care of the documentary heritage, and undertake many other important activities.

To fulfill such roles successfully would enable the State Historical Records Advisory Boards to become important vehicles in assisting the meeting of the archival profession's goals and objectives. These state boards could partially serve as entities for the national planning committee to work with and to encourage to take on projects. The boards must expand their membership beyond just archivists and their colleagues to records users, legislators, creators, supporters, and members of the concerned public; they must possess a clear commitment to statewide archival planning and be able to relate their state plans to national professional goals and plans; and, finally, they must be able to influence the larger and key repositories within

---

[24]One could argue that the National Archives has played such a role in the past. This is undoubtedly true for the formative years of the profession, as shown in Donald R. McCoy, *The National Archives: America's Ministry of Documents 1934-1968* (Chapel Hill: University of North Carolina Press, 1978), and Trudy Huskamp Peterson, "The National Archives and the Archival Theorist Revisited, 1954-1984," *American Archivist* 49 (Spring 1986), 25-33. There is little evidence today, however, that the National Archives considers this to be one of its responsibilities or desired roles.

[25]Larry J. Hackman, "The Historical Records Program: The States and the Nation," *American Archivist* 43 (Winter 1980), 17-32, and F. Gerald Ham, "NHPRC's Records Program and the Development of Statewide Archival Planning," *ibid.* 43 (Winter 1980), 33-42.

the states to support the national plan. The existence of such boards or, in their place, other coalitions or consortia, offers the possibility of carrying the national archival planning and development from a national plane to the arenas of the states. The state arena is more appropriate for many of the initiatives that the archival profession needs undertaken. In New York, for example, the State Historical Records Advisory Board has conducted studies, issued reports, sought legislation, and gained increased State funding for many efforts for managing Court, local government, and private archival records.[26] It is also true, however, that the main impetus for this has come from the state archives itself, with the board generally responding to this leadership.

Regional archival associations, formed in the early 1970s as an alternative to the SAA for professional activities and support, have become extremely important in keeping archival issues before a broader constituency and have assumed, as well, some of the SAA role of providing basic archival training and education. Some of the larger associations have served as forums for the testing and development of ideas later brought into national focus, and two have successfully supported important journals for archival research and writing.[27]

There must be some basic changes in these associations, however, for them to play a greater role in state and national archival planning and development. For one, their support of the GAP Task Force report and the present SAA planning committee could extend to modelling their annual and semi-annual meetings around specific activities in the task force's report, encouraging the preparation and critique of formal papers on these subjects that could contribute to the profession's advancement. Furthermore, these associations should serve as an introduction for the newer members of the profession to the broader vision and needs of the archival community and as a means of attracting wider audiences of records users and creators that can consider, debate, and formulate new strategies for the preservation of America's documentary heritage. Admittedly, much of this has occurred as the GAP report was initially discussed widely throughout the profession and as SAA has recently adopted one avenue for

[26]The state that has tried hardest, with some success, to reconstitute its historical records advisory board into a statewide planning body is New York. See Larry J. Hackman, "From Assessment to Action: Toward A Usable Past in the Empire State," *Public Historian* 7 (Summer 1985), 23-34.

[27]Patrick M. Quinn, "Regional Archival Organizations and the Society of American Archivists," *American Archivist* 46 (Fall 1983), 433-40.

strengthening the profession, certification of individual practitioners. More fundamental changes are still needed.

The regional associations could also play a number of other roles in archival planning and development. They could serve as mechanisms for encouraging high priority research projects on a regional level or for tracking and disseminating information about important projects and their results. And the associations can extend beyond the specific needs or interests of their regions, developing cooperative strategies for the implementation of certain professional goals. Certainly this last role is the regional archival associations' greatest potential contribution to the process of archival planning and the continuing development of the profession.[28]

Although such a national planning committee is essential to the continued growth of the archival profession, no one body or group will bring about the changes necessary to commit the profession to ongoing, dynamic, and essential priorities and activities. All levels or aspects of the archival profession must make this commitment - from the institutional repository[29] to the university training ground to statewide and regional groups -if the archival profession is to continue to grow, identify needs, and adapt to the changing society in which it is a member and that it endeavors to document and to serve. Considering the weakness of the archival profession's theory and literature, all of these groups could simultaneously attack the needs described in the task force report. It will be helpful to consider how a few elements of the report could be coordinated by a planning committee and then to discuss how the CGAP has thus far tried to provide such coordination and what success it has met with a few years after the publication of the task force's report.

One of the strategies in the appraisal goal is "promote the development of coordinated and cooperative collecting strategies," and there are six activities supporting it.[30] In this case, various segments of the profession could easily

---

[28]Although many regional associations discussed the GAP report when it was in draft, few of these groups have continued any serious consideration of the report's recommendations. One exception was the Long Island Archivists Conference which featured a series of keynote addresses on the themes of the report and the implications of the report's priorities and suggested activities for this regional group.

[29]For one effort to suggest ways that individual repositories could make use of the GAP report, see Gregory S. Hunter, "Filling the GAP: Planning on the Local and Individual Levels," *American Archivist* 50 (Winter 1987), 110-115.

[30]*Planning for the Archival Profession*, 11.

concentrate upon each of these activities. For example, the study of "existing cooperative arrangements such as networks and consortia" could be a subject of full analysis by graduate archival students, whereas the evaluation of "geographical and topical case studies to determine how cooperative collecting strategies can be developed and carried out" could be a focus of the meetings of regional archival associations. Some of the suggested activities are much more difficult. The study of the "creation of interconnected documentation . . . to determine if coordinated retention decisions can be made" will never be resolved unless the archival repositories make a stronger commitment to the work of research and development. The staffs of state archives are aware of the interconnection of federal, state, and local records, for example, but generally continue, for a variety of reasons, to make appraisal decisions on an individual basis. Such issues can be resolved only if state archives and the National Archives allow staff the time to investigate such matters, propose procedures that enable more effective appraisal, and carry out the necessary activities.[31]

Goal two, "the administration of archival programs to ensure the preservation of all records of enduring value," is, in some ways, the heart of the task force report. It aims at the basic needs for the development of the archival profession. For example, one of the strategies is to "promote the continuing development of a body of professional literature,"[32] a need that all segments of the profession must work to meet. The national and regional archival associations need to evaluate whether the present means of publishing studies and reports is sufficient. Are the *American Archivist, Midwestern Archivist, Provenance*, and *Archivaria* an adequate number of journals for North American archivists to publish? Can archivists find suitable outlets for the publication of monographs, festschrifts, and other such volumes that would strengthen the profession's theory and practice? Would it be possible for expanded State Historical Records Advisory Boards to encourage research by

---

[31]The framework for such cooperation has been laid, and there are some promising signs that inter-repository cooperation in appraisal may occur. Seven states have been cooperating in developing the means to share appraisal information concerning state and local public records via the Research Libraries Information Network (RLIN). Their work has helped generate interest in more cooperative efforts. The National Archives has also recently proposed some projects to determine how the relationship between federal and state government records can be better accommodated in its appraisal work.

[32]*Planning for the Archival Profession*, 18.

providing funds to focus upon specific statewide needs? Would not institutional research and development units, described earlier in this essay, better support the encouragement of "archival institutions and granting agencies to publish case studies of projects or other studies in archival science?"

The final area of access is, perhaps, one of the easiest goals of the report to conceptualize and consider, although not necessarily the easiest to deal with, since it concentrates upon communication. One of the strategies is to "develop communications between archivists and the user community,"[33] an area often discussed but seldom adequately studied.[34] The regional archival associations, for example, could make an effort to attract wider participation of user groups in their organizations and at their meetings. The State Historical Records Advisory Boards need to include as full participants representatives of the user communities. And archival graduate programs could have students carefully analyze the past and present uses of archival materials in special repositories or across broad topical areas to assist archivists in planning for the future.[35]

A national archival planning committee could monitor work being done in such areas as those mentioned above, identify gaps, encourage individuals, institutions, and associations to fill those gaps, and then report on the progress. This is precisely what CGAP has attempted to do thus far during its brief existence, and the results have been promising.

---

[33]*Planning for the Archival Profession*, 27.

[34]Elsie T. Freeman, "In the Eye of the Beholder: Archives Administration from the User's Point of View," *American Archivist* 47 (Spring 1984), 111-23, and William L. Joyce, "Archivists and Research Use," *ibid.* 47 (Spring 1984), 124-33. For the nature of continuing problems in archivists' general lack of knowledge about researcher needs and their relationship with researchers, see the 1989 study of research use in the National Archives written by Page Putnam Miller.

[35]Studies are needed such as Clark A. Elliott, "Citation Patterns and Documentation for the History of Science: Some Methodological Considerations," *American Archivist* 44 (Spring 1981), 131-42 and Paul Conway, "Research in Presidential Libraries: A User Survey," *Midwestern Archivist* 11, no. 1 (1986), 35-56. An excellent model for studying researcher use of archival models has been suggested by Paul Conway, "Facts and Frameworks: An Approach to Studying the Users of Archives," *American Archivist* 49 (Fall 1986), 393-407.

A Brief Commentary on the Short History of CGAP

It is, of course, impossible to determine the long-term impact of a body that has existed only a little over three years. On the other hand, CGAP's accomplishments bode well for the future of planning in the American archival profession. As CGAP's most recent chair wrote in early 1988, "it is clear that the planning process, which the Task Force on Goals and Priorities began, has now pervaded the society."[36]

Since CGAP was officially established by SAA Council in 1986, it has accomplished a great amount. The NHPRC has endorsed the Task Force's original report, using it as a basis for setting some of its own funding priorities. SAA Council has become more concerned with profession-wide priorities, and how SAA fits into the overall profession and its mission. CGAP established planning groups in five important areas - appraisal and documentation strategies, automated records and techniques, institutional standards and evaluation, management training for archivists, and the educational potential of archives, all issuing reports on needed priority actions.[37] CGAP sponsored three sessions on research agendas in the principal goal areas of the task force report at the 1987 SAA annual meeting, and the publication of these papers in a special issue of the 1988 *American Archivist* has done much to continue discussion about certain needed actions to strengthen the archival profession. And, finally, the CGAP has issued one of its promised annual reports on progress that the profession has made in selected priority areas.[38]

Because of the demonstrated value of the CGAP, SAA Council in June 1988 re-authorized the committee for an additional three years, through 1991. The reconstituted CGAP was given three charges:

1. Purpose, maintain, refine, and distribute statements of goals and priorities for the archival community.

---

[36]Charles Palm to Donn Neal, 4 March 1988, copy in possession of the author.

[37]SAA Committee on Goals and Priorities, *An Action Agenda for the Archival Profession: Institutionalizing the Planning Process; A Report to SAA Council* ([Chicago]: Society of American Archivists, August 31, 1988).

[38]John Fleckner, "The SAA Committee on Goals and Priorities; A Report to the Profession: June 1987," *SAA Newsletter*, July 1987, 6-8.

2.   Report annually to the SAA, the archival community, related professions, and the general public.

3.   Promote action to achieve recommended objectives, especially in areas of high priority.

It is clear from these charges that CGAP has an important responsibility within the American archival community, one that would be sorely missed if CGAP did not exist. Without an effective national planning committee, the chances for the improvement of the profession's status or resources - or even self-image - are significantly poorer. Archivists seem to realize that national planning is important and that such planning needs to be an active and continuous process.

One major area of uncertainty still exists, however, with CGAP. This SAA body does not yet fully represent the archival profession or provide an adequate means for related professions to work together to preserve America's documentary heritage. CGAP is still a body with members completely appointed from among SAA's ranks, although it was originally conceived to be a group that would consist of representatives of other related professional associations. This broader representation is especially important as other professional associations, such as the American Association for State and Local History, form long-range planning committees and wrestle with how to manage other aspects of America's cultural resources.[39]   CGAP is likely to expand the breadth of its mission as it continues its important work. Nevertheless, CGAP, even as it is now organized, represents an important new commitment to archival professional leadership.

[39]Ellsworth H. Brown, "Foundations for the Future: Initial Report of the AD Hoc Committee on Planning for the American Association for State and Local History," *History News* 41 (September/October 1986), 28-33; Lonn W. Taylor, ed., *A Common Agenda for History Museums: Conference Proceedings February 19-20, 1987* (Nashville: American Association for State and Local History and Washington, D.C.: Smithsonian Institution, 1987).

FOUR   **FAILED OPPORTUNITIES:**
        ARCHIVAL LEADERSHIP AND
        LOCAL GOVERNMENT RECORDS[1]

Introduction: The Importance of the Locality in American
History and the Paradox of Local Government Records

One of the more interesting trends of the American
historical profession has been its recurring "discovery" of the
importance of local history. The very dawn of professional
history in the latter decades of the nineteenth century carried
with it an intense, if short-lived, interest in local history and
the establishment of ties between the new professionals and the
traditional antiquarians and local community leaders; this was
typified by the labors of historians like Herbert Baxter Adams.[2]
Not quite half a century later, in a period of awakening
interest in cultural and community history, professional
historians again discovered local history. Constance
McLaughlin Green, in a now classic essay, stated that a "true
understanding of American cultural development . . . must be
told by details."[3] More recently, Kathleen Neils Conzen wrote
that the "history of life at the local level emerged in the 1970s
as one of the most lively and promising areas of historical
inquiry in the United States," all the more promising because
she believed that this new interest "coincided with and fed
upon the dramatic upsurge in popular historical awareness
within the United States during the 1970s."[4]
Although local government records are essential to
documenting and understanding local history in the United
States, the periodic awakenings of interest in local history seem
to have had little impact on their management and
preservation. The deplorable condition of local government
records in the 1980s differs little from their condition in the

---

[1]This essay was originally published as separate essays in the *Public
Historian* 3 (Winter 1981), 49-63; Lisa B. Weber, ed., *Documenting America:
Assessing the Condition of Historical Records in the States* ([Albany]:
National Association of State Archives and Records Administrators, [1984]),
19-36; and the *Midwestern Archivist* 10, no. 1 (1985), 33-41.

[2]John Higham, "Herbert Baxter Adams and the Study of Local History,"
American Historical Review 89 (December 1984), 1225-39.

[3]"The Value of Local History," in *The Cultural Approach to History*, ed.
Caroline F. Ware (New York: Columbia University Press, 1940), 275.

[4]"Community Studies, Urban History, and American Local History," in
The Past Before Us: Contemporary Historical Writing in the United States,
ed. Michael Kammen (Ithaca: Cornell University Press, 1980), 270, 273.

early twentieth century. The Public Archives Commission and the American Historical Association, the Historical Records Survey, and the committees of the Society of American Archivists (SAA), the National Association of Government Archives and Records Administrators (NAGARA), the Association of Records Managers and Administrators (ARMA), and the American Association for State and Local History (AASLH), and the very recent state assessment and reporting projects sponsored by the National Historical Publications and Records Commission (NHPRC) all have reached a similar conclusion about the condition of American local government records over the past eight decades - that these records are mismanaged and neglected.

The explanation of the devastating neglect of these records is complex. Local governments have failed to accept the responsibility for properly managing their own records.[5] Society in general has not valued its own heritage enough to cope with the large costs required to preserve the historical records of the political subdivisions. Still, a large portion of the blame for the condition of local government records rests with the American archival profession itself, if only because this profession wants and assumes the responsibility for managing and preserving the documentary heritage. Archivists may not have carried these records off to the dumps and incinerators or fed them to vermin, but they have failed to stop this destruction, at least partly because they have failed to develop and pursue any consistent strategy for caring for local government records in this country. If efforts like SAA's Committee on Goals and Priorities show a renewed vitality in national archival leadership, then the poor condition of America's local government records reveal how far this archival leadership has to develop. This essay considers the past and present work and future needs of archivists in caring for this important element of America's documentary heritage.

The History of Managing Local Government Records

Attempts to administer local government records in the United States have been as varied as they have been unsuccessful. The earliest plans called for centralizing local records in the newly-created state archival repositories, an arrangement based on the convenience of historical researchers

---

[5]Bruce W. Dearstyne, "State Programs for Local Government Records: Agents for Change," paper presented at the 1983 annual meeting of the Society of American Archivists.

and the assumption that these institutions could provide better care for these records. This was, of course, an unrealistic system proposed by eager and optimistic state archivists seeking to establish their institutions.[6] The development and improvement of micrographics systems offered an alternative to the centralization of original records, but the immense resources required to support such a program were beyond the means of most state archives. The Historical Records Survey (HRS) of the depression years promoted the idea that merely inventorying these records could help convince local officials to care for them better; surprisingly, the 1970s witnessed the resurrection of such efforts in a number of states,[7] even in the face of the obvious failures of the HRS.[8] None of these efforts have resulted in the development of a completely viable means of resolving the problems of administering local records in the United States.

The recognition of these failed attempts led many archivists, beginning in the 1940s, to urge the local maintenance of these records. Eventually, some state archivists expanded their role to provide leadership for the pressing needs of local governments. The concept of such a partnership emerged in the 1950s, was advanced by Ernst Posner in his *American State Archives* in the mid-1960s, and seemed firmly established by the following decade. Published manuals, workshops, outreach programs, and even state run regional networks became accustomed features among the state archives, and the

[6]Solon J. Buck, "Local Archives: Should They Be Centralized at the State Capital? Advantages and Disadvantages of Such a Centralization," American Historical Association *Annual Report*, 1913, I, 268-71; Theodore C. Pease, "The Problem of Archive Centralization with Reference to Local Conditions in a Middle Western State," American Historical Association *Annual Report*, 1916, I, 151-54; and Leon De Valinger, Jr., "The Place of County Records in the State Archival System," *American Archivist* 11 (January 1948), 37-41.

[7]Luther H. Evans and Edythe Weiner, "The Analysis of County Records," *American Archivist* 1 (October 1938), 186-200; J. M. Scammell, "Local Archives and the Study of Government," *ibid.* 2 (October 1939), 225-43; Dale A. Somers, Timothy J. Crimmins, and Merl E. Reed, "Surveying the Records of a City: The History of Atlanta Project," *ibid.* 36 (July 1973), 353-59; and Mary S. Pearson and Robert S. LaForte, "The Eyes of Texas: The Texas County Records Inventory Project," *ibid.* 40 (April 1977), 179-87.

[8]Not only was the improvement regarding these records transitory, but the archival profession managed to ignore the HRS inventories and other publications for over thirty years. See Leonard Rapport, "Dumped from a Wharf into Casco Bay: The Historical Records Survey Revisited," *American Archivist* 37 (April 1974), 201-10.

notion of state leadership and responsibility is, perhaps, the closest there is to a consensus for working with local government records.[9]

State archival leadership has proven to be the most effective approach thus far for the administration of local government records. Instead of struggling to centralize these records, some state archives have developed programs that concentrate upon the education of local officials in records matters and the creation of local programs that can be heralded as models for others to emulate. Leadership, as understood in this context, is the recognition by state archives that they alone cannot resolve all the problems or meet all the needs of local governments, that local governments have a fundamental responsibility for the care of their records, and that the most important goal is the preservation of the historical records of local governments regardless of whether accomplished locally or in a state institution.

Fortunately, there are some energetic and innovative programs succeeding in the management and preservation of local public records,[10] but such programs are far too rare when compared to the volume of local government records requiring attention. The archival profession has still not completely embraced or accepted the importance and necessity of state leadership in the management and preservation of these

---

[9]Howard W. Crocker, "The New York State Local Records Program," *American Archivist* 20 (January 1957), 31-40; Charles E. Hughes, Jr., "Problems in Administering Local Records," *ibid.* 25 (April 1962), 151-57; David C. Duniway, "Where Do Public Records Belong?" *ibid.* 31 (January 1968), 49-55; Ernst Posner, *American State Archives* (Chicago: University of Chicago Press, 1964), 335-37, 340-41, 363-64; H.G. Jones, "North Carolina's Local Records Program," *American Archivist* 24 (January 1961), 25-41; John A. Fleckner, "Cooperation as a Strategy for Archival Institutions," *ibid.* 39 (October 1976), 447-59; and David Levine, "Regional Depository Systems: The Complications of Compromise," *Georgia Archive* 7 (Fall 1979), 6-9; Jones, *Local Government Records: An Introduction to Their Management, Preservation, and Use* (Nashville: American Association for State and Local History, 1980); "Assault on Paper Mountain," *History News* 38 (April 1983), 21-23; and Bruce W. Dearstyne, "Principles for Local Government Records: A Statement of the National Association of State Archives and Records Administrators," *American Archivist* 46 (Fall 1983), 452-57.

[10]The development of the North Carolina local public records programs in the 1950s is one of the best documented examples of what can be accomplished; the most recent account is H.G. Jones, "Clio in the Courthouse: North Carolina's Local Records Program at Age Twenty-five," *American Archivist* 49 (Winter 1986), 41-51. But other innovative efforts have continued to appear, including New York's and Kentucky's use of funds from the National Historical Publications and Records Commission to foster the creation of model local programs.

records.[11] That some states have developed creditable programs
for local government records is commendable, but in the
absence of a strong archival profession committed to a national
agenda for these records, such efforts will remain exceptions
rather than the rule. National leadership is needed to promote
strong standards that local government officials can follow in
the administration of their records. This leadership assumes
the inherent relationship of all information generated and used
by local, state, and federal levels of government. It supports,
as well, leadership by the state archives. Just as state
archival leadership is all too often missing, the lack of national
archival leadership contributes to the poverty of local
government records in the United States.

The Need for National Archival Leadership

A sustained national leadership in records administration is
important for the development of effective local government
records programs. Educational and instructional materials and
courses for local government officials are essential but lack
credibility until the archival profession strengthens its own
educational standards. Rigid standards and definitions of
certification - for both individual archivists and archival
institutions - will aid local governments in procuring the
information and individuals they need for creating records
programs. Even now, national leadership could provide local
governments with models of strong state or local programs
while working toward national standards. National leadership
is needed to create and promote the standards of archival
administration in a manner that not only strengthens the
archival profession but clearly communicates to all that there
is a profession capable of administering all records regardless
of format or location. There is a need for a national
mechanism to sustain strong professional standards, cooperate
with related professions, and clearly communicate to political
subdivisions the rudiments of good records programs.

National leadership is also necessary for identifying what
local government records need to be preserved for historical
research. Appraisal is generally regarded as one of the
weakest components of archival theory, in part because
appraisal decisions are being made in virtual isolation,

[11]H.G. Jones, "The Pink Elephant Revisited," *American Archivist* 43
(Fall 1980), 473-83.

although there is evidence of significant improvements.[12]   Over
a decade ago one well-known urban historian argued that only
a selective preservation of significant and representative local
public records was required by the scholarly research
community, and, very recently, an archivist posed the same
issue as part of "statewide archival documentation plans."[13]
Despite the value of such records to each locality, state archival
resources are inadequate for providing comprehensive care for
all of them. Archivists must carefully identify local government
records based upon purposely composed appraisal criteria and
the willingness of political subdivisions to cooperate in such
programs.[14]   Such selection decisions require intrastate
appraisal policies to ensure that the records of historical trends
and developments are being salvaged for future research use.
National leadership is a minimum requirement for the
coordination of such a broad appraisal strategy.

A national plan or agenda is necessary for coping with
many issues specifically affecting local government records.
Two examples of such issues should suffice. First, nearly all
local governments that desire assistance with their records
problems desire help with *all* of the records. Unfortunately,
the management of current records and archival administration
have become separated functions over the last several decades,
although there seems to be some movement back to the
reunification of these functions. To preserve the historical
records of local governments, archivists must offer a
comprehensive records administration program that promises
cost-savings, efficient retrieval of information, and the cultural
benefits of the preservation of that government's memory.[15]

---

[12]Richard J. Cox and Helen W. Samuels, "The Archivist's First
Responsibility: A Research Agenda for the Identification and Retention of
Records of Enduring Value." *American Archivist* 51 (Winter/Spring 1988),
18-42.

[13]Sam Bass Warner, Jr., "The Shame of the Cities: Public Records of
Metropolis," *Midwestern Archivist* 2, no. 2 (1977), 27-34; and Dearstyne,
"State Programs for Local Government Records."

[14]As Dearstyne and others have argued, the development of public
records programs at the local level would allow state archival institutions
to utilize their resources more effectively in other needed areas such as
statewide documentation strategies and public outreach programs.

[15]Above all we must have balanced programs. For examples of what
happens with records programs skewed one way or the other, see Ian E.
Wilson, "A Noble Dream: The Origins of the Public Archives of Canada,"
Archivaria 15 (Winter 1982/83), 16-35, and Richard J. Cox, "The Need for

Second, historical records are deteriorating rapidly and an efficient and effective preservation program must be developed. Such an effort, of course, would require tremendous resources, but, and even more important, national, regional, and state coordination. Few state archival institutions can care in this way for their own records and local governments have even less of a chance to develop adequate programs. Selective microfilming projects and regional conservation centers are perhaps among the most viable alternatives for coping with this problem, but they require significant cooperation among archival institutions and a stronger national leadership.

Despite the poor condition of local government records in the United States, there has been some progress in very recent years. The National Historical Publications and Records Commission (NHPRC) has generously supported the development of some effective programs, most notably the establishment and strengthening of municipal archives, the support of regional networks, and the development and publication of manuals and inventories. With the assistance of the NHPRC, NAGARA and AASLH have both provided a stronger national focus on these records with promises of greater things to come. Still, even stronger national leadership is needed that reaches down through the states into the localities and both educates and equips the local officials to work effectively with their records. A strong and steady commitment to a national agenda for the improvement and development of local government records programs is a precondition for major changes.

Four such agendas were proposed in the 1980s. In 1982, NAGARA adopted a platform that it hoped would provide a basis for discussion of "ways to improve and strengthen the management of local government records throughout the United States," intending "to encourage a working partnership between state and local officials" with the state archives as the responsible leader for promoting this. That same year the AASLH sponsored the Joint Committee on the Management, Preservation, and Use of Local Government Records. The committee met, deliberated, and concluded that the lack of leadership by the archival profession on both national and state levels was a primary cause for the poor administration of local government records. Perceiving that a major reason for this was the lack of tools and resources, the AASLH committee recommended the creation of an audiovisual program, pamphlet, guide, training packet, independent study programs, and a clearinghouse of information. Another agenda evolved out of the mid-1983 meeting in Atlanta that evaluated the first round of NHPRC-sponsored state assessment and reporting projects. Participants again underscored the leadership role of state archival institutions and the need for improved legislation, education, program standards, and resources. And, finally, Bruce Dearstyne's paper at the 1983 meeting of the SAA in Minneapolis summarized and evaluated these earlier agendas, but stressed that local officials themselves possess the "first line" of responsibility for adequately managing their records.[16]

Unfortunately, all of these agendas lack one major element: a stronger commitment by the archival profession to work with local governments. The evaluation of the assessment projects led to adoption of the principle that "at least one prominent national organization or institution should assume national leadership responsibility in redressing the imbalance in archival and records management priorities which hinder progress in local records issues." Although this is, at best, only a generalized statement, it hits upon the fact that without committed national leadership, archivists are left with little more than pronouncements devoid of practical action. The work of the Joint Committee, for example, has led to the production of materials that still requires leadership, on all levels, to be effectively used. Effective leadership requires a clear commitment to a precise strategy, but even the best strategy is useless without dynamic and aggressive leadership. The condition of local government records is a national problem and requires national leadership for resolution.

American Municipal Records as a Case Study

The management and preservation of American municipal records is typical of that provided for local government records in general, with two major differences. The records of the larger American municipalities pose greater problems for the archival profession than that of most local governments due to their size, greater complexity in government, and broader sense of independence. In addition, but on a more encouraging note, these challenges, in very recent years, have received increasing attention from the archival profession. An examination of American municipal records reveals both the difficulties of

---

[16]Dearstyne, "Principles for Local Government Records" and "State Programs for Local Government Records"; "Assault on Paper Mountain," *History News*; and Weber, ed., *Documenting America*, 64.

managing these records and potential successes in caring for this part of America's documentary heritage.

For the past half century the United States has been considered an urban nation. For at least as many years professional archivists and historians have been concerned about the records of American municipal government. By the 1980s, however, only a small number of municipalities sponsored records management programs and fewer provided for the care of their historical documents. The condition of American municipal records is a national disgrace. What follows is a description of the efforts and failures of municipal officials and theorists, archivists, and historians to manage these important records. Perhaps by perceiving what has been done already with these records, plans can be made for remedying this serious problem.

The first English settlers in America brought with them a specific concept of incorporated municipal government. A municipality was a commercial organization. Regulating commerce, measures, prices, and product quality was the extent of its activity. Except in New England towns, which were founded as religious communities, the government of American cities conformed to the pattern of the English commercial model until the mid-eighteenth century. The expansion of the cities by that time was accompanied by a greater social mobility and new problems of health and fire protection, street maintenance, and lighting, that made the traditional municipality obsolete. By the time of the American Revolution, the largest cities did more than regulate commerce.

After the American Revolution, the state became the chief governmental unit and the municipality was subjugated to it. For a generation this meant little, as urbanization stabilized and state legislatures exercised few restrictions. After 1820, with the beginning of the dramatic population increases of American cities and the concomitant increased demands for improved municipal services, states were forced to consider a more active role. Throughout the first half of the nineteenth century, rural-dominated state legislatures consistently were unresponsive, uninformed, and even hostile to the peculiar problems of city life. The result was limited municipal government unable to cope with immense urban problems. Until well into the century most municipal functions were voluntarily performed, and restricted by the state legislatures, municipal services were inadequate for the growing population. In this void, machine ward administrations were organized in many cities. Although many of these machines helped provide solutions to the urban problems, these solutions often were tainted by corruption.

A city which was badly managed and often corrupt could not play an important role in the nation's life. Municipal reform began slowly to gain momentum. By the end of the nineteenth century, state investigators, taxpayer associations, muckrakers, and municipal reference bureaus had proliferated. By the early twentieth century, the first effects on the structure of American municipal government were visible. The most important legacy of the reformers was the spread of the commission or council-manager plan of municipal government, reflecting both the scientific management principles of business corporations and professional bureaucrats, and the independent mayor-council structure with decreased state involvement.

Despite this municipal reform movement, most urban problems were only partially or temporarily resolved. The introduction of automobiles and mass transit created suburbs and metropolitan regions, accelerating the process of inner-city decay by removing much of the revenue that the cities required to retard and correct such problems. The Depression overwhelmed the municipalities and forced them to appeal to the federal government for assistance. By the 1960s the federal-municipal relationship was secure and few cities had budgets and bureaucracies not dominated by federal funds and requirements.[17]

---

[17]The history of American municipal government has been thoroughly researched. Some important studies include Kenneth Fox, *Better City Government: Innovation in American Urban Politics, 1850-1937* (Philadelphia: Temple University Press, 1977); Mark I. Gelfand, *A Nation of Cities: The Federal Government and Urban America, 1933-1965* (New York: Oxford University Press, 1975); Bradley Robert Rice, *Progressive Cities: The Commission Government Movement in America, 1901-1920* (Austin: University of Texas Press, 1977); Martin J. Schiesl, *The Politics of Efficiency: Municipal Administration and Reform in America 1800-1920* (Berkeley: University of California Press, 1977); Richard J. Stillman, *The Rise of the City Manager: A Public Professional in Local Government* (Albuquerque: University of New Mexico Press, 1974); Jon C. Teaford, *City and Suburb: The Political Fragmentation of Metropolitan American, 1850-1970,* Johns Hopkins Studies in Urban Affairs (Baltimore: Johns Hopkins University Press, 1979); and Jon C. Teaford, *The Municipal Revolution in America: Origins of Modern Urban Government 1650-1825* (Chicago: University of Chicago Press, 1975). Although outdated, the volumes by Ernest S. Griffith also are good sources: *History of American City Government: The Colonial Period* (New York: Oxford University Press, 1939); *A History of American City Government: The Conspicuous Failure, 1870-1900* (New York: Published for the National Municipal League by Praeger Publishers, 1974); *A History of American City Government: The Progressive Years and Their Aftermath 1900-1920* (New York: Published for the National Municipal League by Praeger Publishers, 1974); and with Charles R. Adrian, *A History of American City Government: The Formation of Traditions, 1775-1870* (New York: Published for the National Municipal League by Praeger

Since the appearance of the reformers a century ago, their persistent theme was that municipal corruption and inefficiency were rooted in the structural weaknesses of municipal administration. The result was the emergence of municipal law, municipal political science, and the municipal expert. One might expect that a concern for records would have been reflected in this new municipal thought. Such has not been the case: both municipal theorists and officials have ignored the subject. Such incongruities account for the pessimism that many urban historians have brought to their writings. Sam Bass Warner, one of the most eminent recent urbanists, is convinced that the American city represents a "long tradition" of "endless failures."[18] Warner also is one of the few historians who has lamented the poor condition of municipal records, characterizing this problem as the new "shame of the cities."[19]

Neglect by municipalities of their records results partially from the neglect by municipal theorists. Without a solid philosophical tradition to draw upon, administrators have concentrated upon other areas. Despite myriad published textbooks and journal articles since the late nineteenth century, the literature on records is meager and superficial. William B. Munro's 1934 textbook is the earliest to consider records and its discussion is limited to a few pages. Later textbooks provide little additional information.[20] In periodicals, scanty

Publishers, 1976).

[18]*The Urban Wilderness: A History of the American City* (New York: Harper and Row, 1972), 3.

[19]"The Shame of the Cities: Public Records of the Metropolis."

[20]The textbooks examined include Charles R. Adrian and Charles Press, *Governing Urban America*, 4th ed. (New York: McGraw-Hill, 1972); James D. Banovetz, ed., *Managing the Modern City* (Washington, D.C.: Institute for Training in Municipal Administration, 1971); Dorman B. Eaton, *The Government of Municipalities* (New York: Published for the Columbia University Press by the Macmillan Company, 1899); Charles M. Kneier, *City Government in the United States* (New York: Harper and Brothers, Publishers, 1934); Carol A. McCandless, *Urban Government and Politics* (New York: McGraw-Hill, 1970); Stuart A. MacCorkle, *American Municipal Government and Administration* (Boston: D. C. Heath and Company, 1948); Austin F. MacDonald, *American City Government and Administration* (New York: Thomas Y. Crowell Company, 1929); David R. Morgan, *Managing Urban America: The Politics and Administration of America's Cities* (North Scituate, Massachusetts: Duxbury Press, 1979); William Bennett Munro, *Municipal Administration* (New York: Macmillan Company, 1934), 89-95; William Bennett Munro, *Municipal Government and Administration* (New

attention was given to this subject before the 1920s. Since the 1940s, the journals have featured essays on micrographics, indexing and filing systems, and a very few on the importance of preserving records for administrative and historical purposes. One would face a difficult search before locating a statement on a comprehensive records program.[21] Surprisingly, even the literature of the national municipal organizations has been poor on records. Only the International Institute of Municipal Clerks and the International City Management Association have emphasized this subject, primarily because of the clerk's traditional role of managing legislative files.[22]

The current sorry condition of municipal records programs is not unexpected, considering such neglect. In the mid-1970s only a few American cities operated programs, but even their commitment was suspect, with an average of four staff and less than a fifty thousand dollar annual budget.[23] Today

York: Macmillan Company, 1923); Thomas Harrison Reed, *Municipal Government in the United States*, rev. ed. (New York: D. Appleton-Century Company, 1934); *The Technique of Municipal Administration*, 4th ed. (Chicago: Published for the Institute for Training in Municipal Administration by the International City Managers' Association, 1958); and Lent D. Upson, *Practices of Municipal Administration* (New York: Century Company, 1926).

[21]Munro's municipal bibliography of 1915, for example, included no section on records and not one indexed reference to this subject; William Bennett Munro, *A Bibliography of Municipal Government in the United States*, 2nd ed. (Cambridge: Harvard University Press, 1915). The conclusions here are based upon a careful scrutiny of the *American City* (now *American City and County*), one of the oldest of the municipal periodicals. Typical of its articles are the following: M. L. Carr, "The Protection of Public Records," 25 (July 1921), 5-8; Charles A. Jortberg, Jr., "Perpetuating City Records by Microfilm," 59 (March 1944), 62-63; John G. Krieg, "The Case for Microfilming City Records," 68 (December 1953), 118-19; Perry W. Rodman, "Collecting Taxes Through Punched Holes," 60 (February 1945), 91-93; Walter C. Peterson, "Indexing Council Minutes," 61 (January 1946), 80-81; John B. Andosca, "Case Histories in Open Shelves Double Filing Capacity," 70 (August 1955), 110; and Herman F. Robinson, "Shall Counties Store Old Town Records?" 61 (March 1946), 108.

[22]Robert N. Vernon, *A Master Filing System (Decimal)*, Technical Bulletin no. 16 (Pasadena: International Institute of Municipal Clerks, n.d.); *Indexing and Filing of Council Minutes*, Technical Bulletin no. 2 (Pasadena: International Institute of Municipal Clerks, n.d.); H. B. Bond, *Records Disposition Management*, (N.p.: Technical Institute of Municipal Clerks, n.d.); and Bruce W. Dearstyne, *Records Management*, ICMA MIS Report 18 (May 1986).

[23]Patricia Adduci, "Municipal Governments Records Management Survey," *Records Management Quarterly* 11 (January 1977), 44-47.

considerable progress is evident. A more substantial portion of American cities have programs, most of which have been established in the past decade. Although many of these local governments have a records center of some type and provide records storage, micrographic services, scheduling, and even published records manuals, the degree of commitment remains questionable. Again, financing is limited given the size of municipal budgets. The nature of archival programs is very restricted; most transfer very selective records to museums, state archives, local libraries, historical societies, or universities. More appalling, however, is that cities as large as Pittsburgh and Fort Worth have no records program whatsoever. The reason for this is a lack of interest, and knowledge, by municipal management.[24]

The malformed nature of American municipal records programs is encouraged by weak records legislation. Chicago, Detroit, and Phoenix have virtually no legislation governing their records; Chicago (like other Illinois municipalities) is only required to provide a records clerk and the destruction of license records older than twenty years.[25] Cleveland, Indianapolis, and Memphis are authorized to have local records commissions for the review of disposable records and final review by the respective state archives.[26] Boston, Dallas, Houston, San Antonio, Honolulu, Los Angeles, San Diego, and San Francisco also may transfer records to the state archives.[27] Such legislation is consistently passive, depending upon the municipalities to initiate action and the state archives to be responsive. Since as late as 1978 (and matters have not significantly improved since then) ten states did not even have local archives programs and over half that did were less than two decades old, it is easy to surmise that many state archives

---

[24]Based upon the results of a survey, conducted by the author in 1980, of cities having a population of over two hundred thousand or the largest cities in states.

[25]Illinois Annotated Statutes (1962), Chapter 24, section 3-10-7-8.

[26]Ohio Revised Code Annotated (1978), title 1, chapter 149.39; Indiana Statutes Annotated Code Edition, title 5, article 15; Tennessee Code Annotated, title 10, chapter 7.

[27]Annotated California Codes, article 4, section 12226; Annotated Revised Civil Statutes of the State of Texas (1969), title 114, article 6574b, sections 4 and 5; Hawaii Revised Statutes, chapter 94, section 1 and 3; Annotated Laws of Massachusetts (1978), chapter 66.

will not precipitate action.[28] Of the largest American cities only
Baltimore, Philadelphia, and New York have significant track
records in providing comprehensive records programs; all three
established municipal archives in the 1950s, a rarity on the
American archival scene.

Why is it that some cities have developed their own records
programs and the majority of American cities and towns have
not? Religious and town meeting traditions and a generally
smaller town government account for informal maintenance of
records in clerks' offices and local historical societies in New
England.[29]   Even when a town evolves into a city, these
traditions often remain. Boston's records have continued to be
treated like those of the smaller New England towns. The only
serious effort before the 1980s to gather, describe, and preserve
its records involved the reports of the city records
commissioners of 1876 to 1909. New England's regard for its
past has concentrated, in the case of this region's greatest city,
upon private manuscript collections, to the abysmal neglect of
the public archives.[30]

The Bostonian predicament offers no explanation for other
municipalities; Chicago is very unlike this New England city
except for its lack of a municipal archives. Although Chicago
appeared two centuries after Boston and has supported in the
past decade a large archival community, a municipal records
program has never developed beyond the stage of a written
proposal and discussion. According to one commentator,
archivists and other concerned individuals have simply failed
to impress the municipality with the potential administrative
value of a municipal archives.[31] A more recent commentary
clearly delineated the political problems, now being overcome,

[28]Based upon the *Directory of Archives and Manuscript Repositories in
the United States* (Washington, D.C.: National Historical Publications and
Records Commission, 1978).

[29]Based upon a random sampling of New England towns surveyed by
the author in late 1980. Their records programs consist of little more than
storage vaults, microfilming for preservation, and the placement of selected
records in local institutions.

[30]*Reports of the Records Commissioners of the City of Boston*, 39 vols.
(Boston: Rockwell and Churchill, 1876-1909); L.H. Butterfield, "Bostonians
and Their Neighbors as Pack Rats," *American Archivist* 24 (April 1961),
141-59. A recent effort, funded by the National Historical Publications and
Records Commission, has finally persuaded the city to establish a small
records program.

[31]Patrick M. Quinn, "Windy City Blues: An Archival Profile of Chicago,"
Midwestern Archivist 2, no. 1 (1977), 3-13.

that have delayed the development of an effective Chicago records management archival program.[32]

In stark contrast to Chicago are the relatively successful programs of Baltimore, Philadelphia, and New York. The essential reasons for their successes may only be a matter of time and opportunity. Chicago's archival lobby has developed only recently in comparison. New York's initial efforts started in 1926, were reintroduced with a mayoral study commission in 1939, and were finally successful in 1950. Philadelphia's municipal archives developed fortuitously with the extensive revision of its home rule charter in 1951 and under the early direction of competent professionals. The origins of Baltimore's program go at least as far back as 1874 although it was not explicitly spelled out in an ordinance until eighty years later; it was not until 1978 and the hiring of the city's first professional archivist that the features of this ordinance were fully applied.[33]

Unfortunately, the greater success of Baltimore, Philadelphia, and New York has not been replicated, partly because of the general emphasis by professional archivists on national and state levels to the neglect of municipalities. Because of this, examples such as Chicago's recent efforts are relatively rare. For three generations archivists have surveyed the municipal problem and done little to resolve it. A review of these efforts is quite illuminating.

In light of the preceding comments, it may seem surprising that archivists have been concerned about municipal records from the very dawn of their profession. The Public Archives Commission, created in 1898 by the American Historical Association and in existence until the 1920s, stimulated the organization of many early state archives, sponsored the first gatherings of archivists, introduced archival principles, and considered the condition of American municipal records. The commission was to concentrate its energy on state records and, if the "opportunity may offer," it would also examine the "records of some of the more important municipalities in the

[32]John Daly, "State Archives and Metropolitan Records: The Case of Chicago" *American Archivist* 51 (Fall 1988), 470-74.

[33]For further information on these cities refer to Jason Horn, "Municipal Archives and Records Center of the City of New York," *American Archivist* 16 (October 1953), 311-20; James Katsaros, "Managing the Records of the World's Greatest City," *ibid.* 23 (April 1960), 175-80; Charles E. Hughes, "Philadelphia's Program," *ibid.* 21 (April 1958), 131-42; and Richard J. Cox, "The Plight of American Municipal Archives: Baltimore, 1729-1979," *ibid.* 42 (July 1979), 281-92, and "The Need for Comprehensive Records Programs in Local Governments."

different sections of the country."[34]

Actually, the early Public Archives Commission devoted considerable attention to municipal records. Reports on New York, Syracuse, Brooklyn, Long Island, Philadelphia, Athens and Augusta (Georgia), and St. Augustine (Florida) were prepared.[35] More importantly, however, was the serious concern expressed by this body about the condition of American municipal records. Calls for action were repeatedly sounded. In 1900 the commission concluded that the "problem of the preservation of [New York] town records is a serious one. Only three towns [out of nineteen surveyed] have town halls. In the others the older records [were] stored wherever and however convenience dictates . . . . Two towns have deliberately burned their old material, and others may be expected to follow the example from time to time."[36] In 1901 Herman V. Ames urged that Philadelphia's municipal records be turned over to the Historical Society of Pennsylvania or the municipal law department "in order that they might be rendered accessible to the investigator, or placed where they will be preserved."[37] Three years later U. B. Phillips summarized the condition of the records of Athens, Georgia as being "now extant" with "many signs of neglect" and that a portion may have been destroyed "as rubbish."[38] In 1906 the dictum was formulated that "if carelessness in keeping our public records is an index to government, Arkansas cities are poorly governed."[39] After its first decade, however, the Public Archives Commission concentrated on archival principles and on the establishment of

[34]Report of the Public Archives Commission 1900, American Historical Association *Annual Report 1900*, 2: 9, 23.

[35]Report of the Public Archives Commission 1900, American Historical Association *Annual Report 1900*, 2: 159-61, 166-99; 1901, AHA *Annual Report 1901*, 2: 231-344; 1904, AHA *Annual Report 1904*, 591-96; 1906, AHA *Annual Report 1906*, 2: 159-64.

[36]Report of the Public Archives Commission 1900, American Historical Association *Annual Report 1900*, 2: 150.

[37]Report of the Public Archives Commission 1901, American Historical Association *Annual Report 1901*, 2: 232.

[38]Report of the Public Archives Commission 1904, American Historical Association *Annual Report 1904*, 592.

[39]Report of the Public Archives Commission 1906, American Historical Association *Annual Report 1906*, 2: 48.

a national archives,[40] and the condition of municipal and other local records apparently receded in importance.

The onset of the Depression provided another opportunity for attending to American municipal records. As part of the Historical Records Survey, started in 1935 and ended in 1942 due to the Second World War, a large number of town and municipal records were described. Among the HRS survey forms extant, thirty states and over two thousand municipalities are represented. There was little impact, at least none that has been documented, on municipal record keeping techniques. The vast majority of these surveys were forgotten or even destroyed when the project ended abruptly. Baltimore's records were surveyed, for example, during these years. Except for a valuable name index to several hundred thousand documents, the work of the HRS was forgotten and unused even after the formation of a records management program a decade later.[41]

At the time of the beginning of the HRS, the Society of American Archivists was formed, remaining the dominant national professional archival organization to the present. Logically one would assume that the SAA would coordinate action regarding municipal and other local government records. Since the demise of the HRS, the society has promoted several studies of this subject; in each case, like the earlier Public Archives Commission and the HRS, these efforts have contributed little to resolving the problem of municipal records. In 1955 the report of the SAA's Committee on Municipal Records was published and distributed. Its chairman, Richard Ruddell, lamented that archivists and the cities have neglected these records, but believed there was then an "awakening interest" and that the time was "ripe for positive and vigorous action."[42] Ruddell's upbeat tone was premature. In 1963 Leon de Valinger, Jr. published an article describing an "apathetic activity" for municipal records and urged a full-scale city study similar to that on the state archives then being prepared by Ernst Posner. As an assessment of the state of municipal

---

[40]Report of the Public Archives Commission 1911, American Historical Association *Annual Report 1911*, 1: 316-17.

[41]For information on the HRS records, see Loretta L. Hefner, comp., *The WPA Historical Records Survey: A Guide to the Unpublished Inventories, Indexes and Transcripts* (Chicago: Society of American Archivists, 1980).

[42]"Recent Developments in Municipal Records," *American Archivist* 18 (July 1955), 255-66.

records, this article is regrettably still current.[43] Perhaps as a response to de Valinger's report, an SAA Ad Hoc Committee on Municipal Archives was formed and issued a report in 1964. This survey refuted the poverty of attention portrayed by de Valinger, finding nearly a quarter of municipalities having archives, although it still urged stronger action by the SAA.[44] This report never fully considered the nature of these archives, and the identification in 1978 of only eight such programs in the *Directory of Archives and Manuscripts Repositories in the United States* seriously challenged its validity.[45]

The only significant progress in American municipal records started in the last few years of the 1970s and was directly attributable to the National Historical Publications and Records Commission. Founded in the 1930s and reorganized in 1950 as the National Historical Publications Commission, this body emphasized grants to and supervision of editorial projects, both letterpress and microfilm. In the mid-1970s, it also expanded to records projects and suitably expanded its name. Between 1976 and early 1980, the NHPRC awarded thirty-nine grants totaling over one million dollars to municipal records projects; since then there has been a steady awarding of records grants to municipalities. These grants provided for study projects regarding the development of municipal programs, record surveys and inventories, preservation, and microfilming. Regardless of whether all of these projects have been transformed into continuing, permanent programs, NHPRC's efforts represent the most significant archival activity on behalf of municipal records. Through NHPRC's work there is now a community of municipal archivists and others sensitized to the need to manage these records.[46]

---

[43]"Municipal Archives in the United States," *Archivum* 13 (1963), 3-12.

[44]*Report of the Chairman, Ad Hoc Committee on Municipal Archives* (N.p.: Society of American Archivists, 1964).

[45]These cities were Albany, Baltimore, Dallas, Honolulu, Los Angeles, Milwaukee, New York, and Philadelphia.

[46]As an example of the breadth of NHPRC efforts, the following municipalities received grants through 1980: Birmingham, Alabama; Tucson, Arizona; Los Angeles and Sacramento, California; Morgan City, Louisiana; Baltimore, Maryland; Newton, Massachusetts; Detroit, Grand Rapids, and Kalamazoo, Michigan; Brooklyn, Buffalo, Islip, Medina, New York City, Rochester, Saratoga Springs, and Schenectady, all New York; Dayton, Ohio; Guthrie, Oklahoma; Portland, Oregon; San German, Puerto Rico; Providence, Rhode Island; and Memphis, Tennessee. There were several other grants to state archives for the development of statewide local records programs.

Perhaps the most visible product of NHPRC's early emphasis on municipal and other local government records is H. G. Jones's *Local Government Records* published in 1980 and funded by an NHPRC grant. Jones, a leading archivist of the past third of a century, wrote a treatise aimed at persuading local government officials to manage better their records. The book provided a full picture of the types and value of such records and the necessary components of adequate records management and archives programs. *Local Government Records* was also a telling indictment of the archival profession's neglect of such records. His view of the predicament of municipal records was quite accurate. "The absence of adequate archival facilities provided by the state places a direct obligation upon counties and municipalities to organize and preserve their own archival records." "In the final analysis," Jones continued, "local records management will be as good or as bad as the county or municipality chooses it to be." That Jones's ideas may seem to run against the mainstream of archival practice does not make them wrong, but is a response to the continued poor condition of American municipal records.[47]

Archivists have often told themselves that they should be leading historians and other scholars to new sources and, hence, opening new vistas of research. That, of course, has almost never been the case; the opposite is the norm. This is an additional reason for the neglect of municipal records. Historians have only begun to work on American municipal government in very recent years.

Interest in the history of American cities commenced in the early decades of the nineteenth century. Their rapid population growth, increasing commercial significance, and dramatic industrialization meant that American cities could not be ignored. The growth of the city's importance as a center of the arts and learning also made it inevitable that city histories would be researched and compiled; for one, most American historical societies, proliferating rapidly by the middle years of that century, were located in cities and their members often contributed urban history essays.[48]

These early city histories of the nineteenth century generally followed one of two forms. Antiquarians provided excessive

[47]*Local Government Records*, 79, 103.

[48]Between 1790 and 1890, New York City had seventeen historical societies, Philadelphia, sixteen, and Boston, ten. David D. Van Tassel, *Recording America's Past: An Interpretation of the Development of Historical Studies in America 1607-1884* (Chicago: University Press, 1960), 181-90.

description, little or no discrimination among competing facts, little analytical interpretation, an elitist view, and a florid display of community pride. Many of the antiquarian histories also were molded by the booster tradition. These works promoted the cities as their first responsibility and emphasized the future so excessively that the past often was overshadowed and twisted.[49] These usually unsophisticated histories so dominated writing about American cities that by the 1890s most of the most serious national histories relegated the city to a few insignificant pages.[50]

The professionalization of historical studies in this country, starting in the last two decades of the nineteenth century, is naturally assumed to have wiped away the work of antiquarians and amateurs; urban history should now be flourishing under the direction of the new historians. Such, of course, was not the case. For many years the history of American cities was ignored, written off as the domain of amateur local historians. Frederick Jackson Turner's emphasis on the frontier and the revelation of the 1920 census that the United States was actually an urban nation gradually brought historians to a reanalysis of the city. Traditionally, the beginning of professional urban history has been dated to the 1930s with the work of Arthur M. Schlesinger. By the late 1940s the first classes on this subject were appearing. And by the 1960s, fueled by the "urban crisis" and mounting dissatisfaction with the standard interpretations of the history of the city, American urban history was clearly established as an important field of inquiry. Even by the early 1970s, however, its parameters and definitions were not clearly

[49]For some appraisals of these studies, see Stephen Clark, "Gabriel Furman: Brooklyn's First Historian," *Journal of Long Island History* 10 (Spring 1974), 21-32; Deborah Dependahl Waters, "Philadelphia's Boswell: John Fanning Watson," *Pennsylvania Magazine of History and Biography* 98 (January 1974), 3-52; Daniel Horowitz, "The Meaning of City Biographies: New Haven in the Nineteenth and Early Twentieth Centuries," *Connecticut Historical Society Bulletin* 29 (July 1964), 65-75; Blake McKelvey, "A History of Historical Writing in the Rochester Area," *Rochester History* 6 (April 1944), 1-24; and R. Richard Wohl and A. Theodore Brown, "The Usable Past: A Study of Historical Traditions in Kansas City," *Huntington Library Quarterly* 23 (May 1960), 237-59.

[50]Egal Feldman, "The American City: From George Bancroft to Charles A. Beard," *Societas* 2 (Spring 1972), 121-41.

established.[51]

One result of the relatively recent scholarly interest in the history of American cities is the paucity of literature on municipal government. Except for New England towns, which are now being analyzed from every conceivable angle, few histories of cities contain adequate information on the municipal government or reflect serious research in this area. Ernest S. Griffith's 1938 opus on colonial municipal government was the only major work on this aspect of local government until the mid-1970s. Since that time many valuable and innovative histories of municipal government have been published.[52]

The lack of adequate municipal archives and municipal records in state repositories and the appalling condition of such city records have probably discouraged many a potential researcher. This neglect has not caused historians to encourage improvement. As has already been mentioned, Sam Bass Warner's 1971 paper at the Society of American Archivists' annual meeting still ranks as one of the few efforts by an historian to address the problem of urban records. Warner perceptively blamed the "focus and habits of both the historical and archival professions," although his suggestion for specialized subject archives has many difficulties.[53] Had American historians expressed the same lack of interest in national records as they have shown municipal records to date, there almost certainly would never have been a National Archives; American municipalities require individuals in the image of a J. Franklin Jameson, the professional historian who

---

[51]Eric E. Lampard, "American Historians and the Study of Urbanization," *American Historical Review* 67 (October 1961), 49-61; Charles N. Glaab, "The Historian and the American Urban Tradition," *Wisconsin Magazine of History* 47 (Autumn 1963), 12-25; Glaab, "The Historian and the American City: A Bibliographic Survey," *The Study of Urbanization*, eds. Philip M. Hauser and Leo F. Schnore (New York: John Wiley and Sons, Inc., 1965), 53-80; Dwight W. Hoover, "The Diverging Paths of American Urban History," *American Quarterly* 20 (Summer 1968), 296-317; Bayrd Still and Diana Klebanow, "The Teaching of American Urban History," *Journal of American History* 55 (March 1969), 843-47; Richard C. Wade, "An Agenda for Urban History," *The State of American History*, ed. Herbert J. Bass (Chicago: Quadrangle Books, 1970), 43-69; Eric E. Lampard, "The Dimensions of Urban History: A Footnote to the 'Urban Crisis,'" *Pacific Historical Review* 39 (August 1970), 261-78; and Stephen Thernstrom, "Reflections on the New Urban History," *Daedalus* 100 (Spring 1971), 359-75.

[52]See footnote 17 for some citations to such studies.

[53]"Shame of the Cities."

provided the main source of leadership in securing the establishment of the National Archives.

The neglect by the municipalities, archivists, and historians does not mean it is too late for American municipal records. If progress is continued as has come with the recent NHPRC grants, the situation can be significantly rectified in a generation. But it must be understood that significant progress must be made soon.

The Future of American Local Government Records: Local Initiatives and Archival Leadership

The examination of American municipal records is revealing of the complexity of properly managing local government records. The diversity of local governments, the vast quantity of political subdivisions, and the mixture of local officials, researchers, and citizens interested in these records suggest that there are no easy characterizations of the problems and, obviously, no easy solutions. Just as many are involved in causing the problem of poor local records management, many also need to be involved in the solutions of these problems. Local officials must be persuaded to administer better their records, state archives must be better able to provide assistance to the local governments for this purpose, and there must be stronger archival leadership on both state and national levels. Fortunately, there is evidence of efforts in all of these areas, beginning first with the national level.

The issue of leadership and the origins of the Joint Committee on the Management, Preservation, and Use of Local Government Records are inexorably intertwined. The catalyst for the creation of the committee was H. G. Jones's book on local government records, a book initiated and published by AASLH. Jones took as a major theme the necessity of national and state leadership, emphasizing that its absence was the major reason for the continuing poor management of these records.[54] The original grant proposal written by AASLH staff and submitted to the NHPRC in 1981 essentially paraphrased Jones's conclusions, which were repeatedly supported by members of the Joint Committee during its meetings and reflected in the final report of the first phase of the effort completed in 1983. The committee justified a second grant in 1983 on the grounds of working toward providing the necessary leadership. The second proposal stated that "there is no voice of national leadership prepared to begin taking the steps

---

[54]Jones, *Local Government Records*, 20.

necessary to solve these problems" and concluded that the initial work of the committee could only succeed if it "secures the support of all the professional associations that should be interested in good local records management . . . ."[55]

The formation of the Joint Committee was completed with very careful attention paid to its role as the "voice of national leadership." Aside from the few individuals selected because of their experience and expertise managing or using local government records, the members of the committee consisted of representatives of the Association of Records Managers and Administrators, International Institute of Municipal Clerks, National Association of County Recorders and Clerks, National Association of Government Archives and Records Administrators, National Center for State Courts, and the Society of American Archivists (a representative of the International City Management Association was added in 1985). The group was designed to avoid the problem that archivists and records managers have traditionally fallen prey to, communicating only within their own ranks and neglecting the very people whose records and concerns they are attempting to address.[56] This committee - composed of creators, archivists and records managers, and records users - wrestled with some crucial questions. What did local officials perceive as their needs in records administration? Why did they so frequently avoid seeking the assistance of state archival institutions? How can local officials and archivists cooperate in resolving the problems of administering local public records? How can the professional associations of local officials assist in resolving the neglect of local records in this country?

The committee's first phase of work resulted in a series of productive and stimulating meetings about the management, preservation, and use of local government records in the United States. The product of these meetings was a report that suggested promoting the benefits of properly managing local government records; encouraging state agencies to assume stronger and more active leadership toward political

[55]Copies of records of the Joint Committee are in the possession of the author, a member of the committee from 1982 to 1986. Those seeking additional information about the nature of the project should contact the AASLH.

[56]This was a problem even in the NHPRC-sponsored assessment and reporting projects. Few state archives made efforts to work closely with local government professional associations and officials but, instead, continued to emphasize communication with professional archivists and historians.

subdivisions; developing new, and improving existing, orientation and training programs for local officials and records custodians; and developing guidelines for state and local legislation that strengthens the management of public records. None of these concerns were really new and, at best, merely echoed the thoughts and opinions of a score of archivists over the past generation and more.

The difference in the work of this committee, however, was its commitment to national leadership. It called for a national body, armed with sufficient resources, to monitor efforts at the local level, to study appropriate issues, and to set and revise priorities concerning local government records. Led by the AASLH, a total of $200,000 was obtained from the National Historical Publications and Records Commission and the Andrew Mellon Foundation to continue the work of the committee through 1985; subsequent grants have kept the project going into the late 1980s.

The committee's agenda, established in 1984, included several major objectives. First, the committee produced a brief, general audiovisual program, with accompanying pamphlet, that attractively presented the advantages and elements of records administration to local officials and records custodians. Second, it prepared a more extensive manual on local public records administration that defined and described the nature of these records, outlined the benefits of effective public records management and the techniques of such management, presented who is responsible, and provided a bibliography and other leads for further assistance. And, finally, the committee established a clearinghouse that local officials and others were able to use in seeking assistance to resolve their records problems and concerns. The audiovisual program, manual, and clearinghouse were intended to foster the support of other professional associations in this important work.

The agenda of the Joint Committee was an ambitious one, and its initial progress was commendable. The audiovisual program and accompanying pamphlet were completed and available for use in 1985. A professional multi-media firm packaged the audiovisual program. Also, in 1985, the clearinghouse, renamed the National Information Center for Local Government Records (NICLOG), became operative with two staff members at AASLH headquarters to run it. Their primary responsibilities included marketing the audiovisual program and pamphlet, issuing press releases and updates on the work of the Joint Committee and other activities regarding the administration of local government records, and fielding inquiries requesting advice and assistance. Finally, the manual was prepared and published in 1988, followed in 1989 by a series of technical leaflets expanding on its content.[57] By 1988, then, there was an important assemblage of tools and advice available for local government officials and records custodians to supplement existing model state manuals, archival and records administration handbooks, and training and educational programs.

The implications for national leadership should be readily obvious. There are already professional associations and state archival agencies ready to use these tools to supplement existing outreach programs or to create the nucleus of one. With a large free distribution of pamphlets and modestly-priced manuals, a large portion of the political subdivisions in this country will have received some exposure to the rudiments of proper records administration. And it is also anticipated that local governments will apply some pressure on state archival institutions to provide statewide leadership. For some state archives, this will provide an opportunity to harness support that could be used to acquire sufficient resources and authority to develop effective local government records programs. For other state archives, the interest might be unpleasant, but it could lead to effective local government records programs. The purpose of the Joint Committee was to awaken or strengthen the state leadership needed for improving the administration of local government records.

The success of the new effort is, of course, dependent upon the continued existence of something like the Joint Committee and the national information center. Unfortunately, the Joint Committee and NICLOG went out of business in late 1989 primarily because of the lack of funding, and the long-term impact of this effort is decidedly uncertain. If only a few tools are created but no national mechanism to promote them, improvement in the administration of local government records may be marginal. To some degree, the sustained interest of other professional associations, like the International Institute of Municipal Clerks, may prevent this from happening. A number of prospects are also possible. Additional projects may be identified that could be attractive to funding sources like the NHPRC and the Mellon Foundation. Associations that are

---

[57]Bruce W. Dearstyne, *The Management of Local Government Records: A Guide for Local Officials* (Nashville: American Association for State and Local History, 1988). The local government records technical leaflet series covered such topics as developing a records management program, starting an archives, microfilming, files management, preservation, records inventorying, records retention and disposition schedules, records centers, vital records, micrographics, environmental controls, and machine-readable records.

represented on the Joint Committee might finance the ongoing work of the committee, especially the national information center. Other associations, like NAGARA, might have the resources to assume some of the responsibility for the work. Equally promising, perhaps, is the work of other associations with similar concerns for national leadership, such as the Society of American Archivists' Committee on Goals and Priorities.

The New State Leadership and the NHPRC-State Assessment and Reporting Projects

It is possible, of course, that the role of the former Joint Committee needed to be only a temporary one, since there seems to be a stronger commitment by state archives to assisting local governments. Such new commitment was articulated during the NHPRC-sponsored state assessment and reporting projects, funded in two phases in 1982-83 and 1984-85, which examined the nature and condition of local government records. The common thread to the recommendations for action with local government records was the understanding that state archival institutions must provide revitalized or new leadership in rectifying the neglect of these valuable records. Nearly every recommendation proposed in these reports relates to the issue of state leadership.

Legislation was the first priority for action, with every state report returning to this matter again and again. The various recommendations usually included plans for the clarification of the role of the state archives, the elimination of confusing and miscellaneous statutes, improved instructions for the scheduling and disposition of records, and the establishment of standards in technical aspects of local government records. Some of the reports also urged the creation of more authority for the local governments to work effectively with their own records, provided that state review and guidance are part of the process, and others, that have stronger legislation already, stressed the adoption of procedures so that these laws can be enforced. The latter was, perhaps, the most discouraging note of the degree to which local government records legislation is flawed.

Not surprisingly, the reports devoted considerable space to improved and increased state services to local government for the better management and preservation of their records. Some recommendations were quite predictable and no different from what all archivists have always been seeking - more local records staff, increased micrographics aid, and more money. Other reports urged the preparation of local government records

manuals and other publications and the training of local
records custodians via workshops, consultations, lectures,
professional meetings, and the development and advertisement
of model programs.   These are all practices that have
increasingly gained use and acceptance in the past decade and
that are aimed at gaining the cooperation and assistance of
local governments in preserving and managing their records.
The California report described the goal of this training not to
be the turning out of '"archivists' and 'records managers' but to
inform, educate, and convince local officials that the proper care
of their records is not only good ethics but also good
business."[58]   The most promising of these recommendations
was, however, that the state archival institution should
mobilize support through other local government professional
organizations, a mechanism of communication and proselytizing
that most states have ignored for too long.   The Mississippi
report aptly summed it up by saying that state archives must
conduct "consciousness-raising campaigns."[59]   The era of the
stereotypical quiet and scholarly archival repository must be
forgotten, according to these reports.
     Many of the other recommendations resemble more
traditional archival concerns.   A few reports urged that local
governments assume the responsibility for creating their own
finding aids, but most see the state archives as providing
leadership here again, generally via the creation of a central
data base or union lists useful to both records administrators
and researchers.   One wonders why archivists and researchers
have not raised a storm of protest about the absence of useful
finding aids portrayed in the reports.   The Minnesota report
bluntly stated that "although the historical value of local
records should be unquestioned, some historians, some
archivists, and some records managers seem content to ignore
them."[60]   Nearly every report also devoted attention to
improving the local government records storage conditions.   It
was nearly unanimous that these records should be placed in
public local records centers, private historical societies and
libraries, or in regional network systems *and* that the state
archives be responsible for the composition and enforcement of

[58]California report, draft copy, viii, 160.

[59]*The Management and Preservation of Mississippi's Historical Records:
Problems and Potential* ([Jackson]: Mississippi State Historical Records
Advisory Board, [1983]), 19.

[60]*Historical Records in Minnesota* (St. Paul: Minnesota State Historical
Records Advisory Board, March 1983), 11.

guidelines to ensure that these records are well cared for. These storage recommendations are further evidence of the shift in emphasis to state-directed local government records programs.

This focus of the state assessment reports is supported by the new emphasis of state archives on local government records. Within the second half of the 1980s a number of state archives have turned to producing manuals for the use of local governments in the management of their records, more energetically surveying and identifying local records having historical value, pursuing comprehensive legislation governing the care and management of these records, and establishing fully-staffed programs to assist the local governments.[61]

The most encouraging feature of this renewed support by the state archives is its greater emphasis on the maintenance of local records in the governments themselves, and the acceptance by many of the state archives that this is the only viable manner to ensure that these records are adequately maintained. This seems to have led to the greater development of new local records initiatives, although it is difficult to accurately measure the actual level of interest. However, examples abound throughout the country. In Georgia, state legislation mandating the creation of local records programs caused the establishment of some innovative local records operations, such as the joint program of the City of Rome, Floyd County, the Rome City Board of Education, and the Floyd County Board of Education. In Kentucky, spurred on with seed money from the NHPRC, the Department for Libraries and Archives was able to establish a large regrant program for funding local public records projects throughout the state. In New York, a similar regrant program also led to the establishment of records programs in some counties and towns, as well as helping to redirect the state archives program to assisting local governments care for their own records. More recently in New York, a strong State law requiring the development of local government records programs and creating a local government records advisory council was enacted.[62]

---

[61]The development of these new initiatives and programs can be tracked in NAGARA's quarterly newsletter, *Clearinghouse.*

[62]See the report of this council, *The Quiet Revolution: Managing New York's Local Government Records in the Information Age* (Albany: New York Local Government Records Advisory Council, December 1, 1987). For a specific case study of one of the success stories in New York, see Robert W. Arnold, III, "The Albany Answer: Pragmatic and Tactical Considerations in Local Records Legislative Efforts," *American Archivist* 51 (Fall 1988), 475-79.

Finally, it is more difficult to estimate changes in interest and activity on the local level. New and energetic programs seem to be appearing quite frequently. In nearly every state local officials are seeking more assistance and advice on how to care for their records. Many local governments seem ready to invest funds in establishing and maintaining local records programs. Others are receiving and responding to pressure from local historians, genealogists, preservationists, and others to protect the documentary heritage of their localities. Perhaps, spurred on both by new interest on local and state levels and the desire by national associations of archivists, records managers, historians, and others, the appalling legacy of failure in protecting these important records can be overcome and forgotten.

Conclusion

Local government records are among the most fundamentally important of all records to the history and lives of individuals, neighborhoods, communities, towns, and cities. If they are not better managed and preserved, an important element of America's documentary heritage will be lost. Yet, the management of local government records in the United States and the preservation of those having historical value is an immense challenge. Much of the work still lies ahead. For local government records to be properly administered there must be a stronger state and national emphasis on their care, greater opportunities to assist local officials, stronger professional standards for archivists that will enhance their work with the local governments, a broader appraisal and documentation strategy that incorporates local records into a universe of documentation and that enables these records to be more practically worked with, a reunification between records managers and archivists that will provide ongoing comprehensive care for local government records, and improved state and regional preservation programs that will have more potential benefit for the records of America's local governments. Although this represents an immense amount of work, the decade of the 1980s has been the most promising one thus far for improving the care of local government records in the United States.

FIVE ARCHIVAL EDUCATION IN THE UNITED STATES: OLD CONCERNS, BUT NEW FUTURE?[1]

Introduction

The education of its practitioners has long been a preeminent issue for concern, debate, and action by the archival profession in the United States. From the very emergence of the profession in the early twentieth century until the present, there has been a steady stream of sessions, conferences, and publications about what archival education should be.[2] Since the heart of any profession is its knowledge of practice and theory, it is not surprising that as much attention has been devoted to educating individuals to be archivists; indeed, consider the number of references to this topic in this volume. What *is* surprising, however, is the fact that so many of the concerns and issues about archival education have remained virtually unchanged for nearly half a century. The placement of archival education programs, what archivists should know, and the identity of archivists (are they historians, librarians, information specialists, or archivists?) continue to be the major topics of discussion, as they have almost since the formation of the first state archives in the initial decade of this century.[3] Despite these persistent or nagging matters, however, there is little question that archival education in the United States has been undergoing considerable change *and* strengthening over the past decade. These changes have included the adoption of stronger graduate education guidelines by the Society of American Archivists

[1]This essay was originally published in different versions in the *Journal of the American Society for Information Science* 39 (September 1988), 340-43, and *Archives* 20 (Winter 1989), 33-42.

[2]From the early twentieth century until the mid 1980s, over one hundred articles have been published concerning the education of archivists in the United States. While this topic does not rank as the top subject in archival literature, it is certainly one of the most important aspects of the literature. These comments are based on my "An Annotated Bibliography of Studies in English on Archival Education," an unpublished paper prepared for the Society of American Archivists' Committee on Education and Professional Development, March 1986, and the chapter in this volume on archival literature.

[3]Many of these concerns, for example, were prominent in the writings and activities of Waldo Leland, a pioneer in the formation of the archival profession in the first few decades of the twentieth century. See, for example, his "American Archival Problems," American Historical Association *Annual Report 1909* (Washington, D.C.: Government Printing Office, 1911), 342-48.

(SAA), the emergence of more ambitious multi-course graduate programs, the establishment and development of a continuing education office at SAA, and adoption by SAA of certification for individual archivists. Stepping back from and viewing archival education in the United States, it is not difficult to perceive that it is a mix of old concerns and new prospects for the future.

The purpose of this essay is not to reiterate all of the old concerns; for these there is a large and interesting literature, along with plenty of opportunities to rehash these arguments at professional conferences and gatherings. My main objectives are to review the recent transformation of archival education in the United States, and the continuing discussion about it, and comment on the issues that must be resolved to continue the improvement of archival education and its role in carrying out the archival mission in modern society. Throughout this essay I consider archival education in all its forms, emphasizing continuing education *and* graduate programs.

The Present State of Archival Education in the United States

The history of archival education in the United States has been broadly sketched out in a number of essays,[4] but it is worth a brief review here. In the early days of the profession, archivists were primarily trained through graduate history programs. As the archival community grew and matured, it recognized a variety of skills and knowledge that the traditional history programs did not provide. On the job training programs, short-term institutes, and workshops were developed to meet these needs, and remnants of these offerings and efforts survive to this day.[5] More ambitious graduate programs were also proposed, and the long standing debate

---

[4]See, most notably, Richard C. Berner, "Archival Education and Training in the United States, 1937 to Present," *Journal of Education for Librarianship* 22 (Summer/Fall 1981), 3-19; Jacqueline Goggin, "That We Shall Truly Deserve the Title of 'Profession': The Training and Education of Archivists, 1930-1960," *American Archivist* 47 (Summer 1984), 243-54; and H.G. Jones, "Archival Training in American Universities, 1938-1968," *ibid.* 31 (April 1968), 135-54.

[5]The most famous example of this is the Modern Archives Institute offered by the National Archives for nearly half a century. Although the presenters have obviously changed (along with some of the topics), the basic premise of providing a crash introduction to historical records administration remains as the Institute's most important purpose and the Institute continues to be in continuing demand and oversubscribed.

about whether graduate archival education should be based in history or library schools emerged.

For many years, then, the education of archivists has been a volatile topic and the source of much hand-wringing and debate. This is especially evident with graduate archival education. Only a decade ago, in the late 1970s, graduate archival education was described as being a "field in flux," in a "medieval state," "unfinished business," and in its "infancy, at best in adolescence."[6] It is difficult to know how to describe precisely the condition of that education today, because while there have been gains in many areas, significant unresolved issues (such as those described in this and the next essay in this volume) affecting the education of the professional archivist remain.

Still, at least a general consensus about archival educational content seems to be developing, replacing the only former area of agreement -- the need for improved education of individuals preparing to become archivists and for those who are already embarked on archival careers. Prospective archivists, it is now thought, need a firm understanding of the nature of information, records, and historical documentation; history and the continuing role of archives in modern society; basic archival functions such as appraisal and acquisitions, arrangement and description, preservation management, reference and access, and advocacy and outreach; the legal and ethical implications of records administration; cooperative ventures like automated descriptive networks and documentation strategies; and basic management principles such as organizational theory and practice, program planning, human resources management, and resource development.[7]

---

[6]Ames Sheldon Bower, "Whence and Whither: A Survey of Archival Education," *Georgia Archive* 5 (Summer 1977), 54-55; James W. Geary, "A Fading Relationship: Library Schools and Preappointment Archival Education Since 1973," *Journal of Education for Librarianship* 20 (Summer 1979), 26; Philip P. Mason, "Archival Education: The Need for Standards," in *Symposium on Archival Education, School of Library and Information Science, University of Western Ontario, Saturday, July 28th, 1979*, eds. Janet Fyfe and Clifford Collier (London: School of Library and Information Science, University of Western Ontario, 1980), 67; and Larry J. McCrank, "Prospects for Integrating Historical and Information Studies in Archival Education," *American Archivist* 42 (October 1979), 443.

[7]This is essentially a brief summary of the new SAA guidelines for archival education adopted in early 1988. There has been some debate about these guidelines' statements on management. However, this aspect of education remains due to the fact that a large portion of archivists become managers, whether in one person shops or in larger archival programs as they advance. The guidelines do not advocate that archivists

Central to the present notion about archival education is a stronger conviction that archivists have their own specialized knowledge.[8] Although archival training must include courses in related fields -- historical methodology, public or applied history, information science, conservation, business and public administration, records management, historical editing, and oral history -- historical records administration has its own theoretical foundation and fundamental principles, even though these principles require additional clarification.[9]

A concomitant trend with developments in graduate archival education has been the strengthening of continuing archival education, both basic and advanced, although its relationship to graduate archival education programs remains fuzzy at best. The SAA recently established an Education Office, with its first full-time Education Officer, to develop short courses in "archival fundamentals," a hallmark of SAA's work since the mid-1970s, and "advanced archival training," especially oriented to mid-career archivists. SAA, led by its Committee on Education and Professional Development and new Education Office, is preparing a comprehensive plan for archival education that relates basic institutes and workshops to graduate education and advanced training and the archival profession's other educational needs. Other related professional associations have taken similar steps and new, more ambitious efforts will likely emerge in the next few years.[10]

---

must receive this training from other experienced archivists; they can certainly receive it from public administration experts and similar authorities.

[8]There is still debate about this, but this author strongly contends that the archivist possesses specialized knowledge and theory. For the debate contrast Frank G. Burke, "The Future Course of Archival Theory in the United States," *American Archivist* 44 (Winter 1981), 40-46 with John W. Roberts, "Archival Theory: Much Ado About Shelving," *ibid.* 50 (Winter 1987), 66-74.

[9]The contention here is very simple. Archival administration is a distinct profession, not a subset of history or information science, with a distinct mission. The author is comfortable with the idea of archival administration being viewed as part of a broader "public history" consortium because there are some advantages to this, such as presented in my chapter on "Archivists and Public Historians" in this volume.

[10]For example, the National Association of Government Archives and Records Administrators has held a multi-week advanced institute for state archival administrators and the New England Archivists, with support from the National Historical Publications and Records Commission, has created a series of basic and advanced workshops for its membership.

Present Issues Affecting Archival Education in the United States

Despite the new vitality, archivists face a number of important issues regarding their education and training. All remain important concerns since education and training forms the quality of the professional corps of archivists managing this country's historical records.

One of the major obstacles facing the sound development of graduate and continuing archival education is the general condition of the profession itself, both the way that archivists view themselves and the manner in which society looks at and understands (or misunderstands) the nature of the archival mission. Thanks to the work of past SAA president David Gracy and the Archives and Society Task Force archivists now know for certain that resource allocators -- archivists' bosses and the ones that control the resources available to archivists -- value the work of archivists no more than that of "other" technicians and do not understand the full implications of the value of archival records to their organizations and broader society.[11] Greater public support for the archival mission is crucial for the strengthening of archival education because this education requires increased resources and commitment by the universities for providing the necessary strong base. The best route for continuing education is one that can complement solid graduate archival training programs.

But a major portion of the obstacle to improved archival education has been due to the way in which archivists view themselves. Many archivists label themselves historians or librarians or records managers, devote significant portions of their professional careers to interests far removed from the archival calling, use their archival positions for personal research or as a steppingstone for other positions that may only be tenuously connected to the archival profession, do not support their main professional associations, and do not feel inclined to contribute to their literature that is essential for a sound profession and adequate education.[12] These are not new problems. The SAA Committee for the Seventies nearly two

---

[11]See Gracy's "Our Future is Now," *American Archivist* 48 (Winter 1985), 12-21 and "What's Your Totem? Archival Images in the Public Mind," *Midwestern Archivist*, 10, no. 1 (1985), 17-23.

[12]Leland, "American Archival Problems"; Theodore C. Blegen, "Problems of American Archivists," *Bulletin* of the National Archives, no. 2 (November 1936), 3-4; Lester J. Cappon, "Tardy Scholars Among the Archivists," *American Archivist* 21 (January 1958), 3-16; and my own, "Professionalism and Archivists in the United States" in this volume.

decades ago, for example, squarely lay the blame for the weaknesses in archival education at the doorstep of the profession itself. "In the absence of leadership and direction provided by the Society," this report mentioned, "the matter of education and training has been left to the initiative of concerned members."[13] The results were the "wide range" and "diversity" of programs *and* most of the problems that now hinder the development of sound graduate level archival education programs.

This weakness of professional leadership, cited by the SAA Committee for the Seventies, has resulted in a number of persistent, lingering problems relative to the education of archivists, such as follows:

Regulation of the Quality of Archival Educational Programs. The new SAA graduate guidelines only "guide" archival educators. SAA, with allied professional associations like the American Library Association, need to consider accreditation of graduate archival programs and regulation of other education methods to ensure the continuing quality of archivists. Communicating more effectively to other disciplines that seek a role in educating archivists about the required knowledge and training of prospective archivists, such as public history and library science, is equally as important. This is no small task, since it will require not only tremendous political skill in convincing most universities that archival education should be taken seriously but persuasive abilities among the ranks itself of the archival profession. Any kind of standards for accreditation likely to be adopted would not endorse most of the existing archival education programs.[14]

The Impact of Individual Certification on Archival Education. There appears now to be sharply opposing views about the value of certification for archival education and the profession, some arguing it will weaken the continuing development of formal graduate education and others

[13]Philip P. Mason, "The Society of American Archivists in the Seventies: Report of the Committee for the 1970's," *American Archivist* 35 (April 1972), 206.

[14]There are, for example, a large number of "programs" that consist only of a single introductory course and a practicum requirement. It is unlikely that an accreditation effort would approve these programs. Minimum standards for accrediting graduate archival education programs would have to consist of multi-course efforts or the accreditation effort would be a waste of time.

contending it will strengthen all forms of archival education. Certification can strengthen the educational preparation of prospective archivists, if it is not viewed as a replacement for education but as another means by which to ensure the competency of practicing archivists. Certification can result in the more precise definition of archival work, continued improvement of archival literature, and creation of a higher profile of archival administration; in short, certification can be a powerful impetus for more and improved archival education programs. It can provide a tool to go with accreditation of graduate and other continuing education programs, while at the same time providing some breathing room for such an accreditation apparatus to be developed.

Attracting Qualified Individuals to Become Archivists. Although there appears to be a lack of sufficiently qualified candidates for archival positions at entry, intermediate, and upper level positions, there are now no formal efforts to attract undergraduate students to consider careers in archival administration. Individuals generally learn about archival careers at the graduate level and then only by happenstance. This problem is further compounded by a continuing weak public image of the archival profession. Archivists, led by their associations like SAA and NAGARA, need initiatives that communicate to undergraduate students -- in all fields -- the nature, opportunities, and importance of archival careers.

Distinguishing Educational Requirements for Areas of Archival Specialization. At present, there is little distinction made in archival education for individuals who work as para-professionals, technicians and specialists, or as administrators.[15] The archival profession must consider the differing needs of such individuals and direct them to appropriate existing training courses and programs or create the courses and programs needed. Archivists also need better definition of the necessary qualifications and duties of these various positions. Such definition is crucial to developing the appropriate post-employment archival education courses that will aid the profession's management of the documentary heritage. Some of what needs to occur may come through the development of a much more comprehensive, far-reaching continuing education

---

[15]European archival educators have emphasized such levels; see Michael Cook, "An International Standard for the Training of Archivists and Records Managers," *UNESCO Journal of Information Science, Librarianship and Archives Administration* 4 (April-June, 1982), 114-22.

program designed more for advanced and mid-career professionals than the beginning and early career archivists that such courses have traditionally been designed for.

The Place of the Practicum in Archival Education. A fundamental aspect of archival education has been the practicum, an opportunity for the student to obtain first-hand experience in an archival repository. Although the SAA adopted guidelines for the practicum in 1980,[16] there has been virtually no evaluation of the benefits of this component of archival education.[17] Some argue that the practicum has extremely limited value, gives the impression that archival work is more craft than profession, minimizes the importance of theory in archival administration, and has not been carefully monitored or regulated. More serious attention has to be given to the continuing role of the practicum in archival education. If the practicum is to have a place in the future graduate education of archivists, than it must be expanded in scope and sophistication to match the growth of the profession.

Archival Research and Development and Education. With a few exceptions, there is little in the archival profession resembling organized research and development, although there are plenty of needs for such work. At least one archival commentator has argued forcefully for the need for graduate archival education programs to fill this need.[18] These programs must urge their students to conduct serious research in important archival subjects, and archival educators should have the time and resources for doing research and writing on archival theory and practice. The development of graduate archival educational programs must go hand in hand with the establishment of research and development units in the larger archival repositories, the creation of sabbatical programs for individual research on archival topics, and the emergence of

[16]"Program Standard for Archival Education: The Practicum," *American Archivist* 43 (Summer 1980), 420-22.

[17]Virtually the only article about this aspect of archival education is William G. LeFurgy, "The Practicum: A Repository View," *American Archivist* 44 (Spring 1981), 153-55.

[18]Burke, "Future Course."

archival programs that emphasize research and publication on important archival issues.[19]

The Continuing Role of the Archival Profession in the Modern Information Society. In this matter, archivists face the same challenges as librarians, data processors, management information systems personnel, and other groups concerned with society's information needs and uses. Will there be one information profession that includes all of these now related "information" fields, or will they simply have similar educational programs and professional agendas? Records management educators are already redefining their focus to a broader information resource management (IRM) concept.[20] Archivists also need to do the same, maintaining their distinctive mission -- the identification, selection, preservation, and management of information of enduring value. Individuals training to be archivists in the future will have more exposure to IRM, records management, and other library and information science courses. These related fields must also gain an increased awareness about the preservation of information with continuing value to information creators, users, and society. Archivists have the responsibility to ensure that this occurs.

The Need for Expanded Graduate and Other Archival Educational Programs; or, Alternatives to Such Programs

This last issue is closely related to the matter of expanding and strengthening graduate archival education programs in the university. This is more than an issue, however, it is the whole crux of where we are and should be heading with archival education in the United States. With a few exceptions,[21] the existing graduate archival education programs

---

[19]There are some promising signs in this regard, but they still represent only modest improvement. The National Archives and Records Administration and the Minnesota Historical Society have both established sabbatical programs, but these programs are far too few to benefit substantially the archival profession, except as an encouragement to other historical records and archival programs to offer similar opportunities to their staffs.

[20]Robert V. Williams, "Records Management Education: An IRM Perspective," *Records Management Quarterly* 21 (October 1987), 36-40, 54.

[21]And for this we have to go outside of the United States. Terry Eastwood, "The Origins and Aims of the Master of Archival Studies Programme at the University of British Columbia," *Archivaria* 16 (Summer 1983), 35-52.

consist of no more than three courses (similar to that outlined in the 1977 SAA guidelines) - a general introductory course, an advanced course of some kind, and a practicum or internship. Those programs purporting to have more courses related to or part of archival administration are deceiving. In a library and information school, they are often courses on philosophy of librarianship or social science bibliography; in a history department, they are likely courses on historiography and historical editing.[22] The problem is not that these courses are not useful for individuals equipping themselves to practice as archivists, but that we are shortchanging the archival profession's need to have detailed courses on archival theory and practice.

What should a comprehensive graduate archival education program look like in terms of the courses that it offers and the requirements that it insists upon? Although there is no question that any such program must draw upon the expertise of other fields such as library and information science and history, there is still the need for specialized courses that cover the major practices, functions, and theories of archival administration. What follows is a brief discussion of some of the varieties of courses that I mean and that are not being offered in graduate archival programs in the United States at present. What follows is not a comprehensive sequence of courses - that could be built off of the recent SAA guidelines - but some suggestions about the *kinds* of courses that the archival profession needs developed and offered.

The archival profession needs, first and foremost, full courses on the identification and selection of information with enduring value. Appraisal has been called the archivist's "first responsibility," because it shapes the records which archivists and manuscript curators administer and determines much of the nature of their subsequent duties.[23] Such a course should review the basic principles that archivists have developed for appraisal, from broad approaches such as "documentation

[22]For this insight, I am indebted to Timothy L. Ericson, former Education Officer for the Society of American Archivists.

[23]For the range of work needing to be done on appraisal see Richard J. Cox and Helen W. Samuels, "The Archivist's First Responsibility: A Research Agenda to Improve the Identification and Retention of Records of Enduring Value," *American Archivist* 51 (Winter/Spring 1988), 28-42 and *Planning for the Archival Profession: A Report of the SAA Task Force on Goals and Priorities* (Chicago: Society of American Archivists, 1986), 8-13. The kind of full course on appraisal described here was taught by the author in 1989 and a commentary on this experience is being prepared for publication.

strategies" to more specific applications such as sampling, and guide students through a series of case studies and exercises. Such a course should also compare archival appraisal to the manuscript curator's focus on an acquisition policy and to similar responsibilities in other disciplines such as library and information science (collection management/development), museum administration (artifact selection), and history (analysis of documentary evidence for interpretation of the past).[24] There is certainly no way to introduce properly a student to the complexities of archival appraisal in the few hours or days that archivists now devote to it in their archival education courses.

Although arrangement and description and reference are generally well-represented in existing introductory and advanced courses and emphasized during practica and internships, these are topics that could serve the profession better if they were focused into at least a single course. For one thing, this would allow students to receive an in-depth introduction to the basic principles of archival arrangement and description, their practical application, and their connection to the reference and use of these materials. In such a course, students would be expected to master the principles of archival arrangement, description, and reference; complete a series of case studies; and visit historical societies, government archives, institutional archives, and other repositories. Doing this would also accomplish other important objectives for the archival profession, including allowing practica to stress functions other than arrangement and description, giving students a better and broader introduction to the archival profession, and providing a forum for more in-depth analyzing of these functions.[25]

[24]There are a wide range of studies now available about such areas. See, for example, the following: Ross W. Atkinson, "Selection for Preservation: A Materialistic Approach," *Library Resources & Technical Services* 30 (October/December 1986), 341-53 and Thomas J. Schlereth, "Defining Collecting Missions: National and Regional Models," in *A Common Agenda for History Museums: Conference Proceedings February 19-20, 1987*, ed. Lonn W. Taylor (Nashville: American Association for State and Local History and Washington, D.C.: Smithsonian Institution, 1987), 24-31.

[25]Both reference and description have become centers of attention by the archival profession. In the area of reference, archivists have been challenged to know who uses their records, how they use these materials, and how they should encourage greater and more significant use of their records; see, for example, Paul Conway, "Facts and Frameworks: An Approach to Studying the Users of Archives," *American Archivist* 49 (Fall 1986), 393-407. In the area of description, archivists have become motivated to adopt stronger standards, following the example of their Canadian colleagues. Refer to *Toward Descriptive Standards: Report and*

It is difficult to imagine in the late 1980s that students preparing to be archivists would not receive a good introduction to the issue of preservation,[26] but that generally remains the case. Although a few programs, mostly in library and information science schools, provide a single course introduction to this function, it is nevertheless true that most archivists have received their training in this area from SAA workshops and similar short-term institutes. Any graduate program purporting to be training students to work as archivists should have a course that surveys the basic principles, issues, and practices of archival manuscript and library preservation. Students should be able to distinguish between preservation management, conservation, and restoration[27] and have the opportunity to visit library and archival preservation laboratories, a regional conservation facility, and a micrographics facility.

Since many recent graduates of archival education programs can soon expect to have some administrative responsibility in the institutions in which they work, mainly because so many historical records repositories are small, graduate archival education schools should have courses on the administration of archival and historical records programs. Such courses should introduce students to the subject of developing and administering historical records programs, covering topics such as writing mission statements, developing long-range plans, acquiring resources for support of basic archival and manuscript functions, winning increased institutional support, developing public programs for increased public recognition, staffing and continuing staff development , and so forth.[28] In such a course students should also learn about the differences,

---

Recommendations of the Canadian Working Group on Archival Descriptive Standards (Ottawa: Bureau of Canadian Archivists, December 1985) and for why such standards are needed, Avra Michelson, "Description and Reference in the Age of Automation," *American Archivist* 50 (Spring 1987), 192-208.

[26]For an example of the magnitude of the problem, refer to *Preservation Needs in State Archives* (Albany: National Association of Government Archives and Records Administrators, 1986).

[27]Such as outlined in Mary Lynn Ritzenthaler, *Archives & Manuscripts: Conservation; A Manual on Physical Care and Management* (Chicago: Society of American Archivists, 1983).

[28]An example of the range of functions in administering a historical records program can be found in [Richard J. Cox and Judy Hohmann], *Strengthening New York's Historical Records Programs: A Self-Study Guide* (Albany: New York State Archives and Records Administration, 1988).

needs, and requirements of various archival and manuscript repositories such as local historical societies, corporate archives, government archives, and college and university special collections.

Finally, as another example of the kind of courses that students preparing to become archivists should be able to take, archival education programs should have a single course on archival history and development. Understanding the history of archives is one gateway by which students can gain insight into the nature, problems, issues, and mission of the modern archival profession. Such a course could concentrate on the development of historical records programs and archival institutions in the United States, although it should also review the origins and development of archives in the ancient world, Europe and elsewhere and relate this to the development of related professions like history and library science.[29]

If such broad, comprehensive archival education graduate programs - ones that support the types of courses just outlined - cannot be developed, for whatever reason, than at least two other alternatives need to be explored. The first is the most obvious, an expansion of the SAA's continuing education program to fill the gap. There is no doubt that a sufficient battery of courses, both basic and advanced, can be developed, since SAA is well on its way to having such a battery already.[30] If the nascent individual certification program is a success, than there will be an even greater impetus to the creation and ongoing support of a full range of basic and advanced archival courses. These courses could be offered to individuals already armed with relevant graduate degrees in library science and history, even those who have had an introductory course or two in archival administration, and allow students to receive a more indepth introduction to certain aspects of the administration of historical records.

The other alternative approach resurrects an idea first proposed many years ago, but not given any real serious attention in twenty years at least. The clearest articulation of this concept, a national institute for archival administration training on the graduate level, was written by H. G. Jones in

[29]For the potential of archival history, see my "On the Value of American Archival History" in this volume.

[30]Consider, for example, the existing courses on appraisal. SAA has already sponsored the development of courses and seminars on the basics of appraisal, developing collecting policies, and documentation strategies, totalling up to a far more in-depth introduction to the subject than is offered in any existing graduate program.

the late 1960s. According to Jones such an institute would be staffed by eminent individuals in the history, archival, and records management fields; located in Washington, D.C. and draw on the resources of the major archival repositories like the National Archives and the Library of Congress; administered by a governing board, in cooperation with a Washington-based university; and include a full curriculum that would prepare a student for assuming responsibility for the administration of archives.[31] Archivists may be nearing the time, if their graduate programs cannot assume the primary responsibility for broader and more indepth training, when such a national school, admittedly similar to what other nations already do, should be established.

Conclusion: Prospects for the Future of Archival Education in the United States

Looking into the future is at best chancy, if not foolish. But, as I have already tried to suggest, the prospects for archival education seem better than ever before. Although the archival profession will always be small when compared to its relations like librarians, the archival profession will show steady growth in the next decade or so. There are increasing demands for archival skills and perspective by government, business, and other information consumers. This is not due to any growing public historical consciousness - that remains hard to ascertain - but because of the archivists' expertise in the selection and management of information with enduring value.

What does all this mean? By the early 1990s, there could be at least a half-dozen multi-course graduate programs in archival administration, located in history, public or applied history, and information/library science programs, each having its own unique and valuable focus. These programs might annually prepare from fifty to one hundred archivists qualified to fill specialist or administrative posts. At the same time, continuing education programs could be flourishing at both basic and advanced levels. The basic courses will be providing introductions to individuals training for archival para-professional or support positions or to other professionals seeking short-term introductions to archival administrative principles and practices, and the advanced courses constituting a well-rounded program for archivists in mid-career. If these

---

[31]H. G. Jones, *The Records of a Nation: Their Management, Preservation, and Use* (New York: Atheneum, 1969), 217-222.

programs develop, the archival profession's image, practice, and mission will be stronger than ever.

But what if these programs do not develop? What will be the state of the archival profession and its mission in the United States? America's documentary heritage will be at severe risk because the archival profession will remain small, its influence meager, and its public profile uncertain. There is little question, then, that the average American citizen's notion of information will not include that contained in historical records. The *unique* perspective of the archivist will be lost, along with America's documentary heritage. The education of the archivist is fundamental to the well-being of the archival profession and the preservation and management of historical records in the United States. To improve archival education in this country the archival profession requires significantly stronger and more comprehensive graduate programs and an expanded continuing education program that primarily offers intensive courses on advanced topics; these programs must be accredited and their graduates certified based on standards set by the professional associations. Archivists must show remarkable progress in these areas over the next decade to meet the challenges of preserving America's documentary heritage. A more aggressive research agenda about the nature and needs of archival education is one possible starting point.

SIX

A RESEARCH AGENDA FOR ARCHIVAL EDUCATION IN THE UNITED STATES

Education and the Archival Profession: Introductory Comments

The education of individuals preparing to work as archivists and the in-service or continuing education of practicing archivists have long been concerns of the archival profession in the United States and North America. This interest is evident from the prominence of articles on education and professional development in the archival literature. From 1937 through 1988 over seventy articles on archival education in the United States appeared (see Table One).[1] Over half of these articles were published in the last decade, reflecting an increased recent interest in archival standards and competencies. Despite this interest in archival education, the issue of what archivists know about their own educational needs and approaches is a matter requiring closer scrutiny. There has been little research,[2] significant or otherwise, completed on this topic. The majority of writing about archival education has been devoted to descriptions or informal case studies of educational programs, arguments or opinion pieces about the nature of archival education, historical analyses, and proposals for particular methods to train archivists. The most in-depth research has consisted of three surveys[3] of what practicing archivists thought about archival education and what archival educators were teaching and several historical studies that used primary sources to answer questions about the origins and development of archival education.[4] A more recent analysis of

---

[1]Many of these articles also consider Canada. If essays concentrating on Canadian archival education were also included, the number would be much higher but the patterns described here would certainly hold. The articles on archival education in the United States are certainly typical of those on Canada and sufficient for my points about the nature of the literature.

[2]By research I mean the effort to "solve problems in a systematic" manner "or to confirm the validity of the solutions to problems others have presumably resolved." The research process includes the formulation of questions, careful planning, hypotheses, and the testing of the hypotheses through the accumulation and interpretation of data. See Paul D. Leedy, *Practical Research: Planning and Design*, 3rd ed. (New York: Macmillan Publishing Co., 1985), 4-7.

[3]The most recent survey is Ames Sheldon Bower, "Whence and Whither: A Survey of Archival Education," *Georgia Archive* 5 (Summer 1977), 44-61.

[4]These historical studies are cited in the next section of this essay.

the marketplace for archivists suggests that research on archival topics may be maturing.[5]   Even these better researched investigations pose more questions than they answer and require substantial additional research.

Since education partly defines *and* ensures any profession's well-being through providing competent practitioners,[6] it is essential that the archival profession ensure that its education is of the highest quality and meets the discipline's needs for the carrying out of its societal mission.   This is especially important since the 1980s has been a turbulent decade of self-assessment for the archival profession,[7] bringing with it a proliferation in educational programs at the same time as archival competencies and standards are being reviewed and, in many cases, are being defined for the first time.   The commencement of a program for the individual certification of archivists in the United States in 1988,[8] and continuing debate about this issue in Canada, has both typified and accentuated the changes affecting the profession and pressuring for change in the education of archivists.   The archival profession needs to develop and carry out a research agenda concerning the education of its practitioners.   The results of this research will provide a firmer basis for developing the proper curriculum, curriculum materials, and teaching methods (among other things) needed by the archival profession.

[5]Constance B. Schulz, "Analysis of the Marketplace for Educated Archivists: State Archives as a Case Study," *American Archivist* 51 (Summer 1988), 320-29.

[6]Andrew Abbott's *The System of Professions: An Essay on the Division of Expert Labor* (Chicago: University of Chicago Press, 1988) gives knowledge, defined and nurtured in the university, a central role in the shifting contests between competing professions over jurisdictions and the status of that profession in society. A more traditional sociological analysis emphasizing knowledge is Eliot Freidson, *Professional Powers: A Study of the Institutionalization of Formal Knowledge* (Chicago: University of Chicago Press, 1986). For a summary of earlier sociological writings on professions and how they relate to archival administration, refer to chapter two in this volume.

[7]For a sense of the change occurring in the archival profession, refer to Larry J. Hackman, "A Perspective on American Archives," *Public Historian* 8 (Summer 1986), 10-28.

[8]For the first serious analysis of the certification effort in the United States, see William J. Maher, "Contexts for Understanding Certification: Opening Pandora's Box?" *American Archivist* 51 (Fall 1988), 408-27.

TABLE ONE

LITERATURE ON AMERICAN ARCHIVAL EDUCATION,
1937-1988

	Case studies	Opinion	Historical	Methods	Surveys	Total
1930s	1	2				3
1940s	2	3				5
1950s	3	2				5
1960s		5	1			6
1970s	3	11		2	3	19
1980s	9	18	4	2	1	34
Total	18	41	5	4	4	72

Source: Richard J. Cox, "An Annotated Bibliography of Studies in English on Archival Education," prepared for the Society of American Archivists' Committee on Education and Professional Development, March 1986; Paul Conway, "Archival Education and the Need for Full-Time Faculty," *American Archivist* 51 (Summer 1988) 254-65.

Other professions have conducted more substantial research on their educational programs and provide leads to what archivists should evaluate about their own educational programs. Even though many librarians have lamented the quality of research being done in their profession,[9] they have conducted and published substantially more on their educational programs than archivists.[10] The similarity of

[9]See, for example, Mary Jo Lynch, "Research and Librarianship: An Uneasy Connection," *Library Trends* 32 (Spring 1984), 367-83 and W. Boyd Rayward, "Research and Education for Library and Information Science: Waples in Retrospect," *Library Quarterly* 56 (October 1986), 348-59. For an historical overview of library research, refer to the introductory chapter in Charles H. Busha, ed., *A Library Science Research Reader and Bibliographic Guide* (Littleton, Colorado: Libraries Unlimited, Inc., 1981). In this paper, I have primarily concentrated on the past decade of library education research. The nature and variety of research during this period is sufficient for comparison for the development of a research agenda in archival education.

[10]There are many reasons for the differences in research in the two professions. Librarianship represents an older and larger profession supported by independent professional schools and possessing tremendous outlets for publication. For a recent history of library education that reveals some of these differences, refer to Donald G. Davis and Phyllis

missions, functions, and practices between the two professions, along with the fact that an increasing number of archivists are educated in library and information science schools, makes a comparison of library science educational research to archival education that more important.[11] Education professionals have, of course, devoted considerable time and attention to research methods and activities. Some of their research models and practices have also been drawn upon in developing a research agenda for archival education.[12]

A final introductory word about the scope of archival education considered in this essay needs to be made. Throughout the history of the archival profession in the United States, the education of archivists has been characterized by diversity and debate (something of the flavor of this will be seen in the next section). There has been no monolithic educational system for archivists. They have been trained on the job and in continuing education workshops and institutions. On the graduate level they have been educated in history programs, library schools, and in dual history-library graduate programs. Some individuals have even come into the field and received no more training than what they have learned on the job, through diligent reading of journals and textbooks, and through occasional attendance at professional association meetings. The purpose of this paper is not to argue *what* archival education should look like or what form it should take; this paper acknowledges that all these means of learning about the basic principles and methods of archival administration

Dain, eds., "History of Library and Information Science Education," *Library Trends* 34 (Winter 1986), 357-531.

[11]For a sense of the similarities and differences between librarianship and archival administration, see Robert L. Clark, Jr., ed., *Archive-Library Relations* (New York: R. R. Bowker Co., 1976) and Lawrence J. McCrank, ed., *Archives and Library Administration: Divergent Traditions and Common Concerns* (New York: Haworth Press, 1986).

[12]I have been much more highly selective in drawing upon the educational research than that of librarianship for two reasons. First, there is a vast literature that is far too great to discuss in an essay of this type. Second, many of the library research efforts mentioned here have drawn upon educational research methodologies and models. For example, Mary Kingsbury, in her analysis of library school faculty evaluation, noted that such studies have been rare in her profession. "To find any research on tenure and promotion practices, it is necessary to review the literature of higher education in general"; "How Library Schools Evaluate Faculty Performance," *Journal of Education for Librarianship* 22 (Spring 1982), 221. Kingsbury's approach is typical of individuals doing research on library education.

exist and *may* have continuing value to the profession. Rather, this essay urges that the varieties of archival education be studied to determine their effectiveness and to provide an empirical basis for the strengthening of archival education and the archival profession.

A Brief History of Archival Education in the United States as an Example[13]

Since the purpose of this essay is to define an appropriate research agenda for archival education, there is no attempt here to provide a detailed history of archival education. The most important aspect about its development for the subject of this essay is the checkered history of archival education that has contributed to a general lack of understanding about matters of fundamental importance for the education of archivists. The deficiency of comprehensive archival education programs and the shortage of full-time archival educators are partly why serious research about the nature and quality of archival education has not been undertaken. Moreover, there are a few excellent historical reviews of the development of archival education in the United States that interested individuals can turn to for more information. These have been cited throughout the essay. There are also numerous comments in other sections of this essay that suggest the pertinent features of the historical outlines of archival education.

When the profession was born with the founding of the Society of American Archivists fifty years ago, there was immediate debate about whether prospective archivists should be educated as librarians or historians. There has continued to be debate since then about the professional identity of archivists. Because archival education was part of the education of another field, the immediate focus, lasting for better than a generation, was on in-service training and continuing education. The predominant source of knowledge about archival administration through the 1940s until well into

[13]The primary difference between archival education in Canada and the United States is the Canadian archival profession's strong support of developing a major archival education program at one university, the University of British Columbia. This program's Master's in Archival Studies has had a significant impact on archival education, theory and practice in both the United States and Canada, especially due to the study of archival administration undertaken by its students in their thesis requirement. See Terry Eastwood, "Nurturing Archival Education in the University," *American Archivist* 51 (Summer 1988), 228-52.

the 1970s was on-the-job or in-service training. All through the early years of the archival profession, however, solitary graduate courses on archival administration were developed and offered. There was only one course in 1938, but by thirty years later there were eight multiple course programs; the growth in the size of the profession in the 1970s was likewise accompanied by a proliferation in the number of one or two course sequences, from 23 in 1973 to 59 in 1986.[14] As one archival educator stated, "by 1970, specialized training, usually on the graduate level, was gaining widespread acceptance as a prerequisite for employment in most beginning archival positions."[15] That acceptance has continued, although not at a rate fast enough to satisfy many archivists. There continues to be many "professional" archival positions filled by individuals with *no* appropriate graduate education as well as sentiment by some members of the profession that there is no need for stronger graduate archival education.

Such graduate courses were, and have continued to be, supplemented by short-term institutes, the most famous of which is the Modern Archives Institute offered since 1945 in conjunction with the National Archives.[16] During the 1970s, when the Society of American Archivists (SAA) emerged as a stronger, more dynamic national professional association and the profession's numbers increased dramatically, the first official adoption of graduate education guidelines only stipulated a three course program, consisting of introductory and advanced courses and a practicum. In-service training and continuing education were still to be heavily relied upon for producing competent archivists. It has *only* been in the 1980s that the SAA and other archivists have begun to consider the need for more extensive and accredited education programs (although accreditation elicits divided reactions). The more

---

[14]Summarized in Paul Conway, "Archival Education and the Need for Full-Time Faculty," *American Archivist* 51 (Summer 1988), 256. For the best history of the early development of archival education see Jacqueline Goggin, "That We Shall Truly Deserve the Title of 'Profession': The Training and Education of Archivists, 1930-1960," *ibid.* 47 (Summer 1984), 243-54.

[15]Philip P. Mason, "Archival Education: The Need for Standards," in *Symposium on Archival Education, School of Library and Information Science, University of Western Ontario Saturday, July 28th, 1979*, eds. Janet Fyfe and Clifford Collier (London: School of Library and Information Science, University of Western Ontario, 1980), 65.

[16]Frank B. Evans, "Educational Needs for Work in Archival and Manuscript Depositories," *Indian Archives* 21 (July/December 1972), 20-22.

(although accreditation elicits divided reactions). The more precisely-defined 1988 graduate education guidelines reflect this new interest.[17] The adoption of these guidelines comes at a time, however, when basic short-term institutes and in-service training and continuing education still strongly predominate. The only major change, although it is a significant one, has been the 1988 start of a program of certification of individual archivists (initially rejected in 1982) pushing the formalization of comprehensive education programs.[18] Richard Berner, in his review of the history of archival education, stated that if archival education had been "appropriately placed in an academic setting [at the beginning], the required interaction and development of theory and practice would have deliberately moved ahead"[19] and the at times confusing configuration of workshops, institutes, graduate courses, and other educational and training opportunities might have been more coherently developed. There might also have been little need for an essay such as this one describing the paucity of research on archival education and the general lack of codification of archival principles and methodologies that support this education.

The need for a systematic research agenda on archival education should be obvious to any archivist (and any educator in a related field). For more than two generations archivists have debated, lamented, and, in some cases, whined about the state of archival education. In the mid-1960s, thirty years after the organization of the profession, archivists were continuing to write about their education in the following ways: "Of all the activities in which archivists engage, none, I believe, is in greater need of strengthening and enlarging than that of education,"[20] and "we archivists have failed in our responsibility

---

[17]"Society of American Archivists Guidelines for Graduate Archival Education Programs," *American Archivist* 51 (Summer 1988), 380-89.

[18]Virginia J. H. Cain, "Archives By Degree: Personal Perspectives on Academic Preparation for the Archival Profession," *Provenance* 2 (Fall 1984), 39.

[19]"Archival Education and Training in the United States, 1937 to Present," *Journal of Education for Librarianship* 22 (Summer/Fall 1981), 4. This view has been supported by a number of others, most importantly Paul Conway's "Archival Education and the Need for Full-Time Faculty," cited earlier. In that essay, Conway shows the roles that archival educators can best play, including the preparing of textbooks, monitoring the quality of education for archivists, and recruiting and educating individuals to work as archivists.

[20]Allen du Pont Breck, "New Dimensions in the Education of American Archivists," *American Archivist* 29 (April 1966), 173.

to our profession . . . to provide adequate, regular, and comprehensive training."[21] A decade *after* that, comments such as the following were being made: "Archival education . . . is only recently maturing into comprehensive, systematically-designed curricula."[22] Despite such concerns, however, little research has been done to aid the strengthening of archival education. Archivists know very little about such *basic* things as how individuals enter the profession or the needs and desires of archival employers.

This essay examines ten components of archival education requiring more research than has been done (see Table Two). These elements have been identified through the years by many archival educators although little to no empirical study has been made of them. They can be grouped conveniently into four major characteristics of archival education: basic knowledge and theory, students, archival employers and their institutions, and the nature and success of graduate and continuing educational programs. These groupings are not intended to represent a comprehensive notion of education, but they reflect the major themes and concerns that archivists have focused upon over the last half-century.

Research into these areas will undoubtedly suggest other topics requiring research, but adequate study in the ones described in this essay would significantly improve what archival educators and practicing archivists need to know in order to strengthen graduate and continuing education in this profession.

[21]H.G. Jones, "Archival Training in American Universities, 1938-1968," *American Archivist* 31 (April 1968), 148.

[22]Lawrence J. McCrank, "Present Developments in Archival Education: The Future Care of the Past," in *Symposium on Archival Education*, 11.

TABLE TWO

ESSENTIAL RESEARCH AREAS OF ARCHIVAL EDUCATION

Basic Knowledge and Theory
1. Archival Knowledge & Competencies
2. Theory & Practice

Students
3. Recruitment
4. Learning Traits & Styles

Archival Employers and Institutions
5. Employers' Needs & Hiring Practices
6. Effectiveness of In-service Training
7. Work Levels & Specialized Education

Educational Programs
8. Effectiveness of Graduate Programs
9. Archival Educators
10. Textbooks, Curriculum Materials, & Tools

THE RESEARCH AGENDA FOR ARCHIVAL EDUCATION

Basic Knowledge and Theory: Archival Knowledge and Competencies

Attention on matters such as whether archivists are historians or librarians and where graduate archival education should be placed has diverted a great deal of attention away from the matter of what archivists, to be competent, should know. Nearly half a century ago, Solon Buck called archival administration "an applied science rather than a pure science . . . compounded of parts of many other sciences or fields of knowledge, together with certain principles and techniques derived from practical experience."[23] Buck's interdisciplinary view has been echoed a number of times since then, but it is a perspective that remains as one of only many alternative ways of looking at the profession's educational requirements. Only a decade ago Francis Blouin still felt obliged to urge archivists to accept *themselves* as professionals so that they would focus not "on the problem of who or what we are, but rather on how we can best prepare men and women to make reasoned and correct judgments when confronting problems in

---

[23]"The Training of American Archivists," *American Archivist* 4 (April 1941), 85.

the administration of modern archives and manuscript libraries."[24]

The decade of the 1980s has been a time when Blouin's suggestion seems to have been followed. Terry Eastwood has firmly (and perhaps finally?) placed the notion of archival *knowledge* at the center of archival education in an essay describing the graduate archival program at the University of British Columbia. Eastwood urged "defining, refining, and disseminating a body of archival knowledge."[25] The revision of SAA's graduate archival education guidelines resulted in a more vigorous effort to define a basic archival knowledge. SAA's Committee on Education and Professional Development is now using these guidelines as a starting point to define competencies more fully. These new efforts are at least partly attributable to SAA's adoption of a post-employment individual archival certification program; the efforts to develop a certification examination has promoted greater interest in basic archival knowledge as has fear (as of yet, unjustified) in some quarters that the certification program will weaken graduate archival education programs.

Graduate archival education programs can be used to spur on the development of archival knowledge. Faculty members are, of course, a key to this, but a handful of full-time archival educators who have the time for research will hardly change this situation in any dramatic fashion. But the development of multi-course programs with specialized courses on appraisal, arrangement and description, and reference that attract advanced students who can study proposed models and procedures should significantly improve the quality of the research literature that the profession now processes.[26] The

[24]Francis X. Blouin, Jr., "The Relevance of the Case Method to Archival Education and Training," *American Archivist* 41 (January 1978), 37.

[25]"Nurturing Archival Education in the University." In the same journal issue Timothy L. Ericson wrote: "Archivists also have paid too much attention to the *form* of archival education, and not enough to its *content*. Too much time is spent thinking in terms of workshops, seminars, and institutes, and too little considering what techniques and skills archivists need to learn"; "Professional Associations and Archival Education: A Different Role, or a Different Theater?" *American Archivist* 51 (Summer 1988), 299.

[26]An excellent example of this is Janice E. Ruth, "Educating the Reference Archivist," *American Archivist* 51 (Summer 1988), 266-76. Ruth lays out a number of possibilities for students to conduct research that could benefit the profession. The context for this happening is a full course

small number of full-time faculty and, more importantly, the fact that most graduate archival education programs consist of only a few courses at best also places a strain on what should be taught and the depth of that teaching; both have a detrimental effect on the continued development of archival knowledge.[27]

Librarians have devoted more time to debating, defining, and refining basic knowledge and competencies for their field. Although it is certainly true that they have not advanced as far as most librarians have wished for, there is much that archivists can learn by what librarians have or have not accomplished in this area. Because of major efforts to define competencies in library science, that profession has been able to discuss *both* what the basis of library knowledge is *and* how it can or should be assessed as competencies that can be explicitly described, measured, and evaluated. The King Report, basing library competencies on a survey of literature, use of experts, and observation in the work place, stimulated most of the discussion about library knowledge and competencies during the past decade.[28] Although the King Report raised debate about its methodology and assumptions, many still see it as a useful compendium that helps the "design and redesign of instructional programs in library and information science" and aids the "administration of libraries and information centers."[29]

The sharper focus on competencies, because of their measurability, has led to a number of interesting research efforts in librarianship. Two recent studies of academic librarians reflect the utility of this approach. The first study gathered information that defined fifty-six knowledge bases and ranked them in order of perceived importance. This study concluded that many such skills were not being acquired in the

[27]This problem is also very clearly presented in Susan E. Davis, "Development of Managerial Training for Archivists," *American Archivist* 51 (Summer 1988), 278-85.

[28]Jose-Marie Griffiths and Donald W. King, *New Directions in Library and Information Science Education* (White Plains, New York: Knowledge Industry Publications, Inc. for the American Society for Information Science, 1986).

[29]Lawrence W. S. Auld, "The King Report: New Directions in Library and Information Science Education," *College & Research Libraries* News 48 (April 1987), 178-79. For another reaction see Herbert S. White, "Basic Competencies and the Pursuit of Equal Opportunity, Part 1," *Library Journal* 113 (July 1988), 56.

library school.[30]   A follow-up study asked where, then, such skills "can be most conveniently and effectively acquired." A group of academic librarians were queried about how the twenty most important skills were being gained. Library schools, other degree programs, internships, continuing education, staff development, and on-the-job training and experience were the major sources considered.[31]

Other noteworthy competency studies have also been done. An analysis of children's librarians employed a methodology similar to those used in the studies on academic librarians. Forty-five perceived competencies selected from the literature from the previous twenty years were presented to selected children's librarians. A Likert scale was used to measure attitudes towards the competencies with the aid of a Multiple Classification Analysis Regression.[32]   Another analysis employing a two-round Delphi technique surveyed librarians and information scientists in order to identify the most essential library science competencies. The generic competencies, selected from the literature, were reviewed and strong agreement on the major competencies resulted.[33] The perceptions of employers, users, and librarians have also been ascertained through surveys in order to identify significant areas of agreements and disagreements.[34]

It is not the purpose of this essay to state that the library profession has resolved all of the major issues concerning its fundamental knowledge and competencies. A reading of the library literature indicates quite the opposite. However, the library profession has at least made the effort to define knowledge *and* to test out the validity of that knowledge, whereas the archival profession has done little more than to sketch the general parameters of that knowledge that require

[30]Ronald R. Powell and Sheila D. Creth, "Knowledge Bases and Library Education," *College & Research Libraries* 47 (January 1986), 16-27.

[31]Ronald R. Powell, "Sources of Professional Knowledge for Academic Librarians," *College & Research Libraries* 49 (July 1988), 332-40.

[32]Julie Beth Todaro, "Competencies of Children's Librarians: An Attitudinal Assessment," D.L.S., Columbia University, 1984.

[33]Adele E. Friedrich, "Competencies for the Information Professional in the Coming Decade: A Delphi Study," Ph.D., University of Pittsburgh, 1985.

[34]Such as Cleopatra Whittington Johnson, "A Study of Selected Competencies of Elementary School Library Media Specialists As Perceived by Three Groups of Educators: Principals, Teachers, and Library Media Specialists," Ph. D. dissertation, Georgia State University, 1977.

greater definition as well as research on the validity of the definitions. Neither that research nor definition has occurred. In the library profession studies weak on methodology, such as the Conant Report, are assailed,[35] whereas archivists have generally not yet conducted any real research at all.

The archival profession needs to define better its basic knowledge, such as is reflected in the graduate archival education guidelines, and to test it in the work-place and in the graduate schools educating prospective archivists. The existing archival literature could be analyzed to develop some general list of competencies. Those identified competencies could then be evaluated by use of expert panels, analysis of job descriptions, ranking by archival practitioners, and on-the-job observation. The King Report issued as part of its final report two brief volumes on archivist and museum and records and information manager professional competencies which could be used as a starting point for the elaboration of archival competencies; surprisingly, even though they seem to have many problems, these volumes have been ignored by the archival profession.[36] The drafting of archival competencies sponsored by the Society of American Archivists' Interim Board on Certification to make up the content of the certification examination could also be used to build consensus about archival knowledge, to identify archival tasks and functions, and to break those tasks and functions into the parts necessary for them to be tested, measured, and evaluated. Such research should lead to a stronger base of archival knowledge, perhaps the most needed element to ensure a healthy archival profession.

Basic Knowledge and Theory: Theory and Practice in Archival Education

Closely related to archival competencies and knowledge is the relationship between theory and practice in archival education. For as long as can be remembered, the practicum has been considered an essential component of graduate archival education, although its effectiveness has never been

[35]James D. Ramer and others, "The Conant Report: Three Deans Speak Out," *Journal of Education for Librarianship* 22 (Summer-Fall 1981), 89-99.

[36]Jose-Marie Griffiths, Paula Meise Strain, and Ellen A. Sweet, *New Directions in Library and Information Science Education Final Report* (Rockville, Maryland: King Research Inc., 1984), vols. 8 and 9.

studied or evaluated.[37] The relationship between theory and
practice is something that continues to elicit strong comments.
In 1983 one archivist stated that "one becomes an archivist by
doing it rather than reading about it."[38] Frank Burke, in two
essays, squarely challenged that notion. In the mid-1970s he
urged archivists to stop dealing only with "mechanics" and to
develop a coherent theory of practice.[39] Five years later he
articulated specific areas of theory that needed to be
investigated and developed.[40] Eastwood has stated that the
practicum and thesis in his Canadian archival education
program are the "heart and soul" of archival education as he
sees it, "because they express the two sides of archival
education, the essence of which is the interplay between
practice and theory . . . ."[41] Ruth Helmuth shared this
conviction when she stated that "theory is essential, but
without the practicum it will not an archivist make. . . . only
in the practicum can students build confidence in applying
those theories to the slippery realities of life."[42]

Although the emphasis on the practical has been a fixture
in archival education and training, the practicum has nearly
always been the only alternative for receiving practical
experience other than in-service training (which is considered
below). The one exception has been the National Historical
Publications and Records Commission Mellon Foundation
Fellowship program offered since 1985. This program is
designed to assist "midcareer" archivists enhance their
managerial experience and skills. Although seemingly
successful, the program is quite small and has reached only a

[37]Virtually the only relevant essay on the topic is the brief opinion
piece by William G. LeFurgy, "The Practicum: A Repository View," *American
Archivist* 44 (Spring 1981), 153-55.

[38]David Alsobrook in Cain, "Archives By Degree," 49.

[39]Burke, "Similarities and Differences," in *Archive-Library Relations*, ed.
Robert L. Clark, Jr. (New York: R. R. Bowker Co., 1976), 64.

[40]"The Future Course of Archival Theory in the United States,"
American Archivist 44 (winter 1981), 40-46.

[41]"Nurturing," 244.

[42]"Education for American Archivists: A View from the Trenches,"
American Archivist 44 (Fall 1981), 298. For other views in favor of the
practical training of archivists see W. Kaye Lamb, "The Modern Archivist:
Formally Trained or Self-Educated," *ibid.* 31 (April 1968), 175-77.

limited number of programs and individuals.[43] Moreover, in recent years it has had difficulty attracting large numbers of individual and institutional applicants. It is also difficult to understand, partly because of the lack of any evaluation of the practicum in specific and archival education in general, what this fellowship program actually contributes to the education and training of archivists.

There has been the same tension between practice and theory in library education as well. In fact, librarians have argued about this far longer than archivists, suggesting that this is a common feature on the landscape of many applied fields. As with many other issues, this one has not been resolved in the library profession. Herbert S. White aptly noted that the main reason for this continuing debate is the failure to distinguish between education and training. Education occurs *before* training, White has argued, it "prepares you to accept a professional job, not to perform it."[44] Regardless of the reasons, many of the significant reform efforts in the history of library education have concentrated on the relationship between theory and practice. From the late nineteenth century to the ground breaking 1923 Williamson Report on library education, the practicum, internship, or fieldwork was the major element of the education of librarians. Even so, Williamson noted that in a period when practical work constituted the highest portion of the student's time, library educators still lacked a "clear understanding of the underlying pedagogical principles involved."[45]

Although the practical training of librarians has certainly slipped in prominence as librarianship has professionalized and emphasized its knowledge base, there has been a continuing appearance of research articles and studies on the general issue of theory versus practice in this field. The most common efforts have been surveys of ALA-accredited library programs to determine their attitudes and commitments to practica, internships, and fieldwork, along with occasional historical

[43]Judith E. Endelman and Joel Wurl, "The NHPRC/Mellon Foundation Fellowship in Archives Administration: Structured Training on the Job," *American Archivist* 51 (Summer 1988), 286-97.

[44]"Defining Basic Competencies," *American Libraries* 14 (September 1983), 520.

[45]Charles C. Williamson, *Training for Library Service: A Report Prepared for the Carnegie Corporation of New York* (New York: Carnegie Corporation, 1923), 54.

reviews of the issue. These surveys have revealed some interesting characteristics. One study of accredited graduate library schools noted that the main reason for excluding field experience was not "primarily in the question of its value, but in the difficulties of administration, and in its academic priority in an already crowded curriculum."[46] Five years after this study, another survey concluded that the wide variety of policies and practices, the lack of really strong statements for or against experience, the contradictory statements about it all suggest that there are few hard data on the effect of preprofessional library experience and that little is known about evaluating that experience. Thus library schools do not seem to feel free to require or ban experience, but rather tend merely to encourage, or in a few cases, discourage it. Perhaps it is because we know so little about how students differ as result of experience or lack of experience that little is done to cope with the subject.[47]

Several other approaches have been used effectively by librarians to analyze the importance of the dynamic between theory and practice in library graduate education. John Richardson and Peter Hernon attempted to determine how library students viewed practice and theory by having them rate fifteen general statements on theory and practice. This research effort also considered the impact on these views by such variables as age, sex, status (full or part-time student), previous library experience, and other degrees.[48] There have also been efforts to determine *how* library school graduates, after sufficient experience, evaluate the effectiveness of their education as preparation for practical library work.[49] Another

[46]Laurel Grotzinger, "The Status of 'Practicum' in Graduate Library Schools," *Journal of Education for Librarianship* 11 (Spring 1971), 338.

[47]Virginia Witucke, "Library School Policies Toward Preprofessional Work Experience," *Journal of Education for Librarianship* 16 (Winter 1976), 171-72.

[48]"Theory vs. Practice: Student Preferences," *Journal of Education for Librarianship* 21 (Spring 1981), 287-300.

[49]Virgina Mary Crowe, "Guidelines for Curriculum Revision Based on Selected Role Competencies Perceived as Valuable by Graduates of the Library Science Program at Edinboro State College," Ph.D. dissertation, University of Pittsburgh, 1973; George F. Hodowanec, "Comparison of Academic Training With Selected Job Responsibilities of Media Specialists," Ed.D. dissertation, Temple University, 1973; Marion W. Taylor, "The Assessment of a Program for the Preparation of Media Specialist: A Follow-Up Study of Graduates of the Master's Degree Program at Chicago State University, 1955-1975," Ph.D. dissertation, Southern Illinois University,

interesting effort involved literally developing a theory of library and information science. Here a group of more than 1500 English-language definitions from the literature were gathered, formed into a topology, and assessed by a group of librarians and information scientists.[50]

Although the quality and quantity of research done by librarians in the matter of the relationship of theory and practice leaves much to be desired, this research nevertheless suggests some avenues of study for the archival profession. There has never been a survey of the attitudes of archival educators, both regular full-time and adjunct part-time, toward theory and practice in the education of prospective archivists. Such a survey would be helpful in understanding how and what these individuals teach. There also has not been much of an effort to isolate and evaluate a core of archival theory. The debate generated by the Frank Burke proposal for developing an archival theory has been helpful, but even it has resulted in personal or philosophical responses rather than any real attempt to codify an appropriate archival theory.[51] There also has been no earnest evaluation of the practicum in archival education and training despite its supposed importance in preparing individuals to function as archivists. Whether individuals are archivists because of what they know or do or both, there is little understanding about what the practicum actually results in. What do students do during the practicum? How helpful do they find this experience in first professional appointments and their later career? How does the experience relate to what is taught in the classroom? These and other similar questions have not been addressed systematically at all by archivists despite the decade-long existence of guidelines for the practicum.[52]

1977.

[50]Alvin Marvin Schrader, "Toward A Theory of Library and Information Science," Ph.D. dissertation, Indiana University, 1983.

[51]See Lester J. Cappon, "What, Then, Is There To Theorize About?" *American Archivist* 45 (Winter 1982), 19-25; John W. Roberts, "Archival Theory: Much Ado About Shelving," *ibid.* 50 (Winter 1987), 66-74; and Gregg D. Kimball, "The Burke-Cappon Debate: Some Further Criticisms and Considerations for Archival Theory," *ibid.* 48 (Fall 1985), 369-76.

[52]"Program Standard for Archival Education: The Practicum," *American Archivist* 43 (Summer 1980), 420-23. Theses guidelines are currently being re-evaluated by SAA's Committee on Education and Professional Development.

Students: Recruitment of Prospective Archivists

A few years ago a recent graduate of an archival administration program remarked that "there was no one out there promoting the archival profession and recruiting promising students into established [archival education] programs."[53] This is not a new complaint, as Karl Trevor lamented this over forty years ago![54] It is also equally true that there is a lack of understanding about *why* individuals, not being recruited, choose to become archivists. For years it was understood that most entered the archival profession as an alternate career choice (mostly from history because of its poor employment prospects) or by accident. There has been no study about whether this has changed or even whether how accurate it was, and continues to be, as an assessment. In fact, twenty years ago in a study of archival education it was noted that information about students was the most difficult of all data to gather.[55]

There is a fairly substantial amount of research on students and recruitment completed by librarians. The simplest and most common research has been surveys of entering students to determine how and why they came into graduate library programs. One study of students coming into the Indiana University School of Library and Information Science identified reputation of the school, in-state tuition costs, geographic location, offers of financial aid, friends' attendance, the curriculum, tuition benefits, reputation of faculty members, and resources of the school as reasons for matriculation. These studies have also determined that previous positive contacts with practicing librarians were often major factors in their decisions to attend library schools.[56] One of the more

---

[53]Anita K. Delaries in Cain, "Archives By Degree," 44.

[54]"The Organization and Status of Archival Training in the United States," *American Archivist* 11 (April 1948), 160.

[55]Robert M. Warner, "Archival Training in the United States and Canada," *American Archivist* 35 (July/October 1972), 353-54.

[56]Barbara I. Dewey, "Selection of Librarianship as a Career: Implications for Recruitment," *Journal of Education for Library and Information Science* 26 (Summer 1985), 16-24. See also Agnes L. Reagan, "A Study of Factors Influencing College Students to Become Librarians," *ACRL Monographs* no. 21 (Chicago: Association of College and Research Libraries, 1958); Patricia Reeling, "Undergraduate Women as Potential Recruits to the Library Profession," in Katherine Heim, ed., *The Status of Women in Librarianship: Historical, Sociological, and Economic Issues* (New

interesting and complex research areas has been using quantifiable information such as undergraduate grade point averages and graduate record examination scores to predict the success of students in library schools.[57]

Librarians have also devoted a considerable amount of energy in trying to determine future needs and present supplies of librarians in this country. Such research provides the needed context for understanding student recruitment successes and failures. The survey technique has been extended to library employers to gather data that can be purposively used to induce students to enter library schools. A recent effort in California accumulated information about numbers of librarians, types of library positions, salaries, educational backgrounds, minority status, and expected openings to provide such information to individuals considering librarianship as a career.[58] Here librarians have been able to draw upon the studies and statistical reports that the federal government releases on education and professions because librarianship represents a fairly sizeable community and is often treated separately in these sources. Nancy Van House's recent series of studies have been extremely useful, if at times disturbing, examining projections of newly trained librarians, the economic value of the MLS degree, and what factors determine librarians' salaries. Her research, and studies by others, have been prepared in the conviction that they will provide necessary information in the recruitment of prospective

York: Neal-Schuman Publishers, Inc., 1983), 67-98; Rose Mary Magrill, "Occupational Image and the Choice of Librarianship as a Career," Ph.D. dissertation, University of Illinois, 1972; and Mary Louise D. Meder, "Student Concerns in Choice of Library School," *Journal of Education for Librarianship* 21 (Summer 1980), 3-24.

[57]Judith B. Katz, "Indicators of Success: Queens College Department of Library Science," *Journal of Education for Librarianship* 19 (Fall 1978), 130-39; Rose Mary Magrill and Constance Rinehart, "Success in Library School: A Study of Admission Variables," *ibid.* 19 (Winter 1979), 203-22; Richard I. Blue and James L. Divilbiss, "Optimizing Selection of Library School Students," *ibid.* 21 (Spring 1981), 301-12; and Abraham Bookstein and Eve B. Podet, "Predicting Graduate Library School Performance Using a Probabilistic Retrieval Model," *Library Quarterly* 56 (October 1986), 370-88.

[58]Katie Scarborough and Constance W. Nyhan, "Meeting the Need for Librarians: The California Library School Recruitment Project," *Library Journal* 113 (October 15, 1988), 44-49.

librarians and the development and refinement of graduate education programs.[59]

It is unlikely that archivists can begin to prepare in the near future the kinds of research that individuals like Van House have done for librarianship. Such work will require the development of a much stronger data base about the archival profession and, just as likely, some advocacy work to begin to develop the kinds of information regularly gathered by and reported on by such agencies as the Bureau of Labor Statistics. At the least, however, archivists can begin to determine factors, such as positive contacts with individuals in the field or expected job satisfaction and the like, that have led people into their profession, to see if these can be capitalized upon for better recruitment practices. Surveys of entering graduate students and recent graduates of appropriate education programs would be a useful (and relatively easy) first step in determining why and how individuals choose to enter the archival profession. Efforts to project archival employment possibilities and trends, research that has never been done in a way that is very useful to the archival field itself, also need to be completed if the profession expects to attract the best and most potentially capable individuals to the profession. Selective surveys of government agencies, corporations and businesses, public and academic libraries, historical societies, and museums about their recent and anticipated hiring practices might assist the profession in determining its educational program needs as well as aid it in luring qualified students.

Students: Learning Traits and Styles of Prospective and Practicing Archivists

Given the vast quantity of research done on individual learning styles, it is ironic that virtually no such research in this area has been done in the archival profession. Over thirty years ago it was likely that archivists would chalk up ideal qualities of archivists to purely genetic causes. "Some of the qualities most desired in archivists," wrote one leading archivist, "are those most difficult to find and to assess. Many are inborn or depend on inborn psychological traits. Most are

---

[59]See her "Projections of the Supply of Librarians," *Library Quarterly* 54 (October 1984), 368-95; "The Return on the Investment in Library Education," *Library & Information Science Research* 7 (January 1985), 31-52; "Salary Determination and Occupational Segregation Among Librarians," *Library Quarterly* 56 (April 1986), 142-66; and "Labor Market Segmentation and Librarian Salaries," *ibid.* 57 (April 1987), 171-89. Her articles cite earlier similar studies in librarianship and related fields.

insusceptible of measurement."[60]   In fact, as late as 1981 the President of the Society of American Archivists openly declared that "good archivists are born, not made."[61] Even discounting such statements based on no empirical research, it is true that there is little consensus about *how* archivists should be trained. Some archival educators have looked, for this reason, at other "more established professions" to see how they handle the education of their practitioners. The fullest proposal was one for a case method approach, similar to that used by the legal profession, because "archives is not a precise science governed by rules" and archival administration is governed by a "small group of important principles."[62]

There has been some effort (considerable in comparison to what has been done in the archival profession) by librarians to use psychological testing methods to identify the various personality traits of library practitioners.   One study, for example, used standardized personality tests to compare the personality traits of superior library students to the traits of the general adult public.[63] Enough research has been done, in fact, that some have dismissed the approach as having little to offer or have pointed out that the standardized tests at least need to be used more carefully.[64] Regardless of these problems, it seems that reasonable historical and contemporary profiles of library students can be formulated based on the research completed, a task that would be extremely difficult for the

[60]G. Philip Bauer, "Recruitment, Training, and Promotion in the National Archives," *American Archivist* 18 (October 1955): 291. These views occasionally still reappear such as when David Alsobrook said in 1983 that "archival duties can be performed best by people who are precise, logical, inquisitive, thorough, and persistent"; Cain, "Archives By Degree," 51.

[61]Ruth W. Helmuth, "Education for American Archivists: A View from the Trenches," *American Archivist* 44 (Fall 1981), 298.

[62]Blouin, "The Relevance of the Case Method."

[63]Andrew H. Gibbons, "Personality Traits of Superior Library Media Graduates Using Cattell's 16PF and Fitts' TSCS," Ed.D. dissertation, University of Northern Colorado, 1977. For another example of the kind of research, see Aileen Barnett Helmick, "Two Cognitive Styles Among Library Science Students: Field-Dependence/Independence and Tolerance-Intolerance for Ambiguity," Ph.D. dissertation, Florida State University, 1982.

[64]David P. Fisher, "Is the Librarian a Distinct Personality Type?" *Journal of Librarianship* 20 (January 1988), 36-47 and John Agada, "Studies of the Personality of Librarians," *Drexel Library Quarterly* 20 (Spring 1984), 24-45.

archival profession to do any time in the near future.[65] Among
the most interesting research projects that have been done in
this area are those that have tried to determine and compare
the cognitive styles of library students with other students and
to ascertain the implications for library education, including
teaching approaches and curriculum content.[66]

Determining the cognitive styles that prospective archivists
bring to the graduate programs is a subject worth further
exploration.   Such research might provide additional insight
into   the   characteristics   of   people   that   archival   graduate
programs attract and provide an interesting basis of comparison
to other professions.   What kinds of students is the archival
profession attracting?   What does this mean for archival
education?   This research might also help improve how these
individuals are taught.   In a number of aspects of graduate
archival education courses, such as the relationship of the
practicum to other courses, knowing how students learn would
be advantageous in directing individual students as well as
structuring complete programs.   If a student was determined
to be one who learned more from the application of principles
than through theoretical discussions, why couldn't that person
be persuaded to participate in an extended period of field work
to support his or her classroom learning?   Although using this
research for such purposes might be too difficult, information
gained through such research would nevertheless be helpful in
developing case studies and exercises that could be used in the
classroom to illustrate practical uses of archival theories and
principles. The lack of any information about archival students
at this point considerably weakens how archival educators
approach their education.

*Archival Employers and Institutions: Employers' Needs and
Hiring Practices*

It may seem remarkable that the archival profession has
done so little research into the hiring practices of archival
employers (although it probably won't seem remarkable at all
for those readers who have made it to this point in this essay).

---

[65]See, for example, Adele M. Fasick, "Library and Information Science
Students," *Library Trends* 34 (Spring 1986), 607-21 and William Landram
Williamson, "A Century of Students," *ibid.* 34 (Winter 1986), 433-49.

[66]Barbara L. Stein, James D. Hand, and Herman L. Totten,
"Understanding Preferred Cognitive Styles: A Tool for Facilitating Better
Communication," *Journal of Education for Library and Information Science*
27 (Summer 1986), 38-49.

Constance Schulz's analysis of the employment of archivists in
state archives, mentioned earlier in this essay, was undertaken
because of the fact that "although much attention has been
paid to the form of the education and training, relatively little
has been paid to the needs of the workplaces hiring trained
archivists." She concluded that the "discussion of the form,
location, content, and duration of archival education might be
much illuminated by systematic study of the institutions
employing newly trained or retrained archivists."[67] Although
her effort was hardly conclusive, it is better than archivists
have had, which is now generally speculation. One archivist
suggested, for example, that archivists' fears about "superficial"
archival training in public history education programs is only
viable in a "nonrational" employment market. A rational
market is one in which "informed employers [make] decisions
. . . guided by such criteria as the quality and extensiveness of
an applicant's training and/or work experience, the strengths of
professional recommendations, and the suitability of personal
traits."[68] The problem is, of course, that archivists generally
know little about the market.

It is easy to argue for the need for research in this area.
For example, the archival profession has little or no relevant
data on personnel turnover, how government civil service
policies impact on hiring practices, what affirmative action and
minority recruitment do to a profession that is largely
Caucasian, and how peculiar local policies such as residency
requirements affect the employment of qualified archivists.[69]
These and other areas are all worth some exploration.
Knowing more about such practices should enable archivists to
redirect, where necessary, their educational programs to make
their graduates more attractive to employers. This is especially
important in sectors like business and government that need
archival expertise but are also looking for individuals who can
function in the realm of records management, information
resources management, and the management of information
systems. It is possible that to get individuals with archival
expertise into the workplace in the first place, these same
individuals will have to have skills enabling them to function

[67]"Analysis of the Marketplace," 320.

[68]Allan Kovan, "Helping Friends: Archives Training for Public
Historians," *American Archivist* 51 (Summer 1988), 315.

[69]Many of these issues were identified in the various essays in Herbert
S. White, ed., *Education for Professional Librarians* (White Plains, New
York: Knowledge Industry Publications, Inc., 1986).

in a much more complex and technical information environment.[70] Although the archival profession knows that employers *like* archivists once they have them, these same employers also tend not to give archivists sufficient authority or justified rewards.[71] More detailed information about what employers prefer cannot but assist archivists to position themselves for a more influential role in individual workplaces and society at large.

The library profession has supported some studies on employer preferences that are worth considering by archivists, both for their results and methodologies, for adaption to meet their own needs and objectives. One driving force behind such studies has been the fact that although librarianship has been a feminized profession, women have in general been underpaid and given less opportunity for choice administrative, faculty, and other leadership positions.[72] Since the archival profession also appears to have become increasingly feminized in the past twenty years, such studies are even more relevant. Individual researchers have extended their focus to the workplace, gathering information through surveys and other means that reveal gender differentiations in salary and promotion. Others have looked at the personal and social backgrounds of individual librarians to ascertain factors for their success or lack of success in the field.[73] Assisting such research on gender

[70]Some have even argued that the future of the archival profession depends on making archivists better equipped to deal with a wide range of information technology and uses. See, for example, Richard M. Kesner, *Information Systems: A Strategic Approach to Planning and Implementation* (Chicago: American Library Association, 1988).

[71]Sidney J. Levy and Albert G. Robles, *The Image of Archivists: Resource Allocators' Perceptions* (Chicago: Society of American Archivists, 1984).

[72]See Kathleen Weibel and Kathleen M. Heim, *The Role of Women in Librarianship, 1876-1976: The Entry, Advancement, and Struggle for Equalization in One Profession* (Phoenix: Oryx Press, 1979).

[73]For examples of recent studies of this type, see David R. Dowell, "Sex and Salary in a Female Dominated Profession," *Journal of Academic Librarianship* 14 (May 1988), 92-98; Betty Jo Irvine, *Sex Segregation in Librarianship: Demographic and Career Patterns of Academic Library Administrators* (Westport, Connecticut: Greenwood Press, 1985); Kathleen M. Heim and Leigh S. Estabrook, *Career Profiles and Sex Discrimination in the Library Profession* (Chicago: American Library Association, 1983); Kathleen Carrick, "Silk v. Corduroy: The Status of Men and Women in Law Librarianship," *Law Library Journal* 78 (Summer 1986), 425-41; Roma M. Harris, Susan Monk, and Jill T. Austin, "MLS Graduates Survey: Sex Differences in Prestige and Salary Found," *Canadian Library Journal* 43

issues has been the strong tradition in librarianship of compiling annual and biennial surveys of salaries and placements. Whereas archivists have done major profiles of their professional members only half a dozen times in the past third of a century (1956, 1966, 1972, 1973, 1979, 1982, and 1989), with some inconsistencies from survey to survey that make comparison difficult at best,[74] librarians have *regularly* conducted comprehensive data gathering efforts.[75]

Whether being accustomed to such research is the explanation for this or not, librarians have tended to come up with other interesting approaches for analyzing employers' hiring practices that they are then able to relate back to their graduate education programs. Herbert S. White and Marion Paris had the administrators of medium and large-sized special, public, and academic libraries rate a list of specific courses as requirements for entry-level professionals.[76] Michael Koenig queried information professionals in large industrial institutions about courses they had taken and the importance of those courses to their present positions.[77] Roxanne Sellberg analyzed salaries of recent library school graduates to determine the

(June 1986), 149-53; and Joy Marilyn Greiner, "A Comparative Study of the Career Development Patterns of Male and Female Library Administrators in Large Public Libraries," Ph.D. dissertation, Florida State University, 1984.

[74]Ernst Posner, "What, Then, Is the American Archivist, This New Man? *American Archivist* 20 (January 1957), 3-11; Philip P. Mason, "Economic Status of the Archival Profession, 1965-66," *ibid.* 30 (January 1967), 105-22; Frank B. Evans and Robert M. Warner, "American Archivists and Their Society: A Composite View," *ibid.* 34 (April 1971), 157-72; Mabel E. Deutrich, "Women in Archives: Ms. Versus Mr. Archivist," *ibid.* 36 (April 1973), 171-81; Mabel E. Deutrich and Ben Dewhitt, "Survey of the Archival Profession - 1979," *ibid.* 43 (Fall 1980), 527-35; and David Bearman, "1982 Survey of the Archival Profession," *ibid.* 46 (Spring 1983), 233-41. The 1989 survey results will be available in 1990.

[75]See, for example, the public library biennial surveys conducted since the early 1960s; the most recent is Kay F. Jones, "Sex, Salaries, & Library Support, 1987," *Library Journal* 112 (October 15, 1987), 35-41. For another example, see Jean Ray, Meyer Rubin, and Angela Battaglia, "Pay Equity for Women in Academic Libraries: An Analysis of ARL Salary Surveys, 1976/77 - 1983/84," *College & Research Libraries* 48 (January 1987), 36-49.

[76]"Employer Preferences and Library Education Curriculum," *Library Quarterly* 55 (January 1985), 1-33.

[77]"Education for Special Librarianship," *Special Libraries* 74 (April 1983), 182-96.

impact (there was none) on salaries of whether they matriculated from one or two year programs.[78]   And Desretta V. McAllister compared what was taught in library schools regarding technical services with employers' expectations (academic library technical services administrators), revealing a good deal of similarity between reality and expectations.[79]

What these studies suggest for archivists, of course, is a much more deliberate effort to assess attitudes of employers about what they are looking for in new or replacement personnel and to study actual employment practices. What kinds of archival courses should they have? What other kinds of skills should these individuals possess?   Is practical experience weighed more heavily than classroom education that may emphasize basic principles and theories?   Without more reliable information from employers that can inform archival educators responsible for developing courses, these educators play a kind of Russian roulette with the futures of their students. How can archival educators be assured that they are properly equipping their students with the perspectives and skills that archival employers want?

Archival Employers and Institutions: The Effectiveness of In-service Training and Continuing Education

In-service (or on-the-job) training has been a mainstay for preparing individuals to work as archivists and archival technicians. The impetus for the development of such training was the growth in the number of archival programs and the concomitant demand for qualified archivists *before* archival administration courses were regularly taught at the graduate level.   In-service training has remained, in various different forms, at most major archival institutions in this country, most notably the National Archives.   After the National Archives was placed under the General Services Administration in 1949 and the nationwide system of Federal records centers was established a year later, a "thoroughgoing inservice training program" was set up.   The creators of this system viewed this as "formal" training because of its classroom components

[78]"Two-Year Master's Degree Programs and Salaries of New Library School Graduates," *Journal of Academic Librarianship* 13 (January 1988), 336-39.

[79]"Education for Technical Services: Five Case Studies," Ph.D. dissertation, University of Pittsburgh, 1981.

making it "less fragmentary" and "usually more thoughtful and more fundamental."[80]

A more prevalent form of archival "in-service" education (if it can be really called that) has been self-training. Richard Berner had harsh words about this, suggesting that archivists "entering as neophytes . . . have concentrated on learning the then current state of the archival art . . . . Too few have raised themselves above narrow mastery of mere techniques borrowed from myriad institutional settings."[81] Despite Berner's skepticism, it is hard to refute that the following comments made in the mid-1960s are still not generally relevant: "The archivist . . . does not grow in a vacuum; he is rather the product of certain forces, certain educational forms, and some sort of on-the-job training."[82] Most surprising may be the fact that the archival profession's reliance on in-service training has been so great for so long. Ernst Posner, looking at European archival education nearly half-a-century ago, wrote that "postappointment training [is] generally less desirable because the professional fitness of the appointee remains untested."[83]

Despite the long tradition of in-service training in archival administration there has been little completed research that attempts to evaluate the effectiveness of such training. A fairly sizeable literature of case studies describing how such training is offered has accumulated over the past half-century (these are evident in the writings on this topic cited in this paper), but most of this has been valuable primarily for understanding the historical evolution of archival education. Even using this literature has been difficult, however, because it has tended to be more promotional than evaluative. Essays by individuals at the National Archives about that institution's in-service education, for example, are rarely critical or objective enough. A few years ago an archivist noticed this problem when he wrote that although the "*American Archivist* [the leading journal in the archival profession] has consciously broadened its criteria for full-length articles, . . . its regular

[80]Everett O. Aldredge, "Archival Training in a Record Center," *American Archivist* 21 (October 1959), 402-03.

[81]"Toward National Archival Priorities: A Suggested Basis for Discussion," *American Archivist* 45 (Spring 1982), 171.

[82]Breck, "New Dimensions," 175.

[83]"European Experiences in Training Archivists," *American Archivist* 4 (January 1941), 37.

contributors possess more interest in presenting their own
institutions and techniques as models than in conducting
critical analysis and offering original, provocative thought."[84]

The same is true for continuing education in the archival
profession. Although archivists have not clearly distinguished
the differences between in-service and continuing education,
librarians have and their distinctions are being used here. The
differences can be understood this way. "A distinction has
been made between *professional* development, which is training
that benefits the individual, and *inservice*, which benefits the
organization."[85] Or, as stated by another, "staff development
involves the systematic development of employees' skills,
competencies, and attitudes in order to enhance organizational
effectiveness. Continuing education can be described as
individual learning experience often, but not necessarily
resulting in increased organizational effectiveness."[86]

Over the past fifteen years one of the hallmarks of the
programs of the Society of American Archivists has been
continuing education. Continuing education programs have
expanded to such a degree that nearly every regional and state
archival association (there are nearly sixty of these groups), as
well as other statewide institutions and colleges and
universities, offer a wide-range of continuing education courses,
from basic to advanced.[87] In the past continuing education
programs were viewed as an intermediary step until graduate
archival education programs were established and developed to
the point that a sufficient supply of archivists was available.[88]
Regardless of how they have been viewed, continuing education
programs have supplemented and supported archival

---

[84]Peter J. Wosh, "Creating a Semiprofessional Profession: Archivists
View Themselves," *Georgia Archive* 10 (Fall 1982), 6-7.

[85]Philip M. Turner, "In-service and the School Library Media Specialist:
What Works and What Doesn't," *School Library Media Quarterly* 16 (Winter
1988), 106. For a full statement on this distinction, see Barbara Conroy,
*Library Staff Development and Continuing Education: Principles and
Practices* (Littleton, Colorado: Libraries Unlimited, 1978). Another useful
reference, with a good bibliography, is Lynn Elliott, "Professional Staff
Development in Academic Libraries," *Journal of Librarianship* 15 (October
1983), 237-53.

[86]J.J. Groarck and M.R. Yerburgh, "Staff Development for Academic
Librarians: The Art of the Possible," *Bookmark* 38, no. 3 (1979), 143.

[87]See for example James E. Fogerty, "The Minnesota Basic Workshops
Project," *American Archivist* 44 (Summer 1981), 237-40.

[88]Breck, "New Dimensions," 184.

institutions in training individuals already on the job. Only a decade ago, one archival leader called for SAA to offer a "short institute with a faculty of experienced practitioners" and "advanced institutes on particular archival functions," these being "essential for the continuing education required by the professional archivist."[89] Even in the late 1980s, the statement that "the archival profession has within its ranks many who, for whatever reason, never received a basic *archival* education before they were employed" remains, unfortunately, an accurate one. This means that continuing education cannot be relegated only to introductory education, as some have continued to insist, but must continue to offer a wide variety of courses to supplement and, in essence, to build a full curriculum that enables practicing archivists to improve their knowledge base and to keep up with the rapid change of professional theory and practice.[90] Continuing education has also proved to be invaluable in certain newly emerging specialized areas, such as automation, that have outgrown what graduate archival education programs have been able to offer; developing advanced continuing education courses have aided archival educators to bring new skills and perspectives into their classrooms.[91]

There is no doubt that the nature, use, and effectiveness of in-service training and continuing education have been major issues for librarianship. In some specialized functions, such as cataloguing and classification, there is a "general feeling" that individuals are "being short-changed in library school training"[92] and that in-service training or continuing education is absolutely essential for the welfare of the profession and its institutions. Such concerns tie directly back to the long-standing tension between theory and practice, prompting a variety of research efforts to understand how in-service training and continuing education functions in librarianship. It is further reflected in the fact that continuing education is a

---

[89]Frank B. Evans, "Postappointment Archival Training: A Proposed Solution for a Basic Problem," *American Archivist* 40 (January 1977), 73-74.

[90]Ericson, "Professional Associations and Archival Education," 300.

[91]Lisa Weber, "Educating Archivists for Automation," *Library Trends* 36 (Winter 1988), 501-18.

[92]Judith Hudson, "On-the-job Training for Cataloguing and Classification," *Cataloguing & Classification Quarterly* 7 (Summer 1987), 73. The entire issue of this journal is devoted to "Education and Training for Catalogers and Classifiers," pointing out the various facets of tension in classroom education versus on-the-job training.

relatively recent phenomena in librarianship, primarily the creature of the last two decades' fast moving technological changes and increased specialization.[93]

In their research, librarians have mainly devoted themselves to surveying sample library populations about how they utilize continuing education opportunities. Esther Green Bierbaum's survey of museum, arts, and humanities librarians placed their continuing education needs in the context of their career perceptions and objectives and professional development. Her work shows a high degree of activity in continuing education and strong similar interests in the specifics of that education despite barriers such as lack of released time and financial support.[94] Similar surveys on continuing education have also been conducted of librarians in other specialties, working within certain geographic areas, and of those who administer libraries and decide upon the role that continuing education might play in their institutions. A survey undertaken in Kansas rural libraries looked at continuing education needs and participation in light of the type of library, community size, age and sex of the librarians, income, weekly hours of library service, education, and experience.[95] Another survey solicited the opinions of public library administrators in Florida toward continuing education, with a strong preference for formal efforts such as workshops, courses, and seminars rather than attendance at professional associations or reading professional

[93]Joan C. Durrance, "Library Schools and Continuing Professional Education: The DeFacto Role and Factors That Influence It," *Library Trends* 34 (Spring 1986), 679-96 and Elizabeth W. Stone, "The Growth of Continuing Education," *ibid.* 34 (Winter 1986), 489-513.

[94]"Museum, Arts, and Humanities Librarians: Careers, Professional Development, and Continuing Education," *Journal of Education for Library and Information Science* 29 (Fall 1988), 127-34.

[95]Nancy A. Starke, "Library Continuing Education Needs in Kansas: The Rural Perspective," *Rural Libraries* 8, no. 1 (1988), 39-70. See also Suzanne H. Mahmoodi and Mary F. Lenox, "Continuing Education for Missouri Librarians: A Report of An Educational Needs Assessment," *Show-Me Libraries* 39 (Summer 1988), 32-41. For earlier studies, see Jacqueline Ruth Wolff, "A Survey of Training Patterns and Perceived Priority Professional Needs of School Library Media Professionals in Selected Illinois School Districts," Ph.D. dissertation, Michigan State University, 1975 and Janet Sue Salvati, "Modes of Continuing Library Education: An Investigation Into the Practices, Perceptions, and Preferences of Professional Personnel in Academic Libraries of West Virginia," Ph.D. dissertation, University of Pittsburgh, 1976.

literature.[96]   In Massachusetts academic librarians surveyed revealed that continuing education is highly valued; here the researcher used Spearman correlation procedures to test the correlation between use and perceived effectiveness and between preference and perceived effectiveness.[97]   In contrast, a study undertaken in Great Britain showed that attitudes towards continuing education sharply divided along library management levels, with the management viewing it as the responsibilities of individuals and lower levels seeing it as the responsibility of the library.[98]   One surprising finding in such studies has been that although library faculty could not agree about the manner in which theory relates to practice in graduate library education, they nevertheless supported practica, internships, and a wide variety of continuing education activities.[99]

There has also been some interesting research, again employing the survey method, aimed at evaluating some of the common assumptions about continuing education, rather than seeking to ascertain needs for planning continuing education that many of the studies have concentrated upon.   In Canada two researchers surveyed the participants of nine workshops to see if five basic assumptions about continuing education held

[96]John Anthony McCrossan, "Public Library Administrators' Opinions of Continuing Education Activities," *Public Libraries* 27 (Spring 1988), 47-49.   See also James G. Neal, "Continuing Education: Attitudes and Experiences of the Academic Librarian," *College and Research Libraries* 41 (March 1980), 128-33; Karlene K. Edwards and Isabel Schon, "Professional Development Activities as Viewed by School Library Media Specialists," *School Library Media Quarterly* 12 (Spring 1986), 138-41; and Jacqueline C. Mancall and Linda H. Bertland, "Step One Reported: Analysis of AASL's First Needs Assessment for Continuing Education," *School Library Media Quarterly* 16 (Winter 1988), 88-98.

[97]Lethiel Carol Parson, "Continuing Professional Education of Academic Librarians in Massachusetts: Practices, Perceptions and Preferences," Ph.D. dissertation, Texas Woman's University, 1988.

[98]T. Konn and N. Roberts, "Academic Librarians and Continuing Education: A Study of Personnel Attitudes and Opinions," *Journal of Librarianship* 16 (October 1984), 263-80.

[99]Jerry Dale Saye, "Continuing Education for Library Educators: An Inquiry Into the Current Practices, Perceptions, Preferences and Opinions of Selected Library Educators," Ph.D. dissertation, University of Pittsburgh, 1979.   See also JoAnne Hardison Bell, "An Investigation of Attitudes About Continuing Professional Education Programs in Library Schools Held by Faculty Members and Deans of Library Schools With Accredited Masters' Programs," Ph.D, dissertation, University of North Carolina, 1980.

up. These assumptions included the higher percentage of management in attendance, the ability of higher rank librarians to get released time and other support, the solitary interest of library managers in management, the deterrence of high fees for attendance, and the participation in continuing education of a "small and select group of library personnel." This study suggested that most of these assumptions were correct, except for the deterrent effect of fees.[100]

In-service training or staff development in librarianship has taken all kinds of forms, such as having one library division staff share with another division what they do, educating staff about certain library-wide functions, and using interactive video and other distance learning techniques to provide up-to-date advice on specific library functions and situations.[101] Although librarians seem to have adequately defined what in-service training is and its parameters, the quality and quantity of evaluative research literature seems to be somewhat weaker here than in other areas of education for librarianship. Still, there are some studies that archivists might wish to consider and to emulate. In one research effort, for example, a training program for improving personnel effectiveness at the circulation and reference desk at a mid-sized midwestern college was developed, offered, and evaluated. The focus of the training program was to inculcate into library personnel the importance of their positions in the overall library functions and to offer advice on "specific verbal and nonverbal behaviors" in good service and on "interpersonal strategies" and procedures for "handling stressful situations." Evaluation occurred by administering to the college students using the library, questionnaires both before and after the training program to determine if library personnel effectiveness and behavior had improved.[102] Because staff development is

[100]John Wilkinson and Carolyn Murray, "Continuing Education for Librarianship: Who Benefits and Why," *Canadian Library Journal* 45 (February 1988), 42-46.

[101]Tara Lynn Fulton, "Reference Librarianship: Sharing Our Knowledge with Technical Service Colleagues," *RQ* 27 (Winter 1987), 210-19; Jennifer Cargill, "The Library Financial Picture: Educating the Staff," *Wilson Library Bulletin* 62 (January 1988), 51-53; and Blaise Cronin, "The Electronic Academy," *Aslib Proceedings* 36 (September 1984), 345-66. For some studies on the use of distance learning see the *Journal of Education for Library and Information Science* 27 (Spring 1987), 219-94.

[102]Charles J. Hobson, Robert F. Moran, Jr., and Arena L. Stevens, "Circulation/Reserve Desk Personnel Effectiveness," *Journal of Academic Librarianship* 13 (May 1987), 93-98. See also Betty J. Morris, "Student

inexorably tied to the problem of adequately replacing staff and with the low growth rate of certain types of librarians, there have also been proposals for cost models to determine the overall effectiveness for staff development programs. Such proposals have suggested means of weighing various approaches for providing continuing training to staff.[103] There have been, likewise, suggested models for staff development, ranging from needs assessment or analysis to final evaluations.[104] Such models provide the necessary basis for additional research.

Library research in these areas certainly suggests some directions for archivists. Simple surveys about how archivists and their employers view continuing education and inservice training would provide information that is not now available and that could be extremely helpful in designing effective programs in the future. More in-depth study of the value of such educational offerings and in-service programs is also needed. What aspects of archival administration are best left to the classroom or to the archival workplace rather then to more advanced workshops and institutes after a sufficient amount of experience has been gained by an individual? At this time, the archival profession has only conjecture and informed opinion and no hard data. A follow-up study of participants in formal in-service training programs such as at the National Archives and in the continuing education programs such as offered by the Society of American Archivists would help clarify the place of such instruction in the education of archivists.[105]

Assistants in Academic Libraries: A Study of Training Practices," Ph.D. dissertation, University of Alabama, 1984.

[103]Such as Jana Varlejs, "Cost Models for Staff Development in Academic Libraries," *Journal of Academic Librarianship* 12 (January 1987), 359-64.

[104]James W. Hill, "A Model for Staff Development," *Journal of Library Administration* 1 (Spring 1980), 31-40.

[105]A study of the impact on individuals and institutions of SAA's preservation/conservation workshops is now being done with funding support by the National Endowment for the Humanities. The results of this project should serve as a model for other research that can be used to evaluate continuing education and in-service training.

Archival Employers and Institutions: Professional Work Levels and Specialized Education

Archival programs can be complex operations, requiring diverse skills and experiences for their satisfactory management. For at least a generation or more, the archival profession retained a somewhat static portrait of the archivist and, consequently, his or her training, even though shortly after the formation of the Society of American Archivists proposals were made for educating different "classes" of archivists. The Bemis report of the late 1930s suggested two classes, distinguished by the place of work - "major municipal, state, and national archives" or "small municipal divisions, county, state and special commissions, authorities, and establishments of minor political significance, as well as archivists for business firms, corporations, banks, and other private enterprises." The first class required a Ph.D. in history and the other a "Master's degree in the social sciences, with a support in library technique."[106] Nothing came of the Bemis proposal. Perhaps the first indication that the perspective of a static, monolithic archivist was not viable was the emergence of records management as a distinct discipline in the 1950s. Everett Aldredge, one of the leaders in the new records management field, described the different requirements for training archivists and file clerks. "The work of the archivist is," he stated,

> distinguished from that of the file clerk [because the archivist] has not participated in the creation or accumulation of the noncurrent records with which he must deal. He must therefore learn about their content, structure, functional significance, and administrative origin by research in all available printed sources and in the records themselves or by methodical inquiry among the officials whose operations resulted in their creation or accumulation.[107]

Aldredge's direction has been followed, and the records management field does seem to possess a stronger sense of

---

[106]Samuel Flagg Bemis, "The Training of Archivists in the United States," *American Archivist* 2 (July 1939), 158-59.

[107]"Archival Training," 406-07.

different "levels of proficiency."[108] There is certainly now a growing stronger sense of different educational requirements for different archival positions. Paul McCarthy's rough approximation of the different competencies required for entry-level, middle level manager, and executive level archivists is but one example of this kind of thinking.[109] The advent of automation and automated techniques, greater awareness of immense preservation challenges, and other similar trends and developments have contributed to the heightened sense of the need for various skills and specialized positions in archival institutions. The day of the archival generalist may be over, although the archival profession's continued separation from records managers and its uneasiness over newer fields such as public history may indicate that this view continues to linger and to influence many aspects of the archival profession.

Archivists in North America over the last several decades have seemed to opt for the notion of a uniform definition of a archivist, and consequentially for fairly uniform training, regardless of the nature of the archival program. This may have been partially a reaction to an earlier tendency to emphasize the diversity and lack of standardization of operations between programs. Whatever the reason, there needs to be study about the different educational needs of archivists in different positions *and* kinds of repositories. Some European archivists have made efforts to identify distinctive categories of repositories and their features and to define appropriate educational requirements for individuals working in those repositories. Lionel Bell's concept of "traditional or primitive," "pioneering," and "establishment" archives does not appear to translate well to American soil, but his effort to identify appropriate education (ranging from emphases on

---

[108]Susan M. Bronder has urged the adoption, for example, of four levels, ranging from records clerk to the records manager who plans and directs the records program, each with differing educational requirements, ranging from high school degree to a bachelor's degree. See "Gaining Professional Status: The Leadership Role of the Institute of Certified Records Managers," *Records Management Quarterly* 18 (January 1984), 20-22, 24-26, 32. It is possible that this better defined sense of work levels results from the fact that the bachelor's, rather than master's, degree is seen as the entry level educational requirement for records managers. This field also seems to have more potential for career advancement from individuals starting in paraprofessional or support positions such as file clerks.

[109]"The Management of Archives: A Research Agenda," *American Archivist* 51 (Winter/Spring 1988), 56-57.

apprenticeship training to more formal and comprehensive education) to the staffs of these programs is worth emulating.[110]

All of this is closely related to the matter of generalization in graduate education in applied fields like archival administration. For example, although graduate archival education continues to operate on a rather primitive plane in comparison to other professions, there is little question that a master's degree in library science or history is the preferred entry-level requirement. But should the archivist have other subject specializations? Although there has been no research on this, the experience of special librarians suggests that this is probably relevant, at least as an issue requiring investigation, for archivists. Elin B. Christianson recently wrote that "subject specialization is a basic characteristic of corporate libraries and is the one most often perceived and addressed by both library educators and corporate library managers." The diversity of special library settings in business and industry and the service to their parent corporations require such specialization.[111] Such concern about specialization is apparent in other areas like the preservation of research resources and history-based education. In the past decade a separate preservation profession has seemed to be emerging. Some, like Lawrence McCrank, have argued strongly for its close association with library and archival graduate education programs.[112] Although history has traditionally been seen as a bedrock for archival education and administration, it has been suggested that the primary research skills of historians are so weak as to work against the argument that historians are qualified to work as archivists or to train them.[113]

Turning to the library profession, we find a discipline that has worked more diligently to define levels of professional and

[110]"The Professional Training of Archivists," *UNESCO Bulletin for Libraries* 25 (July-August 1971), 191-97.

[111]"Corporate Libraries," in White, *Education for Professional Librarians*, 96; for a specific case study, see Genevieve M. Casey, "Energy Information Specialist Program: A Feasibility Study," *Journal of Education for Librarianship* 24 (Summer 1983), 53-61.

[112]"Conservation and Collection Management: Educational Problems and Opportunities," *Journal of Education for Librarianship* 22 (Summer/Fall 1981), 20-43.

[113]Lawrence J. McCrank, "Public Historians in the Information Professions: Problems in Education and Credentials," *Public Historian* 7 (Summer 1985), 10-12. See also Margaret F. Steig, "The Information Needs of Historians," *College and Research Libraries* 42 (1981), 549-60.

supportive library staff. This should not be surprising.
English librarian David Baker recently wrote that, "in general,
it is not the *type* of work that non-professionals do but the
levels at which they undertake tasks that separates them from
professional staff."[114]   A 1970 statement by the American
Library Association defined senior librarians, librarians, library
associates, library technical assistants, and clerks. This brief
statement also provided for lateral as well as vertical
advancement.   "Highly qualified persons with specialist
responsibilities in some aspects of librarianship - archives,
bibliography, reference, for example - should be eligible for
advanced status and financial rewards without being forced to
abandon for administrative responsibilities their areas of major
competence."[115]

There is more than guiding statements in librarianship as
well. Library research is replete with studies looking at the
perceived needs and actual educational offerings of library
schools for various specialties in librarianship. One of the most
common approaches has been surveying various populations of
the library profession to match perceptions and needs. A
survey of "media educators," for example, sought their
evaluation of the education programs using existing descriptions
of competencies and certification requirements.[116]   Another
survey examined whether there was any existence of career
ladders in academic libraries corresponding to the ALA
statement, *Library Education and Personnel Utilization*. This
study identified factors which worked for and against such
career ladders and concluded that the ALA statement had little
bearing on what actually exists in certain kinds of libraries.[117]

There have been more in-depth analyses of the levels of
work in a variety of library settings. Donald P. Gould used
the Time-Stratified Systems Theory to examine a large variety

---

[114]"Training and Education of Technicians and Assistants in Library
Work," *Library Management* 8, no. 6 (1987), 5.   Baker's perspective is
certainly formed by the stronger tradition in English library education of
in-service training.

[115]*Library Education and Personnel Utilization* (June 30, 1970), 5. For
the context of this statement, see Baker, "Training and Education," 34-44.

[116]Linda Hall Heller, "A Comparison of Current Curriculum Offerings
of School Media Education Programs in Oklahoma, Kansas, Missouri, Texas,
and Arkansas As Perceived by Media Specialists," Ed.D. dissertation,
Oklahoma State University, 1983.

[117]Bonnie Jackson Clemens, "Career Ladders for Support Staff in
University Libraries," Ph.D. dissertation, Florida State University, 1983.

of professional and non-professional library positions in four academic libraries. This research required intensive interviews with these staff and their superiors to gather qualitative data about their tasks, actual work, and degree of abstraction in their work. Gould compared his findings to ALA's statement on *Library Education and Personnel Utilization*, discovering a wider range of personnel categories.[118] Advertisements for certain kinds of library positions have been examined to identify variations over time, as have the actual graduate education patterns of these library positions.[119] Other attributes, such as behavior styles and values identified through the use of standardized tests, such as the Position Analysis Questionnaire, of various library professionals have also revealed some interesting differences with implications for education.[120]

More has probably been done on the status and uses of paraprofessionals than on any other single aspect of library education, possibly reflecting the increasing use of these individuals in the changing nature of the library workplace wrought by factors such as automated systems and various vendors' services. There have been studies on how nonprofessional personnel are used, the effectiveness of their work, the impact of technology on the reliability of support staff, and how all of this fits into library education and training.[121]

---

[118]"An Examination of Levels of Work in Academic Library Technical Services Departments Utilizing Time-Stratified Systems Theory," Ph.D. dissertation, University of Southern California, 1984. See also Gould, "Measuring Levels of Work in Academic Libraries: A Time Based Approach," *College and Research Libraries* 46 (May 1985), 236-48. For another similar study see David Michael Boals, "Levels of Work and Responsibility in Public Libraries," Ph.D. dissertation, University of Southern California, 1985.

[119]Joseph Abram Jackson, "A Documentation and Analysis of Status and Employment Variabilities in Job Descriptions Among Academic Librarians," Ed.D. dissertation, George Peabody College for Teachers of Vanderbilt University, 1985 and Pamela Rae Palmer, "Graduate Education of Academic Librarians," Ed.D. dissertation, Memphis State University, 1985.

[120]Suzanne O. Frankie, "The Behavioral Styles, Work Preferences and Values of an Occupational Group: A Study of University Catalog and Reference Librarians," D.P.A. dissertation, George Washington University, 1980.

[121]Laura M. Boyer and William C. Theimer, Jr., "The Use and Training of Nonprofessional Personnel at Reference Desks in Selected College and University Libraries," *College and Research Libraries* 36 (May 1975), 193-200; Egill A. Halldorsson and Margorie E. Murfin, "The Performance of Professionals and Nonprofessionals in the Reference Interviews," *ibid.* 38

Despite the long-term recognition of the diversity of skills required by archivists, there has been little research into what levels of archival work exist or how those levels should be defined and what this implies about the requirements for archival education programs.   Likewise, there has been no study about the movement by archivists from practice of specialized skills to management.   One reason for this may have been the profession's overriding emphasis on the notion of the "lone arranger," suggesting both that all archival skills need to be reflected in one solitary individual *and* that the chief archival skill is arrangement and description work.   The closest to any articulation of differing educational requirements for different levels of responsibilities have appeared in the case studies written by staff of the larger archival programs.[122]   And, as noted elsewhere, such essays often provide little real advice or assistance for the profession in general, lacking evaluation and often being applicable to only a small number of similar institutions.   The archival profession needs to define levels of archival work and to study in the work-place how archivists actually function, the educational needs that may vary for differing positions, the nature of work that professionals and non-professionals can and should do, and so forth.   At this point, each graduate archival education program has been left on its own to define what it is educating individuals to do as archivists.   And, as well, there is no general unifying scheme for what continuing education and in-service training should be contributing to the overall education of archivists.

Educational Programs: Effectiveness in Educating and Training Individuals to Work as Archivists

One of the persistent themes in archival education has been the debate about the placement of educational programs,

(September 1977), 385-95; Roger L. Presley and Carolyn L. Robison, "Changing Roles of Support Staff in an Online Environment," *Technical Services Quarterly* 4 (Fall 1986), 25-39; Norman J. Russell, "Professional and Non-professional in Libraries: The Need for a New Relationship," *Journal for Librarianship* 17 (October 1985), 293-310; Dana Grove Gould, "A Study of the Current Role and Status of the Paraprofessional As Perceived By Selected Academic and Public Library Administrators," Ph.D. dissertation, University of Southern Mississippi, 1974; and Charlotte Marie Mugnier, "The Library Assistant: High Level Paraprofessional," D.L.S. dissertation, Columbia University, 1976.

[122]See, for example, G. Philip Bauer, "Recruitment, Training, and Promotion in the National Archives," *American Archivist* 18 (October 1955), 291-305.

primarily whether archivists should be trained as historians or librarians. The first report on archival education that came out of the Society of American Archivists reflected and perpetuated the debate when it stated that there was a "distinct danger in turning over archives to librarians who are not at the same time erudite and critical historical scholars" because "they tend to put the emphasis upon cataloguing and administration" and "mechanics."[123]   This is closely related to the matter of archival identity. There is no question that this is a shop-worn as well as winless (perpetual?) debate; through the years there have been numerous persuasive and logical arguments for locating archival education in either history *or* library schools.[124]   But the debate does raise the issue of *effective* evaluation of existing archival education programs, both at the graduate level and in its various guises of continuing education. At one point there was discussion about whether graduate archival education programs should be accredited. This was dropped because of the great variety of such graduate programs and because the majority of people entering the profession did so at mid-career only with the benefit of short-term training.[125]

Whereas archivists have done little work in this area, the library profession has done considerably more research. Two researchers at the University of Sheffield studied graduates of masters programs in librarianship in a number of areas, including their reactions to the value of their graduate education.[126]   Two American researchers surveyed 45 "randomly-selected library school faculty members" to determine criteria of a "high-quality" MLS program. Although their results revealed a genuine lack of clarity in criteria - "all that *is* clear

---

[123]Bemis, "Training of Archivists," 157.

[124]John C. Colson, "On the Education of Archivists and Librarians," *American Archivist* 31 (April 1968), 167-74; Colson, "Modifying Library School Curricula: Archivists and Education," *RQ* 12 (Spring 1973), 267-72; Janet Fyfe, "Archival and Library Education: The Case for Proximity," in *Symposium on Archival Education*, 1-10; Nancy E. Peace and Nancy Fisher Chudacoff, "Archivists and Librarians: A Common Mission, A Common Education," *American Archivist* 42 (October 1979), 456-72; T.R. Schellenberg, "Archival Training in Library Schools," *ibid*. 31 (April 1968), 155-65.

[125]Helmuth, "Education for American Archivists," 301.

[126]Brendan Loughridge and Jane Sutton, "The Careers of MA Graduates: Training, Education and Practice," *Journal of Librarianship* 20 (October 1988), 255-69.

is that very little is clear" - the results are disturbing enough to prompt additional research and clearer definitions of quality.[127] Most of this research has been prompted by the long existence of an ALA-accreditation program for graduate library schools.

Since the library profession has had an accreditation program for over three decades, it is a logical step to try to see what they have learned about this process. The serendipitous variety of graduate archival education programs has formed during these same years. More recently, partly as a result of having basic guidelines for these programs and partly due to discussion about whether individual certification will be post- or pre-employment, there has been increasing sentiment for some form of regulation of the nature *and* quality of these programs. Although there has been considerable criticism levelled against the library school accreditation process for having weak standards or being under the aegis of the American Library Association or for being a purely voluntary process, the effort to regulate the quality of library education seems to be a logical objective for archival education. The present library standards seek "to identify the indispensable components of good library education" as well as to be "sufficiently flexible to allow for future developments." These standards cover "program goals and objectives, curriculum, faculty, students, governance, administration, and financial support, and physical resources and facilities."[128] The most disturbing news has been that ALA's Committee on Accreditation (COA) standards were not factors in the recent closing of four library schools. "The evidence overwhelmingly indicates that in all four of the cases, accreditation by the American Library Association did not, and could not, guarantee the survival of library education programs on campuses where administrators had determined to eliminate them." Other factors worked against the continuance of these schools,

---

[127]Mary Biggs and Abraham Bookstein, "What Constitutes a High-Quality M.L.S. Program? Forty-five Faculty Members' Views," *Journal of Education for Library and Information Science* 29 (Summer 1986), 28-46 (quote p. 46). See also Herbert S. White, "Perceptions by Educators and Administrators of the Ranking of Library School Programs," *College and Research Libraries* 42 (May 1981), 191-202; White, "Perceptions by Educators and Administrators of the Ranking of Library School Programs: An Update and Analysis," *Library Quarterly* 57 (July 1987), 252-68; and Abraham Bookstein and Mary Biggs, "Rating Higher Education Programs: The Case of the 1986 White Survey," *ibid.* 57 (October 1987), 351-99.

[128]*Standards for Accreditation 1972* (Chicago: American Library Association, 1972), 3.

however, and accreditation still appears to be a viable (perhaps the best) means of self-evaluating and regulating educational quality. Yet, other research needs to be conducted on such vital questions. "Is the accreditation process sufficiently reliable and valid to ensure that each program has an equitable review? Does the process measure what it purports to? Do the membership of the Committee on Accreditation and library educators at large know what the *Standards* purport to measure?"[129]

Looking at the issue of accreditation has caused some librarians to worry about the number and distribution of graduate library education programs. There is some impressionistic evidence that there may be too many programs. The evidence is stronger that the geographical distribution of these programs is woefully inadequate.[130] As graduate archival education programs seem to be on the verge of serious development, the archival profession would do well to study such issues. Twenty years ago, H.G. Jones called for ten universities, in "widely separated geographical areas" to offer "full-year [archival] courses."[131]

Some efforts have been made to distinguish educational requirements for certain archival positions in different institutions. For example, one archivist recently stated that "when properly done, archives training offered as part of a public history program can help prepare students for careers as generalists in county historical societies and smaller public libraries and museums, where responsibilities may include the part-time processing and maintenance of small archives and manuscripts collections along with other historical agency or library responsibilities."[132] Such opinions, while making a certain amount of sense, completely lack any substantive supporting data.

At the least, then, the archival profession needs to consider researching the effectiveness of its various educational programs. Follow-up studies of graduates of these programs would be a worthwhile task, evaluating the experience of archivists about the strengths and weaknesses of their

---

[129]Marion Paris, *Library School Closing: Four Case Studies* (Metuchen, New Jersey: Scarecrow Press, Inc., 1988), 149, 154.

[130]Such as Herbert White in *Education for Professional Librarians*, 181-83.

[131]"Archival Training," 152-54.

[132]Kovan, "Helping Friends," 316.

educational preparation. Moreover, there definitely needs to be research (closely tied to research conducted into manpower needs in the archival profession) done about the geographical placement of the existing and developing multi-course graduate archival education programs. Where are their students coming from and where are they taking jobs? How many comprehensive graduate education programs are needed? Finally, the whole issue of regulating archival graduate education programs needs to be carefully thought about and researched. Archival employers need to be surveyed about their desires in this area and about whether they would restrict hiring to graduates of "accredited" graduate programs.

Educational Programs: Archival Educators

One theme that has persisted from the very beginning of the American archival profession is debate over who should teach. In the early years, this was part of the broader debate about whether archivists are historians or librarians and, consequentially, where their educational programs should be anchored. Richard Berner noted appropriately that "archivists must be the teachers 'initially' because the quality of archival literature is so uneven and diffuse that only an experienced archivist can compensate for its difficulties."[133] However, Berner did not fully consider this issue, and neither has anyone else. James Geary, in his effort to argue for library schools to take up more seriously the education of archivists, considered this problem in a slightly different context. He believed that the most qualified individual to teach would have a Ph.D. in history *and* archival experience, but that this still posed a problem for library schools:

> The possession of a history Ph.D., even when combined with a broad exposure to primary source material and relevant work experience, might nevertheless prove insufficient for appointment to a library science faculty. . . .
> Without an M.L.S., library schools would understandably hesitate to hire even an extremely qualified individual since he would lack the desired educational background for articulating the basic differences and similarities between archives and libraries to library science students.

---

[133]"Toward National Archival Priorities," 173.

Still another reason why this individual should possess an M.L.S. is because he might be expected to teach courses in traditional areas of library science in order to meet the normal course load requirements expected of all faculty members in that unit.[134]

Although some of these concerns might be compensated for by the fact that the new SAA education guidelines suggest programs of more than three courses and, thus, heavier teaching loads on archival topics, this still relates to another concern of library educators - generalization versus specialization in the M.L.S. degree.[135] Some archivists have very different views. One argued versus the "library school model," because there "gradually instruction has divorced itself from reality."[136]

Librarians have also been concerned, of course, about the quality and quantity of their educators. This concern has led to a number of studies about faculty recruitment, productivity, and activity. There has been research, for example, on the scholarly productivity of faculty in library schools. Variables such as the highest degree, gender, size of faculty, teaching load, and program prestige have been found to be determining factors on the amount of research that faculty members undertake.[137] Closely related to these studies have been efforts

---

[134]James W. Geary, "A Fading Relationship: Library Schools and Preappointment Archival Education Since 1973," *Journal of Education for Librarianship* 20 (Summer 1979), 31.

[135]See, for example, Jane Robbins-Carter and Charles A. Seavey, "The Master's Degree: Basic Preparation for Professional Practice," *Library Trends* 34 (Spring 1986), 561-80; Herbert S. White, "Generalization versus Specialization in the MLS," *Library Journal* 113 (February 15, 1988), 148-49; and Robert V. Williams and Martha Jane K. Zachert, "Specialization in Library Education: A Review of the Trends and Issues," *Journal of Education for Library and Information Science* 26 (Spring 1986), 215-32. The debate about the sixth year and two year graduate programs also includes the issue of specialization and generalization; see Alice Gullen Smith, "A Survey of the Sixth-Year Program in Library Schools Offering the ALA Accredited Master's Degree," *Advances in Library Administration and Organization* 6 (1986), 197-220.

[136]Helmuth, "Education for American Archivists," 301.

[137]Kathleen Garland and Galen E. Rike, "Scholarly Productivity of Faculty at ALA-Accredited Programs of Library and Information Science," *Journal of Education for Library and Information Science* 28 (Fall 1987), 87-98; Jana Varlejs and Prudence Dalrymple, "Publication Output of Library and Information Science Faculty," *ibid.* 27 (Fall 1986), 71-89; Robert M.

to determine how library schools evaluate their faculty. Classroom teaching, research and publications, work with students, service, competing job offers, and personal attributes such as personality were examined and weighed through a survey of library school deans and administrators.[138]   There have also been some assessments of how library school faculty are recruited.[139]   Some of the more intriguing studies have examined library school faculty workload and activities in the areas of teaching, research, and service.   These research projects surveyed faculty at library schools, while a more recent project analyzed over twenty weeks the activities of a single faculty member.[140]   Other studies, such as one looking at the nature and percentage of doctorates on library school faculties,[141] reveal other means by which the library profession has sought to study its educators.   That some library schools have consciously made efforts to bring practitioners on faculties not only as adjuncts but as special or temporary lecturers *and*

Hayes, "Citation Statistics as a Measure of Faculty Research Productivity," *Journal of Education for Librarianship* 23 (Winter 1983), 151-72; Christine A. Korytnyk, "Comparison of the Publishing Patterns Between Men and Women Ph.D.s in Librarianship," *Library Quarterly* 58 (January 1988), 52-65.

There have also been cautions about depending on such measures; see Bert R. Boyce and Youngsuck Cho, "Tracking School of Library and Information Science Faculty Productivity," *Journal of Education for Library and Information Science* 29 (Summer 1988), 63-65.

[138]Kingsbury, "How Library Schools Evaluate Faculty Performance." That fundamental questions remain regarding such research can be seen in Kathleen M. Heim's "Dimensions of Faculty Public Service: A Policy Science Approach to Questions of Information Provision," *Journal of Education for Library and Information Science* 26 (Winter 1986), 154-64.   In this essay Heim questions the traditional notion of public service and attempts to relate the research function of faculty to the development of public information and library policy.

[139]James D. Ramer, Philip M. Turner, and J. Gordon Coleman, "Recruitment of Library School Faculty," *Journal of Education for Library and Information Science* 27 (Fall 1986), 100-04.

[140]J.F. Wyant and P.D. Morrison, "A Faculty Workload Survey," *Journal of Education for Librarianship* 12 (Winter 1972), 155-61; E.S. Gleaves, "Faculty Teaching Loads in Graduate Library Schools in the Southeast," *ibid.* 14 (Summer 1973), 32-42; L.G. Denis, "Full-time Faculty Survey Describes Educators," *Canadian Library Journal* 36 (June 1979), 107-21; and Virgil Diodato, "Faculty Workload: A Case Study," *Journal of Education for Librarianship* 23 (Spring 1983), 286-95.

[141]Raymond Kilpela, "Library School Faculty Doctorates: A Statistical Review," *Journal of Education for Librarianship* 22 (Spring 1982), 239-59.

to evaluate their impact shows how the concern for practice-theory or education-training continues to affect what library schools do.[142]

Carrying over the kind of research done in the library profession to the archival discipline is fraught with problems. There are no separate schools of archival studies. There are less than ten full-time archival educators in North America as of this writing. Graduate archival education is divided into a wide variety of history, applied or public history, and library school programs. It is these unique aspects of graduate archival education that ought to be studied. For example, given that such a large portion of graduate archival education is borne on the shoulders of adjunct or visiting professors, how is the quality of that education affected? Are these individuals viewed and evaluated in the same fashion as tenure-track or tenured professors? What control or influence do they have over what they teach and the placement of students in the archival profession? What should library schools (and other schools) look for in regular faculty to teach in this area since there is no doctorate in archival administration? The studies on library school faculty provide some interesting bases for comparison.

Educational Programs: Textbooks, Curriculum Materials, and Teaching Tools

There has long been a concern for this issue in the archival community. In 1909 Waldo Gifford Leland recommended to the first Conference of Archivists that a general manual be prepared, a project accepted but never completed.[143] The later success of UNESCO's Records and Archives Management Program (RAMP), an operation that has produced innumerable research studies and publications aiding both international archival education as well as education in the United States, underscores the need for textbooks and curriculum materials.[144] Although there is no question that the quantity and quality of

[142]For example, see the interesting case study by Richard Barlow and Andrew Green, "Practitioners as Lecturers: Benefits, Advantages and Practicalities," *Journal for Librarianship* 18 (July 1986), 165-79.

[143]Frank B. Evans, "Educational Needs for Work in Archival and Manuscript Depositories," *Indian Archives* 21 (July-December 1972), 16.

[144]For a description of RAMP, see Frank B. Evans, "UNESCO and Archives Development," *UNESCO Journal of Information Science, Librarianship and Archives Administration* 4 (July-September 1982), 162-73.

archival literature has improved considerably in recent years,[145] the phenomenal recent changes in information technology has threatened to undo even this progress. Not only are information technology's potential uses increasing, its similarities to human thinking have changed the potential for information generation.[146] How do archivists keep up with such changes *and* educate individuals to enter the profession?

Unfortunately, the library profession offers less help here than in other areas. There have been some studies on the effectiveness of teaching methods and tools, but such research seems to have been rare. The potential for research here should be great. For example, one study on the various methods of teaching basic subject cataloguing determined that there were some significant differences in results from microcomputer programmed instruction, television lecture, and printed test.[147] Another study evaluated the seminar and workshop approaches in raising conservation awareness among library school students by offering pretests and posttests to students participating in the training program.[148] A few efforts examining educational materials have appeared in the literature from time to time. One research project surveyed American and Canadian library school faculty about the use of instructional materials and textbooks, finding a wide range of opinions on the materials available to them.[149] A more valuable study examined, among other things, various influences (such as the authors' education and experience) on the production of

[145]For an overview of the change in the nature of the archival literature, see chapter seven in this volume.

[146]See, for example, Albert L. Lorenzo and Kul B. Gauri, "Educational Implications of Technological Innovations: A Perspective," *Library Hi Tech* 6 (Spring 1988), 55-59.

[147]Patricia Elaine Jensen, "The Effectiveness of Three Methods of Instruction in the Teaching of Basic Subject Cataloguing," Ph.D. dissertation, University of Connecticut, 1983.

[148]James E. Twomey, "Descriptive Analysis of a Conservation Awareness Program," *Journal of Education for Library and Information Science* 29 (Winter 1989), 197-208.

[149]Lois Mai Chan, "Instructional Materials Used in Teaching Cataloguing and Classification," *Cataloging and Classification Quarterly* 7 (Summer 1987), 131-44.

textbooks on government publications management.[150]   But in general librarians have paid little attention to such concerns. Philip A. Metzger recently wrote that although "from its beginnings, university-level library education has generated much literature on the subject of its own curriculum . . . . the subject of the tools to be used in that work - i.e., primarily textbooks - has been nearly ignored."[151]

Archivists need to research their curriculum needs and teaching tools for both graduate and continuing education. Are there sufficient textbooks, for example, for the development of graduate level courses and continuing education workshops and institutes?   What are educators using for teaching?   Is the curriculum for archival education being shaped more by existing textbooks and the literature than by archival competencies and knowledge?   Surveys of what archival educators use and desire to use, attitudes of students to the materials, and other similar research could potentially strengthen the quality of education that prospective and practicing archivists receive.   Perhaps more than anything else the placement of regular faculty specializing in archival administration and opening up the possibilities for graduate level research on archival topics has to help improve research studies and publications that can be used in educating individuals to practice as archivists.   In the period from 1973 through 1981 only six of one thousand library science dissertations completed in the United States related to archives in this country.   It is unlikely that this has changed very much in recent years.[152]   Such a trend hardly suggests the possibilities of improved textbooks, curriculum materials, and teaching tools.

Conclusion

The question now arises as to where and how archivists should get started in such an ambitious, even if highly

---

[150]John V. Richardson, "Paradigmatic Shifts in the Teaching of Government Publications, 1895-1985," *Journal of Education for Library and Information Science* 26 (Spring 1986), 249-86.

[151]"An Overview of the History of Library Science Teaching Materials," *Library Trends* 34 (Winter 1986), 469.

[152]The source for this is Gail A. Schlachter and Dennis Thomison, *Library Science Dissertations, 1973-1981* (Littleton, Colorado: Libraries Unlimited, Inc., 1982).   For another study I noted that *Dissertation Abstracts International* volume 44 (1983/84) reported 62 dissertations on library science topics and only one on an archival topic.

specialized, research agenda concerning their education. Is there a logical starting place in the varied topics in such an agenda? What are the most likely and most suitable players for sponsoring and carrying-out this research agenda? How should the research results be disseminated and used for maximum benefit for the archival profession? How does this research agenda relate to all the other agendas proposed in the past few years?

This agenda should start, obviously, where the archival profession is at present. The major issues today are the continued establishment of the certification of individual archivists, the impact of individual certification on education and employment, and the defining or codifying of archival competencies and knowledge for the preparation of certification examinations. This is an excellent beginning point for a research agenda on archival education. Studies of the views of archival educators and practitioners about a core body of archival knowledge, analyses of the content of job announcements, assessments of what archival employers are looking for, and similar efforts would increase the depth of knowledge about the archival field and aid continued development of education programs.

There is also the need for funded major research efforts on some specific aspects of archival education, probably under the sponsorship of the national professional associations like the Society of American Archivists and the National Association of Government Archives and Records Administrators. Topics for such study could include the use and viability of the practicum as a fundamental component of graduate archival education (since SAA's Committee on Education and Professional Development is already at work on this), archival employers' needs and practices, and the determination of future employment needs of archivists in government, colleges and universities, cultural organizations such as museums and historical societies, and industry. Joint cooperative efforts with other related associations such as the American Library Association, American Association for State and Local History, National Association for Government Archives and Records Administrators, and the National Council on Public History - all stakeholders in the education of archivists - also seem to be excellent possibilities.

Library schools and history departments educating individuals to practice as archivists also could undertake some modest research that could expand the knowledge about archival education. Surveys and reports on why students are taking archival and related courses, how they came to take such courses, how they were recruited (if they were), and their cognitive styles and other characteristics could provide information about the potential future pool of archival practitioners and their education and training needs. Doctoral students in history, library science, and information science should be encouraged to undertake substantive research on archival topics. The almost universal lack of graduate research on archival topics continues to hamper the development of archival theory and practice and, of course, education.

There also needs to be an increased effort at advocacy to persuade government agencies and related bodies to undertake and report on research relative to the archival profession. Cultural resources, such as historical records, are vital to all Americans and the increasing number of federally-subsidized studies on information use and policy need to be expanded to include data about the profession that is primarily responsible for these resources. The national professional associations need to lobby for federal surveys on professions, for example, that include information of use for archivists in planning for educational programs and other aspects of their profession. These same associations, through sponsoring sessions at their meetings and other means, need to encourage archival employers to report on in-service and continuing education programs, needs, and possibilities. Finally, these associations need to continue to apply pressure and offer support to the National Archives to expand the Archives Research Information Center, located at the archives, into a more effective clearinghouse that does not just report on research, but identifies and encourages research needs and possibilities.[153]

Prioritizing this particular research agenda among all the agendas recently proposed and presently facing the archival profession is a more difficult task. Recommended studies on appraisal, management, and use of historical records and archives, to name just three, are all vitally important to the archival profession.[154] But if there is a common theme

---

[153]ARIC developed out of the report sponsored by the National Association of Government Archives and Records Administrators with funding by the National Historical Publications and Records Commission to develop an improved means for the dissemination of information relative to the archival profession. See Victoria Irons Walch, *Information Resources for Archivists and Records Administrators: A Report and Recommendations* (Albany: National Association of Government Archives and Records Administrators, 1987).

[154]Richard J. Cox and Helen W. Samuels, "The Archivist's First Responsibility: A Research Agenda to Improve the Identification and Retention of Records of Enduring Value," *American Archivist* 51 (Winter/Spring 1988), 28-42; McCarthy, "The Management of Archives,"

connecting these other agendas, it is the need for better educated archivists and continuing education opportunities for practicing archivists that assists the profession to grapple with such issues and concerns. Archivists have become used to being challenged by their colleagues to explore new areas, to understand themselves and their profession, and to develop and try new methods and techniques. Undertaking a research agenda on archival education is another challenge worthy of serious consideration.

ibid., 52-69; and Lawrence Dowler, "The Role of Use in Defining Archival Practice and Principles: A Research Agenda for the Availability and Use of Records," *ibid.*, 74-86.

SEVEN

ARCHIVAL RESEARCH AND WRITING: EXPANDING HORIZONS AND CONTINUING NEEDS, 1901-1987[1]

Introduction

Over the past few years there has been an increasing interest in understanding the origins and present condition of the American archival community; one sign of this is the intensive profession-wide planning that has come to be accepted as crucial for meeting the archival mission. The essay that follows is intended to be a contribution to such understanding and planning. American archival literature, one significant measure of the health of the archival profession, has shown steady and considerable improvement over the years, especially since the early 1970s. Although archivists should be pleased with the progress of their literature in the United States, archivists must also recognize that they face serious challenges to continue the strengthening of their literature and profession.

In examining archival literature this essay considers anything written and published about the archival profession, its mission, and its technical procedures. Descriptive writings, reports, case studies, historical accounts, and theoretical treatises are all reviewed. All of these publications are important to the American archival profession because they are essential to the formation and nurturing of the knowledge and theory that gives the profession its distinctiveness and supports its practical work. The quality of archival knowledge is mainly attributable to the literature that defines, debates, and refines the profession's practices and the reasons for these practices. Even literature that is purely descriptive or historical can contribute to the development of a profession's theoretical knowledge.[2]

This essay reviews the history of archival writing in the United States, analyzes the development of this literature, evaluates obstacles to its continued development, and recommends actions for its improvement. The discussion is limited to archival literature in the United States because archival writing viewed on an international scale is too complex

---

[1]This essay was originally published in the *American Archivist* 50 (Summer 1987), 306-23.

[2]For the importance of theory in the archival profession, see my, "Professionalism and Archivists in the United States" in this volume.

for easy characterization, given the varying archival traditions of American, European, and third world nations. Nevertheless, the implications of this study for archival literature world wide are many, since over the past half-century the writings of American archivists have had a progressively wider influence on the international archival scene.[3]

There have been at least three distinctive phases in the evolution of archival literature in the United States, each marked by particular characteristics and recognizable dividing points. The first period of archival literature commenced at the turn of the twentieth century with the establishment of the first state archives and ended in 1936 with the organization of the Society of American Archivists (SAA). This was a time of gestation. Significant writings on archival topics were rare. Many publications were composed with an eye to the future formation of archival institutions or to provide practical guidelines directing the basic functions of these repositories.

Next came the formative era in the development of an American archival literature. During this period, American archival writing slowly formed into a significant corpus, although it remained uneven at best. This era ended in 1972 with the publication of the report of the SAA Committee for the 1970s, which called for the SAA to sponsor, besides the publication of a quarterly journal, the production of a basic professional literature.

The final phase of archival writing has extended from 1972 to the present. In this very short time span American archival literature has matured. In the early 1970s archival educators taught an archives administration course armed with a few

---

[3]The differences in the international archival community have been most clearly shown in the writings on archival education. American archivists have emphasized modern records with a bias for practical on-the-job training, while European archivists have been traditionally trained more intensively in historical methodology oriented to earlier records. In contrast to both, third world countries have required more basic assistance and often blended both American and European traditions. See Michael Cook, "Professional Training of Archivists: Problems of Modernization and Harmonization," *UNESCO Journal of Information Science, Librarianship and Archives Administration* 2 (July/September 1980), 150-58; Ruth W. Helmuth, "Education for American Archivists: A View from the Trenches," *American Archivist* 44 (Fall 1981), 295-303; William J. Orr, "Archival Training in Europe," *ibid.* 44 (Winter 1981), 27-39; Wilfred I. Smith, "The ICA and Technical Assistance to Developing Countries," *American Archivist* 39 (July 1976), 343-51; and Anne Thurston, "The Training of Archivists from Developing Countries: A Commonwealth Perspective," *Archivaria* 20 (Summer 1985), 116-26.

basic texts, most likely the products of T. R. Schellenberg or heavily influenced by him; in the late 1980s they now must choose from numerous manuals, essays scattered in a variety of archival, library science, and historical journals, and an assortment of monographs.

Archivists are now beginning a fourth period of archival writing, part of what one archivist recently has called the "Age of Archival Analysis,"[4] to which this present volume definitely belongs and from which it takes its title. This *new* writing is more concerned with professional standards, recognizes the value of evaluating and assessing the archival profession, is committed to collective action to preserve America's documentary heritage, and accepts the need to communicate to the public the importance of historical records. The long-term impact on and benefits for the archival profession of this new literature can only be conjectured at this point, but it promises to strengthen the archival profession and to transform what and how archivists write about.

The Beginning of Archival Writing, 1901-1936

The long, thirty-five year gestation of an archival literature was the natural result of the archivist's quest for a separate identity. Operating under the aegis of professional historical associations, archivists had no distinctive educational requirements. Their hopes for composing a body of archival theory were lost amid the pressures of establishing archival repositories, especially the long drive for a national archives. More importantly, perhaps, archivists did not even possess adequate outlets for publishing their work except the limited space *historical* journals provided for essays on archival subjects. It would have been remarkable indeed if an important corpus of archival literature had appeared during these years.[5]

Between 1901 and the mid-1930s archival writings were few, scattered widely in various journals and institutional publications, and generally descriptive rather than theoretical or prescriptive in tone and content. The few manuals of sorts that were published during these years were quickly outdated

[4]Bruce W. Dearstyne, "Archivists and Public History: Issues, Problems, and Prospects: An Introduction," *Public Historian* 8 (Summer 1986), 2.

[5]The best characterization of this period remains William F. Birdsall, "The Two Sides of the Desk: The Archivist and the Historian, 1909-1935," *American Archivist* 38 (April 1975), 159-72.

and remain of interest now only as historical curiosities.[6] Nevertheless, a few notable essays and volumes appeared that had a lasting influence on archival practice. Waldo G. Leland probably made the strongest contributions during these years. Leland served as a conduit for European ideas about archival administration, urged - although unsuccessfully - the drafting of a manual on archival principles, and co-authored several model finding aids.[7] Although Margaret C. Norton began writing her most important essays in the later part of this period, her efforts would have a greater impact many years later as archivists rediscovered her writings.[8] More typical of the archival literature of these years was the 1932 Public Archives Commission publication on local government records, which was written to encourage historians to use local records but did not explain the administration of these materials.[9]

It is easiest to summarize the archival literature of the first three decades of the twentieth century by examining two evaluations of the archival community, one written at the beginning and the other at the close of this period. In 1909 Leland addressed the subject of "American archival problems." He discussed, among other things, the need to establish a foundation for an "archive economy, sound in principle, and in practice adapted to American conditions, in conformity to which all our public archives, federal, state, county, municipal, and town, and perhaps even our private archives, shall in time come to be administered." Leland envisioned an archival

---

[6]For example, John C. Fitzpatrick, *Notes on the Care, Cataloguing, Calendaring and Arranging of Manuscripts* (Washington, D.C.: Government Printing Office, 1913, 1921, and 1928) and Cassius C. Stiles, *Public Archives: A Manual for Their Administration in Iowa* (Des Moines, 1928). For a discussion of the work during this period, see Richard C. Berner, *Archival Theory and Practice in the United States: A Historical Analysis* (Seattle: University of Washington Press, 1983), chapter 2.

[7]For a description of Leland's career see Rodney A. Ross, "Waldo Gifford Leland: Archivist by Association," *American Archivist* 46 (Summer 1983), 264-76.

[8]Her most famous essay, "The Archives Department as an Administrative Unit in Government," was published at the end of this period in 1930. See Thornton C. Mitchell, ed., *Norton on Archives: The Writings of Margaret Cross Norton on Archives & Records Management* (Carbondale: Southern Illinois University Press, 1975), 3-12.

[9]*The Preservation of Local Archives* (Washington, D. C.: American Historical Association, Public Archives Commission, 1932).

literature contributing to this construct.[10]　In 1935 Theodore C. Blegen returned to Leland's concerns, lamenting the lack of archival literature and calling for further investigation into archival systems and production of a glossary.[11] Thus little progress had been made during the years between Leland's and Blegen's essays.　Archivists still had no distinct identity, despite Leland's work the European literature was inaccessible to most American archivists, and American archival repositories remained in the shadow of the antiquarian tradition of the historical societies-collecting haphazardly with only modest concern for control or the intellectual integrity of records and record keeping systems.

The Formation of an Archival Literature, 1936-1972

Two events, the founding of the National Archives in 1934 and the organization of SAA two years later, led American archivists into a new phase of thinking and writing about their work. From the mid-1930s into the early 1970s, when the SAA Committee for the 1970s set an aggressive new agenda for an American archival literature, archivists slowly emerged as a distinctive community, creating in the process a larger and more varied collection of writings.[12]

The story of archival writing in these years is essentially the story of the National Archives and the SAA. The National Archives became the largest archival employer in the country and dominated, with mixed results, the Society.　Both the institution and the association provided a national focus and outlets for the publication of archival practices and theory. The *American Archivist*, established in 1938, was and remains the premier archival journal in the United States. The journal revolutionized archival writing and the archival profession, providing a forum for the archival writings that prior to 1938 had had little chance for publication, as well as giving considerable space for reviews and news.　The *American*

---

[10]American Historical Association, *Annual Report, 1909*, I, 302-08.

[11]*Problems of American Archivists*, National Archives Bulletin no. 2, November 1936.

[12]For some understanding of this period, see J. Frank Cook, "The Blessings of Providence on an Association of Archivists," *American Archivist* 46 (Fall 1983), 374-99.

Archivist was the chief professional bond for archivists, the "voice of the profession."[13]

In addition to providing crucial support for SAA's quarterly journal, the National Archives was also fertile ground for other archival writings. Cognizant of creating a new institution and profession, many staff members of the National Archives endeavored to establish both through writing. The National Archives' annual reports, *Bulletins*, and *Staff Information Papers* - along with the *American Archivist* - "made available to archivists the first substantial American contributions to the preservation and administration of archives."[14] Many of the profession's chief principles and practices were born or refined in the heady atmosphere of the young National Archives, led by such archival pioneers as T. R. Schellenberg, Oliver Wendell Holmes, and Philip C. Brooks. Schellenberg's staff writings alone, later brought together in his two extremely influential manuals, did much to mold the nature of the archival world.[15]

There were, of course, other important influences on American archival literature. One significant contribution was the Historical Records Survey (HRS) conducted from 1936 to 1942. In recent years much attention has focused on the voluminous finding aids, and their abysmal neglect, produced by this massive federal effort. But the HRS also appears to have left behind some literature about archival methodology that was absorbed into archival practice.[16] From the founding of the National Archives until the early 1970s some of the first truly American archival manuals were published, as well as a small group of monographs and collections of essays that revealed a growing sense of archival identity and vigor. The history of the profession was one concern, as modern archivists

[13]Karl Trever, "The American Archivist: The Voice of a Profession," *American Archivist* 15 (April 1952), 147-55.

[14]H. G. Jones, *The Records of a Nation: Their Management, Preservation, and Use* (New York: Atheneum, 1969), 20.

[15]Schellenberg, *Modern Archives: Principles and Techniques* (Chicago: University of Chicago Press, 1956) and *The Management of Archives* (New York: Columbia University Press, 1965). For a recounting of Schellenberg's career, see Jane F. Smith, "Theodore R. Schellenberg: Americanizer and Popularizer," *American Archivist* 44 (Fall 1981), 313-26.

[16]This aspect of the importance of the HRS on the developing archival profession needs more study. For some of these writings, see Frank B. Evans, comp., *Modern Archives and Manuscripts: A Select Bibliography* (Chicago: Society of American Archivists, 1975), 136.

sought to understand the origins of their work; these efforts produced a few outstanding writings.[17] Such historical writings and other festschrifts and essay collections[18] were indicators that the maturing archival community was gaining some sense of retrospection. Schellenberg's manuals, already mentioned, only added to the profession's developing maturity.

The most interesting aspect of this second period was the spate of writings in the 1960s that endeavored to define specific aspects of the condition of the American archival profession and to recommend changes for improvement. The volumes of Walter Muir Whitehill on historical societies, of Ernst Posner on state archives, and of H. G. Jones on the National Archives remain classic statements and analyses of their respective topics. Walter Rundell's study on American historical research could be added to this group because of its sensitivity to the work of archivists in supporting research into the United States' past.[19] These works share several common characteristics: a broad approach to their topic, the support of national professional associations and foundations, and an optimism that improvement would result from their work, its distribution, and reading. They are, perhaps, typical products of the 1960s, a time of available and abundant research monies, increasing societal change, and agitation for wide reform and improvement.

[17]Leslie W. Dunlap, *American Historical Societies, 1790-1860* (Madison, Wisconsin: privately printed, 1944); Roscoe R. Hill, *American Missions in European Archives* (Mexico: Instituto Panamericano de Geografia e Historia, 1951); H. G. Jones, *For History's Sake: The Preservation and Publication of North Carolina History, 1663-1903* (Chapel Hill: University of North Carolina Press, 1965); and Ernst Posner, *Archives in the Ancient World* (Cambridge: Harvard University Press, 1972).

[18]William B. Hesseltine and Donald R. McNeil, eds., *In Support of Clio: Essays in Memory of Herbert A. Kellar* (Madison: State Historical Society of Wisconsin, 1958); Ruth Anna Fisher and William Lloyd Fox, eds., *J. Franklin Jameson: A Tribute* (Washington, D.C.: Catholic University of America Press, 1965); and Ken Munden, ed., *Archives & the Public Interest: Selected Essays by Ernst Posner* (Washington, D. C.: Public Affairs Press, 1967).

[19]Walter Muir Whitehill, *Independent Historical Societies: An Enquiry Into Their Research and Publication Functions and Their Financial Future* (Boston: Boston Athenaeum, 1962); Ernst Posner, *American State Archives* (Chicago: University of Chicago Press, 1964); Jones, *Records of a Nation*; and Walter Rundell, Jr., *In Pursuit of American History: Research and Training in the United States* (Norman: University of Oklahoma Press, 1970).

Although this period produced some memorable and important archival literature, it is questionable if it, in fact, laid a solid foundation for the American archival profession. In actuality, the preponderance of writing by the archival community were finding aids and reports of institutional activities, which avoided to a large extent the more difficult, theoretical issues.[20] Although archival practice showed a gradual movement toward common practices, these practices did not constitute standards or theory. Most revealing was that action on the recommendations of the reports by Whitehill, Posner, and Jones was slow in coming, when it came at all. Posner's book was accepted immediately as a reference book instead of a call to action.[21] Whitehill's study, judging by more recent evaluations of American historical societies, had little impact.[22] In addition, the archival profession suffered during these years its only major schism, the split between archivists and records managers. This separation not only slowed the development of a strong archival theory for such functions as appraisal, but it severely hurt the work of the modern records manager. The literature of both occupations was weakened as a result.[23]

[20]This can be seen in two ways. First, all through these years and up to the present, the quantity of publications on more theoretical issues like appraisal and professional education have been far below the number of writings on arrangement and description, repository studies, and the like. Second, there were a number of articles during this second period that highlighted the importance of institutional reports: C. C. Crittendon, "Publications Policies for Archival and Historical Agencies," *American Archivist* 3 (October 1940), 245-50; Leon De Valinger, Jr., "Preparation of Annual Reports," *ibid.* 16 (April 1953), 161-63; Morris L. Radoff, "Reports of State Archivists," *ibid.* 17 (October 1954), 331-39; Crittendon, "Reports of State Archivists," *ibid.* 18 (October 1955), 309-15; and Howard H. Eddy, "Reports of State Archivists," *ibid.* 20 (January 1957), 13-18.

[21]H. G. Jones, "The Pink Elephant Revisited," *American Archivist* 43 (Fall 1980), 473-83.

[22]Charles Phillips and Patricia Hogan, *A Culture At Risk: Who Cares for America's Heritage?* and *The Wages of History: The AASLH Employment Trends and Salary Survey* (Nashville: American Association for State and Local History, 1984).

[23]This topic requires much more analysis. The schism is evident in numerous essays on this subject in the *American Archivist* during the 1950s and 1960s. The damage to the work of records managers can be seen in the general weakness of their literature on historical records issues. Many archivists remain uncomfortable with records management despite its potential for identifying and selecting records having enduring value. Despite closely related missions, archivists and records managers remain

The condition of American archival literature from the mid-1930s to early 1970s is perhaps best summed up by the only self-reflective analysis on archival writing produced during these years. In his 1957 SAA presidential address Lester J. Cappon emphasized the need for archivists to contribute to historical scholarship, primarily by producing finding aids and other tools that encouraged the use of archival holdings. Many today might argue that Cappon's tie of archivists to historians was far too limiting, considering the recent strengthening of connections between archivists and librarians and other information professionals; however, Cappon was chastising his colleagues for being little more than "tardy scholars," producing few finding aids and writing little in general. Archival scholarship and hence its literature still had significant areas for improvement.[24]

The Maturation of Archival Literature, 1972-1986

SAA's Committee for the 1970s recognized the deficiencies of archival scholarship. The committee's report, published in 1972, provides the clearest delineation of stages in the historical development of an American archival literature. The report offered several recommendations concerning archival literature, including:

*   strengthening the *American Archivist*, especially expanding it in "scope and content";

*   publishing an SAA newsletter six times a year;

*   publishing a "pamphlet series" on "practical archival and technical problems" for the beginning archivist;

*   publishing, on an occasional basis, "manuals, technical pamphlets, and other archival studies to meet the varied needs of our membership and carefully edited readings which would be of particular value to students of archives administration and allied subjects";

*   publishing directories and publicity brochures;

largely divided into two camps, characterizing each other as records destroyers or antiquarian packrats.

[24]"Tardy Scholars Among the Archivists," *American Archivist* 21 (January 1958), 3-16.

    *   hiring a fulltime SAA editor.[25]

This remarkable document precisely laid out SAA's publications program of the past decade, a program that has become the cornerstone of a modern American archival literature.

    The publication efforts by the SAA have been the major achievement in the history of an American archival literature during the 1970s and early 1980s. In 1951 it was said that the *American Archivist* "remains . . . the Society's major venture in the field of professional publication."[26] A quarter of a century later, the journal was but one part of its publication program. Armed with grants from the National Historical Publications and Records Commission, the Society started and has sustained a series of publications intended to be the basic building blocks of professional theory and practice.[27] This "Basic Manual Series" has been supplemented with other publications on such diverse topics as Native American archives, business archives, and basic education workshop guidelines.[28] SAA's publications program has helped the archival profession to begin to define better its basic work, provided many of the basic references needed for archival

    [25]Philip P. Mason, "The Society of American Archivists in the Seventies: Report of the Committee for the 1970's," *American Archivist* 35 (April 1972), 193-217.

    [26]Trever, "The *American Archivist*," 147.

    [27]This series includes the following: Maynard Brichford, *Appraisal and Accessioning* (1977); David B. Gracy, II, *Arrangement and Description* (1977); Sue E. Holbert, *Reference and Access* (1977); Timothy Walch, *Security* (1977); John A. Fleckner, *Surveys* (1977); Gail Farr Casterline, *Exhibits* (1980); H. Thomas Hickerson, *An Introduction to Automated Access* (1981); Ralph Ehrenberg, *Maps and Architectural Drawings* (1982); Ann Pederson and Gail Casterline, *Public Programs* (1982); Carolyn Hoover Sung, *Reprography* (1982); Mary Lynn Ritzenthaler, *Conservation* (1984); Mary Lynn Ritzenthaler, Gerald J. Munoff, and Margery S. Long, *Administration of Photographic Collections* (1984); Margaret L. Hedstrom, *Machine-Readable Records* (1984); and Gary M. and Trudy Huskamp Peterson, *Law* (1985).

    [28]A few examples include Edie Hedlin, *Business Archives: An Introduction* (1978); Thomas C. Pardo, *Basic Archival Workshops* (1982); William Deiss, *Museum Archives: An Introduction* (1984); and John A. Fleckner, *Native American Archives: An Introduction* (1984).

education, and given SAA and archivists a higher profile among related professions and some of their constituencies.[29]

During these years the SAA was joined by other organizations which established archival or closely-related subject journals that have provided a much broader base for archival publication. *Prologue, Midwestern Archivist, Provenance* (formerly *Georgia Archive*), *Archivaria*, and the *Public Historian* are, or should be, essential reading for any archivist. Several non-archival journals have become more open to essays on archival topics. Although library science and history journals have always included a few archival essays, higher quality essays treating important archival issues now seem to be appearing regularly in these publications. The increased interest of these journals is certainly partly due to the budget-cutting climate in the federal government that has seriously threatened archival, historical, and library programs alike, uniting these professions in the face of a common enemy.[30] Also, the shift by regional archival organizations from a complete preoccupation with basic, practical concerns to the consideration of professional issues like archival image, certification, and educational standards has caused the production of more publishable papers that can be submitted to the journals interested in featuring essays on archival subjects. And, finally, more (although not enough) archivists, primarily as a result of the growth of the profession and attitudinal changes to realize the importance of research and its dissemination, appear to be writing than before. It is, therefore, no surprise or coincidence that the summer 1986 issues of the *Public Historian* and *Journal of Library Administration* were special volumes on archives.[31] The

[29]For some evaluation of this publication program, see Philip Mason, "Archives in the Seventies: Promises and Fulfillment," *American Archivists* 44 (Summer 1981), 204; and Terry Abraham, "Publishing for the Archival Profession," *Scholarly Publishing* 15 (April 1984), 266-67. For a recent evaluation of the archival profession over the last decade, see Larry J. Hackman, "A Perspective on American Archives," *Public Historian* 8 (Summer 1986), 5-23.

[30]Almost every issue of the newsletters of the American Historical Association and Organization of American Historians includes substantial information about archival issues.

[31]The *Public Historian* issue, edited by Bruce W. Dearstyne, explored the place of archival administration in public history. The *Journal of Library Administration* issue, edited by Lawrence J. McCrank, contains essays on various aspects of the relationship between archives and libraries. I would like to re-emphasize that the total portion of archivists writing for publication is still too small for the good of the profession.

simultaneous publication of two such journal issues is unprecedented in the history of American archival literature.

There has also been a rapid and dramatic increase in the number of monographs on archival subjects, published on a wide variety of subjects by an equally diverse group of publishers. There have been significant contributions on the formulation of standard practices, a new interest in theory, volumes on automation, explorations in interprofessional cooperation, a new interest in local public records, and some excellent writings on the origins and development of certain aspects of the archival profession. These publications have been issued by the presses of historical associations, universities, library-information science publishers, and, occasionally commercial publishers.[32] In addition, the National Archives has seemed to revitalize its publishing program,[33] and archivists are more committed than ever to wrestling with the significant issues and problems confronting the profession and its mission. Largely deriving from the efforts of the National Historical Publications and Records Commission, SAA, and the National Association of Government Archives and Records

---

[32]Some of these publications include Ken Duckett, *Modern Manuscripts: A Practical Manual for Their Management, Care, and Use* (Nashville: American Association for State and Local History, 1975); Robert L. Clark, Jr., ed., *Archive-Library Relations* (New York: R. R. Bowker Co., 1976); Edmund Berkeley, Jr., *Autographs and Manuscripts: A Collector's Manual* (New York: Charles Scribner's Sons, Inc., 1978); H. G. Jones, *Local Government Records: An Introduction to Their Management, Preservation, and Use* (Nashville: American Association for State and Local History, 1980); Burl Noggle, *Working With History: The Historical Records Survey in Louisiana and the Nation, 1936-1942* (Baton Rouge: Louisiana State University Press, 1981); Victor Gondos, Jr., *J. Franklin Jameson and the Birth of the National Archives, 1906-1926* (Philadelphia: University of Pennsylvania Press, 1981); Nancy Peace, ed., *Archival Choices: Managing the Historical Record in An Age of Abundance* (Lexington, Massachusetts: Lexington Books, 1984); and Richard M. Kesner, *Automation for Archivists and Records Managers: Planning and Implementation Strategies* (Chicago: American Library Association, 1984).

[33]See, as examples, Maygene F. Daniels and Timothy Walch, eds., *A Modern Archives Reader: Basic Readings on Archival Theory and Practice* (Washington, D. C.: National Archives and Records Service, 1984) and Patricia A. Andrews and Bettye J. Grier, comps., *Writings on Archives, Historical Manuscripts, and Current Records: 1979-1982* (Washington, D. C.: National Archives and Records Administration, 1985).

Administrators, writings have appeared that instill in archivists the sense of a new and fuller agenda.[34]

This new interest has also suggested that archivists may have largely completed the task of "basic" writings (although the profession could benefit from the preparation of a comprehensive basic primer on archival administration) and need to continue moving towards the resolution of the tougher problems and theoretical issues presented by operating in and trying to document modern society.

Present Challenges

Although the archivist now can lay claim to essential writings comprising more than a single bookcase shelf, there are numerous significant problems remaining to be addressed in the continued development of an American archival literature. At least seven challenges remain for the archivist. These include (1) the continuing lack of adequate archival theory; (2) the need for more opportunities for research and writing; (3) the need for more energetic national leadership in the support and dissemination of archival literature; (4) archivists' lingering doubts about their identity; (5) limitations of archival education; (6) the need to find suitable outlets for scholarly publication; and (7) archivists' inability to write for broader audiences. All of these issues require serious attention in order to protect the health of the American archival profession and to ensure its continued growth.

Concern about archival theory has been the subject of recent debate. In an important essay published in 1981, Frank Burke lamented that archival theory was not flourishing in the United States because such "theory can only grow in the cool and contemplative conditions of the cloister, i.e., in the classroom and its concomitant academic setting."[35] In this essay, which has generated more response than most archival writing, Burke presented to his colleagues a series of theoretical questions and topics deserving exploration. Some

---

[34]Lisa B. Weber, ed., *Documenting America: Assessing the Condition of Historical Records in the States* ([Albany]: National Association of State Archives and Records Administrators in cooperation with the National Historical Publications and Records Commission, [1983]); Committee on the Records of Government, *Report* (Washington, D. C.: March 1985); and *Planning for the Archival Profession: A Report of the SAA Task Force on Goals and Priorities* (Chicago: Society of American Archivists, 1986).

[35]"The Future Course of Archival Theory in the United States," *American Archivist* 44 (Winter 1981), 42.

have felt that Burke was splitting hairs between practice and theory and others have tried to build on his ideas.[36] Burke is correct, however. Without any commitment to the development of theory, the archival community lacks one of the essential features of a profession and weakens its incentive for improving practice and meeting its mission to document society. The archival profession is more than just a service occupation or a subset of other disciplines, as some seem inclined to argue; it has a theoretical basis for practice and it needs to continue the development of that theoretical foundation.[37]

Most archivists would agree with Burke's assessment that archival theory building is severely restricted because of the lack of time and opportunity for archivists to devote to research, the second challenge confronting the archival profession. Nor do archival educators have much time to inspire and encourage graduate students to do research. The first priority of the archival profession should be to place experienced and capable archivists in fulltime academic positions, where they can challenge students to address neglected topics in archival literature, as well as have time for their own archival writing. This seems, at last, to be occurring. A fulltime teaching archivist has been hired in the library school at the University of Texas, and there are plans for employing a second. The University of British Columbia *now* has two internationally known and respected archival educators. The library school at the State University of New York at Albany has recently hired one of the foremost experts on records management and has hired an archivist. The School of Library and Information Science at the University of Pittsburgh is now developing a comprehensive graduate education program as well. Archival education appears to be on the threshold of new and exciting developments that have tremendous implications for the entire profession's continuing growth, especially its body of literature.

Besides the appointment of full-time archival educators, the American archival profession must obtain considerably greater support for research and development. The recent SAA Goals

[36]Lester J. Cappon, "What, Then, Is There To Theorize About?" *American Archivist* 45 (Winter 1982), 19-25 and Gregg D. Kimball, "The Burke-Cappon Debate: Some Further Criticisms and Considerations for Archival Theory," *ibid.* 48 (Fall 1985), 369-76.

[37]It should be obvious that I strongly disagree with the views expressed by John W. Roberts, "Archival Theory: Much Ado About Shelving," *American Archivist* 50 (Winter 1987), 66-74.

and Priorities Task Force report identifies this as a priority activity, urging more opportunities for such work along with the "establishment of a national foundation to coordinate and promote archival research and development."[38] The Bentley fellowship program, funded by the National Endowment for the Humanities and the Andrew Mellon and other foundations, is a viable model already having generated a sizeable amount of research and writing.[39] But more such incentives are needed. If NHPRC's funding base could be increased, it could develop a program for individual research, such as that offered by the NEH, a program which has not appeared to be used to advantage by archivists. Other possibilities that have long been ignored are the creation of research and development units in archival institutions, the development of sabbatical programs with release time, and temporary exchanges of staff among archival programs facilitating additional research. Without increased professional support and emphasis, archival theory and literature will remain seriously limited, unable to profit from the obvious talents of individual archivists.

The absence of a strong national institutional leader is the fourth obstacle to a developing and vibrant American archival literature. The National Archives fulfilled that role for a very long time, and there are renewed hopes that with its recently won independence it will reassume this position. Former Archivist of the United States, Robert M. Warner, stated that its independence was essential for "assisting the American archival community." "The National Archives is in the best possible position of any archival institution to provide this service because of its size, its variety of activities and records, as well as its ability to experiment while drawing on the widest pool of expertise."[40] Most archivists continue to hope. Even stronger leadership from the national professional associations is also essential. SAA should expand its publications program beyond basic texts and carefully evaluate the effectiveness of its present publications program, including the *American Archivist*. Stated simply, are SAA's publications meeting the needs of modern archivists? NAGARA has made

---

[38]*Planning for the Archival Profession*, 33.

[39]Much of the early work of the Bentley fellows focused on appraisal; for example, see the Spring 1985 issue of the *American Archivist*. A number of other important essays completed by the fellows have also appeared in subsequent issues of the *American Archivist*.

[40]"The National Archives at Fifty," *Midwestern Archivist* 10, no. 1 (1985), 30.

some very interesting contributions in recent years, especially its analysis of government records preservation needs and issuance of guidelines in areas such as local government and governors' records,[41] but it cannot mount an ambitious program unless it builds its financial base or develops stronger cooperative ventures with other organizations such as the SAA.

A much more serious problem inhibiting the development of archival literature is the way in which archivists view themselves. David Gracy has written about how others see archivists, suggesting that some of the image problems are due to archivists' own perceptions of what an archivist should be.[42] Building on what Gracy has written, it is logical to wonder if too few archivists seem to think of themselves as archivists, compelling many not to think seriously about writing on archival subjects. In one of the few essays on archival research and writing, the author suggested that archivists do historical research; there also have been ideas about specializations in administrative history.[43] Although well intentioned, such efforts seem misdirected. There are too many gaps in the profession's theory and literature for archivists to squander their energies on interesting, but tangential areas unless they are made more essential to the mission of the archival community. Although existing archival literature has been characterized as too "nuts-and-bolts,"[44] practical case studies and reports about special projects and initiatives are still needed in many areas. Max J. Evans found this lack of case studies "ironic" and problematic: "It is ironic that although we are a profession concerned primarily with documentation, we have not created a permanent body of documentation, or precedent, upon which we can base future decisions and which we can use to train future generations of

[41]Such as *Preservation Needs in State Archives* (Albany: National Association of Government Archives and Records Administrators, February 1986).

[42]"What's Your Totem? Archival Images in the Public Mind," *Midwestern Archivist* 10, no. 1 (1985), 17-23 and "Our Future is Now," *American Archivist* 48 (Winter 1985), 12-21.

[43]David Mycue, "The Archivist as a Scholar: A Case for Research by Archivists," *Georgia Archive* 7 (Fall 1979), 10-16 and Arthur D. Larson, "Administrative History: A Proposal for a Re-evaluation of Its Contributions to the Archival Profession," *Midwestern Archivist* 7, no. 1 (1982), 34-45.

[44]Peter J. Wosh, "Creating a SemiProfessional Profession: Archivists View Themselves," *Georgia Archive* 10 (Fall 1982), 6-7.

archivists."[45]   There is much excellent work being done in archival institutions that is not being effectively reported. This must change if the profession is to continue to be strengthened to meet its mission of documenting society.

The condition of archival education and training accounts for the sixth major barrier to a healthier archival literature. Although there is evidence of new growth and strength, the persistent challenge is to persuade graduate students to study archival issues and topics. Most professions derive significant new ideas or testing of ideas from the work of its novice practitioners, who bring fresh perspectives and insights. Yet serious research by students on archival topics is rare. There are hundreds of theses and dissertations on history and library science for every one on an archival subject.[46] The American archival profession must have strong graduate training programs extending far beyond the traditional infatuation with practical, craft-like concerns to interest in theory and research. Thus far, only two graduate archival education programs (the University of Maryland and the University of British Columbia) have shown any proclivity for such research and writing; this is obviously too small a number to have much of an impact on archival literature and theory.[47] As of yet, there is no viable model to be emulated, and archival literature is the less for it.

Finally, archivists face the same challenges in publishing scholarly works as members of other related professions. Publishing major monographs is now difficult due to increasing costs of production and severely limited sales.[48] The real problem, however, may be the tendency of many professionals to write only for each other, rather than addressing wider

---

[45]"The Visible Hand: Creating a Practical Mechanism for Cooperative Appraisal," *Midwestern Archivist* 11, no. 1 (1986), 9.

[46]The actual impact of graduate archival education programs on archival research and writing is yet another topic deserving more attention. A crude measurement is an examination of one year of *Dissertations Abstracts International*.   Using volume 44 (1983/84) of that publication revealed the following: a total of 62 dissertations reported on library science topics; a total of one dissertation on an archival topic.

[47]There are positive signs. Some archival educators have directed their students to researching and writing about more substantive topics. Frank Burke seems to have turned his students to analyzing some of the concerns raised in his "Future Course" essay, some of which have been published; see Kimball, "Burke-Cappon Debate," and Wosh, "Creating a SemiProfessional Profession." Others seem intent to follow this example. The brochure on Western Washington University's archival program states that "thesis topics involving the history of archives administration and records management, or emerging problems in these disciplines, are encouraged."

[48]"The Crisis in Scholarly Publishing," AHA *Perspectives* 24 (March 1986), 7-8, 10.

issues in readable ways that would interest a broader public. Although the care and management of our documentary heritage is a vital public issue, archivists have to present a case for this in a way that the public can comprehend and be persuaded to support. More subventionary grants must also be actively sought to ensure the completion and publication of scholarly archival works. Equally important, archivists must write both scholarly and popular works. If this occurs, archival theory will be strengthened and resources, necessary for supporting work on such theory, will improve.

Conclusion

What is the present condition of archival literature in the United States? A summary review such as this reveals significant progress. The improvements in the archival literature in the United States correspond with overall improvements in the profession. But archivists face some serious challenges if such progress is to continue. Not all archivists need or want to write, but more should. Not all archival work must be described in publication, but more should. Not all archivists need to grapple with weighty theoretical issues, but more should. The condition of the literature indicates much about the condition of the archival profession. Strengthening the literature will make better archivists, both now and in the future.

EIGHT

**ON THE VALUE OF ARCHIVAL
HISTORY IN THE UNITED
STATES[1]**

Introduction

Over thirty years ago Jesse Shera wrote a cogent essay
entitled "On the Value of Library History." Libraries, he
reasoned in his watershed essay, must be examined as a vital
part of society.[2] Prior to his writing, library history consisted
mainly of narrow institutional histories and superficial
commemorative accounts. Now this field includes a large
quantity of excellent studies that employ sophisticated historical
methodologies and feature differing schools of thought;
individuals other than librarians are increasingly interested in
the subject as well.[3] Archival history, closely related to library
history, has lagged far behind in research, but now appears to
be the object of new interest and activity. Archival history,
chronicling humanity's efforts to preserve its documentary
heritage, is a subject deserving as much serious attention as
the nature and development of libraries.[4]
When Shera wrote his essay in the early 1950s, most
archivists presently at work in the United States had not yet
entered grade school. The archival profession is a young
discipline.[5] Although the first repositories of historical records
in this country date back to the late eighteenth century, the

---

[1]This essay was originally published in *Libraries & Culture* 23 (Spring
1988), 135-51.

[2]*Library Quarterly* 22 (July 1952), 240-51.

[3]For contrasting views, see Michael H. Harris, "Antiquarianism,
Professional Piety, and Critical Scholarship in Recent American Library
Historiography," *Journal of Library History* 13 (Winter 1978), 37-43 and
Phyllis Dain, "A Response to Issues Raised by the ALHRT Program, 'The
Nature and Uses of Library History,'" *ibid.*, 44-47.

[4]By "archival history," I do not mean just the history of the archival
profession which can be dated from the early twentieth century or, as some
do, from the founding of the National Archives and the Society of American
Archivists in the mid-1930s. Archival history encompasses the history of
all efforts to preserve and manage historical records. However, the focus
of this essay is primarily on the twentieth century formation and
development of the modern archival profession in the United States.

[5]A 1982 analysis of the archival profession in the United States
concluded that "archivists are young: more than half are under forty, two-
thirds are under fifty." Even this represented substantial aging since a
similar study conducted a few years before. See David Bearman, "1982
Survey of The Archival Profession," *American Archivist* 46 (Spring 1983),
233.

staffs of these institutions for many years remained well-meaning amateurs more interested in antiquarian, patriotic, and even xenophobic activities than in developing systems or theory to guide the management of their historical collections. Not until the twentieth century, with the appearance of well-trained historians and the establishment of the first publicly supported archives, did a distinct archival profession begin to emerge.[6] The Society of American Archivists (SAA) was not founded until 1936, sixty years after its counterpart, the American Library Association. Partly because of its youth and the press of other concerns and issues, the archival community did not begin to show any interest in its own past and antecedents until recently.   Despite a growing number of articles and some monographs on archival history, there remains a distinct lack of any sense - at least any precise definition - of the value of archival history.

It is not exceedingly difficult to determine when and why a profession like that of archivists or librarians, might turn to its past. When a profession is first developing, it might attempt to define its origins and antecedents. Rarely, however, does such writing have any lasting usefulness or relevance, other than as a historical source on the profession's origins.[7] Interest in the history of a profession sometimes appears when it encounters serious challenges or crises or undergoes periods of immense change that threaten, or appear to threaten, it and its practitioners.[8] A profession often turns to its own past as it

---

[6]William F. Birdsall, "The Two Sides of the Desk: The Archivist and the Historian, 1909-1935," *American Archivist* 38 (April 1975), 159-73 and "Archivists, Librarians, and Issues During the Pioneering Era of the American Archival Movement," *Journal of Library History* 14 (Fall 1979), 457-79.

[7]Public historians have looked back, for example, to the individuals associated with the pioneering historical societies and archival repositories as their ancestors. This was done to legitimize the newly emerging field, but it has also alienated many practitioners of these "older" disciplines. What has passed thus far for a history of public history, only little more than a decade old, has really been the history of archivists, historical society leaders, historic preservationists, oral historians, and others. There still is no adequate history of the early development of this new field. For an essay that touches upon some of these matters, see my "Archivists and Public Historians in the United States" in this volume.

[8]The historical profession is a good case in point.   It has a tremendously large literature on its history, which often seems to grow during times of stress. There has been a literal explosion of such writings over the past decade as the historical profession has weathered declining student enrollment, a lessening of the number of teaching positions, and a

reaches some new level of maturity; at the least, a profession seems interested in its past on certain commemorative dates, evident in the many histories of professional associations and institutions and biographies of individuals.[9]

A profession also turns to its own past when its self-identity or self-image improves, especially as educational requirements, the very heart of professionalism, are expanded and strengthened.[10] Finally, a profession can be the subject of research by sociologists, historians, and other outsiders. One examination of the recent interest in professions noted that the "study of the professions derives much of its impetus from the commonplace observation that professionals have become a dominant force in contemporary society, a group whose numbers greatly exceed what anyone could have predicted a century ago and whose influence reaches far beyond what their numbers would indicate."[11] Perspectives from outsiders can greatly enrich a profession's own knowledge of itself.

Motives for examining the history of a profession determine the quality and value of such studies. The strength of a profession's educational standards and prominence that attracts outside attention lead to more important studies than research conducted only to commemorate anniversaries. The most crucial catalyst for serious historical research is a well-developed sense in a profession's practitioners of the value and relevance of their own past and development. Archivists are only now, despite their close alliance with historians, beginning to grasp the importance of their profession's history. Their primary concern within the past decade about the public's

shrinking readership of its work. See, for example, Joan Hoff Wilson, "Is the Historical Profession an 'Endangered Species?'" *Public Historian* 2 (Winter 1980), 4-21.

[9]The centennial of the American Library Association brought with it an outpouring of library history studies in the mid-1970s, as reflected in the annual reviews in The Journal of Library History and Michael H. Harris and Donald G. Davis, Jr., *American Library History: A Bibliography* (Austin: University of Texas Press, 1978).

[10]Nathan Glazer, "The Schools of the Minor Professions," *Minerva* 12 (July 1974), 346-64, and, for a historical case study, Stephen J. Kunitz, "Professionalism and Social Control in the Progressive Era: The Case of the Flexner Report," *Social Problems* 22 (October 1974), 16-27.

[11]Matthew Ramsey, "History of a Profession, *Annales* Style: The Work of Jacques Lenard," *Journal of Social History* 17 (Winter 1983), 320. See also Burton J. Bledstein, "Discussing Terms: Professions, Professionals, Professionalism," in *Prospects: An Annual of American Cultural Studies*, ed. Jack Salzman, 10 (1985), 1-15.

understanding of the archivist's mission has been reinforced more recently by studies about earlier efforts to promote the preservation of historical records.[12]   The recent golden anniversaries of the founding of the National Archives and the SAA have brought renewed attention to the archival profession's history.[13]   Unfortunately, very few archival education programs encourage students to write theses or dissertations on archival topics and few outside the archival profession are interested in its history.[14]   Literature on the history of the archival profession, at least in the United States, remains extremely uneven in quality and coverage. Little has been written from a national perspective, and the history of the archival profession continues to consist of episodic views, from widely different angles, that do not constitute a complete portrait.[15]   Archivists, let alone outsiders to the profession, still possess an insufficient appreciation of the value of archival history.

On the Value of Archival History

Archival history has two general values. Its first benefit is

[12]For recent concerns about the public image of the archival profession's mission, see David B. Gracy, II, "Our Future Is Now," *American Archivist* 48 (Winter 1985),   12-21.   For a history of an earlier archival public outreach effort, see James Gregory Bradsher, "Taking America's Heritage to the People: The Freedom Train Story," *Prologue* 17 (Winter 1985),   229-45.

[13]Such as Timothy Walch, ed., *Guardian of Heritage: Essays on the History of the National Archives* (Washington, D.C.: National Archives and Records Administration, 1985).

[14]A rare exception of a first-rate study in archival history by a non-archivist is Donald R. McCoy, *The National Archives: America's Ministry of Documents 1934-1968* (Chapel Hill: University of North Carolina Press, 1978).   McCoy's effort is virtually alone as an archival history by an academic historian. In most histories of historical research and writing, even those confined to the twentieth century, the advent, development, and importance of the archival profession is ignored.

[15]For a survey of the nature of archival historical research, see Richard J. Cox, "American Archival History: Its Development, Needs, and Opportunities," *American Archivist* 46 (Winter 1983),   31-41. The archival study with the closest to a national perspective is Richard C. Berner, *Archival Theory and Practice in the United States: A Historical Analysis* (Seattle: University of Washington Press, 1983). Berner's book has been criticized by some of his colleagues for not being broad enough; see Ann Pederson, "Analysis or Prescription? Richard Berner on Archival Theory and Practice," *Midwestern Archivist* 9, no. 1 (1984),   35-43 and William L. Joyce's review in the *American Archivist* 47 (Summer 1984),   299-301.

to the archival community itself. Research into the history of the care of the documentary heritage can assist archivists in understanding themselves and their institutions, provide an outlet for research and writing, and satisfy a normal and healthy interest in their past. Archival history can also be a means to answer a number of fundamental questions about the nature and significance of recorded information, how that information actually relates to decision making and policy formulation, and, finally, how historical records are really perceived by society, past and present. The implications of this, of course, extend far beyond the archival profession. We already know a considerable amount about the history of historical research and writing and about the origins and development of libraries and that knowledge has helped us to understand much more about ourselves and our culture. Archival history holds the same promise; our quest to collect and preserve recorded remnants of the past extends back hundreds of years and seems imbedded, even if we do not completely understand why, in human nature.

Contemporary Issues. *Archival history is extremely important for addressing the contemporary concerns and issues of the archival profession.* Any profession, at a given moment, is usually beset with a number of important, sometimes crucial, issues and concerns. Archivists have been debating in the 1980s the certification of individual practitioners, graduate education, control over entry into the profession, their public image, and their effectiveness in promoting the importance of preserving the nation's documentary heritage. For most archivists these probably seem like new concerns or, in the case of certification, go back little further than the early or mid-1970s. Such present-mindedness is the natural consequence of the youthful nature of the archival community, leading sometimes to a distortion of reality. It is wiser to examine present issues and debates from the historical perspective to understand the origins of issues and to be able to distinguish between transient and more important ongoing concerns. Two examples will suffice to demonstrate this.

It has long been recognized that many of the problems of the National Archives came from its placement, in 1949, under the General Services Administration, a situation that archivists and their allies long worked to remedy.[16] Success in the

---

[16]See Walter Robertson, Jr., "NARS: The Politics of Placement," *American Archivist* 39 (October 1976), 485-92 and H.G. Jones, *The Records of a Nation: Their Management, Preservation, and Use* (New York: Atheneum, 1969), chapters 11 and 12.

National Archives independence movement in 1984 brought forth a number of self-congratulatory pieces that attempted to show archivists that they had the ability to achieve significant political success if only they organized better and tried harder.[17] As efforts to persuade archivists to become more effective advocates, these essays are quite appropriate, especially considering the more recent brouhaha over the appointment of a new Archivist of the United States.[18] But these essays can also be misleading because they give the impression that such forays into the political arena, especially on the national scene, are new. Their authors have forgotten that the movement to found the National Archives was the result of a long, sustained political campaign largely spearheaded by one individual, J. Franklin Jameson. Jameson's persistence and his ability to take advantage of opportunities and to unify disparate groups, including the members of the fledgling archival community, should be a historical lesson for contemporary archivists.[19] Archivists should also be concerned about why they have had such rare leadership in public advocacy.

The second example is that of archival education. The educational preparation of the archivist has been an increasing concern for this profession for a variety of reasons, primarily because archivists have never completely controlled their own educational standards. Most archivists have been educated in history or library schools with additional archival training in institutes, workshops, and other forms of continuing education or on-the-job-experience. Over the past decade, concerns about professional identity, stronger archival standards, and archival theory have brought education to the forefront of discussions and debates. This has especially occurred in the mid-1980s with the question of the certification of individual archivists, an issue that has prompted persuasive arguments from both

---

[17]Page Putnam Miller, "Archival Issues and Problems: The Central Role of Advocacy," *Public Historian* 8 (Summer 1986), 60-73 and Charlene N. Bickford, *The Coalition to Save Our Documentary Heritage: An Important Lesson in Archival Advocacy*, MARAC Occasional Publication, no. 3 (n.p.: Mid-Atlantic Regional Archives Conference, 1983).

[18]The nomination in 1986 of John Agresto, then acting Chair of the National Endowment for the Humanities, as Archivist of the United States brought strong reactions from the archival and historical communities. The Senate confirmation panel refused to vote on his nomination and the White House withdrew the nomination. Don W. Wilson was nominated and approved as Archivist the following year.

[19]Victor Gondos, Jr., *J. Franklin Jameson and the Birth of the National Archives 1906-1926* (Philadelphia: University of Pennsylvania Press, 1981).

supporters and detractors. One of the strongest arguments against certification has been that it would not be as effective as graduate education in strengthening the profession. The problem with this view, however, is that most archivists are still not even certain whether archivists should be trained in history or library schools.

Here a knowledge of archival history is instructive. Jacqueline Goggin has researched and written an interesting essay on the debate about and development of archival education between 1930 and 1960.[20] What should strike anyone familiar with the archival profession today is that the vexation about archival education has changed very little in substance. The basis of archivists' problems with education remains their concern about location rather than substance, although there are a few exceptions to this in the literature.[21] What archivists could learn from a greater knowledge about their history is that the political issue of educational placement is a short-sighted concern in comparison to determining what archivists should know. Because of the increasing interest in archival identity and the uncertain future of the archival profession in the Information Age,[22] archival education will remain a center stage issue, but (it is hoped) one that has different concerns than *who* provides the education.[23] The history of their education can aid archivists in keeping their present issues in perspective, possibly even assisting their speedier resolution.

[20]"That We Shall Truly Deserve the Title of 'Profession': The Training and Education of Archivists, 1930-1960," *American Archivist* 47 (Summer 1984), 243-54.

[21]Such as, Francis X. Blouin, Jr., "The Relevance of the Case Method to Archival Education and Training," *American Archivist* 41 (January 1978), 37-44 and Lawrence J. McCrank, "Prospects for Integrating Historical and Information Studies in Archival Education," *ibid.*, 42 (October 1979), 443-55.

[22]This is one of several issues that will probably dominate the attention of the archival profession over the next decade or so. For some writings on this, see John A. Vernon, "Technology's Effect on the Role of the Archivist," *Provenance* 3 (Spring 1985), 1-12; Richard Kesner, "Automated Information Management: Is There a Role for the Archivist in the Office of the Future?" *Archivaria* 19 (Winter 1984-85), 162-72; and F. Gerald Ham, "Archival Strategies for the Post-Custodial Era," *American Archivist* 44 (Summer 1981), 207-16.

[23]The main concerns may become the placement of full-time archival educators in the graduate schools, the development of a number of multi-course programs that satisfy the employment needs of the profession, and the accreditation of archival graduate education programs. See the two earlier chapters on this topic in this volume.

Self-evaluation and planning. *Archival history is an important tool to be used in institutional self-evaluation and planning, activities that have become very important to the archival profession.* Self-study and planning have become the hallmark of the archival community in the 1980s; one archivist has suggested that this time may become known as the "Age of Archival Analysis."[24] A historical perspective should be a valuable tool in such work. What was the original mission of the archival institution? What events or decisions most affected achievement of that mission? What have been the most important obstacles to that mission, and how were they resolved or why were they not resolved? What accounts for the archival institution's major successes? These are really historical issues and questions, and the value of such a perspective should be obvious in self-study and planning. Unfortunately, this has not been recognized as such by archivists, although other closely related professions have begun to realize the value of history for self-analysis and planning.[25] We need more examples of the advantages of the historical perspective in the archival profession.

A recent detailed analysis of historical records programs in Alabama is at least one such example. This study was part of a national effort by archivists and their colleagues to assess the condition of historical records and to plan for better management and care of them.[26] Guidance for this work came from the project's funding source, the National Historical Publications and Records Commission, and instructions were uniform for each state. These directions did not ask for any historical evaluation, but Alabama represented a unique case among the forty-two states that eventually undertook such assessment. Alabama was the site of the first state archives, the Alabama Department of Archives and History founded in

---

[24]Bruce W. Dearstyne, "Archives and Public History: Issues, Problems, and Prospects -- An Introduction," *Public Historian* 8 (Summer 1986), 7.

[25]Steven K. Hamp, "Subject over Object: Interpreting the Museum as Artifact," *Museum News* 63 (December 1984), 33-37.

[26]For various conclusions from these assessments, refer to Lisa B. Weber, ed., *Documenting America: Assessing the Condition of Historical Records in the States* ([Albany]: National Association of State Archives and Records Administrators in cooperation with the National Historical Publications and Records Commission, [1983]); Virginia Stewart, "Archives in the Midwest: Assessments and Prospects," *Midwestern Archivist* 10, no. 1 (1985), 5-16 and Edie Hedlin, "Archival Programs in the Southeast: A Preliminary Assessment," *Provenance* 2 (Spring 1984), 1-15.

1901, which had been the archival profession's leader for two decades before entering into a long and sustained decline. By the early 1980s the state was marked by lack of archival professionalism, by few historical records programs with any significant resources, and by a distinct unawareness of its own impoverishment. The NHPRC-funded assessment project was a logical time to ask questions about why this had happened and to determine the historical origins of the present crisis.

Examining the history of Alabama's archives revealed a number of important facts that would not have been understood except through historical study. For one, it taught that ideas thought to be *new*, such as a more prominent profile in the public arena of the value and utility of historical records, had been discussed and acted upon effectively eighty years earlier by individuals like Thomas Owen, the founder of the Alabama state archives. Moreover, although much attention focused upon the need for resources for archival administration, it was soon realized that resources were only one element required for effective archival administration. In Alabama one of the most significant problems had been erosion of leadership in the historical records community after Thomas Owen's death in 1920; Owen's successors were often more interested in matters other than the preservation and management of historical records, and limited resources were diverted among a variety of other activities. Finally, on a more positive note, it was reassuring to discover that an intensive study and issuance of a report could result in something of lasting value. Thomas Owen had evaluated the condition of historical records in 1898-1900, and the Alabama state archives was the result. Perhaps a reinvigorated Alabama historical records community could be the result of similar work in the mid-1980s.[27] What is telling about all of this is that the first review of this report by an archivist suggested that too much time had been spent on the historical study.[28] The archival profession once again demonstrated its lack of appreciation for its own history.

Case studies. *Archival history could be used to develop a body of case studies that would facilitate a better understanding of the life cycle of cultural institutions such as archives.* Archivists who have written about the history of specific

---

[27]*Assessing Alabama's Archives: A Plan for the Preservation of the State's Historical Records* (Montgomery: Alabama Historical Records Advisory Board, 1985) and Richard J. Cox, "Alabama's Archival Heritage, 1850-1985," *Alabama Review* 40 (October 1987), 284-307.

[28]Anne R. Kenney's review in *The Public Historian* 8 (Summer 1986), 106.

archival institutions have tended to treat them in virtual isolation, ignoring how they compare to repositories in other states or how they function in their own cultural milieu. There has also been little effort to use sociological or other organizational models to understand how or why these programs come to be, flourish, change, or die. This is all the more amazing given the vast differences that exist between similar archival institutions in the various states and regions in this country. For example, why is it that some state archives have only one or two staff members while others have over one hundred? Why is it that it took over seventy years for every state to found a state archives? How do we account for the immense differences in the governmental location of these programs when all possess closely related missions?[29] Despite the existence of a sizable number of essays on the development of archival programs, there are none that attempt to compare or understand their differences.

There have been no efforts to review the existing literature on archival programs to determine if there are any patterns or models of development. This is unfortunate. Such a study could tell much about where a particular archival institution is in its development and help it in ascertaining what it needs to maintain or improve its condition. For example, in looking at the institutions that make up the archival profession, it is not difficult to find examples of programs that were established, flourished, moved to a position of professional leadership, and then declined. It is also not especially difficult to find cases of programs that, after a period of decline, were turned around and became stronger than ever before.[30] There is a need to determine patterns of change and why such changes occur, making it possible to detect signs of decline and to take corrective measures. In this, we can turn for inspiration to the archivist's newest colleagues, the public historian, especially those consulting in the business world. Using concepts such as "corporate culture," and examining that culture over time, these individuals are trying to understand why companies succeed or fail and what corrective actions can be taken to prevent

---

[29]Ernst Posner, *American State Archives* (Chicago: University of Chicago Press, 1964) remains the major reference on the nature of these institutions.

[30]Edie Hedlin, "*Chinatown* Revisited: The Status and Prospects of Government Records in America," *Public Historian* 8 (Summer 1986), 56-59.

failure.[31]   Archivists could profitably take the same route and enrich their own growing interest in the management of their institutions.

Graduate studies. *Archival history is an excellent means of introduction for graduate students preparing to be archivists.* Until recently, students in archival education programs were not encouraged to write theses or dissertations on archival subjects.   Whether in history or library science graduate programs, students preparing to be archivists have completed little research on archival topics. The recent strengthening of graduate archival education has, however, brought hope for change. Until recently, the most common academic preparation for archivists was a three course program consisting of an introductory course, an internship, and an advanced course, although a large portion of archivists are still trained by a combination of courses, practical workshops and institutes, and on-the-job experience.   Stronger multicourse (beyond three courses) educational programs are now being established, and these generally include more encouragement of research on archival subjects. The description of the Western Washington University's history master's degrees with a concentration in archives and records management includes an incentive for students to prepare theses on "topics involving the history of archives administration and records management, or an emerging problem in these disciplines. . . ."[32] Most promising in this regard are the theses being completed at the youthful Master of Archival Studies Program at the University of British Columbia, some of which have already turned up in the published literature.[33] It is precisely for this reason that the most recent SAA guidelines on graduate education include a strong statement promoting archival research.[34]

There may be no better introduction to the archival profession for students than to have them investigate present archival issues from the historical perspective. Tackling issues in education, appraisal, arrangement and description, and

---

[31]Charles Dellheim, "Business in Time: The Historian and Corporate Culture," *Public Historian* 8 (Spring 1986), 9-22.

[32]Quotation from brochure describing the program.

[33]Terry Eastwood, "Abstracts of Theses in Archival Studies at the University of British Columbia," *Archivaria* 21 (Winter 1985-86), 269-74.

[34]"Society of American Archivists Guidelines for Graduate Archival Education Programs," *American Archivist* 51 (Summer 1988), 387.

preservation and examining them over time will provide students not only with a better understanding of present concerns and problems but also with an introduction to the origins and past practices of the archival community.

This is extremely helpful for several reasons. First, the archival profession is still young enough that many of the ideas and principles of archival practice written about a quarter or even a half-century ago are still adhered to in some degree.[35] Second, since the literature on archival history is relatively sparse, graduate students can make unique contributions to the archival writings and enrich the profession's comprehension of its origins and nature. It is not difficult to find neglected areas for students to investigate.[36] Third, students who study historical aspects of the archival profession may be able to determine needs in current archival practice and take up those areas for further work and study. It is not inconceivable that a student might turn - and profitably so - from historical analysis of a particular archival principle to examination of the theory underlying that principle. The historical study of archival practice might help to identify weaknesses in that practice by engaging the student's interest in it beyond the historical perspective.

The nature of records. *Archival history is a gateway through which to examine some fundamental questions about the nature of records and information.* Perhaps the most important essay on an archival topic in the 1980s was Frank

[35]For example, the concept of record group has dominated thinking on archival arrangement and description for nearly forty years, although it is now beginning to be challenged as a result of the increased use of automation in records creation. Until the mid-1980s, a historical review of the origins and development of the record group idea would have also been an introduction to the accepted principles of archival arrangement and description.

[36]A glance at *Planning for the Archival Profession: A Report of the SAA Task Force on Goals and Priorities* (Chicago: Society of American Archivists, 1986) will reveal a host of subjects and issues that have been barely touched by historical analysis. A more specific example is Ernst Posner's plea, made over twenty years ago, for historical research on state archives: "To write a full history of the development of American state archives would require many and detailed preliminary studies. The record-making and record-keeping practices of colonial America should be investigated, with particular attention to their relationship to the practices of the respective mother countries; so should the practices of the states during the nineteenth and twentieth centuries. We also need histories of individual archival agencies, their struggles, and their achievements" (*American State Archives*, 7). Little has been accomplished, however, relative to Posner's call.

G. Burke's brief article on the need for a stronger archival theory. Burke not only lamented that archivists had most often been concerned with "what" and "how" and not "why," but suggested an agenda for studying the nature of records and record-keeping, the value and use of information in decision making, and other such "why" issues.[37] Burke's essay has been answered in two ways. Some respondents have dealt with the broader issue of the nature and role of theory in the archival profession.[38] Others have grappled with specific elements of Burke's research agenda, most notably the matter of whether records adequately reflect decision making, policy making, and actual activities and events.[39] It is precisely in the latter area that archival history again offers some value. Why can't analyses of archival institutions help archivists gain a better conception of the general role of records and information in documenting actual events and in assisting decision making and policy setting?

The historical study of archival institutions can help archivists understand how decisions have been made, whether correctly or not, and how effectively all of this has been captured in the records. Archival repositories reflect the nature and characteristics of modern institutions. If archivists used their own programs as laboratories they might learn how to strengthen these programs and gain insights that would help archivists work with other professions and records-creating entities. At the least, archivists would come to grips with the serious problem of their own inadequately documented profession, since many archival institutions care for their own records as a secondary responsibility.[40] Even the archival

---

[37]"The Future Course of Archival Theory in the United States," *American Archivist* 44 (Winter 1981), 40-46.

[38]Lester J. Cappon, "What, Then, Is There to Theorize About?" *American Archivist* 45 (Winter 1982), 19-25; Gregg D. Kimball, "The Burke-Cappon Debate: Some Further Criticisms and Considerations for Archival Theory," *ibid.* 48 (Fall 1985), 369-76.

[39]Michael A. Lutzker, "Max Weber and the Analysis of Modern Bureaucratic Organizations: Notes Toward a Theory of Appraisal," *American Archivist* 45 (Spring 1982), 119-30; JoAnne Yates, "Internal Communication Systems in American Business Structures: A Framework to Aid Appraisal," *ibid.* 48 (Spring 1985), 141-58.

[40]This is an impressionistic conclusion based on experiences in institutions that I have worked in and conversations with other archivists. The scantiness of writing on archival history by outsiders suggests that this might indeed be the case.

community's main professional organization, SAA, cares for its historical records a bit too informally, relying on the voluntary efforts of that organization's officers and other leaders.[41] An effort by a staff member to chronicle the development of the most recently created state archives, New York, even caused him to worry that critical events of only ten years before had been lost because of inadequate documentation.[42]

The archival profession should better care for its own records and heritage if it is really committed to preserving the historical documents of other professions and occupations. There is little question about the archival community's interest in such work with many articles about its importance.[43] But the archival profession will weaken its aim of helping other disciplines if it has not learned how to take care of its own records or failed to set an adequate example. At the least, success in documenting their own profession will help archivists' larger mission to document society. At the worst, archivists appear hypocritical if they do not care for their own records.

[41]SAA's executive office files have been formally appraised and scheduled and are regularly transferred to the SAA's official archives at the University of Wisconsin-Madison. However, the papers of individuals or the records of committees are solicited informally, and there is no oral history program for prominent leaders of the profession. Some of these issues are now being discussed by the recently-formed Archival History Round Table.

[42]Bruce Dearstyne, in reviewing the formation of the New York State Archives in the 1970s, wrote that "there is no history of that program. No one on the State Archives staff has taken an interest in recovering and analyzing that history. Many of the records that would be needed to reconstruct program development, or even key events, are lost or their location is unknown. Moreover, even a study of the files for the period since 1975 -- the year the first State Archivist was hired -- would not reveal the dynamics of program development, the ways in which the program found support, and how it actually developed. If that history is to be recovered at all, it would have to be recovered by interviewing the chief actors.... Even then, it would be difficult to construct an accurate picture, or to draw clear lessons about the development of the program that would really be useful in understanding its present-day makeup and its likely course for the future." From "Archives in the Empire State: A Political History," an unpublished paper presented at the Fall 1983 meeting of the Mid-Atlantic Regional Archives Conference.

[43]The most recent and most important effort has been on behalf of the records of science and technology. See Clark A. Elliott, ed., *Understanding Progress as Process: Documentation of the History of Post-War Science and Technology in the United States* (Chicago: Society of American Archivists, 1983); Joan K. Haas, Helen Willa Samuels, and Barbara Trippel Simmons, *Appraising the Records of Modern Science and Technology: A Guide* (Cambridge: Massachusetts Institute of Technology, 1985).

Scholarly interests. *Finally, archival history can provide an outlet for the scholarly interests of individual archivists.* Many archivists have an interest in historical research and writing. Although the archival code of ethics dissuades archivists from using their own collections for personal research,[44] a considerable number of archivists maintain active scholarly careers in other specializations and do research in other repository holdings. There is no question that such activity can benefit individual archivists and the archival profession. Research skills are kept sharp, scholarly qualifications and credibility are maintained, and valuable knowledge for administering historical records holdings is gained. The real issue is, however, whether such peripheral scholarly activity is more a reflection of an inadequately developed professional archival self-image or a misuse of already severely limited time for research and writing.[45] Some archivists seem to have discovered the means to do both, but the truth is that too few archivists write about archival administration, and the archival profession has been the poorer for it.[46]

What does archival history really offer for the archivist as scholar? Thirty years ago archival scholarship was largely viewed as the production of finding aids; it was a time when archivists were generally considered as servants or, more charitably, assistants to the academic historian.[47] The times have changed. More archivists see themselves as constituting an independent profession. Alliances or partnerships with historians, librarians, or other colleagues are necessary, but the

[44]"Commentary on Code of Ethics," SAA *Newsletter*, July 1979, 14.

[45]There have been many essays by archivists attesting to the value of such historical research. The most recent and blunt argument about this is David Mycue, "The Archivist as Scholar: A Case for Research by Archivists," *Georgia Archive* 7 (Fall 1979), 10-16. The major weakness with Mycue's essay, and with others of this ilk, is that its main concern seems to be establishing archivists back within the historical profession, not encouraging them to write about archival topics and their own profession. A thorough knowledge of historical methodology and historical research trends is, of course, valuable to the archivist, but *more* valuable may be an understanding of the archival profession, its theoretical principles, and its practices.

[46]See the essay on archival research and writing in this volume.

[47]Lester J. Cappon, "Tardy Scholars Among the Archivists," *American Archivist* 21 (January 1958), 3-16.

stress is on the equality of roles.[48] Archival history provides an
opportunity for serious research, requiring the standard array
of historical sources and the best skills in interpretation and
writing. The various values of archival history -- illuminating
contemporary concerns and issues, assisting institutional self-
evaluation and planning, helping understand the development
and decline of cultural institutions, introducing graduate
students to the nature of archival administration, and clarifying
the nature of records and information -- can only be achieved
if this subject is treated seriously and respectfully by archivists
and other scholars such as historians and librarians.

*Making Archival History Relevant to the Archival Profession
and to Others*

If the values of archival history can be agreed upon by the
archival profession and others, it is important to determine how
to promote the study, discussion, and publication of archival
history. The time seems ripe for exploring the archivist's past.
The archival profession is maturing, entering the period of its
greatest challenge (whether the archival community has any
future in the Information Age), and being strengthened by the
acceptance of more complex and specific educational standards.
Archival history, as a topic of inquiry and the focus of some
energy, needs to be a part of the archival profession's continued
growth. What follows are some recommendations to support
archival history as a legitimate professional pursuit.

*There needs to be a mechanism that coordinates and
promotes the study of archival history.* Fortunately, the
prospects for this already appear to be excellent. In late 1985
SAA's governing body adopted guidelines for the formation of
special interest groups or round tables,[49] and nearly a dozen
were in motion by late 1986, including one for archival history.
At the Archival History Round Table's inaugural meeting in
August 1986, nearly forty individuals launched a newsletter,
and began to discuss various projects such as a bibliography of

---

[48]Cox, "Archivists and Public Historians," is one example of this kind
of thinking. That a truly separate archival profession is emerging is
evident by essays that argue for the opposite, such as its subservience to
academic history; George Bolotenko, "Archivists and Historians: Keepers of
the Well," *Archivaria* 16 (Summer 1983), 5-25.

[49]"Roundtables are informal groups of SAA members formed to promote
discussion and communication, exchange information or engage in similar
activities centered around an archival topic"; SAA *Newsletter*, January 1986,
3.

studies and a collection of readings.

An unexpected early benefit of the formation of the Archival History Round Table was the opening of communications with allied colleagues. The chair of ALA's Library History Round Table, who is also an active member of SAA, was in attendance and spoke about the similarities between the two professions and the interest in and values of their respective histories. A closer relationship between the two disciplines in the study of their pasts could provide an interesting opportunity for comparison, publication, and dialogue and aid the library profession in its own historical work. Although there is an increasing quantity of literature on library history, little has been written about the identification and management of library records having historical value.[50] At the same meeting of the Archival History Round Table, the executive director of the International Council on Archives was present and discussed the need for Americans better to understand their European heritage and the increasing interest by Europeans in their own archival history. The SAA Archival History Round Table could promote work on the European origins of American archives and comparisons between the development of archives in various countries; much could be learned about how and why historical records are cared for or neglected.[51]

Graduate archival education must continue to be strengthened and there must be increased opportunities for research. For most professions, certainly for those in the humanities, strong educational programs are a primary source for research and development. Full-time academics have more time to think, do research, and write than do practicing archivists. Graduate students are obligated to spend significant portions of their time doing original research in their chosen field. For the archival profession, this appears to be the future for its educational programs and standards, and archival history, for all the reasons already mentioned, should be an excellent subject for such study. A basic part of graduate archival education should be a separate course on archival history that focuses on the development of archives in the United States and that is attentive to European origins and the

---

[50]Richard J. Cox and Anne S.K. Turkos, "Establishing Public Library Archives," *Journal of Library History* 21 (Summer 1986), 574-84.

[51]That is, there has been no connection between the two although there exist excellent separate historical studies of both European and American archives. For the variety of such studies, refer to Frank B. Evans, comp., *The History of Archives Administration: A Select Bibliography* (Paris: UNESCO, 1979).

parallel or divergent development of archives in other countries.

A stronger graduate education is not enough, however. The archival profession requires opportunities, outside of the academy, for research and development. At present, the profession has only one such opportunity. The Bentley Historical Library of the University of Michigan has sponsored since 1983 -- with the aid of funding from the National Endowment for the Humanities, the Andrew W. Mellon Foundation, and other foundations -- a summer fellowship program for individuals to examine the area of documenting modern society. This single program has been the source of some of the most original and provocative archival thinking and writing in the past few years.[52] The archival community needs more individual fellowship opportunities that enable archivists, historians, librarians, and others to study archival history seriously and to test some of the values that this essay has described (and to discover new ones!).

Finally, the SAA needs to strengthen the institutional self-evaluation program that it started in the late 1970s and to expand it to include historical analysis as a self-study tool. Archivists have been extremely concerned, especially in recent years, with the quality of the nation's archival repositories. The SAA established in 1977 an ad hoc committee "to explore the related questions of establishing standards for archives and establishing an accreditation program for archival institutions." That committee became, in 1980, the Task Force on Institutional Evaluation that two years later issued a brief publication entitled *Evaluation of Archival Institutions: Services, Principles, and Guide to Self-Study* and is now doing some excellent work on the census of archival institutions.[53] Although the original movement toward institutional accreditation seems in limbo, and there is little evidence that more than a few archival repositories ever seriously used the self-evaluation guide or that it has had a very noticeable impact on the archival profession, the *Evaluation of Archival Institutions* is an excellent publication that should be resurrected to play an important role in the profession. One

---

[52]For a sample of these writings, see the Spring 1985 issue of the *American Archivist* on appraisal.

[53](Chicago: Society of American Archivists, 1982); Paul Conway, "Perspectives on Archival Resources: The 1985 Census of Archival Institutions," *American Archivist* 50 (Spring 1987), 174-91. The task force has now become a standing committee. The last act of the Task Force was issuance of Paul H. McCarthy, ed., *Archives Assessment and Planning Workbook* (Chicago: SAA, 1989).

of the major recommendations by the SAA Task Force on Goals and Priorities a few years after this publication was for a greater effort to "develop and adopt standards for archival programs";[54] the *Evaluation of Archival Institutions* and other tools seem to be an excellent base for pursuing that goal.

Unfortunately, one of the main weaknesses of the institutional self-study guide is its distinct lack of historical perspective. Key individuals of historical records repositories and archival institutions, who are the ones likely to use the self-study guide, are directed by it to examine many basic areas of their programs. The guide's self-study questions and its content never direct anyone to examine the repository from a fuller historical perspective. The evaluation, however helpful it may be, is a static snapshot of the archival program's present condition. How can such an institution be understood without a greater understanding of how it reached its current form and what factors have contributed to its successes and failures? A few good questions, placed at several crucial points in the self-study guide, could rectify this problem and, at the same time, help to raise the archival profession's awareness about its own important past. Published reports about the self-study process that utilizes or tests the values of archival history would also be helpful.[55]

Conclusion

The archival profession will not fail in its mission to identify, preserve, and encourage the use of records of enduring value if it does not develop a greater sense or knowledge of its own past. However, a better developed archival history can both enrich and strengthen the archival profession in its quest to accomplish its mission. Archivists are in the business of preserving historical records because these records are valuable to society. The records of their own profession and its precursors are no less significant than the records of other professions. A knowledge of archival history ought to be an essential part of any archivist's training and work. Acceptance of the values of archival history is the sign of a more mature, vital, and healthy archival profession.

---

[54]*Planning for the Archival Profession*, 33.

[55]As of yet not a single evaluation of the process of self-study has appeared in the archival literature. Such studies would do much to assist the archival profession to strengthen its own work and its repositories. Inherent in the nature of self-study is a stronger sense of standards for guiding and regulating the profession in its quest to accomplish its mission.

NINE   **ARCHIVISTS AND PUBLIC HISTORIANS IN THE UNITED STATES**[1]

Introduction

Archivists and public historians face similar challenges, and their fields share common origins. Both disciplines are evolving and, by most standards, neither yet constitutes a profession.[2] Public history, little more than a decade old, was born primarily because of declining employment options for academic historians, and public historians still lack a consensus about their own mission. Though archivists have a much better developed professional identity (the Society of American Archivists celebrated its golden anniversary in 1986), they do not adequately control entry into their field, lack well-defined educational standards, and are weak in theory supporting their work. They also seem confused about their own identity. Are they historians, public historians, librarians, information specialists, or archivists pure and simple? Given their similar problems, archivists and public historians are not working together as closely as they should. This essay describes the possible relationship, and the benefits, of a stronger working accord between archivists and public historians.

It is not surprising that archivists and public historians are often wary or uncertain of each others' intentions. Given their common origins and related missions, however, the two groups can meet some of their own professional goals by focusing upon mutual concerns. Archivists and public historians should jointly work for the identification, preservation, and management of America's documentary heritage, for the promotion of the practical value of historical knowledge to address contemporary social issues and problems, and for resolution of similar professional concerns such as the adequacy of their educational preparation and training. This essay discusses several matters of interest shared by the two fields and should prompt further dialogue, opening avenues leading to cooperation and strengthening the work of both disciplines.

[1]This essay was originally published in the *Public Historian* 8 (Summer 1986), 25-41.

[2]Although I will explain this in more detail below, my full ideas on this topic are found in the second essay in this volume, "Professionalism and Archivists in the United States."

The Current Relationship Between Archivists and Public Historians

The logical place to begin a discussion about the relationship between archivists and public historians is with their common ancestry as professional historians. Archivists emerged as a distinct element in the historical community in the early twentieth century, gained their own identity with the founding of the Society of American Archivists and the National Archives in the 1930s, and started on their way to becoming an independent profession. Chronicling this history is an extensive, but uneven, series of articles and books.[3] Even with this literature it is difficult to compare accurately and fully the formation and growth of public history with the older archival profession. Public history is so recent as to have no real literature charting its development. Public history's adherents have tried to create an almost mythological past for it, christening it a "new-old focus in history"[4] and tracing its origins to the birth of state historical societies and state history programs in the late nineteenth century.[5] This analysis fails to provide an adequate perspective for serious comparison between public historians and archivists. The chief difference seems to be that employment of professional historians was the catalyst for public history, whereas the archival discipline developed from a combination of influences that supported the preservation and management of historical records. Furthermore, nearly three quarters of a century separates the founding of the two disciplines. These historical variations account for some of the perceptions that archivists and public historians hold about each other today.

Most public historians seem to believe they have co-opted archives administration into their own field. In the first issue of *The Public Historian*, G. Wesley Johnson, Jr. said that public history "stands as a convenient way of bringing together a number of endeavors which are not now present in the standard historical curriculum, but which are essential for relating historical skills to the larger society." This explanation

---

[3]See my "American Archival History: Its Development, Needs, and Opportunities," *American Archivist* 46 (Winter 1983), 31-41.

[4]Wesley Johnson, Peter N. Stearns, and Joel A. Tarr, "Public History: A New Area of Teaching, Research, and Employment," *American Historical Association Newsletter* 18 (March 1980), 8.

[5]"First National Symposium on Public History: A Report," *Public Historian* 2 (Fall 1979), 60-61.

of public history included archives and records management as one of its eight basic "sectors."[6] Johnson's definition has remained a prevalent one for public history. In 1980, in a comprehensive description of this field, *The Public Historian* published a review of university and college courses on public history, the majority either including an archives component or else being an archives program reclassified as public history.[7] Such descriptions of public history curriculum and the purposes of training have remained commonplace over the past decade.

Public historians see themselves as bridging across disciplines, and stress their ability to train individuals for archives administration. One public historian has suggested, for example, that the identity of professors of applied history rests in their main fields, whether that be in "historical societies, archives, museums, editing projects, or businesses, or more generally, as 'popularizers' of historical knowledge and analysis for the broadest possible nonprofessional audience."[8] Another public historian has argued that the distinguishing characteristics of his colleagues are their products; instead of books and articles they produce museum exhibit research projects, museum catalogs, historical editing projects, bibliographies, and historical records management plans.[9]

The problem with such a broad definition of the public history field is that it has arisen, almost arrogantly, with little regard for or understanding of many of the professions it presumes to include within its own parameters. Most revealing of this is the major publication of the National Council on Public History, *The Craft of Public History*, a bibliography that identifies the content of public history with chapters on archives, records management, and information management; genealogy and family history; historical editing; historical resource management; library science; oral history; and so

---

[6]Editor's preface, *Public Historian* 1 (Fall 1978), 6-7.

[7]Of thirty-seven graduate programs, twenty-two either included archives administration or were archival education specializations; on the undergraduate level, the tally was four of ten. "Public History in the Academy: An Overview of University and College Offerings," *Public Historian* 2 (Fall 1979), 84-116.

[8]Kendrick A. Clements, "Promotion and Tenure Criteria for Faculty in Applied History," *Public Historian* 6 (Spring 1984), 57.

[9]Brit Allan Storey, "Who and What are Public Historians?" *OAH Newsletter* 12 (May 1984), 22-23.

forth.[10]   An astute reviewer of *The Craft of Public History*
perceived that the book "accurately mirrors the difficulties
public historians have defining and distinguishing their field."
David E. Kyvig went on to say that the "chapters on archival
administration and library science . . . provide excellent
introductions to the technical literature and current debates in
these fields.   Yet while the importance of each field to
historians is unquestionable, the practitioners of each regard
theirs as a distinct profession with responsibilities, training,
and credentialing which distinguish it from history."[11]   Public
historians have formed their discipline with little effort to seek
cooperation from affected professionals like archives.[12]

Why have public historians so firmly grasped these other
disciplines? There is much evidence that a major stimulant for
public history was the 1970s job crisis of academic historians;
public history "has strongly emerged organized around
employment instead of audience."[13]   As a result, its proponents
naturally gravitated to other disciplines like the archival
community (and the larger state and local history movement)
with their long tradition of rewarding employment.   Such a
development is certainly not surprising since there had been a
steady succession of academic historians, like Herbert Baxter
Adams in the 1880s, promoting similar potential employment
since the advent of professional history.[14]   Archivists and the
state and local history community have been viewed primarily
as inviting sources of employment.   The mission of public
history has remained loosely specified to take advantage of
such opportunities. This also explains why the main focus and
definition of the public history movement has remained within

[10]David F. Trask and Robert W. Pomeroy, III, eds., *The Craft of Public History: An Annotated Select Bibliography* (Westport, Connecticut: Greenwood Press, 1983).

[11]*Public Historian* 6 (Summer 1984), 98-99.

[12]I do not mean to imply that practicing archivists have not been consulted or, in many cases, employed to teach within the applied history programs.   However, there seems to have been little serious discussion between the various professional associations about standards and principles.

[13]Bruce Fraser, "A Methodology Based on Limits: The State Humanities Councils and Public History," *Newsletter of the National Council on Public History* 2 (Summer/Fall 1984), 3.

[14]W. Stull Holt, ed., *Historical Scholarship in the United States, 1876-1901: As Revealed in the Correspondence of Herbert B. Adams* (Baltimore: Johns Hopkins Press, 1938), 55.

the academy, retarding the drafting of a comprehensive mission statement for public history. The National Council on Public History, founded in 1979 and the professional hub of public history, continues to struggle to prescribe its mission, membership, and relationship to other organizations.[15]

Considering the rapid emergence of public history and its implications for archivists, surprisingly little has been written by archivists about public history. Even this sparse literature, however, reveals general attitudes. Over the past decade only one essay on public history has appeared in the *American Archivist*, the primary journal of the archives field. David A. Clary termed public history the latest "fad" of the academic historian, a field invented to resist the "declining fortunes of academe," and a "cynical effort to inflate enrollments by enticing students with vague promises of immediate and profitable employment after graduation."[16] Three archivists have also written on this topic. In 1982 Edward Weldon penned an essay that basically described the work and world of the archivist, built around a thesis that "public historians and archivists share a common asset and a common problem: wide public interest in their efforts and limited institutional support." Despite its title, however, the article did not deeply explore the nature of the relationship between public historians and archivists.[17] A year later I wrote a brief paper that attempted to argue how the public history movement could strengthen the labor of archivists.[18] In the most important writing to date, archivist and librarian Lawrence J. McCrank has analyzed in significant detail the connection between public history and the information professions (librarianship, records management, archives administration, and information systems management), especially examining the numerous problems regarding their education and credentials. McCrank concluded that the "public history movement is potentially a healing influence" in archivists' separation from professional history,

[15]"Long-Range Planning Committee Report: A Summary," *Newsletter of the National Council on Public History* 5 (Spring-Summer 1985), 1-4.

[16]"Trouble is My Business: A Private View of 'Public' History," *American Archivist* 44 (Spring 1981), 105-12.

[17]"Archives and the Practice of Public History," *Public Historian* 4 (Summer 1982), 49-58.

[18]"Archivists and Public History," *Institute News: Newsletter of the North Carolina Institute of Applied History* 3 (March 1984), 3-6.

seeing this division as largely the result of archivists' increasing interest in their own professionalism.[19]

These writings reflect some of the various opinions of archivists about public history. Archivists have not openly embraced public history, although some have recognized the common bonds and potential benefits of a stronger relationship between the two fields. At present many archivists resent public historians because of their self-proclaimed expertise in areas where archivists have already worked for a long time. This is the reason why public history sessions at professional archival meetings sometimes have descriptions that sound like panel discussions on preventive medicine: "Public history, an academic discipline that prepares history and library science graduate students for non-teaching careers, emerged ten years ago. While it offers the archives profession challenges and opportunities, it also may create problems. This session will examine public history and its impact on archivists and archives programs."[20]

Archivists have also within the past few years become more conscious of their own sense of professionalism, sought a stronger identity and role separate from historians, librarians, and records managers, and shown an increasing concern with an information society driven by technology that seems to encourage the destruction, in time, of all information, historical or otherwise.[21] Part of this concern derives from recent self-assessments that reveal that archivists' ability to identify, preserve, and manage America's archival records is severely hampered by poor image, lack of resources, and deficient authority in a society that is becoming more complex and difficult to document.[22] Many archivists conclude that they

[19]"Public Historians in the Information Professions: Problems in Education and Credentials," *Public Historian* 7 (Summer 1985), 7-22.

[20]Session entitled "Public History: What Archivists Should Know About It," Midwest Archives Conference, October 4, 1985.

[21]The literature on this is extensive, but for excellent essays on opposite sides of the issue see Hugh Taylor, "Information Ecology and the Archives of the 1980s," *Archivaria* 18 (Summer 1984), 25-37 and Terry Cook, "From Information to Knowledge: An Intellectual Paradigm for Archives," *ibid.* 19 (Winter 1984/85), 28-49.

[22]The literature on this is also ample. For examples, refer to the following: David B. Gracy II, "What's Your Totem? Archival Images in the Public Mind," *Midwestern Archivist* 48 (Winter 1985), 12-21; Peter J. Wosh, "Creating a SemiProfessional Profession: Archivists View Themselves," *Georgia Archive* 10 (Fall 1982), 1-13; and Bruce W. Dearstyne, "The Records Wasteland," *History News* 40 (June 1985), 18-22.

need a more clearly focused identity and mission and incorrectly tend to see public history as only a competitor for already limited resources needed to manage America's documentary heritage.

Despite suspicion about motives, negative experiences, and extant obstacles, the relationship between archivists and public historians needs to improve to take advantage of areas where cooperation can strengthen both disciplines. Identifying these potential nexuses will overcome some of the suspicions and competition between archivists and public historians. Public historians must realize the need to cooperate with archivists in the development of their mission and of a definition of the nature of their field. Archivists must acknowledge that lack of standards in key areas of their profession has encouraged public historians to define their field broadly and that, in any case, the care of America's documentary heritage is a task that requires assistance from other groups like public historians. Reciprocity is required from both disciplines, and both have much to gain by it.

Promoting the Value of Archives

The success of any occupation's mission is dependent upon the public's sanction of its work. Such an endorsement requires the occupation to effectively communicate to the public the content of its mission and to convince the public that the occupation's mission is important or even essential to society.[23]

There is little doubt that archivists have a specific and fairly well-defined mission, the identification, preservation, and use of America's historical records.[24] Despite the vast array of historical societies, libraries, and archival repositories involved in the care of our documentary heritage, however, it is doubtful whether society really understands the value of archives. Indeed, the public's interest in the past may be superficial and more prone towards a mythical history than toward a real

[23]Community sanction of an occupation is considered important by sociologists whether they adhere to a theory that emphasizes the traits of the ideal profession or one that stresses an occupation's movement toward professionalization. For a sampling of the extensive literature on professions, refer to the second essay in this volume.

[24]The SAA Goals and Priorities Task Force adopted this as the profession's mission. For the importance of the group's work and its report, see the essay in this volume on this topic.

understanding of the implications of the past.[25] The lack of fiscal and other support for America's archives suggests that the public really has little comprehension of their value. Archivists have contributed to the problem by too long assuming that what they do is socially significant and failing to see the need to promote greater public understanding of why historical records are important.

Adding to this problem has been the archival community's extremely close relationship to academic historians.[26] Until the past decade or so, many archivists assumed that they were actually historians and that the primary value of their records was for "serious" historical research. As the products of professional history became less accessible to the general public, partly evident in the increasing number of essays by historians struggling with their own relevancy,[27] the public mission of the archivist also suffered. A recent study of the perceptions of administrators who allocate resources for archival programs reveals the consequence of these problems. Archives are given low priority in their organizations because they "hark to the past . . . compared to more current, ongoing, aggressive demands on the budget." Archivists seem "most vital to academic institutions which may be the poorest." Archivists are described as "scholarly" and "apt to be introverted, bookworms, quiet and mousey."[28] As long as such perceptions prevail, there is little hope for the success of the archival mission.

[25]In this I think of, for example, Henry Ford's sentimental and mythical view of the American past, best typified in his enduringly popular Greenfield Village. For an account of its creation see Geoffrey C. Upward, *A Home for Our Heritage: The Building of Greenfield Village and Henry Ford Museum, 1929-1979* (Dearborn, Michigan: Henry Ford Museum Press, 1979).

[26]Mattie U. Russell, "The Influence of Historians on the Archival Profession in the United States," *American Archivist* 46 (Summer 1983), 277-85.

[27]Such as Joan Hoff Wilson, "Is the Historical Profession an 'Endangered Species?'" *Public Historian* 2 (Winter 1980), 4-21. The inaccessibility of scholarly history was primarily caused by the heavy influx of social science and other "scientific" ideas and techniques, making the product of historical research indecipherable to the public; see, for one example of such complaints, Jacques Barzun, *Clio and the Doctors: Psycho-History, Quanto-History & History* (Chicago: University of Chicago Press, 1974).

[28]These quotations are from a report commissioned by the SAA and summarized in the SAA *Newsletter*, August 1985, 5-7.

Archivists have, however, begun to make progress in helping the public understand more fully the value of preserving and using archival materials. The foundation of this progress was laid in the early 1970s with the reorganization of the Society of American Archivists as a much stronger professional association with permanent staff, a commitment to publish basic archival literature, and a determination to play a public advocacy role.[29] During the past few years the Society has supported two extremely important task forces stressing a stronger message to the American people about the importance of historical records. The Goals and Priorities Task Force not only composed a precise set of recommendations for the future success of the archival mission but emphasized the significance of carrying that mission to the public.[30] The Archives and Society Task Force prepared a concise statement about the values of historical records, including research on contemporary problems and issues, administrative continuity, legal documentation, historical research, and education and enrichment.[31] David Gracy, in his 1984 Presidential address to the Society of American Archivists, summarized this new interest among archivists by noting that "archival work no longer is archival work . . . . To increase our service to society, indeed, just to maintain it - just to survive in the highly competitive, fast-changing world of our times - we spend increasing portions of our day reminding our various publics how archival endeavor contributes to their lives."[32] Such efforts have already led to significant results in a few states.[33] Most archivists realize this work has just begun and needs to continue and expand.

[29]Philip Mason, "Archives in the Seventies: Promise and Fulfillment," *American Archivist* 44 (Summer 1981), 199-206. Equally as important has been the role of the National Historical Publications and Records Commission; see F. Gerald Ham, "NHPRC's Records Program and the Development of Statewide Archival Planning," *ibid.* 43 (Winter 1980), 33-42.

[30]For further description of the GAP Task Force and its successor, the Committee on Goals and Priorities, see F. Gerald Ham, "Planning for the Archival Profession," *American Archivist* 48 (Winter 1985), 26-30 and the essay in this volume.

[31]"Archives: What They Are, Why They Matter," Society of American Archivists *Newsletter*, May 1984, 6-7.

[32]"Our Future is Now," 17.

[33]Larry J. Hackman, "From Assessment to Action: Toward a Usable Past in the Empire State," *Public Historian* 7 (Summer 1985), 23-34.

What role should public historians have in all of this? First, since they are users of archival records, they should be vitally interested in archival management and care. Philip Cantelon even predicts that "public historians will become in the next decade the chief users of our national records,"[34] giving then additional incentive to support the preservation of American archives. One historian, who has worked closely with both archivists and records creators, believes the divisions within the community interested in the preservation of historical sources has seriously hampered the chances of gaining "national support" for this purpose.[35] Archivists, public historians, and other users of historical records must realize that the protection of America's archives is a task that should appeal to and draw on the interest and resources of many groups and disciplines.

Public historians have an extremely important stake in the preservation of historical records. One of the highly-touted purposes of public history is to relate an understanding of past events to the formulation of contemporary public policy. *The Public Historian* has featured a growing number of articles related to the historian as expert witness,[36] the historian in government,[37] and the historian in corporations,[38] all recognizing the importance of records. Yet despite the importance of historical records, a recent analysis of government records revealed that their care is extremely poor.[39] Other studies

[34]"Prospects for Public History: Old Reliances, New Alliance," paper presented at the 1984 meeting of the Society of American Archivists.

[35]Anna Nelson, "In Support of History," American Historical Association *Perspectives* 22 (March 1984), 15.

[36]J. Morgan Kousser, "Are Expert Witnesses Whores? Reflections on Objectivity in Scholarship and Expert Witnessing," *Public Historian* 6 (Winter 1984), 5-19, and Paul Soifer, "The Litigation Historian: Objectivity, Responsibility, and Sources," *ibid.* 5 (Spring 1983), 47-62.

[37]Jamie W. Moore, "History, the Historian, and the Corps of Engineers," *Public Historian* 3 (Winter 1981), 64-74; Ronald W. Johnson, "The Historian and Cultural Resource Management," *Public Historian* 3 (Spring 1981), 43-51; and Robert G. Stakenas and David B. Mock, "Context Evaluation: The Use of History in Policy Analysis," *ibid.* 7 (Summer 1985), 43-56.

[38]Julia Niebuhr Eulenberg, "The Corporate Archives: Management Tool and Historical Resource," *Public Historian* 6 (Winter 1984), 21-37 and the Summer 1981 issue on "Business and History."

[39]*Committee on the Records of Government: Report* (Washington, D.C., March 1985).

show that only a small portion of American corporations have adequate systems for the control of their archival records.[40] Public historians should be working closely with archivists to ensure that the information necessary for public policy formulation is being well maintained.

The potential of public history for promoting the value of archival records extends far beyond the realm of public policy making. The recent self-analysis by the National Council on Public History noted that it has been "preaching to the converted" in the academy and government and "has neglected an area of great potential: the promotion of the use and value of history throughout society at large." This report recommended that the NCPH promote aggressively the "application of the historical process and the use of historians throughout society" through workshops, seminars, participation in non-history conferences, popular essays, and cooperative ventures with other organizations like the Society of American Archivists and the American Association for State and Local History.[41] There is a great need for such broad efforts. The successful push to gain independence for the National Archives by a broad coalition of organizations and individuals, including public historians, is the best recent example of the tough advocacy that is needed, and that can succeed in promoting the significance of archival records in society.[42] Raising citizen consciousness about the importance of history will lead to increased support for programs for the preservation and management of America's documentary heritage. Certainly, there is enough necessary labor to be shared by archivists, public historians, and others in this important work.

[40]Douglas A. Bakken, "Corporate Archives Today," *American Archivist* 45 (Summer 1982), 279-86.

[41]The summary of this report is in the Spring-Summer 1985 issue of the NCPH newsletter.

[42]Charlene Bickford, *The Coalition to Save Our Documentary Heritage: An Important Lesson in Archival Advocacy*, MARAC Occasional Publication, no. 3 (n.p.: Mid-Atlantic Regional Archives Conference, 1983) and Page Putnam Miller, "Archival Issues and Problems: The Central Role of Advocacy," *Public Historian* 8 (Summer 1986), 60-73.

Archivists, Public Historians, and the Documentation of Modern Society

Archivists have long been concerned with the appraisal of records, especially since World War II and the rapid proliferation of government and technological systems for information management. Appraisal is the process by which archivists and records managers select records that possess information of permanent value. Archivists conveniently describe these values as being for administration, legal, fiscal, and research purposes. Ironically, however, the theory underlying such selection has been developed extremely poorly, although there is evidence of significant recent progress. One well-known monograph on archival theory declined even to consider appraisal because of the "primitive nature of its development."[43]

The explanation for inadequate appraisal theory can be traced to the archival community's difficulty in grappling with changes in modern society. Archivists have a preoccupation with "collecting" that goes back at least as far as the Renaissance antiquarian-scholars and which was firmly entrenched in the United States in the historical society movement of the nineteenth century.[44] Archivists selected by searching for older records that could be easily evaluated for their research value because of the time that had lapsed between their creation and examination. Like their antiquarian predecessors, many archivists thrilled in the chase of unique and interesting documents. Archivists also remained oriented to older records because of their ease of selection, their usually smaller volume, and, in many cases, their endangered condition. Regardless of when or where a records program is established, the first task of the archivist usually is analysis of older documents and this has often diverted attention away from newer records with equal or greater importance.

Archivists also tend to perpetuate centralized records collection and preservation programs. Most archivists have a vision of the selection of records appropriate for retention and preservation and access in a central repository. The growth

---

[43]Richard C. Berner, *Archival Theory and Practice in the United States: A Historical Analysis* (Seattle: University of Washington Press, 1983), 6-7.

[44]See, for example, Lester J. Cappon, "Collectors and Keepers in the England of Elizabeth and James," in *Sibley's Heir: A Volume in Memory of Clifford Kenyon Shipton* (Boston: Colonial Society of Massachusetts, 1982), 145-71, and Leslie W. Dunlap, *American Historical Societies 1790-1860* (Madison, Wisconsin: Privately printed, 1944), chapter 6.

and increasing complexity of modern society has made such tactics increasingly difficult to pursue. The prime example of this is the failure by state archives to manage sufficiently the records of local government or to encourage local officials to manage their own records.[45]

Changes in the nature of American society in the past four decades have significantly outrun the archival community's means of documenting that society.[46] At a rate that is virtually incalculable, the amount of documentation has expanded remarkably, most noticeably in government. This is the result of the growing size of government and of government being involved in an increasing variety of activities. The birth of modern records management was the result of the increase in the size of the federal government in the 1930s and 1940s.[47] Now a few archivists and records managers are again beginning to ponder techniques that challenge many long-cherished assumptions. For instance, some records that were traditionally kept have become too costly to maintain and their vast bulk has discouraged their use.[48] The expansion of records extends far beyond government and reflects a major characteristic of modern society - the interrelatedness of government, private enterprise, and individuals. Decisions of policy implementation are no longer made unilaterally nor can they be documented in any simple manner.

Furthermore, the nature of records or their information is often dictated or largely molded by governmental requirements or industry-wide regulations and guidelines. A few archivists are now arguing that in order to document even a single achievement, the records of many organizations and government

[45]This is true even for the oldest and best-funded of the state archives; see Edie Hedlin, "Archival Programs in the Southeast: A Preliminary Assessment," *Provenance* 11 (Spring 1984), 6-8.

[46]See Edward Weldon, "Archives and the Challenges of Change," *American Archivist* 46 (Spring 1983), 125-34.

[47]Frank B. Evans, "Archivists and Records Managers: Variations on a Theme," *American Archivist* 30 (January 1967), 45-58.

[48]Leonard Rapport, "No Grandfather Clause: Reappraising Accessioned Records," *American Archivist* 44 (Spring 1981), 143-50 and "In the Valley of Decision: What to Do About the Multitude of Files of Quasi Cases," *ibid.* 48 (Spring 1985), 173-89.

offices should be evaluated.[49]   Spurring on both of these traits
has been the advent of an electronic information revolution,
making it possible to create, manipulate, duplicate, and erase
information in ways unheard of less than a generation ago.
The advent of information technology is an inviting temptation
in the hands of a presentist culture, challenging the idea of
records permanence and the very nature of archival work.[50]

Documenting modern society is, then, very different from the
archivists' traditional approach to appraisal, and has significant
implications for public historians.   Recently, a model of
"documentation strategy" has been proposed that provides some
exciting possibilities for public historians.   A documentation
strategy is defined as "a plan to assure the adequate
documentation of an ongoing issue, activity, function, or subject.
The strategy is ordinarily designed, promoted, and in part
implemented by an ongoing mechanism involving archival
documentation creators, records administrators, archivists,
users, other experts, and beneficiaries and other interested
parties."[51]

Such an appraisal tactic proposes several major changes
from standard appraisal methods and invites the participation
of public historians.   First, it more actively engages records
creators in evaluating entire information systems.   Second, the
documentation strategy strives to identify and compare
documentation that is needed and documentation that exists,
encouraging the creation of new information if necessary.
Third, and finally, a documentation strategy requires the
participation of records creators, custodians like archivists and
records managers, and users and other beneficiaries.   Such an
appraisal system endeavors to take into account the
complexities of modern records by bringing as much expertise
as possible to bear on them.

---

[49]The best work on this has been done in the area of the records of
science and technology. See Clark A. Elliott, ed., *Understanding Progress
as Process: Documentation of the History of Post-War Science and Technology
in the United States* (n.p., 1983), and Joan K. Haas, Helen Willa Samuels,
and Barbara Trippel Simmons, *Appraising the Records of Modern Science
and Technology: A Guide* (Cambridge: Massachusetts Institute of Technology,
1985).

[50]Trudy Huskamp Peterson, "Archival Principles and Records of the
New Technology," *American Archivist* 47 (Fall 1984), 383-93.

[51]Helen W. Samuels, "Who Controls the Past," *American Archivist* 49
(Spring 1986), 109-24 and Larry J. Hackman and Joan Warnow-Blewett,
"The Documentation Strategy Process: A Model and A Case Study," *ibid.* 50
(Winter 1987), 12-47.

Since many public historians hold key positions in or have influence upon government agencies, corporations and other institutions, their expertise will be an added boon to the development of a documentation-oriented approach. Decisions on documentation require an indepth knowledge of records creators,[52] and public historians' involvement with such institutions - as historians, archivists, records managers, policy analysts, or consultants - can provide invaluable insights and guidance. Indeed, many public historians become actively concerned about the fate of their institutions' records as a matter of course.[53] The documentation strategy model offers both a better mechanism for public historians to evaluate the records of their organizations and the possibility of a more influential role in appraisal. Public historians can bring much to this process through awareness of the relationship of their institution and its records to other organizations and their information and by leading towards practical application of this newly developing appraisal technique. It is also in this area of model building and theory construction that public history provides significant opportunities for assisting archivists.

The Challenge of Educating Archivists and Public Historians

A healthy educational system is essential to the well-being of any profession or occupation. A classic sociological analysis of professionalism also emphasized the necessity of a "body of theory" that "serves as a base in terms of which the professional rationalizes his operations in concrete situations."[54] Other sociologists have written that all "well-established" professions have solid bases in the university.[55] Even

[52]JoAnne Yates, "Internal Communication Systems in American Business Structures: A Framework to Aid Appraisal," *American Archivist* 48 (Spring 1985), 141-58 and Michael A. Lutzker, "Max Weber and the Analysis of Modern Bureaucratic Organizations: Notes Toward a Theory of Appraisal," *ibid.* 45 (Spring 1982), 119-30.

[53]For example, George T. Mazuzan, "Countering 'Doublethink': Doing History at the Nuclear Regulatory Commission," *Public Historian* 7 (Summer 1985), 37-38.

[54]Ernest Greenwood, "The Elements of Professionalization," in *Professionalization*, eds., Howard M. Vollmer and Donald L. Mills (Englewood Cliffs, N.J.: Prentice Hall, Inc., 1966), 11.

[55]Bernard Barber, "Some Problems in the Sociology of the Professions," in *The Professions in America*, ed. Kenneth S. Lynn (Boston: Houghton Mifflin Co., 1965), 19-22 and Nathan Glazer, "The Schools of the Minor Professions," *Minerva* 12 (July 1974), 346-64.

sociologists who disagree about the means of determining professional and occupational attributes often cite education and the idea of specialized knowledge as keys to recognition and support in society.[56]

Archival education has improved tremendously over the last two decades. As recently as the early 1970s a person desiring to be trained as an archivist had little option other than to attend a single course or workshops ranging from a few days to a few weeks. Now, an individual seeking basic training will discover a bewildering array of workshops and seminars; single courses with apprenticeships; training in history, applied history or library science departments; joint MA/MLS programs; and post-appointment opportunities. But there are still no well-established standards or clear expectations in the field of archival education.[57]

The emergence of public history has only added to the confusion. No matter how archivists might feel about the encroachment of public historians here, they have little ground for complaint because of their own inadequate standards for education and training. This state of affairs reveals an occupation that still has some uncertainty about its own identity and that has not convinced itself of the need to establish education standards and control over who constitutes an archivist. An English archivist, examining archival education from an international perspective, stated that "although the United States has the oldest professional association [the Society of American Archivists] . . . it is probably the most backward in professional training."[58] What is surprising is how far archival education in the United States has *not* progressed. In the early 1970s, for example, Frank B. Evans and Robert B. Warner pointed out that problems with education were contributing to the lack of archival professionalism: "Its members are drawn from a variety of educational and occupational backgrounds, and they reveal

[56]For example, Julius A. Roth, "Professionalism: The Sociologist's Decoy," *Sociology of Work and Occupations* 1 (February 1974), 6-23; Douglas Klegon, "The Sociology of Professions: An Emerging Perspective," *Sociology of Work and Occupations* 5 (August 1978), 259-83; and Eliot Freidson, "Are Professions Necessary?" in *The Authority of Experts: Studies in History and Theory*, ed. Thomas L. Haskell (Bloomington: Indiana University Press, 1984), 3-27.

[57]For more information on this topic, see the essays on archival education in this volume.

[58]Edwin Welch, "Archival Education," *Archivaria* 4 (Summer 1977), 55-56.

significantly divergent professional training, experience, and interests. The bounds of the profession still remain undefined, and the professional identity of the members is uncertain."[59]

The malformed nature of American archival education, now with some hope of change, has also had a profound effect on archival theory. Frank G. Burke has related the lack of such theory to the problem of archival education.[60] There is virtually no opportunity for the support of researcher-theoreticians among the archival community; indeed, the history of archival development in this country has been especially thin in this regard.[61] With the exception of a single fellowship program, established only in 1983 at the Bentley Historical Library at the University of Michigan, serious thoughts on the *whys* of archival management must be given after work hours, through special grant-funded projects like the Joint Committee on the Archives of Science and Technology, or in institutions where benevolent directors support such work. As long as archival education is weak and archival theory suffers, no one should be surprised about the lack of public recognition of their work and the resultant poverty of resources.

One solution would be improved archival training in the academy, where public history is solidly rooted. Burke believes that archival training through history departments would wean the archival community away from its reliance upon remedial training and emphasis upon learning through practice.[62] There are even more compelling cases for archival education programs that draw upon the strengths of both history and library/information science.[63] Archivists in training need to have a firmer footing in the academy, a grounding in theory *and* practice, and the opportunity to draw upon important related disciplines like library science, information science,

[59]"American Archivists and Their Society: A Composite View," *American Archivist* 34 (April 1971), 172.

[60]"The Future Course of Archival Theory in the United States," *American Archivist* 44 (Winter 1981), 44-45. See also his "Archival Cooperation," *ibid.* 46 (Summer 1983), 303.

[61]There are a few exceptions; see Jane F. Smith, "Theodore R. Schellenberg: Americanizer and Popularizer," *American Archivist* 44 (Fall 1981), 313-26.

[62]"Future Course of Archival Theory," 45.

[63]Lawrence J. McCrank, "Prospects for Integrating Historical and Information Studies in Archival Education," *American Archivist* 42 (October 1979), 443-55.

records management, historical editing, public administration, *and* public history.

Public history represents a promising opportunity to tie archival education and theory to the university. Applied history programs are based in history, and archival work will also need to continue to have such a foundation. The broad perspective of public history allows archives to be related to similar disciplines such as historic preservation and museology. The placement of introductory archival courses in public history programs could be useful to individuals training for administrative positions in institutions that include archival components. Such courses could also provide some training to staff from institutions that are starting archives. The courses could also provide another forum on archival issues, encouraging students - regardless of whether or not they intend to pursue archival work as a vocation - to study and write on these topics. The interdisciplinary nature of that forum could bring other valuable perspectives to bear on archival concerns.

Archivists are learning, for example, from librarians and museum curators tools that they can apply to issues like the documentation of modern society.[64] Public history education provides an excellent arena for an interdisciplinary approach that could study many essential and interesting archival concerns such as the history and degrees of success of record keeping systems, the social and cultural utility of archives, the nature and impulse of collecting, and the future role of the archivists in the age of information technology. Public history education could also be a forum for discussions among people interested in the theoretical footing of archival work and those experienced in its practical applications.

The caveat in all of this is that public historians, especially public history educators, must realize that their educational framework is not the complete solution for the education of archivists. Archivists need more as they move towards individual certification of practitioners, another recent issue among archivists, and the accreditation of archival education programs, an inevitable event. To this point, public history educators have been content to accept the status quo of archival education - a general introductory course and a semester practicum - with little questioning. The changes public historians have made have been generally for the worse:

---

[64]Jutta Reed-Scott, "Collection Management Strategies for Archivists," *American Archivist* 47 (Winter 1984), 23-29 and Harry R. Rubenstein, "Collecting for Tomorrow: Sweden's Contemporary Documentation Program," *Museum News* 63 (August 1985), 55-60.

the teaching of a single public history course that provides a few weeks, at best, of introduction to the work of the archivist. Of course, public historians need to guarantee to their archival colleagues that trained and knowledgeable archivists will teach the archival courses. But public historians also need to be aware of and involved in professional archival associations, their meetings, and their special committees and task forces. Public historians also should concentrate on developing their *own* theory underlying what applied history can and should be, rather than merely appropriating a hodgepodge of other disciplines. A stronger public history profession will provide necessary assistance in the preservation of America's documentary heritage and, perhaps, challenge archivists to adopt stronger standards for themselves.

The Future Association of Archivists and Public Historians

While there is significant potential for cooperation between archivists and public historians, a greater number of unresolved issues need serious discussion by both groups. What follows is a brief list of suggestions for archivists and public historians to consider about their relationship to each other.

First, the main professional associations (The National Council on Public History, Society of American Archivists, and National Association of Government Archives and Records Administrators) need to build stronger mechanisms for discussion and cooperation. The National Council on Public History should invite archivists to identify areas where the participation of archivists would be beneficial. The Society of American Archivists should seek representation from public historians on its essential committees and task forces like the Committee on Education and Professional Development. The SAA Committee on Goals and Priorities should involve the National Council on Public History and individual public historians in the development and carrying out of professional archival goals. The various professional associations need to develop regular program sessions that explore the relationship between archivists and public historians, with a focus on cooperative rather than divisive issues. And, finally, the available professional journals need to encourage the submission and publication of essays that explore the possibilities of a closer bond between archivists and public historians.

Second, these main professional associations need to pool resources and develop ways of carrying to the public the message that history is important and archival records are essential to knowing about that history. The National Council on Public History, Society of American Archivists, and National Association of Government Archives and Records Administrators need to hire people who can effectively utilize the media in communicating such basic concerns. Popular essays, audio-visual programs, and educational materials need to be developed that reach a wider audience. Also, these professional associations need to work harder in lobbying in the nation's capital for the preservation of historical sources and on behalf of issues (like improved access to public records, funds for developing and testing efficient and effective mass preservation techniques, and resources for providing strong and dynamic national leadership in archival matters) that affect their management and use.

Third, and finally, public historians and archivists need to cooperate in the development of stronger educational standards and theory in both fields. Public history education programs need to abandon any presumption that they are solely responsible for training archivists and, instead, should work with archivists in developing training programs for both disciplines. Public historians can use their courses to introduce students and other interested individuals to the nature of archival work and can encourage students to devote time to studying current archival issues and theories. Archivists, in developing their own stronger standards through means like certification, can help public historians to strengthen their own educational programs. Both archivists and public historians should use the academy as a laboratory for developing a stronger archival theory, especially in the selection of archival documentation.

Conclusion

Of all disciplines, archivists and public historians are probably the most closely related in nature and possess the greatest potential for cooperation. Both archivists and public historians are history-based occupations, are involved with the management, preservation, and use of historical records, are primarily located outside of the traditional academic community, and share a future that has some promise for growth and successful employment for their practitioners. The success of archivists and public historians, and their ability to work together, may well determine how well America's documentary heritage is preserved. If that work is truly important, then archivists and public historians need to work to strengthen their own fields and to seek out, wherever possible, opportunities for cooperation, partnership, and even alliances.

TEN   GOVERNMENT PUBLICATIONS AS ARCHIVES: BUILDING A CASE FOR COOPERATION BETWEEN ARCHIVISTS AND LIBRARIANS[1]

Introduction

Archivists have stronger professional ties to historians than to librarians because of the deep roots of the first and most influential archival institutions, the state archives and the National Archives, in the professional historical community. Without "scientific" history and such proponents as J. Franklin Jameson, the emergence of the archival profession would have taken much longer.[2] During the past decade, however, there has been a shift by archivists toward the adoption of library principles and practices accompanied by vigorous expressions of need for cooperation between the two professions. This trend has been fueled by the development of more vibrant professional archival associations and a stronger focus in planning and development.[3] Although Robert Clark's *Archive-Library Relations*, the "first comprehensive book" on the subject, is now a decade old,[4] there are many signs suggesting that archivists and librarians continue to be interested in working energetically together.[5]

---

[1]This essay was originally published in the *Journal of Library Administration* 7 (Summer/Fall 1986), 111-28.

[2]Ernst Posner, *American State Archives* (Chicago: University of Chicago Press, 1964), chapter 1; and Victor Gondos, Jr., *J. Franklin and the Birth of the National Archives 1906-1926* (Philadelphia: University of Pennsylvania Press, 1981).

[3]J. Frank Cook, "The Blessings of Providence on an Association of Archivists," *American Archivist* 46 (Fall 1983), 374-99; Philip P. Mason,"The Society of American Archivists in the Seventies: Report of the Committee for the 70's," *ibid.* 35 (April 1972), 193-217; Mason, "Archives in the Seventies: Promises and Fulfillment," *ibid.* 44 (Summer 1981), 199-206; Larry J. Hackman, "The Historical Records Program: The States and the Nation," *ibid.* 43 (Winter 1980), 17-31; and F. Gerald Ham, "NHPRC's Records Program and the Development of Statewide Archival Planning," *ibid.* 43 (Winter 1980), 33-42.

[4]Robert F. Clark, Jr., ed. *Archive-Library Relations* (New York: R. R. Bowker Co., 1976).

[5]The most prominent example is the adoption of the MARC format for archives and manuscripts; see Richard Lytle, "An Analysis of the Work of the National Information Systems Task Force," *American Archivist* 47 (Fall 1984), 357-65 and Nancy Sahli, "National Information Systems and Strategies for Research Use," *Midwestern Archivist* 9, no. 1 (1984), 5-13. Additional evidence that such a trend is occurring is the recent development

Despite progress in archives-library cooperation, such association is still in an embryonic stage. Past collaboration between the two professions has been minimal compared to unrealized potential. Librarians have shown little interest in acknowledging and building upon the contributions of archivists to the modern information society. Conversely, archivists have failed, especially because of their until recent lack of educational guidelines and standards, to develop a theory that supports such cooperation.[6] Instead, both professions are making unilateral efforts in areas of overlapping interest with only minimal coordination of action or cross-fertilization of ideas, resulting in weaker products than could be achieved by both disciplines working together. The management of government publications is a classic example of this problem.

The Importance of Government Publications

The transition from an oral to a written and from a scribal to a print society wrought tremendous cultural change. Modern information technology is causing change of similar magnitude in the late twentieth century.[7] Government, so

of a reactionary literature that urges archivists to retrench themselves into professional history; see Mattie U. Russell, "The Influence of Historians on the Archival Profession in the United States," *American Archivist* 46 (Summer 1983), 277-85 and George Bolotenko, "Archivists and Historians: Keepers of the Well," *Archivaria* 16 (Summer 1983), 5-25.

[6]The need for stronger archival theory has been well presented in Frank G. Burke, "The Future Course of Archival Theory in the United States," *American Archivist* 44 (Winter 1981), 40-46. For discussions about the problem with archival education see the chapter on this topic in this volume and the following: Richard C. Berner, "Archival Education and Training in the United States, 1937 to Present," *Journal of Education for Librarianship* 22 (Summer/Fall 1981), 3-19; James W. Geary, "A Fading Relationship: Library Schools and Preappointment Archival Education Since 1973," *Journal of Education for Librarianship* 20 (Summer 1979), 25-35; Lawrence J. McCrank, "Public Historians in the Information Profession: Problems in Education and Credentials," *Public Historian* 7 (Summer 1985), 7-22; Frederick J. Stielow, "Continuing Education and Information Management: Or, the Monk's Dilemma," *Provenance* 3 (Spring 1985), 13-22; Hugh A. Taylor, "The Discipline of History and the Education of the Archivist," *American Archivist* 10 (October 1977), 395-402; and Peter J. Wosh, "Creating a SemiProfessional Profession: Archivists View Themselves," *Georgia Archive* 10 (Fall 1982), 1-13.

[7]M. T. Clanchy, *From Memory to Written Record: England, 1066-1307* (Cambridge: Harvard University Press, 1979); Elizabeth L. Eisenstein, *The Printing Press as an Agent of Change: Communications and Cultural Transformations in Early Modern Europe*, 2 vols. (New York: Cambridge

interested in order and administration, quickly adopted printing as a valuable tool. By the time America was settled, government-sponsored printing had become a routine activity. During the colonial era the staple of a printing business was government contracts, which allowed a public printer to branch into commercial publishing.[8] Although publishing by the Federal government did not really take off until the establishment in 1861 of the Government Printing Office, official printing was long beforehand an important part of its work.[9] Most governments, from the Federal to the smallest local level, began publishing during their earliest days. The press publicized and legitimized their work.

The importance of government publications is evident in that so few aspects of the political realm are not documented through printing. Government printing has become essential for information about public administration, both for government's own use and by its citizens. Governments publish to document the legislative process, assist in administration, report completed projects or progress of work, provide information about the activities and condition of its citizenry, generate findings of research undertaken by governmental bodies, and provide general information about the nature and labors of government. A wide variety of government publications support these important functions - maps, research findings, guides, checklists and directories, committee and commission reports, periodicals, decisions and opinions, and audio-visual resources. These publications leave few other types of documents that are unique information sources with different perspectives on governmental operations.[10]

University Press, 1979); and J. David Bolter, *Turing's Man: Western Culture in the Computer Age* (Chapel Hill: University of North Carolina Press, 1984).

[8]Lawrence C. Wroth, *The Colonial Printer* (Charlottesville: Dominion Books, University Press of Virginia, 1964; org. pub. 1931).

[9]Stephen W. Stathis, "The Evolution of Government Printing and Publishing in America," *Government Publications Review* 7A, no. 5 (1980), 377-90 and Jerrold Zwirn, "Federal Printing Policies 1789-1861," *ibid.* 7A, no. 3 (1980), 177-87.

[10]Peter Hernon and Charles R. McClure, *Public Access to Government Information: Issues, Trends, and Strategies* (Norwood, New Jersey: Ablex Publishing Corp., 1984), chaps. 3 and 17, and Terry L. Weech, "The Characteristics of State Government Publications, 1910-1969," *Government Publications Review* 1 (Fall 1973), 29-51.

A recent study about the nature and condition of government records declares their six major functions as:

1. Document the history and intent of public policy.
2. Assure accountability to legislatures as well as the public through documentation of government programs.
3. Retain basic data necessary for research on scientific, medical, and economic problems.
4. Assure the effective administration of ongoing public programs. . . .
5. Assure effective administration within government agencies.
6. Form the basis of a national history and an understanding of American government.[11]

Not only are these functions evident in government publications, they could not be performed without the printed records of government.

Government publications are being more highly touted as a preeminent source of information about government activities, past and present. This has been caused partly by the efforts of libraries to be information purveyors to as wide a community as possible and by the discovery, in the past two decades, of the immense wealth of information in publications of Federal, state, and local governments.[12] More of the general public and the research community are endeavoring to gain access to government publications. Even the renaissance of local history and the immense popularity of genealogy have affected the uses of these publications.[13] Nevertheless, recent user studies of

[11]*Committee on the Records of Government: Report* (Washington, D.C.: The Committee, March 1985), 13-14.

[12]David W. Parish, "Into the 1980s: The Ideal State Document Reference Collection," *Government Publications Review* 10 (March-April 1983), 213-19, and Michael O. Shannon, "Collection Development and Local Documents: History and Present Use in the United States," *ibid.* 8A (1981), 59-87.

[13]See, for example, Jean Ashton, "Into the Swamp: Government Documents for the Literary Historian," *RQ* 24 (Summer 1985), 391-95; Bruce Morton, "U.S. Government Documents as History: The Intersection of Pedagogy and Librarianship," *ibid.* 24 (Summer 1985), 474-81; and Betty Jean Swartz, "Getting to the Source: Government Documents for the Genealogist," *ibid.* 23 (Winter 1983), 151-54. Even popular history guides, such as David E. Kyvig and Myron A. Marty, *Nearby History: Exploring the Past Around You* (Nashville: American Association for State and Local History, 1982), are promoting the potential use of government publications.

government publications reveal that their potential use is very far beyond their actual reference.[14] The introductory comments of a national study on government publications noted that these documents are a "major source of information in practically every field of endeavor and are crucial to informed public decision-making," but they are also "recognized as probably the most neglected and under-utilized information resource available to the public."[15] Regardless of such difficulties, most library administrators believe that government publications in their institutions are necessary and very important. In examining these publications in public libraries, one librarian concluded that "if this information is not provided by the public library, they will turn elsewhere and the public library will become less relevant to the information needs of a part of its population."[16] There is little question or debate about the value of government publications.

The Condition of Government Publications

Given this acknowledged importance of government publications, the extensive problems one sees in their management in libraries and archives today are surprising. The best management is the national depository system for federal documents supervised by the Government Printing Office, but even its effectiveness is questioned when considering

---

[14]Such as Barbara J. Ford, "Reference Use of State Government Information in Academic Libraries," *Government Publications Review* 10 (March-April 1983), 189-99; Nancy P. Johnson, "Reference Use of State Government Information in Law Libraries," *ibid.* 10 (March-April 1983), 201-11; Peter Hernon, "Information Needs and Gathering Patterns of Academic Social Scientists, With Special Emphasis Given to Historians and Their Use of U.S. Government Publications," *Government Information Quarterly* 1, no. 4 (1984), 401-29; Hernon, "Infrequent Use and Non-Use of Government Publication by Social Scientists," *Government Publications Review* 6, no. 4 (1979), 359-71; and Hernon, *Use of Government Publications by Social Scientists* (Norwood, New Jersey: Ablex Publishing Corporation, 1979). Actually, it has been shown that many researchers have difficulty in making effective use of standard information sources, government publications being only one source; see Margaret F. Stieg, "The Information of [sic] Needs of Historians," *College & Research Libraries* 42 (November 1981), 549-60.

[15]Bernard N. Fry, *Government Publications: Their Role in the National Program for Library and Information Sciences* (Washington, D.C.: National Commission on Libraries and Information Science, December 1978), 1.

[16]Gary R. Purcell, "Reference Use of State Government Information in Public Libraries," *Government Publications Review* 10 (March-April 1983), 184.

easy access to information.[17]   The management of state and
local government publications in libraries faces even more
difficulties.   These are programs generally described as
beleaguered, wanting in resources, and indecisive in
management.[18] A national evaluation of state publications in
depository libraries concluded that the latter programs are
hampered because of the notion that each state is unique and
the lack of national minimum standards.[19]

Public archives treat government publications no better than
libraries.   Public archives are supposedly concerned with all
information generated by their governments, whatever its
recorded form.[20]   Unfortunately, government publications have
not held a prominent place in the universe of record keeping.
The first modern American manual on archival administration
mentioned publications but relegated their management to
libraries or advocated their being kept, as found, with other
records.[21]   The result has been a general neglect by archivists
of government publications.[22]   A recent survey of state archives
reveals a sporadic and inconsistent pattern of interest in the

[17]Hernon and McClure, *Public Access to Government Information.*

[18]Yuri Nakata and Karen Kopec, "State and Local Government
Publications," *Drexel Library Quarterly* 16 (October 1980), 40-59 and Paula
Rosenkoetter, "Treatment of State Documents in Libraries," *Government
Publications Review* 1 (Winter 1973), 117-34.

[19]Margaret T. Lane, *State Publications and Depository Libraries: A
Reference Handbook* (Westport, Connecticut: Greenwood Press, 1981).

[20]For a good introduction to the purpose of public archives, see Posner,
American State Archives.

[21]T. R. Schellenberg, *Modern Archives: Principles and Techniques*
(Chicago: University of Chicago Press, 1956), 38, 114, 147-48.

[22]For example, two otherwise fine analyses of local public records
ignored the subject; David Levine, "The Management and Preservation of
Local Public Records: Report of the State and Local Records Committee,"
American Archivist 40 (April 1977), 189-99 and H. G. Jones, *Local
Government Records: An Introduction to Their Management, Preservation,
and Use* (Nashville: American Association for State and Local History,
1980). This has also caused serious problems to researchers desiring access
to such records; see, for example, Robert D. Armstrong, "The Beast in the
Bathtub, and Other Archival Laments," *American Archivist* 45 (Fall 1982),
375-84.

management of government publications.[23]

The administration of government publications is the victim of the continued lack of systematic coordination and cooperation between libraries and archives. The two professions continue to emphasize, to a considerable degree, their differences rather than similarities. Consider how government publications could be treated "archivally" to the benefit of both professions, opening the door to increased cooperation.

An Archival Model for Appraisal and Selection

In recent years librarians and archivists have advanced parallel emphases in the administration of their materials. Librarians now stress collection management, the "systematic, efficient and economic stewardship of library resources."[24] Collection management is a way that librarians (and archivists) can "control the flood of publications and records and . . . cope with the demands of the emerging information society." Collection planning, good selection, evaluation of holdings, and sharing of resources and cooperative collecting are all aspects of collection management.[25] Archivists have developed complementary approaches to library collection management. During the early and mid-1970s archivists pursued the notion of regional networks based on cooperative collecting.[26] More recently archivists, due to a greater awareness of their limited resources and the enormity of the challenge of documenting modern society, have developed stronger definitions of collection

[23]Richard J. Cox, "State Government Publications and State Archival Institutions," National Association of Government Archivists and Records Administrators *Clearinghouse* 7 (December 1984), 4-5, 16. For an earlier survey that revealed that government documents were generally separated from archival materials and treated differently, see Richard C. Berner and M. Gary Bettis, "Disposition of Nonmanuscript Items Found Among Manuscripts," *American Archivist* 33 (July 1970), 275-81.

[24]Paul H. Mosher, "Collection Development to Collection Management: Toward Stewardship of Library Resources," *Collection Management* 4 (Winter 1982), 41-48 (quote p. 45). See also Murray S. Martin, "A Future for Collection Management," *ibid.* 6 (Fall/Winter 1984), 1-9.

[25]Jutta Reed-Scott, "Collection Management Strategies for Archivists," *American Archivist* 47 (Winter 1984), 23-29 (quote p. 24).

[26]John A. Fleckner, "Cooperation as a Strategy for Archival Institutions," *American Archivist* 39 (October 1976), 447-59 is the classic statement on this approach. See also the special issue on archival networks in the *Midwestern Archivist* 6, no. 2 (1982), 91-240.

policies extending beyond the limits of a single institution.[27]
Work is now underway to define "documentation strategies," a
collecting regimen that requires a constant focus on all
information creators.[28]   What are the implications of these
approaches for the administration of government publications?
For librarians, "collection management" applied to
government publications has stalled on selection. Although
librarians have recognized that the volume of government
publications is growing at an exponential rate requiring
selection, they still retain some fundamental misconceptions in
how they should approach selection. The discovery that the
use of these sources decrease quickly as they get older has
made some build collection management around use.[29]   Other
librarians have defined the selection and maintenance of
government publications more broadly as the public's "present"
information needs plus availability of resources to make these
sources accessible.[30]   The predominant problem with most of
these arguments is that they adhere to the concept that *all*
government publications are somehow perpetually valuable.
Most of the literature on selection of government publications
has been written from the perspective of the Federal depository
system which provides an "out" for the local librarian if a
patron wishes a document that has not been previously selected
by that library - the national system may be able to provide a
back-up copy.[31]   Even guidelines for state government
publications depository systems have adopted a concept of

[27]Faye Phillips, "Developing Collecting Policies for Manuscript
Collections," *American Archivist* 47 (Winter 1984), 30-42 and Frank G.
Burke, "Archival Cooperation," *ibid.* 46 (Summer 1983), 293-305.

[28]Helen W. Samuels, "Who Controls the Past," *American Archivist* 49
(Spring 1986), 109-24; Larry J. Hackman and Joan Warnow-Blewett, "The
Documentation Strategy Process: A Model and A Case Study," *ibid.* 50
(Winter 1987), 12-47; Philip N. Alexander and Helen W. Samuels, "The
Roots of 128: A Hypothetical Documentation Strategy," *ibid.* 50 (Fall 1987),
518-31.

[29]See, for example, Kevin L. Cook, "Circulation and In-Library Use of
Government Publications," *Journal of Academic Librarianship* 11 (July
1985), 146-50.

[30]Charles R. McClure, "An Integrated Approach to Government
Publication Collection Development," *Government Publications Review* 8A,
nos. 1-2 (1981), 5-15.

[31]Yuri Nakata, *From Press to People: Collecting and Using U.S.
Government Publications* (Chicago: American Library Association, 1979),
especially chapter 4.

"archival" collections as being a comprehensive collection.[32] Moreover, the tremendous difficulty in even identifying and acquiring state and local government publications has made premeditated or planned selectivity almost a moot point.[33] Although librarians acknowledge the necessity of selection of government publications, they have little that approaches a system to enable selection to succeed.

Archivists have placed great emphasis on the selection of records possessing historical and other long-term research or administrative values. The first modern archives manual, written by T. R. Schellenberg three decades ago, defined the ideas that continue to shape appraisal decisions. Schellenberg in examining government records identified two broad values: evidential and informational. The former value is the "evidence" of how a government is organized and how it functions. Schellenberg generalized that "all archivists assume that the minimum record to be kept is the record of organization and functioning and that beyond this minimum values become more debatable." But Schellenberg also recognized the interest of the general public and research community in these records, when he devised the idea of informational value. This latter concept acknowledges that almost any record can be found useful for some reason, although not every public record can be saved. The archivist "must show that a careful selection of the documentation produced by a modern government is necessary if he is not to glut his stacks with insignificant materials that will literally submerge those that are valuable," as well as to use "limited" funds "judiciously."[34] Schellenberg's earlier approach to archival appraisal is very close in principle to the more recently invented idea of library collection management.

Unfortunately, archivists have not followed logically the direction they set in appraisal when working with government publications or the publications of any institution. The Society of American Archivists' manual on appraisal states that the "archivist should keep a record set of all publications of his institution," although it does attempt to identify the variety of

---

[32]Lane, *State Publications and Depository Libraries*, 30-31.

[33]Nakata and Kopec, "State and Local Government Publications," 44; Yuri Nakata, Susan J. Smith, and William B. Ernst, Jr., *Organizing a Local Government Documents Collection* (Chicago: American Library Association, 1979).

[34]Schellenberg, *Modern Archives*, 140, 152-53.

publications that possess greater value.[35] Thus, in practice at least, archivists have also subscribed to the idea that all government publications have permanent value. The various approaches to appraisal - sampling, records management scheduling and assistance, adequacy of documentation, reappraisal, and evidential and informational values - have not been uniformly applied to government publications.[36] Appraisal assumes that not all information has long-term or permanent value, that the varying values of information mandates selection so that the most important information is accessible, that costs of maintaining information in its different forms need to be considered, and that information comes in different physical forms and conditions which might govern what is maintained or discarded. Government publications need to be evaluated according to such criteria, especially the newly formed concept of documentation strategies.

Documentation strategies, as a form of archival appraisal, have emerged for two reasons. First, other systems of appraisal have been less effective because they are decentralized, uncoordinated, reactive, passive, and duplicative. The second rationale, containing in it the reasons for the general failure of standard archival appraisal techniques, is that in modern post-World War II society the creation and use of information is spread among a diverse group of records creators from individuals to big government. Archivists are now not only concerned with their limited resources, but also the super-abundance of records and information.[37] To accommodate these needs, archivists have developed definitions of collecting methodologies: 1) collection or acquisition policy prepared by an individual repository although now in tandem

[35]Maynard J. Brichford, *Archives & Manuscripts: Appraisal & Accessioning*, Basic Manual Series (Chicago: Society of American Archivists, 1977), 4-10. Generally, such practices have been followed in other settings as well; see Nicholas G. Burkel, "Establishing a College Archives: Possibilities and Priorities," in *College and University Archives: Selected Readings* (Chicago: Society of American Archivists, 1979), 43. Also, the retention scheduling of government records tends to schedule publications permanently, such as in the *Texas Municipal Records Manual* (Austin: Texas State Library, Regional Historical Resource Depositories and Local Records Division, 1985).

[36]Julia Marks Young, comp., "Annotated Bibliography on Appraisal," *American Archivist* 48 (Spring 1985), 190-216.

[37]See Samuels, "Who Controls the Past," and the Hackman and Warnow-Blewett essay for descriptions of the limitations of conventional archival appraisal and the new challenges confronting archivists in their selection of information of enduring value.

with and respect for what other repositories are collecting; 2) collecting project developed by a group of repositories and individuals to document a specific historic issue or event; and 3) documentation strategy which involves records creators, custodians, and users in a plan to document an ongoing issue or activity such as the operation of a local government or the effort to protect the environment.[38]

The idea of documentation strategy both reveals the reason why government publications have been so difficult to manage and provides a mechanism for dealing with them in the future. First, a documentation strategy draws attention to the fundamental question of what is being documented. In working with government publications, librarians and archivists have been concerned with their information content and not necessarily how that content relates to other information sources. F. Gerald Ham, in an article presaging work on documentation strategies, argued for more disciplined appraisal in our age of abundant information, including "an analysis of the extent to which documentation in print has devalued the information in the archival record."[39] Government publications are the prime example of such "documentation in print." If the goal is to document government, then *all* government information sources must be examined carefully as a whole, requiring its publications to be evaluated in relationship to more traditional archival sources.[40] If the goal is to document an ongoing event or process, such as a scientific or technological project, then government publications should be evaluated in tandem with other information sources.[41]

The concept of documentation strategies also invites the involvement of information creators, administrators, and users

[38]Alexander and Samuels, "The Roots of 128," is an excellent case study of some of the issues that need to be addressed by a new approach to archival identification and selection.

[39]Archival Choices: Managing the Historical Record in an Age of Abundance," *American Archivist* 47 (Winter 1984), 15.

[40]Leonard Rapport has paved the way for this in his development of reappraisal methodology: "No Grandfather Clause: Reappraising Accessioned Records," *American Archivist* 44 (Spring 1981), 143-50 and "In the Valley of Decision: What to Do About the Multitude of Files of Quasicases," *ibid.* 48 (Spring 1985), 173-89.

[41]Joan K. Haas, Helen Willa Samuels, and Barbara Trippel Simmons, *Appraising the Records of Modern Science and Technology: A Guide* (Cambridge: Massachusetts Institute of Technology, 1985), 9, 54-55, 63, 74, and 82.

in comparative efforts. This approach provides a better mechanism in evaluating the selection and use of government publications than has been proposed previously. Since libraries have been traditionally the repository for government publications and public archivists and records managers generally have had responsibility for appraisal, such strategies depend on their bringing these two disciplines together. The adoption of strategies relating to government publications should not be overly difficult since many public archives are already administratively associated with public libraries,[42] and many communities already support a tremendous diversity of libraries, archives, and public agencies.[43]

Another inherent and important assumption in documentation strategies is that their analysis of existing information will discover areas not adequately documented and, if necessary and possible, recommend the creation of needed information. This is a controversial suggestion, cutting across the grain of traditional archival practice. However, given the increasing use of modern information technology, it will probably be given more serious attention in the future. For governments the best and easiest means of creating such documentation is publication. The preparation of published reports, research studies, and administrative and informational documents are already accepted forms of government publications and are excellent choices for completing documentation.

Access to Government Information

Although archival appraisal appears to be an acceptable model for the selection of government publications, the bibliographical control of these documents by archival arrangement and description systems has already been judged by librarians as unsatisfactory. Federal government publications have long been handled through an archival arrangement by issuing agency, type of document, and title, - a system with little universal acclaim because of the difficulty

---

[42]State archival repositories fall into a number of different administration patterns, a major one of which is association with or placement in state libraries; see *Directory of State Archives and Records Management Programs* ([Albany]: National Association of Government Archives and Records Administrators, 1988).

[43]This is especially true in urban areas; see Fredric Miller, "Documenting Modern Cities: The Philadelphia Model," *Public Historian* 5 (Spring 1983), 75-86.

in achieving subject access.[44] Servicing the information needs of the public has raised questions about such an archival approach to government publications. As Bernard Fry wrote,

> the archival heritage . . . is a mixed blessing for government publications viewed today as an important informational resource. For many libraries the decision to follow the principle of archival arrangement has provided a practical way of identification, shelving, and servicing large numbers of varied formats of government documents which did not conform to standard library practice and could not be accessed according to traditional library concepts. However, the resulting failure to catalog, list, index, publicize, and distribute government publications on the same basis as conventional library materials raises a formidable . . . problem for both the document specialist and the potential user.[45]

Such a complaint, however, should be weighed against both the validity of library classification schemes and the continuing development of archival arrangement and description methodologies.

Despite whatever disadvantages archival control might possess, librarians have not developed alternative systems that, in practice at least, have proven more efficient to government information users. A recent study about online catalog use noted that "traditionally, sizable government documents collections in libraries have been less likely to be catalogued than have other library materials," adding that librarians "have treated government documents like the journal literature - by providing access through separate indexes . . . ."[46] The result is a system as clumsy as how librarians have viewed archival description. Even federal government publications are not considered readily accessible, even though their bibliographic

---

[44]Morton, "U.S. Government Documents as History," 476-77. The real reason for this is that most researchers generally go for information which is the most accessible and SUDOCS, the Federal government publications classification scheme, is seen as "too complicated for the scholar [and most researchers] to use on his own"; Stieg, "Information of [sic] Needs of Historians," 553, and Hernon, "Information Needs and Gathering Patterns of Academic Social Scientists," 406.

[45]*Government Publications*, 9-10.

[46]Roseann Bowerman and Susan A. Cady, "Government Publications in an Online Catalog: A Feasibility Study," *Information Technology and Libraries* 3 (December 1984), 331.

control is often more developed than for most other government publications.[47] State and local government publications are covered by a myriad of competing bibliographic systems based both upon subject access and archival description.[48] Basic decisions, such as whether government publications should be separate collections or integrated into the main library holdings, remain unresolved.[49] Some librarians have argued minimally for their intellectual integration so "that government publications have the same levels of physical availability, bibliographic accessibility, professional service, and status as other information resources in the library."[50] Much better administration of government publications seems indicated.

Consider the origins and future prospects of archival arrangement and description for handling government publications. Archival control systems were developed to manage large quantities of records in an efficient and expeditious manner. They open new opportunities for improving other aspects of initial bibliographic control in acquisition.[51] Finally, the archival arrangement and description process is itself undergoing extensive change that will possibly resolve some of the knottier problems of subject access.

Archival arrangement and description is built on several major principles - provenance (maintaining records by the agency of origin), original order (the concept of adherence to

---

[47]Hernon and McClure, *Public Access to Government Information*, 11.

[48]Nakata and Kopec, "State and Local Government Publications"; Rosenkoetter, "Treatment of State Documents in Libraries"; and Russell Castonguay, *A Comparative Guide to Classification Schemes for Local Government Documents Collections* (Westport, Connecticut: Greenwood Press, 1984).

[49]Nakata and Kopec, "State and Local Government Publications," 55; Castonguay, *A Comparative Guide*, 18; Susan Folsom Berman, *Municipal Publications in the Public Library: Guidelines for Collection and Organization* (Westerly, Rhode Island: South County Interrelated Library System, Westerly Public Library, n.d.), 13-15; and Nakata, Smith, and Ernst, *Organizing a Local Government Documents Collection*, 13-18. Generally, archivists have recommended that publications remain with larger archival holdings unless they are "discrete printed items"; see David B. Gracy, II, *Archives & Manuscripts: Arrangement and Description*, Basic Manual Series (Chicago: Society of American Archivists, 1977), 41-42.

[50]McClure, "An Integrated Approach to Government Publication Collection Development," 6.

[51]Hernon notes that bibliographical control includes such elements as location, acquisition, recording of publications, and provision of subject access; *Public Access to Government Information*.

original filing schemes), record group (organizationally related records arranged according to provenance with strict attention to hierarchical relationships of the records), and series (records arranged according to a filing system or maintained as a unit because they relate to a particular subject or function or result from the same activity). For the description of public records, the inventory unites all of these principles by incorporating the record group and series as the primary descriptive elements and adding a history and analysis of the functions of the records creator. The justifications for the use of such a system is the maintenance of evidence about the nature of the records creator, protection of the integrity of the records and their information, better consideration of the nature of the records, and allowance for records to be handled efficiently and effectively. The development of such a system of archival arrangement and description was motivated by the need to handle large quantities of documentary material and, quite naturally, emerged primarily from the National Archives and its staff.[52]

Librarians accustomed to subject control, perceive difficulties with archival arrangement and description because of its dependence upon physical arrangement rather than content of the records. However, the archival originators of this system were from the beginning deeply aware of this problem. Early public archivists endeavored to use, with notable failure, library subject classification systems,[53] later firmly adhering to the idea that "while records may pertain to subjects, they ordinarily do so only to the extent that such subjects are the object of action."[54] T. R. Schellenberg, the leading theoretician from the National Archives, suggested that records being held only for informational content could be "maintained in whatever order will best serve the needs of scholars and government officials"[55] and later acknowledged that abiding by provenance, record group, and series would be opposite of what the users desired -

[52]Richard C. Berner, *Archival Theory and Practice in the United States: A Historical Analysis* (Seattle: University of Washington Press, 1983) is a detailed analysis of archival arrangement and description.

[53]Donald R. McCoy, *The National Archives: America's Ministry of Documents 1934-1968* (Chapel Hill: University of North Carolina Press, 1978), 77-80, 105-09.

[54]T. R. Schellenberg, *The Management of Archives* (New York: Columbia University Press, 1965), 93.

[55]*Modern Archives*, 193.

subject access.[56]   Indeed, over the years a significant body of
literature has developed critiquing the archivist's ability to
provide adequate reference, i.e., efficient subject access, to their
holdings.[57]   However, it is also obvious that the vast quantity
of modern public records and the limited resources of public
archivists will not, for the foreseeable future, allow the
adoption of other systems that are more labor-intensive.[58]

Automation offers the break from this dilemma with the
hopes of allowing better subject access through existing archival
practices of arrangement and description. Not too many years
ago, literature on archival automation was sparse. Just within
the past few years, however, articles and even book-length
studies have appeared rapidly on this subject.[59]   Less than a
decade ago the literature mainly focused on the prospects of
archival automation, both for administration of archival

[56]*Management of Archives*, 91. Schellenberg was vitally concerned with
the problem of subject access, especially after his increased acceptance of
many library principles and practices. One of his last articles struggled
with the need for broad subject control; "A Nationwide System of
Controlling Historical Manuscripts in the United States," *American Archivist*
28 (July 1965), 109-12.

[57]Peter J. Scott, "The Record Group Concept: A Case for Abandonment,"
American Archivist 29 (October 1966), 493-504 and Mario D. Fenyo, "The
Record Group Concept: A Critique," *ibid.* 29 (April 1966), 229-39 are early
criticisms. More recent complaints consist of Mary Jo Pugh, "The Illusion
of Omniscience: Subject Access and the Reference Archivist," *ibid.* 45
(Winter 1982), 33-44 and Elsie T. Freeman, "In the Eye of the Beholder:
Archives Administration from the User's Point of View," *ibid.* 47 (Spring
1984), 111-23.   For related concerns see Frank Boles, "Disrespecting
Original Order," *ibid.* 45 (Winter 1982), 26-32 and Michel Duchein,
"Theoretical Principles and Practical Problems of *Respect des Fonds* in
Archival Science," *Archivaria* 16 (Summer 1983), 64-82.

[58]For a summary of recent reports and studies on this subject, see the
first essay in this volume.

[59]For the growth in this literature compare Richard M. Kesner, comp.
and   ed., *Automation,   Machine-Readable   Records,   and   Archival
Administration: An Annotated Bibliography* ([Chicago]: Society of American
Archivists, 1980) and Kesner, comp. and ed., *Information Management,
Machine-Readable Records, and Administration: An Annotated Bibliography*
(Chicago: Society of American Archivists, 1983). For examples of fuller
studies see H. Thomas Hickerson, *Archives & Manuscripts: An Introduction
to Automated Access*, Basic Manual Series (Chicago: Society of American
Archivists, 1981); Lawrence J. McCrank, ed., *Automating the Archives: Issues
and Problems in Computer Applications* (New York: Published for the
American   Society   for   Information   Science   by   Knowledge   Industry
Publications, Inc., 1981); and Richard M. Kesner, *Automation for Archivists
and Records Managers: Planning and Implementation Strategies* (Chicago:
American Library Association, 1984).

practices and improved access to the information contained in the records.[60] Now case-studies of practice in the use of archival automation are increasingly frequent. The implications for improved subject access are much more obvious today. Automation makes it possible to have both the traditional provenance-based access and subject access, making "debates over which approach is correct unnecessary and misleading."[61]

The key to the prospects for automation is the recent emendations of the US MARC Archival and Manuscripts Control (AMC) format. For years since 1973 when librarians originally adopted a MARC manuscripts format, the archival community avoided its use because of its orientation to the individual item rather than series, collection, or record group. After the work of the National Information Systems Task Force, the AMC format was revised to allow for more customary archival practice. The new format has opened the way for better control over archival sources like government publications. The AMC format includes fields for subject headings and, in addition, provides control over all levels from record group or collection down to item. Government publications could be treated as series or as individual items within record groups (records originators), and researchers could gain better subject access to their information content. The use of the AMC format will allow greater linkage into broader library communication networks, intellectually integrating government publications into the larger collections as many desire.[62]

There are additional distinctive advantages to the control of government publications by the AMC format, primarily in providing increased information about these publications as well as providing a system for more efficient acquisition. The AMC format supports the continued use of the provenance method of archival arrangement and description. For several generations archivists have built a convincing argument that knowledge about records creators and the origins of records is

[60]Such as Richard M. Kesner, "The Computer's Future in Archival Management: An Evaluation," *Midwestern Archivist* 3, no. 2 (1978), 25-36 and "Computers, Archival Administration, and the Challenges of the 1980s," *Georgia Archive* 9 (Fall 1981), 1-18.

[61]W. Theodore Durr, "Some Thoughts and Designs About Archives and Automation, 1984," *American Archivist* 47 (Summer 1984), 171-89.

[62]Nancy Sahli, *MARC for Archives and Manuscripts: The AMC Format* (Chicago: Society of American Archivists, 1985), and Max J. Evans and Lisa B. Weber, *MARC for Archives and Manuscripts: A Compendium of Practice* (Madison: State Historical Society of Wisconsin, 1985).

not only essential to appraisal or the selection of archival records, but it is beneficial to their use.[63]   As Max Evans has argued recently, "the archival approach to the management of records is based on the assumption that context is the key to understanding" and although one manifestation of this assumption, the record group, "is flawed as an access tool," context still remains important and can be adhered to, with the necessary subject access, thorough other means.   Evans, building on an earlier skepticism about the record group concept, and in approaching automation, advocates the use of authority control that includes information about the records creator and the functions of the creator which with automation allows greater subject access to and administrative control of the records.[64]   Thus, government publications would be arranged and described as series and connected to their creating agencies in a way that additional information about their function and purpose is provided and which guarantees more sophisticated subject access.

Adherence to the AMC format and the archival principles of arrangement and description, especially the centrality of series, provides the relief for one of the biggest problems in government information - the acquisition of government publications.   The archival scheme allows for building upon records management principles, specifically scheduling records series.   Tying acquisition to the established government records management programs provides the opportunity to acquire government publications in a systematic and thorough manner. Records managers survey all the records being produced by a particular agency, evaluate these records' value and use, and recommend disposition either ultimately by destruction or transfer to an archives.   Records management is essential for

---

[63]This is evident in archivists' view towards administrative history which has been seen as a unique specialty of the archivist, an outlet for scholarly publication, and a means for appraisal.   See Karl L. Trever, "Administrative History in Federal Archives," *American Archivist* 4 (July 1941), 159-69; Arthur D. Larson, "Administrative History: A Proposal for a Re-evaluation of Its Contributions to the Archival Profession," *Midwestern Archivist* 7 (1982), 34-45; Michael A. Lutzker, "Max Weber and the Analysis of Modern Bureaucratic Organization: Notes Toward a Theory of Appraisal," *ibid.* 45 (Spring 1982), 119-30; JoAnne Yates, "Internal Communication Systems in American Business Structures: A Framework to Aid Appraisal," *ibid.* 48 (Spring 1985), 141-58; and David Mycue, "The Archivist as Scholar: A Case for Research by Archivists," *Georgia Archive* 7 (Fall 1979), 10-16.

[64]"Authority Control: An Alternative to the Record Group Concept," paper presented at the Society of American Archivists meeting, November 1, 1985.

the effective administration of a government's information and is crucial to the successful operation of a government archives as well.[65] Although government publications are often intermingled with other files, they are as likely to be maintained separately for distribution and other administrative purposes. The operation of a government records management program should provide systematic control by and a steady flow to the repository of all publications being created by the government. The only obstacle is the uneven quality of records management programs available in government today.[66]

Recommendations for Cooperation

Margaret S. Child has emphasized the need for cooperation between the library and archives professions while acknowledging their propensity to work independently.[67] Archivists have much to learn in cooperating with each other; nevertheless, the fact remains that archivists and librarians must cooperate in matters like government publications. Some recommendations for promoting cooperation in the administration and use of government publications follow:

1. *Libraries and archives presently responsible for government publications should seek means to cooperate in the selection and administration of government publications.*

   The National Archives is a logical place to investigate how government publications could be handled as part of all government information, since it now has responsibility for the "archival collection"

---

[65]Frank B. Evans, "Archivists and Records Managers: Variations on a Theme," *American Archivist* 30 (January 1967), 45-58 and Richard H. Lytle, "The Relationship Between Archives and Records Management: An Archivist's View," *Records Management Quarterly* 2 (April 1968), 5-8.

[66]Unfortunately, records management in practice has often not worked as well as in principle. See a Canadian perspective which is not far afield from government in the United States; Bryan Corbett and Eldon Frost, "The Acquisition of Federal Government Records: A Report on Records Management and Archival Practices," *Archivaria* 17 (Winter 1983-84), 201-32.

[67]Margaret S. Child, "Reflections on Cooperation Among Professions," *American Archivist* 46 (Summer 1983), 286-92 and "Statewide Functions and Services," in *Documenting America: Assessing the Condition of Historical Records in the States* ed. Lisa B. Weber ([Albany]: National Association of State Archives and Records Administrators in cooperation with the National Historical Publications and Records Commission, [1984]), 47-57.

of government publications and has long been involved in the management of Federal records.[68] As likely a place, however, is the combination of state libraries and state archives, many of which share administrative structures. There should be few obstacles for the staffs of these institutions to develop better working relationships in regard to such shared information sources as government publications.

2. *Professional associations of archivists and librarians should seek stronger working partnerships to resolve problems facing the selection and administration of government publications.*

    National and state library associations have long had government documents round tables. Archivists should involve themselves in these as well as support keener interest in government publications within their own professional groups. These associations should be crucibles for cooperative projects as well as forums for adopting standards to achieve cooperation in the administration of government publications as the norm.

3. *Both library and archival education should encourage stronger professional development to support cooperative management of government publications.*

    Although many universities connect archival and library education, a proximity of programs has not been seen always as an opportunity to develop better understanding of such mutual concerns as government publications. The graduate education of librarians and archivists should be used to develop the theory underlying practice in managing government publications.

4. *A literature of case studies needs development, about the appraisal of government records that incorporates both published and original source materials.*

---

[68]LeRoy C. Schwarzkopf, "The Proposed National Depository Agency and Transfer of the Public Documents Library to the National Archives," *Government Information Quarterly* 1, no. 1 (1984), 27-47. Unfortunately, the separation of the National Archives from the General Services Administration has changed its records management function, although no one is sure of its implications; see Linda Vee Pruitt, "Archives and Records Management in the Federal Government: The Post-GSA Context," *Provenance* 3 (Fall 1985), 87-93.

A substantial literature of case studies already reveals that government publications are not being utilized adequately. However, archivists should produce appraisal analyses that show how and when government publications can be substituted for bulkier archival holdings. Librarians need to study better how information in various types of government publications are used and which ones might have more ephemeral value. Librarians and archivists must become aware of how government publications fit into a broader spectrum of information.

5.　*The US MARC format for Archives and Manuscripts Control (AMC) needs to be evaluated thoroughly for its potential to improve subject access in government publications.*

The growing participation by state archives in national networks that employ the AMC format should make this evaluation possible within a reasonable period. The recent funding by the National Historical Publications and Records Commission to the Research Libraries Group to support state archives in using RLIN to share appraisal information may be the first step in such an evaluation.

Conclusion

The future of rapidly developing information technology and the prospects for the library and archives professions provide a context for considering improved management of government publications. Increasingly government publications are being valued simply for their information and are being moved from traditional paper to machine-readable formats.[69] Modern technology makes it difficult to distinguish between published and unpublished documents.[70] This blurs older distinctions between archives and libraries. The numerous implications of

[69]Margaret T. Lane, "Distribution of State Government Publications and Information," *Government Publications Review* 10 (March-April 1983), 159-72 and Peter Hernon, ed., *New Technology and Documents Librarianship: Proceedings of the Third Annual Library Government Documents and Information Conference* (Westport, Connecticut: Meckler Publishing, 1983).

[70]Lise Hesselager, "Fringe or Grey Literature in the National Library: On 'Papyrolatry' and the Growing Similarity Between the Materials in Libraries and Archives," *American Archivist* 47 (Summer 1984), 255-70.

such changes do not ameliorate the need for archivists and librarians to work together in selecting and administering government publications. Archivists have already determined that their present systems of appraisal and arrangement and description can accommodate the transition to society's greater reliance on automated information.[71] The possibility exists that the current separation between archivists and librarians could disappear because of such information technology. Richard Kesner has called for archivists to "become information specialists drawing upon a wide array of automated tools and analytical techniques in serving our constituents."[72] Librarians already see themselves this way. Cooperation in managing government information and publications is one way of preparing both professions for possible merger and to serve a more vital role in the modern information age.

[71]Carolyn L. Geda, Erik W. Austin, and Francis X. Blouin, Jr., eds., *Archivists and Machine-Readable Records* (Chicago: Society of American Archivists, 1980); Margaret L. Hedstrom, *Archives & Manuscripts: Machine-Readable Records*, Basic Manual Series (Chicago: Society of American Archivists, 1984); and Trudy Huskamp Peterson, "Archival Principles and Records of the New Technology," *American Archivist* 47 (Fall 1984), 383-93.

[72]"Automated Information Management: Is There a Role for the Archivists in the Office of the Future?" *Archivaria* 19 (Winter 1984-85), 162-72.

ELEVEN   CONTENDING WITH THE HYDRA-
HEADED MONSTER:
PRESERVATION SELECTION OF
ENDURING INFORMATION[1]

Introduction

The selection of information of enduring value is not, of course, the only archives and library preservation issue. Archives and library preservation also consists of the development of effective physical treatment and reformatting techniques, the building of cooperative networks to make data about preservation efforts available, the education of archivists and librarians in preservation management, and the acquisition of increased support and resources for the better care of archives and library materials. In all of these areas, archives and librarians have made tremendous strides, especially during the past decade. But these concerns always follow determining what should be preserved. Despite the fundamental nature of the issue, selection remains comparatively underdeveloped, especially in librarianship, both in terms of theoretical constructs and practical analyses of criteria.

This essay, written by an archivist involved in research on selection of records possessing enduring value and a university library preservation coordinator, attempts to form a research agenda for the library community that addresses this singular need. The purpose of the essay is not to criticize or praise librarians and archivists, or to be a comprehensive review of archives and library preservation issues. Anyone familiar with recent literature on library preservation and archival appraisal will recognize a considerable and beneficial exchange of ideas and practices between these two professions. However, in terms of preservation selection, librarians may not yet have considered archival selection models as sources for selection strategies appropriate to library materials. This is another opportunity for different branches of the information professions to cooperate.

The following essay consists of four parts: first, a summary of the challenge that preservation provides for all related information professions; second, a review of major preservation efforts and library selection models that have been recently

[1]This essay was originally published in *Re-Thinking the Library in the Information Age: Issues in Library Research; Proposals for the 1990s* (Washington, D.C.: U.S. Department of Education, 1988), 115-30. The essay was co-authored by Lynn W. Cox.

proposed; third, a discussion of one source for potential solutions; and fourth, an identification of major issues requiring additional research.

The Preservation Challenge

Professionals conscious of the library's role as an information provider have always been challenged by the changing nature, quantity, and constantly shifting demand for information.[2] But an equally important challenge has always been present -- the physical impermanence of all information. More information is being lost at present than entire past generations made and used. This gives the librarian the responsibility to decide, first, *what* information must be saved and, second, *how* it should be preserved. It is not an easy responsibility, likened by Margaret Child to a "hydra-headed monster,"[3] but one that the library profession (and all other information professions, for that matter) must accept and effectively deal with to help society meet its long-term information requirements.

Librarians and other information specialists, such as archivists, have become much more cognizant of the fragility of all information forms. This relatively new concern is partly in response to greater knowledge about the seriousness of the physical threats to information sources. The perils are on all sides: inherent vices of construction, debilitating environmental conditions, and the throw-away mentality of modern culture. Study after study, adding layer upon layer of evidence, has formed an unsettling picture of the magnitude of the effort needed to preserve information.

Printed books: "Typically, one-fourth of the volumes in [the nation's research] libraries are described as brittle - that is, the paper breaks after one or two double folds of a page corner. Further, up to 80 percent of the books in those collections are acid and, without preventive action, eventually all will become brittle." The problem is growing because the majority of book publishers still use acidic

---

[2]F.W. Lancaster, Laura S. Drasgow, Ellen B. Marks, "The Changing Face of the Library: A Look at Libraries and Librarians in the Year 2001," *Collection Management* 3 (Spring 1979), 55-77.

[3]"Deciding What To Save," *Abbey Newsletter* 6, supplement (August 1982): 1.

paper.[4] Great quantities of information housed in libraries are rapidly disappearing.

Archival records: "Most government records created during the past century cannot withstand the rigors of use and time without significant loss in image quality, physical strength, and chemical stability. At the present time no state archives [this is true for other types of archival repositories as well] approaches the goal of providing total preservation care for its permanently valuable records."[5] In surveying the condition of the country's archival records, the primary conclusion reached is that "the United States is in danger of losing its memory."[6]

Machine-readable information: "The danger of losing historically valuable records is greatly increased by the changeover to electronic recordkeeping .... records created on tapes or disks are erased or lost before anyone exercises judgement about their possible value .... given the rapidity of technological change, even information recognized as valuable can be lost because the equipment and skills necessary to retrieve it become obsolete or unavailable."[7] "The turn to computerization in the last thirty years hastens the danger of societies being left with little or no material for the study of their own past."[8]

Other historical records and artifacts: "Historical agencies and museums .... are in the vanguard of collecting and preserving our cultural heritage, yet the majority are doing so without the money, people, and technical know-how they need. Because they lack adequate resources, the physical remains of America's past - documents and artifacts alike -

---

[4]Committee on Preservation and Access, *Brittle Books* (Washington, D.C.: Council on Library Resources, 1986), 7-8.

[5][Howard P. Lowell], *Preservation Needs in State Archives* (Albany: National Association of Government Archives and Records Administrators, February 1986), 7.

[6]*Committee on the Records of Government: Report* (Washington, D.C.: The Committee, March 1985), 9.

[7]*Ibid.*, 10.

[8]Gerhard L. Weinberg, "The End of History?" *Perspectives* 25 (February 1987), 17.

are in peril."[9]

The questions such analyses raise are simple to ask, but extremely difficult to answer. What information about the past and present will be left for future generations? How is information that should be preserved best identified? In what forms should this information be preserved? Is technology friend or foe? Who will supply the resources for preservation? How can society be convinced of the preservation crisis? How will the traditional information role of the library be affected if the deterioration of valuable information is not arrested and reversed?

The issues of information's fragility and the corresponding lack of resources to deal effectively with the problem concern librarians, their colleagues, and all citizens. Clearly, advocacy for improved stability and permanence of information media and for increased resources for library and archival preservation must be accelerated. But the magnitude and urgency of these needs also increase the importance of wise selection. Information specialists must play a proactive role in addressing this issue.

While librarians and archivists have become attuned to the problems of loss of information, the society of which they are a part has become accustomed to thinking of the 1970s and 1980s as the "information" or "electronic" era, and to hearing positive predictions about what fast access to enormous quantities of information means for the quality of life. However, initially optimistic forecasts about the electronic era have recently been qualified. If it is true that we are losing more information than past generations created, it is also true that we can generate and manipulate more information than can be effectively used or managed. There is too much "unrefined, undigested information flowing in from every medium around us."[10] The computer, to name but one information storage medium, leads us to believe that all information possesses equal value, when data are often

---

[9]Charles Phillips and Patricia Hogan, *A Culture at Risk: Who Cares for America's Heritage?* (Nashville: American Association for State and Local History, 1984), 82.

[10]Theodore Roszak, *The Cult of Information: The Folklore of Computers and the True Art of Thinking* (New York: Pantheon Books, 1986), 162. For examples of the more optimistic assessments of the role of information in society, see Alvin Toffler, *The Third Wave* (New York: William Morrow and Co., Inc., 1980) and John Naisbitt, *Megatrends: Ten New Directions Transforming Our Lives* (New York: Warner Books, 1984).

extraneous or ephemeral. In reality, even if it were possible, comprehensive preservation would be undesirable. Librarians and their colleagues must chart a course for preservation selection between the Scylla and Charybdis of excessive loss and extravagant retention of information.

Library Preservation Programs and Literature

The library profession's full awareness of the scale of the physical preservation needs of library collections (primarily books) is relatively recent.[11] Although there is evidence that some librarians worried about preservation as early as the late nineteenth century, the variety of actions emanating from this concern has changed rapidly over the past three decades. Modern library preservation started in the mid-1950s, marked by the founding of the Council on Library Resources. The sixties brought new research studies on paper aging and conservation, development of physical treatment techniques, the first appointments of library conservators, and publication of a few pioneering manuals on library preservation. The 1970s accelerated what had been started, earning the label of the "decade of conservation awareness in librarianship."[12] Manuals proliferated, research on techniques increased, numerous preservation officer positions were created, cooperative efforts (such as regional conservation centers) were initiated, and interest in a national preservation plan was renewed through bodies such as the National Conservation Advisory Council.

The decade of the 1980s has seen a new awareness by librarians of the magnitude of the preservation problem and the threat of irreparable damage to the holdings of this country's libraries, archives, and other information repositories. This awareness has led to greater efforts to understand the specifics of the challenge in individual libraries and, on the other end of the scale, to mount a stronger national effort to find and carefully allocate resources to resolve the problem. During the 1980s there have been serious efforts, such as Yale University's scientific and statistically sophisticated collection survey, to study the condition of holdings in individual libraries in order "to determine the extent and nature of the

[11]The best review of this subject is Pamela W. Darling and Sherelyn Ogden, "From Problems Perceived to Programs in Practice: The Preservation of Library Resources in the USA, 1956-1980," *Library Resources & Technical Services* 35 (January/March 1981), 9-29.

[12]Howard P. Lowell, "Sources of Conservation Information for the Librarian," *Collection Management* 4 (Fall 1982), 1.

deterioration of books."[13]   The Yale study has spawned similar analyses, seeking to identify the variety and extent of preservation problems.[14]   Attention has also been given to the costs of various preservation alternatives, such as the cost-accounting done by the RLG Cooperative Preservation Microfilming Project,[15] and to the development of viable cooperative preservation programs.[16]

The library preservation literature of only a decade ago was firmly built on the premise that all information should be preserved, a foundation that has been shaken a little.   The report by Warren J. Haas on a national preservation system and subsequent efforts to structure such a system accepted comprehensive preservation as a legitimate goal.[17]   This idea has been hard to abandon at both the national and institutional levels.   However, consistent conclusions regarding the pervasiveness of the preservation problem and recognition of the immense resources required have led to an increasing, if still fledgling, interest in the matter of selection.   In the late 1980s, librarians seem to be acknowledging that not all can be saved; the decision to preserve one item is also a decision to allow another to deteriorate.   Criteria for selection must be developed and adhered to institutionally and nationally. Fortunately, this need has been recognized.

The schema that have been proposed for assessing library materials based on the value of information content have been propelled by the growing emphasis on "collection management

[13]Gay Walker, Jane Greenfield, John Fox, and Jeffrey S. Simonoff, "The Yale Survey: A Large-Scale Study of Book Deterioration in the Yale University Library," *College and Research Libraries* 46 (March 1985), 112.

[14]Randall Bond, Mary DeCarlo, Elizabeth Henes, and Eileen Snyder, "Preservation Study at the Syracuse University Libraries," *College and Research Libraries* 48 (March 1987), 132-47; Linda Nainis and Laura A. Bedard, "Preservation Book Survey in an Academic Law Library," *Law Library Journal* 78 (Spring 1986), 243-59.

[15]Patricia A. McClung, "Costs Associated With Preservation Microfilming: Results of the Research Libraries Group Study," *Library Resources & Technical Services* 30 (October/December 1986), 363-74.

[16]Nancy E. Gwinn, "The Rise and Fall and Rise of Cooperative Projects," *Library Resources & Technical Services* 29 (January/March 1985), 80-86, and Margaret S. Child, "The Future of Cooperative Preservation Microfilming," *ibid.* 29 (January/March 1985), 94-101.

[17]*Preparation of Detailed Specifications for a National System for the Preservation of Library Materials* (Washington, D.C.:   Association of Research Libraries, 1972).

... the systematic, efficient and economic stewardship of library resources."[18] The concept of collection management has provided a new source for the improvement of selection for acquisition, and archivists have been influenced by the collection management approach in developing their own selection schemes. Cooperative collecting projects exist at both local and national levels for libraries. Notable among these are efforts sponsored by the Research Libraries Group.   The Conspectus program invites libraries to assume collecting responsibility for specific subject areas, and these commitments have influenced the design of the Cooperative Preservation Microfilming Project.   RLG is sponsoring an intensive investigation into cooperative collecting in two subject areas, and carefully analyzing the extent to which these can be said to be documented in American collections.

While collection management theory has had a significant effect on selection for acquisition, its influence on selection for preservation is less apparent. This may be partly attributable to the way that many institutional preservation programs operate.   Selection for acquisition assumes that subject specialists design and control the strategy for acquisition. In contrast, much preservation activity focuses on evaluating damaged materials already in the library's custody.   The process is often item specific and reactive.   Many library preservation programs are "circulation-driven," responding to damage or deterioration detected after use. Faced with trucks of decaying volumes from diverse subject areas, the tendency is to concentrate on the selection of treatment or reformatting options; strategic analysis of information can seem an unaffordable luxury.

Librarians are aware of the need to gain control over the flood of damaged materials. To this end some preservation selection criteria have been proposed. Some approaches are relatively simple, relying on evaluation of paper and binding condition, or documentation of use.[19] Others consider more

[18]Paul H. Mosher, "Collection Development to Collection Management: Toward Stewardship of Library Resources," *Collection Management* 4 (Winter 1982), 45; Dan C. Hazen, "Collection Development, Collection Management, and Preservation," *Library Resources & Technical Services* 26 (January/March 1982), 6-10.

[19]Rose Mary Magrill and Constance Rinehart, "Selection for Preservation: A Case Study," *Library Resources & Technical Services* 24 (Winter 1980), 45-57; Michael E. Holland, "Material Selection for Library Conservation," *Library and Archival Security* 6 (Spring 1984), 7-21; and Christinger Tomer, "Selecting Library Materials for Preservation," *ibid.* 7 (Spring 1985): 1-6.

factors to guide selection. Dan Hazen has defined a set of criteria that includes user demand, "historical precedent and tradition" (potential use), volume and cost of materials, alternatives to preservation (such as interlibrary loan), and the required information needs of certain disciplines.[20] Lisa Williams has composed a similar list that includes monetary value, intellectual value, aesthetic or artifactual value, projected use, and usability or condition.[21]

The most elaborate and most recent selection model is the one advanced by Ross Atkinson. Atkinson developed a three class structure. The first class represents items of "high economic value," the second higher use items, and the third lower use material, such as specialized subject collection materials, that need more careful evaluation. According to the author, classes one and two represent decisions to be made by the local library, while judgments about the third class can only be resolved by extensive cooperative efforts that identify significant "subject collections in place," as the basis for effective preservation decision making.[22] Although Atkinson's model is the most provocative of those suggested for selection guidance, it also reveals the embryonic nature of library selection criteria; Atkinson's model suggests comprehensive subject preservation through cooperation, an idea that has been questioned by at least one other librarian.[23]

The tendency in library preservation has been to identify first the physical preservation needs of various information media, then to address society's information needs and the information value of the materials in library collections. The process should be reversed. Concern for the physical needs of collections is commendable, but the threat of loss is only half the preservation challenge. Librarians, and all information professionals, must first make the hard choices about what information should be preserved, then seek the appropriate

[20]"Collection Development," 7-10.

[21]"Selecting Rare Books for Physical Conservation: Guidelines for Decision Making," *College and Research Libraries* 46 (March 1985), 153-59.

[22]"Selection for Preservation: A Materialistic Approach," *Library Resources & Technical Services* 30 (October/December 1986), 341-53.

[23]Margaret Child, "Further Thoughts on 'Selection for Preservation: A Materialistic Approach,'" *Library Resources & Technical Services* 30 (October/December 1986), 354-62.

means and resources to accomplish the preservation.[24] The development and use of appropriate information selection criteria remains a daunting task and the resources remain insufficient. Here, however, librarians can make use of the ideas and practices of their archival colleagues.

A Source of Help for the Selection Problem

Archivists have been concerned with selection of records of enduring value -- a process they term "appraisal" -- since the formation of an independent profession over half a century ago. They have long recognized that they cannot save all unique records, and, furthermore, that not all unique records are worthy of preservation. Archivists have also accepted that appraisal is their "first responsibility," requiring careful thought, then action that affects all else they do.[25] The records chosen for preservation determine all other of their administrative functions and responsibilities.

Archivists have also agreed that the selection of records of enduring value is their most difficult work. One prominent archivist recently wrote that

> appraisal is one of the archivist's most intellectually demanding and difficult tasks. Pressure to keep records comes from members of the research community who see value in almost everything. Pressure to destroy comes from the genuine and immediate constraints of limited space, limited resources to preserve, and limited staff to arrange and describe new accessions.[26]

Appraisal has been called "an inexact science, perhaps more an

---

[24]Although this essay refers primarily to selection studies about book preservation, the process is relevant for all library materials. Newspapers, for example, have been generally treated as items that require comprehensive preservation. The U.S. Newspaper Program has, however, shifted its focus to "selective" preservation that includes criteria of research importance, physical condition, intended audience, geographic scope, availability of nearly complete runs, and period of publication; see Jeffrey Field, "The U.S. Newspaper Program," *Conservation Administration News* no. 30 (July 1987), 5, 24.

[25]For the importance of appraisal to the archival profession, see *Planning for the Archival Profession: A Report of the SAA Task Force on Goals and Priorities* (Chicago: Society of American Archivists, 1986), 8-13.

[26]Max J. Evans, "The Visible Hand: Creating a Practical Mechanism for Cooperative Appraisal," *Midwestern Archivist* 11, no. 1 (1986), 9.

art"[27] and an "elusive, subjective process."[28]   This formidable
task has produced, not surprisingly, numerous debates,[29] but
these disagreements have resulted in a dynamic and improving
archival function in the 1980s, the subject of ever more
sophisticated research, testing, and development.

Like library preservation literature and practice, archival
appraisal theory and practice have gone through several
distinct phases. Like their nineteenth century predecessors the
state and local historical societies, modern archival programs
in their earliest years rapidly, and often randomly, collected
everything and anything that seemed to possess historical
relevance, emphasizing older materials.   Much of great value
was saved, along with questionable "historical" curiosities.[30]
The establishment of the National Archives in 1934 and its
difficult task of determining what to save out of massive, and
rapidly increasing, quantities of records[31] led to the first
formally articulated appraisal criteria by the early 1940s.[32]

These basic principles were later codified by T. R.
Schellenberg, the National Archives' principal theoretician.
Schellenberg noted that "public" records have two values --
"primary values for the originating agency itself and secondary
values for other agencies and private users." Schellenberg then
denoted two broad kinds of secondary values -- the "evidence"
the records "contain of the organization and functioning of the
Government body that produced" the records, and the
"information" the records "contain on persons, corporate bodies,

[27]Leonard Rapport, "No Grandfather Clause: Reappraising Accessioned
Records," *American Archivist* 44 (Spring 1981), 149.

[28]Fredric Miller, "Use, Appraisal, and Research: A Case Study of Social
History," *American Archivist* 49 (Fall 1986), 372.

[29]Such as Rapport, "No Grandfather Clause" and Karen Benedict,
"Invitation to a Bonfire: Reappraisal and Deaccessioning of Records as
Collection Management Tools in an Archives -- A Reply to Leonard
Rapport," *American Archivist* 47 (Winter 1984), 43-49.

[30]For a perceptive essay on this subject, see Henry D. Shapiro, "Putting
the Past Under Glass: Preservation and the Idea of History in the Mid-
Nineteenth Century," *Prospects* 10 (1985), 243-78.

[31]For an idea of the scale of the challenge facing these archivists, see
James Gregory Bradsher, "A Brief History of the Growth of Federal
Government Records, Archives, and Information 1789-1985," *Government
Publications Review* 13, no. 4 (1986), 491-505.

[32]The pioneering essay was Philip C. Brooks, "The Selection of Records
for Preservation," *American Archivist* 3 (October 1940), 221-34.

things, problems, conditions, and the like, with which the Government body dealt."[33] Schellenberg's criteria remained the basis for archival appraisal, even for non-government records, for nearly three decades and continue to play a prominent role in archival appraisal systems. Archivists have embellished his criteria, adding such elements as age, volume, form, institutional acquisition policies and intrinsic value,[34] and techniques such as sampling.[35]

Over the past decade, however, archivists have become increasingly concerned about the validity and effectiveness of their selection criteria. This dissatisfaction has come from a variety of directions and for a number of reasons. One, archivists became uneasy that the unilateral application of appraisal techniques by individual records programs was not necessarily adding up to an adequate documentary record of any aspect of the country's past or present.[36] Two, archivists recognized that modern information technology and other changes in modern society, such as the remarkable interrelatedness of government and private records creators, limited the effectiveness of standard archival appraisal techniques.[37] Even a single event or function cannot be satisfactorily documented without examining the records of many records creators. Three, archivists noted that the ideas of Schellenberg, widely followed and applied, were not

[33]*The Appraisal of Modern Public Records, Bulletin* of the National Archives, no. 8 (October 1956), 6.

[34]Maynard J. Brichford, *Archives & Manuscripts: Appraisal & Accessioning* (Chicago: Society of American Archivists, 1977). For the idea of intrinsic value, also developing out of the National Archives, see *Intrinsic Value in Archival Material*, National Archives and Records Service Staff Information Paper, 21 (Washington, D.C.: National Archives and Records Service, General Services Administration, 1982).

[35]David R. Kepley, "Sampling in Archives: A Review," *American Archivist* 47 (Summer 1984), 237-42.

[36]F. Gerald Ham, "The Archival Edge," *American Archivist* 38 (January 1975), 5-13 and Andrea Hinding, "Toward Documentation: New Collecting Strategies in the 1980s," *Options for the 80s: Proceedings of the Second National Conference of the Association of College and Research Libraries*, eds. Michael D. Kathman and Virgil F. Massman (Greenwich, Connecticut: JAI Press, Inc., 1981), 531-38.

[37]F. Gerald Ham, "Archival Choices: Managing the Historical Record in An Age of Abundance," *American Archivist* 47 (Winter 1984), 11-22 and "Archival Strategies for the Post-Custodial Era," *ibid.* 44 (Summer 1981), 207-16; Helen W. Samuels, "Who Controls the Past," *ibid.* 49 (Spring 1986), 109-24.

necessarily applicable to non-government records creators and often did not take into enough account reasons other than legal mandates for records creation and continuing use.[38] Four, archivists determined that many important actions were not being adequately documented in records traditionally saved as the primary sources of information of enduring value.[39] Archival theory presumed that the records of key decision makers or important administrative units fully documented the records creator; in fact, decisions, policy formulation, and actions are often determined by means that are not captured in the records of those key individuals and institutional units.

Although archival appraisal criteria have always emphasized informational or research value as a primary means of selection for preservation, two newly proposed archival appraisal models have reaffirmed the importance of this factor. Both models have been enriched by library collection management ideas.[40] A tripartite model for college and university records appraisal considers the value of information, costs of retention, and the implications of appraisal recommendations. Informational value is the first and most important criteria to be considered, however.[41]

The "documentation strategy" model is another framework that stresses information criteria before all else. This strategy is "a plan formulated to assure the documentation of an ongoing issue, activity, or geographic area." A team of records creators, administrators (including librarians), and users sees that the strategy, constantly refined, is "carried out through the mutual efforts of many institutions and individuals influencing both the creation of records and the archival

---

[38]Frank Boles and Julia Marks Young, "Exploring the Black Box: The Appraisal of University Administrative Records," *American Archivist* 48 (Spring 1985), 121-40; Joan K. Haas, Helen W. Samuels, and Barbara Simmons, *Appraising the Records of Modern Science and Technology: A Guide* (Cambridge: MIT, 1985) and "The MIT Appraisal Project and Its Broader Implications," *American Archivist* 49 (Summer 1986), 310-14.

[39]David J. Klaassen, "Achieving Balanced Documentation: Social Services from a Consumer Perspective," *Midwestern Archivist* 11, no. 2 (1986), 111-24 and JoAnne Yates, "Internal Communication Systems in American Business Structures: A Framework to Aid Appraisal," *American Archivist* 48 (Spring 1985), 141-58.

[40]Jutta Reed-Scott, "Collection Management Strategies for Archivists," *American Archivist* 47 (Winter 1984), 23-29.

[41]Boles and Young, "The Black Box."

retention of a portion of them."[42]   This appraisal mechanism includes in it the once widely regarded as heretical notion that archivists persuade records creators to create documentation where significant information gaps exist, along with a reemphasis on understanding the universe of information before selecting what should be saved.

How can these trends in archival appraisal be of use to librarians, given the many legitimate differences between libraries and archives?[43]   The two kinds of institutions have related, but distinctively different collecting missions, which influence the nature of the materials in their care.   Most library collections (books and periodicals) are not unique by nature.   Additionally, while there is a pronounced trend toward cooperative collection development, libraries will probably always have a significant overlap of collections between repositories in order to serve local constituencies.   The library's mission might be better compared to the combined functions of a records center and archives, because libraries have a mandate to make available information of temporary as well as long-term value.   Yet within the library, the same resources must be used for physical maintenance of ephemeral materials and for information of enduring value.

These differences are not more significant than the preservation challenge faced by both libraries and archives. Both are pressured to preserve by diverse constituencies; both are pressured to destroy (or not to interrupt the process of deterioration) by limited resources.   Libraries and archives share responsibility for materials of artifactual value, and for media chiefly valuable for their intellectual content.   This similarity has prompted both professions to develop reformatting as a preservation technique, as well as to seek to preserve some materials in their original format.[44]

---

[42]Samuels, "Who Controls the Past," 115.

[43]For the full range of differences in the two professions, refer to Robert L. Clark, Jr., ed., *Archive-Library Relations* (New York: R. R. Bowker Co., 1976) and Lawrence J. McCrank, ed., *Archives and Library Administration: Divergent Traditions and Common Concerns* (New York: Haworth Press, 1986).

[44]A decade ago, Pamela Darling sagely advised librarians that they "must learn to distinguish within [their] own collections between those things that are valuable as artifacts quite apart from the information they contain and those that are valuable chiefly - or only - for their intellectual contents." Likewise, archivists have developed the notion of intrinsic value to identify those items that require preservation in their original format in order to maintain all of their essential information. Darling, "Our Fragile

Coping with the insurmountable problems of physical deterioration of information media and evaluating the content of extant collections have motivated librarians and archivists to experiment with new strategies for collection development and appraisal. Archivists are only beginning to explore the idea of a national plan for documentation, selection and preservation, whereas the concept of a national preservation effort is already established among librarians. Librarians have not tested the potential of collection and preservation strategies based on the more ruthless (at least, that is the way many librarians might first view them) collecting models of archival appraisal. This may be the time for libraries to adopt the "information value first" perspective that is currently enlightening archival appraisal and preservation theory and practice. If the difficulties of designing information selection strategies can be resolved, libraries will have one more tool for whittling the preservation problem down to size.

Recommendations for a Library Preservation Selection Research Agenda

1.   *Re-evaluate the concept of comprehensive collecting and preservation.* Libraries have accepted the reality that no single repository can build and maintain comprehensive collections in every discipline. Yet even the premise that shared collection development and preservation responsibility will make possible preservation of all materials in designated subject areas may not be useful in two respects. First, resources for preservation may still be inadequate given the quantity and condition of information to be saved. Second, this approach may waste resources on information of little value. Comprehensiveness might be more profitably defined in terms of quality of information, rather than quantity of material.

2.   *Test the potential of recent library and archival appraisal models for preservation selection.* Models suggested by Atkinson, and archivists Hackman, Samuels, and Warnow-Blewett should be investigated. Archival appraisal models suggest that preservation selection follows information selection,

---

Inheritance: The Challenge of Preserving Library Materials," *The ALA Yearbook 1978: A Review of Library Events 1977*, vol. 3 (Chicago: American Library Association, 1978), xxxv; Trudy Huskamp Peterson, "The National Archives and the Archival Theorist Revisited, 1954-1984," *American Archivist* 49 (Spring 1986), 129.

and propose various methods for systematic evaluation of information content.

3. *Refocus and redesign user studies to assess quality of use as a tool for preservation selection.* While there is disagreement over the weight that documented use should have in determining preservation priorities for research collections, there is little question that use is a significant consideration in determining the value of information. To date, user studies have tended to be descriptive, emphasizing quantity and frequency of use, and research methods. Techniques are needed for more substantive analysis of use, to determine why certain sources are consulted and how information is interpreted and applied.[45] More qualitative analysis of use might enable libraries to publicize information sources in ways that would build increased support for preservation efforts.

4. *Evaluate and work to reconcile local and institutional needs with national preservation efforts.* No matter how sympathetic library administrators are to a national preservation strategy, these sympathies often end up at odds with institutional priorities when the time comes to commit limited resources for preservation. For example, portions of collections that are nationally significant may be in low demand locally, as is frequently the case in an academic library serving both undergraduates and more sophisticated researchers. Forced to choose between constituencies, one highly visible and vocal, the other invisible, many libraries will meet immediate needs at the expense of a long-range preservation strategy. The relationship between local and national preservation concerns is complex and fraught with thorny problems, which must be addressed if the best information resources are to be saved.

5. *Enhance automated systems to facilitate identification and analysis of information of enduring value.* Libraries have been leaders in developing bibliographic systems for access to information sources, including manuscripts and not-textual

---

[45]See especially Paul Conway, "Facts and Frameworks: An Approach to Studying the Users of Archives," *American Archivist* 49 (Fall 1986), 393-407 and Bruce W. Dearstyne, "What Is the *Use* of Archives? A Challenge for the Profession," *ibid.* 50 (Winter 1987), 76-87.

materials. Recent efforts, such as the RLG Conspectus Project[46] should be evaluated[47] and continued, so that automated systems will be of more use in information selection strategies. The proposed addition of preservation information in the MARC format should also be an effective management tool. Other possible enhancements include minimizing the number of databases (automated and manual) to be consulted for preservation information, and concerted efforts to increase the number of repositories reporting their preservation decisions in the automated systems.

6. *Initiate more interaction with other information specialists and other types of repositories for planning and problem solving.* The agenda for constructive interaction with other information professionals is almost limitless. More than token diplomacy, librarians and archivists must pool their intellectual resources to address the toughest components of the preservation challenge. For example, the question of whether technology will insure the future of traditional information formats, or cause the demise of recorded information cannot be ignored.[48] Working together, libraries and archives could better access and control the potential impact of technology on information creation and selection, reformatting options, and preservation management.

7. *Cooperate in statewide assessments of documentation needs and priorities.* State libraries, archives, and other repositories of unique resources should combine forces to survey the quality and condition of local information resources, and to

[46]Nancy E. Gwinn and Paul H. Mosher, "Coordinating Collection Development: The RLG Conspectus," *College and Research Libraries* 44 (March 1983), 128-40.

[47]Several archival institutions with statewide collecting mandates - Minnesota, Wisconsin, and Michigan - have done some analysis of their effectiveness in documenting a state. The New York State Archives worked with a group of archivists, librarians, historians, and others to plan for the effective documentation of Western New York. In each case manageable sets of topics have been used in favor of more complex library classification systems. See, for example, Gloria Thompson, "From Profile to Policy: A Minnesota Historical Society Case Study in Collection Development," *Midwestern Archivist* 8, no. 2 (1983), 29-39.

[48]For two extreme responses to this question, see *Books In Our Future* (Washington, D.C.: Joint Committee on the Library of Congress of the United States, 1984) and Gordon B. Neavill, "Electronic Publishing, Libraries, and the Survival of Information," *Library Resources & Technical Services* 28 (January/March 1984), 81.

determine the framework against which the value of information should be measured. This state-by-state analysis approach has already proven beneficial for historical records programs, by involving records creators and users, and by gathering data useful for local and national preservation strategies.[49] A different geographic perspective on information resources would complement what is known about the subject strengths and condition of collections in individual libraries.

8. *Assess the impact to date of reformatting programs on use and access to information.* Libraries are investing increasing resources in reformatting irreplaceable, damaged materials with high information and low artifactual value. There is little question that this course is wise from a management perspective, but how do the users, who must ultimately support preservation programs, perceive this choice? Are reformatted items as frequently consulted as they were in their original format? Are users following materials from the shelves to the film cabinets, or are they frequenting interlibrary loan offices to locate still usable hardcopy? When is photocopying a wiser use of preservation resources than conversion to microform? Are libraries successfully affording the conversion to microform of materials traditionally used as hardcopy? These and other questions should be answered to determine if our best efforts to save valuable information are serving the audiences for whom the information is preserved. The economics of preservation selection must suit the goals.

9. *Integrate preservation selection with collection management education.* As described in this essay, collection management is the process of both acquiring and preserving information according to a defined strategy. Practically speaking, under the collection management umbrella, library professionals will tend to specialize in either preservation or acquisition, but this specialization should not undermine the

---

[49]For a summary of the statewide assessment reports funded by NHPRC, see Lisa B. Weber, ed., *Documenting America: Assessing the Condition of National Historical Records in the States* ([Albany]: National Association of State Archives and Records Administrators in cooperation with the National Historical Publications and Records Commission, [1983]). For the context and importance of these reports, see Larry J. Hackman, "A Perspective on American Archives," *Public Historian* 8 (Summer 1986), 10-28. One state has already began the process of such broad cooperative analysis on the issue of preservation of information sources. *Our Memory At Risk: Preserving New York's Unique Research Resources* (Albany: New York Document Conservation Advisory Council, 1987) was an out-growth of New York's historical records assessment report published in 1984.

essential interrelatedness of the functions of selecting and preserving information. Library training for collection managers and preservation and subject specialists should reflect this close relationship.

10. *Design interdisciplinary graduate and mid-career training programs in documentation and preservation selection.* Archivists have generally recognized that the best sources of education for them are programs that draw primarily upon library and information science and history.[50] Graduate and continuing education programs should expose librarians to the best of archives and library theory in analysis of information for selection and preservation.

---

[50]See, for example, Lawrence J. McCrank, "Prospects for Integrating Historical and Information Studies in Archival Education," *American Archivist* 42 (October 1979), 443-55 and "Conservation and Collection Management: Educational Problems and Opportunities," *Journal of Education for Librarianship* 22 (Summer/Fall 1981), 20-43.

TWELVE

ANALYTICAL BIBLIOGRAPHY
AND THE MODERN ARCHIVIST: A
COMMENTARY ON SIMILARITIES,
DIFFERENCES, AND PROSPECTS
FOR COOPERATION

Introduction

When I started out in my archival career, I had some rigid
notions of what archivists and other related professionals did
and did not do. One of my strongest presuppositions was
reserved for the rare book collector, specialist, and custodian.
I viewed these individuals in the most pejorative sense of
"antiquarian." It was difficult for me to understand individuals
who seemed mostly interested in fondling old bindings or in the
monetary value of certain rare or unusual printings, despite my
own interests in historical records. With the benefit of
hindsight, it is possible for me to see now that this was a view
derived from my inexperience, my first employment in one of
the older private historical societies, and my contact with rare
book persons that were hardly typical of the field. Nearly
twenty years later, however, it is troubling to me that many,
if not most, archivists still possess such views or, at the least,
have little understanding of what rare book librarianship and
the study of books, such as represented by analytical
bibliography, are really about; I believe it is also true that
those who work with rare books are generally unaware of the
principles and practices of archival administration. This is
partly due to historical events, of course, as archivists,
manuscript curators, and rare book librarians and their
collections followed three generally unique paths of
development, despite some common origins.[1] Regardless of the

---

[1]Thomas R. Adams, for example, sees four different motivations that
have shaped distinctive library collections: 1) the free public library and the
quest to fill all needs; 2) the university research library and the effort to
fill the needs of certain selective elements of society; 3) the historical society
seeking to collect a particular subject or subjects; and 4) the private
collector in quest of satisfying personal desires ("Librarians as Enemies of
Books?" *College & Research Libraries* 45 [May 1984], 197). Archivists or
manuscript collectors add to this diversity by traditionally coming out of
the professional historical community seeking to serve scholarship and now
increasingly out of more narrowly-defined service to governments and
corporations and other profit-making institutions; archivists now just as
likely function as parts of information resources programs or management
information systems along with records managers, data processors,
technicians, and administrators. Adams writes that the place of the
bibliographer "should be somewhere between libraries, museums, and the
history profession. We [bibliographers] partake of some of the

reasons, the poor relationship between the two fields hurts both the archivist and the analytical bibliographer. This essay compares and contrasts the functions, methods, and perspectives of analytical bibliography, one vital component of the rare book librarian's world,[2] to modern archival administration. It continues this volume's examination of archival administration with other information and related professions.

Analytical (sometimes called critical) bibliography, and its related studies of historical, textual, and descriptive bibliography, is the "study of books as material objects." It is a specialty within library and humanistic spheres that studies the book and all its parts in the assumption that any individual book is a representation of the society in which it was produced and that analyzing aggregates of books will assist in understanding the means and circumstances of transmitting ideas and the general nature of past society. "Each book is a monument, great or small, of the civilization of its time and place . . . . [B]y assembling such historical book descriptions we [bibliographers] help to write the history of all the material means and circumstances surrounding the transmissions of ideas."[3] In such study books are appreciated for a variety of

characteristics of each and add to them our own conviction of the importance of something that stands by itself, the book" (p. 200). If that is the case, archivists are probably somewhere between the history profession, librarianship, and information science.

For some other suggestive comments on these origins, see Clifton H. Jones, "Remarks on the Integration of Special Collections," *College & Research Libraries* 45 (November 1984), 437-41; William L. Joyce, "Rare Books, Manuscripts, and Other Special Collections Materials: Integration or Separation?" *ibid.*, pp. 442-45; and Richard C. Berner, "Manuscript Collections, Archives, and Special Collections: Their Relationships," *ibid.*, 446-49.

[2]Throughout this essay I am making the assumption that many rare book librarians contribute to analytical bibliographic scholarship and that analytical bibliography is a skill essential to the rare book librarian's work. Of course, some analytical bibliographers are university-based faculty members or other independent scholars. It is difficult, however, to imagine a rare book librarian functioning adequately without a considerable knowledge of analytical bibliography. This would be akin to an individual working as an archivist with insufficient training in archival theory and methods. Although this may occur, it is hardly an ideal situation.

[3]Roy Stokes, *Esdaile's Manual of Bibliography*, 5th rev. ed. (Metuchen, New Jersey: Scarecrow Press, 1981), p. 11. For a brief introduction to the nature of this work see also Terry Belanger, "Descriptive Bibliography," in *Book Collecting: A Modern Guide*, ed. Jean Peters (New York: R. R. Bowker Co., 1977), 97-115.

reasons, ranging from the artistic expressions of their binders and type setters to their serving as important historical documents fundamental for understanding the past. As analytical bibliography has developed over the years, it has spawned specialized procedures to support its purposes. It has become, furthermore, a cornerstone of the rare book librarian's work.

Archival administration is not focused on the printed book, obviously, but upon the manuscripts routinely generated by individuals and families and the records created by institutions. The archival profession desires to identify and preserve manuscripts and records that have continuing or enduring value for researchers seeking to understand the historical development of society. Archivists also wish to serve a variety of administrative needs of institutional records creators such as businesses and government agencies.[4] As more fully articulated in recent years, the archivist and manuscript curator are also endeavoring to document present society for present and future researchers. The German archival theorist Hans Booms has written that archival appraisal, the function of determining which records should be preserved, is the "archetypal activity of the archivist." He noted that appraisal has "undergone a qualitative transformation in the last generation of archivists. Originally, it consisted of collecting and preserving more or less sparsely and randomly retained 'leftovers.' Then, as the volume of material with the potential of forming part of the documentary heritage began to exceed the limits of what could be physically incorporated into that documentary heritage, this function changed to comprise mainly the acquisition and preservation of material chosen more or less thoughtfully from

---

[4]There are now a number of book-length definitions of the work of the archivist. The classic volumes on this topic are Hilary Jenkinson, *A Manual of Archive Administration*, rev. 2nd ed. (London: Percy Lund, Humphries & Co., Ltd., 1966) and T. R. Schellenberg, *Modern Archives: Principles and Techniques* (Chicago: University of Chicago Press, 1956) and *The Management of Archives* (New York: Columbia University Press, 1965). More recent books have tended to be collections of essays by a variety of authors, such as Maygene F. Daniels and Timothy Walch, eds., *A Modern Archives Reader: Basic Readings on Archival Theory and Practice* (Washington, D.C.: National Archives and Records Service, 1984); Ann Pederson, ed., *Keeping Archives* (Sydney: Society of Australian Archivists, Inc., 1987); and James Gregory Bradsher, ed., *Managing Archives and Archival Institutions* (Chicago: University of Chicago Press, 1989).

out of an overabundant store."[5] Ensuring such documentation also requires, just like analytical bibliography, the use of a wide variety of techniques and methods to sort through a massive quantity of recorded information and to manage effectively that portion of information having enduring value.[6]

There are obvious similarities and differences between the *weltanschauung* and methods of the archivist and the bibliographer. They share many mutual concerns related to acquisition, preservation, security, use, resources, education and training, cataloging, and selection. If nothing else, historical records and rare books are often stored together or administratively placed in proximity to each other in institutions.[7] Consider, for example, statements about the missions of the rare book scholar and the archivist. John Carter wrote this way about the work of the rare book collector (individual or institutional): "It was . . . and is still one of the collector's most significant functions to anticipate the scholar and the historian, to find some interest where none was recognized before, to rescue books from obscurity, to pioneer a subject or an author by seeking out and assembling the raw material for study, in whatever its printed form."[8] A president of the Society of American Archivists also similarly called upon his colleagues to anticipate research trends and needs: "[The archivist] must become the research community's Renaissance

---

[5]"Society and the Formation of a Documentary Heritage: Issues in the Appraisal of Archival Sources," *Archivaria* 24 (Summer 1987), 76. For another effort to place appraisal in its general context in archival administration, see Richard J. Cox and Helen W. Samuels, "The Archivist's 'First Responsibility': A Research Agenda for the Identification and Selection of Records of Enduring Value," *American Archivist* 51 (Winter/Spring 1988), 28-42.

[6]For citations to the literature on archival appraisal techniques and theory, from sampling to institutional acquisition policies to multi-institutional strategies, start with Julia Marks Young, comp., "Annotated Bibliography on Appraisal," *American Archivist* 48 (Spring 1985), 190-216.

[7]See Sidney E. Berger, "What is So Rare . . .: Issues in Rare Book Librarianship," *Library Trends* 36 (Summer 1987): 9-22 and compare with *Planning for the Archival Profession: A Report of the SAA Task Force on Goals and Priorities* (Chicago: Society of American Archivists, 1986). This can also be seen in the many standards and guidelines that have been adopted concerning both rare books and archival materials. See John B. Thomas III, "Standards and Guidelines Prepared by the Rare Books and Manuscripts Section of the Association of College and Research Libraries," *Rare Books & Manuscripts Librarianship* 2 (Fall 1987), 109-12.

[8]*Taste & Technique in Book Collecting* (London: Private Libraries Association, 1970), 6.

man. He must know that the scope, quality, and direction of research in an open-ended future depends upon the soundness of his judgment and the keenness of his perceptions about scholarly inquiry. But if he is passive, uninformed, with a limited view of what constitutes the archival record, the collections that he acquires will never hold up a mirror for mankind."[9] Not only do these views mesh well, but in some ways, in fact, the bibliographer has more in common with archivists or manuscript curators than with librarians.[10]

This essay will initially explore some of these shared and dissimilar aspects of analytical bibliography and archival administration. More importantly, however, this paper will examine how the skills and perspective of the analytical bibliographer can possibly enhance the work of the archivist and manuscript curator, although the modern archivist in the United States has not generally worked with bibliographers or studied bibliographic methods and practices. Indeed, there has been a decidedly noticeable lack of articles on any of the branches of bibliography-related topics in archival journals in recent years. Six articles in a fifty year run of the leading archival journal in the United States, the *American Archivist*, (see Table One) reveals that the relationship between the analytical bibliographer or rare book librarian and the archivist is a relationship that may not be understood very well and that is certainly neglected. Of course, the reverse is also true. Bibliographers have paid little attention to the work of archivists. Over the last twenty years, a time when archival research and literature has begun to expand in both quantity and quality, leading journals on bibliographical research have barely paid attention to such achievement.[11]

This neglected and malformed relationship may be partly due to the relatively recent development of analytical bibliography and the imprecision of even its basic definitions; similar developmental problems in the archival community

[9]F. Gerald Ham, "The Archival Edge," *American Archivist* 38 (January 1975), 13.

[10]See, for example, Daniel Traister, "A Caucus-Race and a Long Tale: The Profession of Rare Book Librarianship in the 1980s," *Library Trends* 36 (Summer 1987), 141-56.

[11]A scanning of the last twenty years of the *Papers of the Bibliographical Society of America* and *The Library* found no reviews on archival publications (except for an occasional review of a published guide to manuscript collections) and few articles on archival-related topics. For an understanding of the changes now underway in archival administration research and writing, refer to chapter seven in this volume.

TABLE ONE

ANALYTICAL BIBLIOGRAPHY IN THE
AMERICAN ARCHIVIST, 1938-87*

Years	Articles		Reviews	
1938-49	216	(0)	292	(3)
1950-59	221	(1)	461	(3)
1960-69	340	(0)	397	(9)
1970-79	217	(2)	432	(22)
1980-87	237	(3)	258	(6)
Totals	1231	(6)	1840	(43)

*   The figures in parentheses represent articles and reviews that have some relationship to rare book librarianship and analytical bibliography.

certainly contribute to the problem. G. Thomas Tanselle has written that "although the listing of books is an ancient activity, the examination of the physical evidence in books was rarely undertaken until relatively recent times . . . . The emergence of analytical and descriptive bibliography as recognizable fields is therefore essentially a twentieth-century phenomenon."[12] Ross Atkinson has also written that although there seems to be general agreement about two broad categories of bibliographical work and study, "what has not yet been sufficiently established . . . is a precise definition of these divisions and subdivisions *in relation to each other*."[13] Another leader in this field, Thomas R. Adams, has also suggested that there has been even a lack of coordinated research within analytical bibliography, resulting in some confusion.

For all too long there has been a tendency in bibliography, particularly analytical bibliography, for each line of research

---

[12]"Bibliographical History as a Field of Study," *Studies in Bibliography* 41 (1988), 34. For example, Fredson Bowers's 1949 book on bibliographical description has been seen as the beginning of modern bibliographical method. See G. Thomas Tanselle, "The Achievement of Fredson Bowers," *Papers of the Bibliographical Society of America* 79 no. 2 (1985), 175-90 and David L. Vander Meulen, "The History and Future of Bowers's *Principles*," *ibid.* 79 no. 2 (1985): 197-219.

[13]"An Application of Semeiotics to the Definition of Bibliography," *Studies in Bibliography* 33 (1980), 59. For other attempts to define bibliography see Lloyd Hibberd, "Physical and Reference Bibliography," *The Library*, 5th series, 20 (1965), 124-34; G. Thomas Tanselle, "Descriptive Bibliography and Library Cataloguing," *Studies in Bibliography* 30 (1977), 1-56; and Tanselle, "Bibliography and Science," *Studies in Bibliography* 27 (1974): 55-89.

to go its separate way, drawing on the work of colleagues only when needed. Little wonder that, today, scholars coming to the subject from outside the field who would like to make full use of the work that has already been done find it something like a mine field in which they are in danger of stumbling over apparently hidden areas of research that can damage the progress of the work.[14]

Archivists may have found it difficult, therefore, to perceive what it is they need to know about a field in such a state of flux. Just as importantly, however, there is little evidence that archivists are even aware of the major texts and references on analytical bibliography and rare books librarianship that could be valuable tools in their own work.[15] This ignorance may also be attributable to the fact that archival administration is a field itself undergoing re-definition and change. The until recent lack of articulation of archival theory or the subject matter that should be taught in graduate archival courses is indication of a profession that might find it difficult to relate to another discipline such as rare book librarianship or research methods such as analytical bibliography.[16]

---

[14]Book review in the *Papers of the Bibliographical Society of America* 79 no. 4 (1985), 578.

[15]There really appears to be no rhyme or reason for what books in the field of rare book librarianship and scholarship get reviewed in archival journals. There are, for example, many references to studies on the preservation and durability of book paper that archivists would naturally be interested in (for example, *American Archivist*, vol. 230, 341-42; vol. 24, 185-87, 187-88), but what else turns up seems to a potpourri of related publications. One volume of *American Book-Prices Current* gets a review (vol. 5, 108-10), one study on bookbinding gets a short notice (vol. 31, 77), and then a analysis of watermarks appears (vol. 36, 253-54). None of the major texts such as those by Stokes or Gaskell are reviewed, even if to point out major differences of approach between the two fields.

[16]Education, along with defined knowledge and competencies, are at the heart of any profession and vital to that profession's continued viability. Two recent studies that relate the importance of these elements to professions are Andrew Abbott, *The System of Professions: An Essay on the Division of Expert Labor* (Chicago: University of Chicago Press, 1988) and Eliot Freidson, *Professional Powers: A Study of the Institutionalization of Formal Knowledge* (Chicago: University of Chicago Press, 1986). Yet, archivists are only now seriously defining their knowledge and competencies and developing comprehensive education programs. To understand the general condition of the archival profession, refer to chapter 2 in this volume, and the continuing debate about the state of archival knowledge or theory: Frank G. Burke, "The Future Course of Archival Theory in the

What follows is a description of the interests and outlooks shared by analytical bibliographers and archivists, skills and perspectives of both professionals that can mutually enhance each other's work, and areas of divergent methodologies and interests that create tensions between analytical bibliographers and the modern archivist. Since I am an archivist, I have written this essay primarily for an audience of archivists. This explains why I have elected to end the paper with suggestions to archivists about how they might gain greater familiarity with the practice of analytical bibliography. However, it is also hoped that individuals managing or studying rare books will find in this essay aspects of archival administration valuable to their own work.

Common Ground, Common Differences

There is considerable ground (meaning functions, perspectives, techniques, and practices) shared by the archivist and analytical bibliographer, although it is also true that any bond between the two may be more a potential than actual one. Both professionals share interest in closely-related forms of recorded information, concern for optimum bibliographic control and efficient research access to the materials they manage, uneasiness about possible future trends of the book and historical record, a desire for increased definition of professional standards and professional culture, and concern with the new milieu and expanding influence of the information specialist. A review of the literature of both fields also indicates that there are obvious differences, even tensions. For example, both the archivist and rare book custodian or scholar "selects" items or collections to add to their holdings or to study, but the premises underlying their selection processes are very different and seemingly contradictory, if not irreconcilable. It is, in fact, relatively easy to identify common areas that archivists and rare book librarians and bibliographers themselves perceive to be major differences.

The common ground shared by archivists and bibliographers is most readily defined by the forms of information that they are responsible for in their institutions and that they use in their research. Although many still seem inclined to divide the

United States," *American Archivist.* 44 (Winter 1981), 40-46; Lester J. Cappon, "What, Then, Is There to Theorize About?" *ibid.* 45 (Winter 1982), 19-25; Gregg D. Kimball, "The Burke-Cappon Debate: Some Further Criticisms and Considerations for Archival Theory," *ibid.* 48 (Fall 1985), 369-76; and John W. Roberts, "Archival Theory: Much Ado About Shelving," *ibid.* 50 (Winter 1987), 66-74.

archivist and manuscript curator from printed items and the librarian from original unique source materials, it is more likely that they will be responsible for both (and other) information forms. Twenty years ago John C. Colson contended with this concern when he wrote about the mutual educational needs of librarians and archivists:

> There was a time when librarians were concerned primarily with books, for most of the world's recorded knowledge was in books. That time has passed. The librarian who ignores the other forms in which knowledge is stored does so at peril to his profession. There was a time when archivists were concerned primarily with official manuscript records. That time has also passed. The archivist who ignores the other forms in which official knowledge is stored does so at peril to his profession.[17]

Colson's comments are useful for an initial view of the bibliographer and archivist. Even though the analytical bibliographer will be studying printed books, much of that study will consider the evolution of the text from the author's manuscript and will also require the use of other manuscript and source material for understanding the production, dissemination, and use of the book. The fact that rare imprints are often found in archival and manuscript collections[18] and that book collections often include many different information forms also means that the analytical bibliographer serving as rare book custodian in a library or researching such collections will have a wider range of responsibilities and options than what narrow interpretations of the fields will normally include. As mentioned earlier, archivists and librarians, including analytical bibliographers, also share common ancestors in the ancient archives of the Middle East and the monastic and secular scriptoria of Europe. The earliest books were manuscripts and the earliest manuscripts were treated as books. This problem can also be

---

[17]"On the Education of Archivists and Librarians," *American Archivist* 31 (April 1968), 170.

[18]See, for example, Robert D. Armstrong, "The Beast in the Bathtub, and Other Archival Laments," *American Archivist* 45 (Fall 1982), 375-84; W. A. Katz, "Tracing Western Territorial Imprints Through the National Archives," *Papers of the Bibliographical Society of America* 59 (1965), 1-11; George W. Belknap, "County Archives as a Resource for Regional Imprints Studies," *Pacific Northwest Quarterly* 66 (1975), 76-78; and Belknap, "Early Oregon Imprints in the Oregon State Archives," *Proceedings of the American Antiquarian Society* 66 (1981), 111-27.

seen in some more modern materials. Federal, state, and local government publications can be treated both as library materials, some of which should be accorded the status of rare and all of which are important to the study of government printing, printing in general, and as archival materials for understanding the development of government and society.[19]

Still, there is little solid advice at present for either the archivist or rare book librarian about what to do with materials normally falling under the other's jurisdiction when they are discovered.[20] Are printed materials transferred from the archives to the rare book collection? Should the materials be kept together as collections with full cataloging information to guide people to the various formats they seek? Some have at least paid attention to the fact that there is a close relationship between the book and manuscript in the history of publishing and record keeping. Francis Blouin, in his review of the Eisenstein study on the development of the printing press in early modern Europe, wrote that the study raises "significant new questions and perspectives on process and form [which influence the use and impact of textual materials], questions which are particularly relevant to archivists and librarians who have primary responsibility in society for the preservation of texts of all sorts." Blouin likened this to the impact of modern information technology on archivists and librarians,[21] a matter that I will consider at several other points in this essay. Such expressions have been rare, however, and they have not been translated to procedures or practices for administering diverse collections.

What concern for similar materials does exist has served to bring closer together the analytical bibliographer and the archivist in another way, bibliographic control of and improved access to the materials that they manage and study. Common interests have especially emerged during the past two decades because of the use of automated bibliographic systems that seem to promise improved access as well as collection

---

[19]See, for example, Ernst Posner, *Archives in the Ancient World* (Cambridge: Harvard University Press, 1972) and Lucien Febvre and Henri-Jean Martin, *The Coming of the Book: The Impact of Printing 1450-1800* (London: Verso, 1984). For the treatment of government publications as archival materials, refer to chapter ten in this volume.

[20]See, for example, Richard C. Berner and M. Gary Bettis, "Disposition of Nonmanuscript Items Found Among Manuscripts," *American Archivist* 33 (July 1970), 275-81.

[21]*American Archivist* 44 (Spring 1981), 158.

management. For both archivists and rare books librarians there was a common initial negative or skeptical response (often caused by a kind of institutional parochialism) when offered the possibility of adapting automated bibliographic systems for providing access to their holdings. The uniqueness of individual items or collections generated an attitude of unilaterally administering these materials. In both fields such hesitancy is quickly breaking down. There are also enormous similarities in the various MARC formats and other automated standards for managing rare books, special collections, manuscripts, and archives. These similarities provide the possibility of stronger standards development, shared resources for developing and using such standards, and integrated data bases that will allow researchers to gain information about books, rare books, manuscripts, photographs and prints, and other materials related to a given topic.[22] The analytical bibliographers, although bringing specific needs and interests to the kinds of information going into these systems, generally stand to find their work made easier by improved access to locating multiple copies of publications that they can use for their more specialized study. Archivists, committed to documenting society and making their holdings widely available for research, have devoted significant effort to creating a national bibliographic database of archives and manuscripts. Archivists and rare book bibliographers and librarians have also expressed interest in providing greater information on their collections than content descriptions; provenance information and physical characteristics are potentially just as important to the users of these materials as their textual or informational content. Unfortunately, the development of the Anglo-American Cataloguing Rules, International Standard Bibliographic Description, and MARC formats have all been accomplished with relatively little influence, at least until recently, from analytical bibliographers, rare book librarians, and archivists and manuscript curators. The significant catch-

[22]See Stephen Paul Davis, "Bibliographic Control of Special Collections: Issues and Trends," *Library Trends* 36 (Summer 1987), 9-22; John B. Thomas, III, "The Necessity of Standards in an Automated Environment," *ibid.* 36 (Summer 1987),125-39; and Melissa C. Flannery, "A Review of Recent Developments in Rare Books Cataloguing," *Cataloguing & Classification* Quarterly 7 (Fall 1986), 55-62.

up work remaining to be done opens the door for increased cooperation between these various disciplines.[23]

Both analytical bibliographers (and, of course, rare book custodians) and archivists also share concern about the spreading use of certain forms of information technology challenging the continued relevance of the book and archival record. Undoubtedly, this shared interest is due at least partly to the common origins of rare books and manuscript collections and the motives of their collectors, individual and institutional.[24] Just as likely, however, concern for the future is a common human characteristic and certainly typical of professions in an increasingly complex society. Archivists have articulated such concern in several different ways. They have expressed anxiety about the continuing status of the archivist, the transformation of archival principles and practice, and the lack of interest to preserve the historically and culturally valuable information in society.[25] Librarians have expressed

[23]For understanding the general interest and role of rare book librarians in the development of these systems, see G. Thomas Tanselle, "Descriptive Bibliography and Library Cataloguing," *Studies in Bibliography* 30 (1977), 1-56. The US MARC Archives and Manuscripts Control Format has been developed and used only in the last decade. For an overview of how the AMC format has been developed and is being used, see David Bearman, *Towards National Information Systems for Archives and Manuscript Repositories: The National Information Systems Task Force (NISTF) Papers* (Chicago: Society of American Archivists, 1987) and Anne J. Gilliland, ed., "Automating Intellectual Access to Archives," *Library Trends* 36 (Winter 1988), 495-623. For a sense of the progress that has been made, individuals should refer to the Winter 1989 issue of the Research Libraries Group *News* that describes RLIN's use of MARC AMC since 1984, efforts to develop a national archival data base, continued cooperation by state archives to share appraisal and other information through RLIN's AMC file, work to develop an integrated system to manage archives and museum information, and continuing work on descriptive standards.

[24]See, for example, William L. Joyce, "The Evolution of the Concept of Special Collections in American Research Libraries," *Rare Books & Manuscripts Librarianship* 3 (Spring 1988), 19-29.

[25]See, for example, F. Gerald Ham, "Archival Strategies for the Post-Custodial Era," *American Archivist* 44 (Summer 1981), 207-16; Richard M. Kesner, "Automated Information Management: Is There A Role for the Archivist in the Office of the Future?" *Archivaria* 19 (Winter 1984/85), 162-72; Trudy Huskamp Peterson, "Archival Principles and Records of the New Technology," *American Archivist* 47 (Fall 1984), 383-93; John A. Vernon, "Technology's Effect on the Role of the Archivist," *Provenance* 3 (Spring 1985), 1-12; John C. Mallinson, "Preserving Machine-Readable Archival Records for the Millenia," *Archivaria* 22 (Summer 1986), 147-52 and Sue Gavrel, "Preserving Machine-Readable Archival Records: A Reply to John

similar concerns about the future of their institutions. As one European librarian recently wrote, the notion of the electronic library is promoted with the conviction that the "libraries that we know today will be museums for an outdated technology - printing technology."[26] Such warnings about a future without books have been voiced for many years of course, as Louis B. Wright once suggested that Babylonians probably worried about their clay tablets in the same way,[27] but never more than in the past decade or so when librarians have been flooded with recorded information *and* the increasing problem of mass preservation. Archivists likewise envision museums of paper records, prey to become less regarded and less supported in an age that values information delivered rapidly and cheaply. Others with broader views, like Lawrence J. McCrank, have foreseen the transformation, not necessarily loss, of certain types of institutions. "Libraries holding research materials beyond current high-use periods," McCrank has written, "will become more archival as document repositories, or museological as cultural institutions stressing public programs, while those with immediate service objectives based on current information needs will behave like document clearing houses similar to records management centers."[28] In the future, then, not only may the archivist and analytical bibliographer work side by side with the older information sources of our civilization, it may become extremely difficult for them to know whether new sources are printed or manuscript.[29]

One already noticeable effect of such developments and concerns for analytical bibliographers and archivists has been the decline in the teaching of historical bibliography and

Mallinson," *ibid.*, 153-55.

[26]Svend Larsen, "The Idea of an Electronic Library: A Critical Essay," *Libri* 38 (September 1988), 159. For similar statements, see Paul Stuges, "Policies and Criteria for the Archiving of Electronic Publishing," *Journal of Librarianship* 19 (July 1987), 152-72 and Ithiel De Sola Pool, "The Culture of Electronic Print," *Daedalus* 111 (Fall 1982), 17-31.

[27]*Of Books and Men* (Columbia: University of South Carolina Press), xviii-xx.

[28]"Conservation and Collection Management: Educational Problems and Opportunities," *Journal of Education for Librarianship* 22 (Summer/Fall 1981), 27.

[29]Lise Hesselager, "Fringe or Grey Literature in the National Library: Or 'Papyrolatry' and the Growing Similarity Between the Materials in Libraries and Archives," *American Archivist* 47 (Summer 1984), 255-70.

related subjects, although some think that historians and other disciplines have picked up some of the slack,[30] as education in librarianship has become more oriented to dealing with broader professional concerns such as management and information technology. As Lawrence McCrank has again characterized it, "the gulf between bookmanship and librarianship is widening with the impact of professionalization and current trends toward information studies in library education." He also stated that "rare book librarianship may be more akin to museology than to the future information center. Or, in other words, cultural and information centers may not be synonymous, and rare books are being relegated to the former and excluded from the latter organizations."[31] Librarians in the field sometimes strongly express a similar lack of interest in historical and cultural studies. It is, indeed, *au courant* to emphasize "information" or management over more traditional concerns such as historical studies. One school librarian asked, typically, if it is

> essential to spend time on the history of libraries, of librarianship, or paper, and of books? . . . We do not have to teach the history of the pencil in order to teach writing: we teach how to shape letters and how to write creatively. There are areas of the library school curriculum that should be left to the curious student to study independently, just as the student who wants more information on the development of the computer may pursue it individually. Such a revision would allow the library school to include units on self-confidence, teaching skills, and leadership and management skills.[32]

Both rare book librarians and archivists have also been caught up in professionalization trends in the 1980s. Although

---

[30]Roderick Cave, "Historical Bibliographical Work: Its Role in Library Education," *Journal of Education for Librarianship* 21 (Fall 1980), 109-21.

[31]*Education for Rare Book Librarianship: A Reexamination of Trends and Problems*, University of Illinois Graduate School of Library Science Occasional Papers No. 144 (April 1980), 4, 6-7. This is the most recent survey report, citing and summarizing the earlier reports. See also McCrank's "Public Historians in the Information Professions: Problems in Education and Credentials," *Public Historian* 7 (Summer 1985), 7-22.

[32]Karen K. Niemeyer, "School Libraries and Media Centers," in *Education for Professional Librarians*, ed. Herbert S. White (White Plains, New York: Knowledge Industry Publications, Inc., 1986), 127.

the features of these movements are very similar, the nature of professionalization itself can sharpen boundaries and drive wedges between related professions. Self-study, planning, standard-setting, individual certification, and advocacy and lobbying have all moved to the fore in national and regional professional library and archival associations.[33] As archivists have concentrated on such issues, rare book librarians and other colleagues such as analytical bibliographers have also characterized themselves as constituting a distinct profession. Sidney Berger started out a recent essay by stating that "only in the past fifty years has rare book librarianship become a profession under critical scrutiny and discussed in professional journals and books."[34] Although it has not been sufficiently studied, these similar issues and interests have certainly accentuated the differences between the archivist and rare books custodian and scholar. Both groups have devoted attention to similar issues, but these issues have also caused divisions rather than a search for common interests and perspectives. Emphasizing needs peculiar to one field can stultify needed efforts to build mechanisms for cooperation that are also just as badly needed.

Besides concerns with professionalization, other matters have widened the gulf between that of the archivist and librarian, including the rare books librarian, and the newly emerging corps of information specialists. There are, at the least, very different cultures evident here. Writing about the information industry, Herbert R. Binberg noted that "unlike libraries, whose role is either acculturation, including the preservation of our cultural heritage, or information service to scientific, technical, business or other specialized fields, the information industry consists of businesses whose objective is to generate profits from the creation and handling of information." His proposal for a revamped library school curriculum includes no component for identifying or preserving information with broader values to society.[35] Such views are why a bibliographer like Thomas Adams has said that he is "on the fringes of the library world" because his "first concern

---

[33]The best introductions to what has been going on in the archival profession are *Planning for the Archival Profession: A Report of the SAA Task Force on Goals and Priorities* and Larry J. Hackman, "A Perspective on American Archives," *Public Historian* 8 (Summer 1986), 10-28.

[34]"What is So Rare," 9.

[35]"The Information Industry," in *Education*, ed. White, 155.

is the book, not information."[36] The archival professionalization trend mentioned earlier has included some orientation to information technologies and services, causing some additional divergence of archivists from analytical bibliographers despite such common origins in the Renaissance interest in humanistic collecting and the custodianship of rare and significant items[37] and their overlapping respective histories since then.[38] The archivist, concerned with documenting society, has found it necessary to try to work with and join forces (or, at least, try to do so) with the modern information society's increasing use of technology or face the loss of valuable historical sources and even the obsolescence of their profession.[39]

As we have seen then, the analytical bibliographer and modern archivist have something of a symbiotic relationship. This relationship is made even more clear when it is understood that there is also considerable stress between the two fields. The archival perspective on appraisal, for example, brings out such tensions, since the analytical bibliographer is seemingly concerned to save every book published. Stokes stated that the "bibliographer is concerned with fact and not with judgment since the fundamental concern is to record, as completely and accurately as is humanly possible, whatever has been written."[40] Such a view is also clear in the writings by Tanselle. Reacting to criticisms that some had made about editions of historical documents (a matter which will addressed

---

[36]"Librarians as Enemies of Books?", 200.

[37]Compare John Feather, "The Rare-Book Librarian and Bibliographical Scholarship," *Journal of Librarianship* 14 (January 1982), 30-44 to the development of archival studies reflected in the studies described in Richard J. Cox, "American Archival History: Its Development, Needs, and Opportunities," *American Archivist* 46 (Winter 1983), 31-41.

[38]In the United States, for example, many of the pioneer antiquarian book dealers were also the agents for acquisition of historical manuscripts for libraries and historical societies; see Madeleine B. Stern, "Henry Stevens: 'G.M.B.,'" *American Book Collector* 6 (May-June 1985), 3-9 and Joseph Rosenblum, "A Tale of Two Savannah Collectors: Israel K. Tefft and Alexander A. Smets," *American Book Collector* 5 (May-June 1984), 13-15, 17-21.

[39]Richard Kesner has written extensively on this very issue. See especially his two books, *Automation for Archivists and Records Managers: Planning and Implementation Strategies* (Chicago: American Library Association, 1984) and *Information Systems: A Strategic Approach to Planning and Implementation* (Chicago: American Library Association, 1988).

[40]*Esdaile's Manual*, 8.

again below) being overly-annotated, focusing on unimportant documents, and reflecting bias in the selection of papers edited and published, Tanselle responded that

> whatever justice there may be to these opinions, they have nothing to do with the quality of the editions themselves. If the annotation is accurate and helpful, it will be of use, and there is little point in wishing there were less of it; and any document or figure is of some historical interest. Individual tastes regarding what material is worth spending time on, and judgments about priorities, will naturally vary; one may deplore another's choice of subject, but it is unrealistic to criticize accomplished work for having usurped time better spent on something else.[41]

Many archivists have, for example, countered that microfilm should be utilized or that funds should be devoted to projects that provide basic care for the original materials rather than their costly publication. Tanselle also noted that the "skilled editor, employing his critical intelligence and fund of historical detail, establishes a text which marks an advance in knowledge over the mere existence of the document itself. Microfilm editions of unedited documents do not obviate true editions; but editing takes time, and one is back at the earlier question of individual priorities for spending time."[42] These seem to be irreconcilable differences between the approach of the archivist and analytical bibliographer.

Collecting is another easily identified source of tension, because the rare books world brings a strong tradition of private collecting that many modern archivists have become increasingly uncomfortable with. Lola L. Szladits, in discussing the collecting of manuscripts and rare books, wrote that "even these days, when vast bodies of archival papers have ended up (one could assume permanently) in public collections, one knows that there is a steady flow of material both through private transfers and public auctions."[43] One senses in her phrasing a lament that such materials are in public repositories! A century ago, in 1894, the English book market was described

---

[41]"The Editing of Historical Documents," *Studies in Bibliography* 31 (1978), 43.

[42]"Editing," 44.

[43]"The Art and Craft of Collecting Manuscripts," in *Book Collecting: A Modern Guide*, ed. Jean Peters (New York: R.R. Bowker Co., 1977), 79-80.

as childlike and prone to speculation resembling a "stock exchange in miniature."[44] A rare book collector recently stated that one of the main reasons a rare books collector collects is "because he wants to, and the acquisitive instinct is inherent in all humans." Even in his definition of rare books as books that are scarce, important, and desireable, this individual deferred considering importance due to "high literary merit, historical significance or invaluable contents," preferring to leave that to each person to set his or her own standards.[45] The modern archivist is, on the other hand, committed to seeing that such documentary sources are available to the research community and the larger public. A.N.L. Munby once captured some of this sentiment when he wrote that the "briefest reflection on the history of institutional collections of manuscripts will confirm the fact that the great majority of libraries, even ones which have a lively tradition of purchasing printed books, expected to be *given* manuscripts."[46] A more unpleasant bit of evidence about the archivist's perspective is his or her concern to replevin public historical documents that have somehow, sometimes it is unknown how, wound up in the hands of private collectors, autograph and book dealers, and even private repositories.[47]

These tensions, and the general separation that remains, between archivists and analytical bibliographers is surprising since most archivists and, conversely, most rare book bibliographers daily face decisions that encroach upon the other's sphere of operation. There are, indeed, skills and

---

[44]Carter, *Taste & Technique*, 26.

[45]George Tweney, "Collecting Rare Books: Ingenuity and Imagination," *Pacific Northwest Library Association Quarterly* 47 (Summer 1983), 24-25, 26.

[46]"The Acquisition of Manuscripts by Institutional Libraries," in *The Bibliographical Society of America 1904-79: A Retrospective Collection* (Charlottesville: Published for the Bibliographical Society of America by the University Press of Virginia, 1980), 385.

[47]For various views on replevin, written when one particular case galvanized the attention of the archival profession a decade ago, see William S. Price, Jr., "Toward a Definition of Public Records: North Carolina's Replevin Action," *Carolina Comments* 25 (November 1977), 127-31; Price, "N.C. v. B.C. West, Jr.," *American Archivist* 41 (January 1978), 21-24; P. W. Filby, "On Replevin," *Manuscripts* 30 (Winter 1978), 30-33; James E. O'Neill, "Replevin: A Public Archivist's Perspective," *College & Research Libraries* 40 (January 1979), 26-30; "Replevin Committee Draft Statement," *SAA Newsletter*, September 1979, 8-9; and Thornton W. Mitchell, "Another View of the West Case," *Carolina Comments* 29 (November 1981), 126-31.

perspectives possessed by both professionals *necessary* to the other; each needs to be more aware of these in order to work effectively and, indeed, to meet their own missions.   The remainder of this paper examines in greater detail these areas and then refocuses on ways that archivists can specifically incorporate these additional skills into their work.

Skills and Perspectives: The Analytical Bibliographer

The primary contributions that the analytical bibliographer can make to archival administration is in expanding its focus through the positing of a different set of questions.   In other words, the bibliographer and archivist have, although working with similar materials and for closely-related purposes, very different perspectives.   These divergent perspectives are most clearly seen in respect to the ways they approach historical documents (printed and manuscript) in their study, preservation, and editing.

One of the most obvious skills seemingly shared by the archivist and the analytical bibliographer is that concerning the study of specific documents and books.   Since the modern archivist's attention has shifted to issues such as the management of electronic records and dealing with voluminous quantities of files,[48] the bibliographer reminds archivists of the importance of studying older documents.   That is, although the archivist is correct in focusing attention on the difficulties and vagaries of documenting modern society, the archivist must also be continually ready to deal with the remnants of older documentation that surface and must be evaluated.   The Canadian guidelines for graduate archival education carefully specify, for example, the need for diplomatics - study of the

[48]See, for example, Frank Boles, "Sampling in Archives," *American Archivist* 44 (Spring 1981), 125-30; Ross J. Cameron, "Appraisal Strategies for Machine-Readable Case Files," *Provenance* 1 (Spring 1983), 49-55; Clark A. Elliott, ed., *Understanding Progress as Process: Documentation of the History of Post-War Science and Technology in the United States* (Chicago: Society of American Archivists, 1983); Joan Krizack Haas, Helen Willa Samuels, and Barbara Trippel Simmons, *Appraising Records of Contemporary Science and Technology: A Guide* (Cambridge: Massachusetts Institute of Technology, 1985); Michael Stephen Hindus, Theodore M. Hammett, and Barbara M. Hobson, *The Files of the Massachusetts Superior Court, 1859-1959: An Analysis and a Plan for Action* (Boston: G.K. Hall, 1979); Nancy E. Peace, ed., *Archival Choices: Managing the Historical Record in an Age of Abundance* (Lexington, Massachusetts: D.C. Heath, 1984); Leonard Rapport, "No Grandfather Clause: Reappraising Accessioned Records," *American Archivist* 44 (Spring 1981), 143-50; Rapport, "In the Valley of Decision: What To Do About the Multitude of Files of Quasi Cases," *ibid.* 48 (Spring 1985), 173-89.

"analysis of the formation, forms, and effects of single archival units" - to be part of this education.[49] The rare book librarian and analytical bibliographer can assist the archivist here. David Woodward, in his work on early maps, for example, has noted the need to use scientific methods for analyzing the fabric and media of *individual* maps, seeing the need to build a data bank of such information. Such a store house of information "would constitute an impressive resource not only for historians of cartography but also for all researchers, conservators, archivists, librarians, and others who need access to precise physical information about the documents that come into their hands."[50] G. Thomas Tanselle likewise made a case for the necessity of including analytical bibliography in studying the past. "The never-ending process of returning to documents of the past for the stimulation that produces new insights, to be recorded in their turn in new documents, cannot be effectively studied without the point of view that analytical bibliography affords, for ideas are affected at every step of the way by the physical means of their transmission."[51] Elsewhere Tanselle has demonstrated this perspective in an area of significant interest to archivists and manuscript curators, the study of paper. Knowledge about the paper used in books and other printed materials is essential not for a dilettante's study of "fine" printings, but for understanding the history of the book trade and printing industry.[52]

Not surprisingly, the modern archivist's ability to deal with individual documents and troublesome manuscripts continues to be relevant. There continue to be periodic spectacular

[49]"Guidelines for the Development of a Two-Year Curriculum for a Master of Archival Studies," Association of Canadian Archivists *Bulletin* 13 (March 1989), 15-16. Other similar areas are generally not included in modern archives administration. For example, in a recent publication on modern archives, the following statement was made: "Also not discussed are the special areas of expertise (paleography, diplomatics, chronology, toponymics, and sphragistics or sigillography) needed by custodians of pre-nineteenth century documents to read, interpret, understand, date, and authenticate old documents and seals"; Bradsher, *Managing Archives*, xv. Obviously, I am arguing that such areas should not be the focus of modern archival education, but they must be known about and generally familiar to the modern archivist.

[50]"The Analysis of Paper and Ink in Early Maps," *Library Trends* 36 (Summer 1987), 105.

[51]"Bibliographical History as a Field of Study," 43.

[52]"The Bibliographical Description of Paper," *Studies in Bibliography* 24 (1971), 27-67.

forgery cases, such as the recent Hitler diaries fiasco,[53] and
there is also the problem of continuing concern with common
facsimiles that only the skills possessed by the critical
bibliographer will help to resolve.[54] The analytical
bibliographer's concern for the breadth of information deriving
from all of the components of a book is a perspective that
archivists need to possess as well. Although archivists have
a fine working definition of the intrinsic value of documents,
noting when "historical materials . . . should be retained in
their original form rather than as copies,"[55] this is a value that
can often be lost in the race to save vast quantities of recorded
information. Indeed, archivist James M. O'Toole, in a
provocative recent essay, has shown how archivists have shifted
from saving "permanent" to "enduring" records, indicating a
greater sense that archival records are "archival" because of the
way that society presently views and uses these records and
that "archival value" can change.[56]

It is not difficult to understand, therefore, that a *useful*
tension exists in the way that archivists and bibliographers
generally approach preservation. Archivists, in league it seems
with the majority of librarians, see microfilming as the primary
manner of preserving *information* found in most documentary
and printed sources.[57] This is undoubtedly due to the fact that
for archivists the "basic unit of archives is not individual
letters, diaries, deeds, ledgers, photographs, or other single
records, but rather a group of items (usually called a record
group) formed around and recording the life and work of their

[53]For a popular account see Robert Harris, *Selling Hitler* (New York:
Pantheon Books, 1986). For an archivist's view see Joseph Henke,
"Revealing the Forged Hitler Diaries," *Archivaria* 19 (Winter 1984-85), 21-
27.

[54]See Leonard Rapport, "Fakes and Facsimiles: Problems of
Identification," *American Archivist* 42 (January 1979), 13-58.

[55]Maygene F. Daniels and Timothy Walch, eds., *A Modern Archives
Reader: Basic Readings on Archival Theory and Practice* (Washington, D.C.:
National Archives and Records Service, 1984), 91.

[56]"On the Idea of Permanence," *American Archivist* 52 (Winter 1989),
10-25.

[57]Nancy E. Gwinn, ed., *Preservation Microfilming: A Guide for
Librarians and Archivists* (Chicago: American Library Association, 1987).

creator."[58]   This outlook draws their attention primarily to mass preservation. Bibliographers and conservators, on the other hand, worry that microfilming will destroy a considerable amount of valuable information. One conservator noted that "there are qualities inherent in the original artifact that transcend mere data. Neither the sense of history embodied in the artifact, nor its mental impact as knowledge is transferred from one generation to another, can survive the transfer to film; only the bare information is transmitted by the reading device."[59]

One has the sense that in dealing with rare printed items, as little as possible should be done to treat the book or change its nature.[60] The statement for the ethical conduct of rare book, manuscripts, and special collections libraries has incorporated this sentiment, noting that the individual responsible for these materials "shall (so far as is economically and technologically feasible) insure that their evidentiary value is not impaired in the work of restoration, arrangement, and use."[61] This applies to archival work as well, although archivists would most likely grasp onto the parenthetical statement of economic and technological feasibility as a way out for dealing with many of their problems, even more recent and voluminous government files.   Many older government records that are excellent candidates for microfilming, as just one example, are recorded in folio-sized binders that are often destroyed when the filming is done. Occasionally, however, careful attention needs to be given to the nature of the bindings themselves. In the Florida State Archives forty volumes bound in alligator skin between 1885 and 1911 were recently discovered. "The intrinsic factors that make the volumes worth preserving in their original format," wrote one archivist, "are the intrinsic use of the skin, gold tooling, and marbled-pattern paper; evidence of technological development; age; and exhibit value.   These factors also provide the basis for research into a wealth of

[58]David B. Gracy II in *Researcher's Guide to Archives and Regional History Sources*, ed. John C. Larsen (Hamden, Connecticut: Library Professional Publications, 1988), 18.

[59]Jack C. Thompson, "Mass Deacidification: Thoughts on the Cunha Report," *Restaurator* 9 (1988), 147.

[60]Helmut Bansa, "Conservation Treatment of Rare Books," *Restaurator* 8, nos. 2/3, (1987), 140-50.

[61]"Standards for Ethical Conduct for Rare Book, Manuscripts, and Special Collections Libraries," *College & Research Libraries News* 48 (March 1987), 135.

subjects: history, binding technology, art, economics, foreign trade, and conservation and preservation."[62]   Such problems have caused some rare books librarians and bibliographers to advocate a careful working relationship between the "curator" and "conservator" to ensure that preservation practices do not, in effect, destroy the very information intended to be saved;[63] the archivist would be wise to do the same.

The editing of literary and historical texts is yet one more apparent difference between the analytical bibliographer and archivist and has already been partially discussed in this paper. Unquestionably, the late twentieth century has seen considerable improvement in the publication of authoritative literary texts. Fredson Bowers wrote that "when the history of scholarship in the twentieth century comes to be written, a very good case should be made for calling it the age of editing."[64]   The past decade has been a time of tremendous discussion and debate about the nature of literary and documentary editing and more systematic ways of editing have been formulated than were available in the past.[65]   Here the archivist is somewhat tangentially involved because of the close affinity with the historical or documentary editor.[66]   The historical editors have tended to favor regularization and modernization of texts, among other things, that have gone against the common approaches of literary editors. G. Thomas Tanselle, one of the most outspoken and learned critics of documentary editing, sees the work of historical editors as

[62]Hal Hubener, "Sunshine State Showpieces: Alligator-Skin Bindings in the Florida Archives," *Provenance* 6 (Fall 1988), 48-49.

[63]Bonnie Jo Cullison and Jean Donaldson, "Conservators and Curators: A Cooperative Approach to Treatment Specifications," *Library Trends* 36 (Summer 1987), 229-39.   This is also the emphasis in McCrank, "Conservation and Collection Management."   See also Karl Dachs, "Conservation: The Curator's Point of View," *Restaurator* 6, nos. 3-4, (1984), 118-26.

[64]"Scholarship and Editing," in *The Bibliographical Society of America*, 514.

[65]See Mary-Jo Kline, *A Guide to Documentary Editing* (Baltimore: The Johns Hopkins University Press, 1987) and Peter L. Shillingsburg, *Scholarly Editing in the Computer Age: Theory and Practice* (Atlanta: University of Georgia Press, 1986).

[66]This can be seen, for example, in that one of the major federal funding sources for archival work is the National Historical Publications and Records Commission (NHPRC).   The NHPRC divides its support equally between archival projects and historical editing work.

paradoxically withholding documentary evidence. He stated
that

> because analytical bibliography developed primarily among
> literary scholars, many historians have not yet come to
> understand the lessons it has taught about the role of
> physical evidence in uncovering textual problems (lessons
> relevant to the study of manuscripts as well as of printed
> books) and therefore have not recognized that the task of
> identifying "the text" read at a given time is often more
> complicated than the simple location of a single copy.[67]

The primary source of this perspective may be the literary
editor's desire to get back to the authentic text that an author
intended for public consumption, something that the historical
editor, dealing most often with manuscripts never intended for
public view, is unaccustomed to thinking about.[68] The
historical editor has been far more interested in getting out a
text that the historian can use, a goal that all archivists agree
with but a means that many question as too slow, too
expensive, and too uncertain as to the success in making
historical sources available for use.[69]

Skills and Perspectives: The Modern Archivist

Archivists also bring a set of skills and perspectives that
the analytical bibliographer (and rare book librarian) might find
useful. At least, there seems to be enough here of value that
the archivists ought to try to work more frequently with
bibliographers and rare book librarians and vice versa. Not

---

[67]"Historicism and Critical Editing," *Studies in Bibliography* 39 (1986),
11. See also his "Recent Editorial Discussion and the Central Questions of
Editing," *ibid.* 34 (1981), 23-65. For a response by a historical editor to
Tanselle's views, see Don L. Cook, "The Short Happy Thesis of G. Thomas
Tanselle" and Robert J. Taylor, "Editorial Practices -An Historian's View,"
Newsletter of the Association for Documentary Editing 3 (February 1981), 1-
8.

[68]See Fredson Bowers, "Transcription of Manuscripts: The Record of
Variants," *Studies in Bibliography* 29 (1976), 212-64 and G. Thomas
Tanselle, "The Editorial Problem of Final Authorial Intention," *ibid.* 29
(1976), 167-211.

[69]I have not seen any published critiques of historical editing by
archivists. My characterization of such views is based upon conversations
with archivists, although I recognize that there are a diversity of opinions
within the archival community on this topic.

surprisingly, the archivist's roles in managing manuscript and archival records are extremely useful functions to the analytical bibliographer who must often use these materials in his or her own research. Many books will not be well understood without resort to these additional research materials. More importantly, the archivist brings an appraisal (selection) tradition that places a premium upon the value of recorded information with the understanding that not all can be saved. Although that seems contradictory to the manner in which the analytical bibliographer approaches the world, it is, as it turns out, something that could still be very worthwhile to the bibliographer.

The relationship between archivist and analytical bibliographer is not one restricted to printed items of course. Analytical bibliographers are concerned with manuscript and archival material related to the history of printing and publishing. An English bibliographer wrote that "the scarcity of printers' account books and ledgers has bedeviled a realistic understanding of eighteenth- and nineteenth-century printing-house practice; such understanding has been further confounded by the equally low survival-rate of other vital documents, notably original printers' copy."[70] Another bibliographer has written about the value of publishers' archives, valuable

> precisely because they contain such a wealth of information, especially correspondence, touching on all aspects of the book-making process - from submission and selection of manuscripts to marketing the finished product and payment of authors' fees and protection of mutual rights, publishers' archives are rich natural lodes for the bibliographical prospector, whether his interest be historical, enumerative, analytical, descriptive or critical.[71]

Moreover, the use of authors' manuscripts - looking at the original paper for such things as transmitted light, watermarks, paper-finish, paper-color, and paper-batch - are often essential for determining the date of authorship and the intended text

---

[70]Gwyn Walters, "The Account Book, 1826-1836, of the Reverend John Parry, Printer and Publisher of Chester," *Journal of the Printing Historical Society* 15 (1980/81), 54.

[71]William E. Fredeman, "The Bibliographical Significance of a Publisher's Archive: The Macmillan Papers," *Studies in Bibliography* 23 (1970), 184-85.

of important writings.[72]   Again, the view of the analytical bibliographer is essential to aid the archivist in being able to evaluate such manuscripts and collections as they are identified.   Just a few years ago, an archivist, writing about the related area of literary manuscripts, noted that there were no real guidelines or literature that

> treats the collecting, accessioning, appraisal, or disposition of literary papers. . . . There is no standard or norm by which curators can judge the rightness of their appraisal decisions; they have neither precedents nor resources upon which to draw. It is difficult to determine what colleagues are doing in the same situation. Does one retain galley proofs? Should these proofs be turned over to the rare-book librarian?[73]

More proactive efforts to document the publishing industry through the development of strategies, surveys, advocacy for the creation of publishing archives, and identification of existing repositories with the interest and resources in acquiring such records are also needed.

The natural survival of materials is a problem that the analytical bibliographer has struggled with and that the archivist can provide assistance with in several ways. Philip Gaskell has written, for example, that the

> rate of survival of copies of early editions is not as a rule a direct indication of their original quantity. On the contrary it is precisely such things as school books, which were printed in the largest numbers but were used to death, which have survived least well, while small luxury editions, much prized but little used, may have survived almost complete.[74]

---

[72]See, for example, Helen Baron, "*Sons and Lovers*: The Surviving Manuscripts from Three Drafts Dated by Paper Analysis," *Studies in Bibliography* 38 (1985), 289-328. See also Robert Thomas Fallon, "Miltonic Documents in the Public Record Office, London," *ibid*. 32 (1979), 82-100.

[73]Philip N. Cronenwett, "Appraisal of Literary Manuscripts," in *Archival Choices: Managing the Historical Record in an Age of Abundance*, ed. Nancy E. Peace (Lexington, Massachusetts: Lexington Books, 1984), 107.

[74]*A New Introduction to Bibliography* (Oxford: At the Clarendon Press, 1972), 162-63.

This problem has recently been given an eloquent and more comprehensive treatment by historian Daniel Boorstin.[75] While there have been a few efforts by analytical bibliographers and rare book librarians to determine criteria for selection, the emphasis of their efforts have been on defining rarity or financial values.[76] Here the archivist brings his or her skill to developing criteria for selection of contemporary informational materials that could assist in identifying even common materials that possess potential historical value.

The archivist has developed a fairly elaborate set of selection criteria, practices, and models that the analytical bibliographer might find of interest. These can be seen as part of a typology of selection approaches that range from individual items and collections to concerns with documenting all of society. Definitions of evidential and informational values, sampling, reappraisal, institutional collecting plans and policies, surveys and collecting projects, and multi-institutional cooperative documentation strategies all provide a lens by which the book can be seen as physical artifact in documenting the past. Archival appraisal approaches provide the means to evaluate a single item as it turns up as well as to identify and select from the recent bulky documentation that should be saved for future researchers. The increasingly cooperative approach of the archivist to the appraisal function can easily be stretched to accommodate the analytical bibliographer's perspective. The archivist will want to know the essential and unique information that may be found in books and other printings, while showing where this information may be duplicated elsewhere in other sources. For example, there already has been substantial work done regarding how reprint collections in the papers of scientists and engineers should be handled as part of the overall documentation of the individual's work and his or her field.[77] The archivist also is increasingly seeking to ask first *what* should be documented, rather than

---

[75]*Hidden History* (New York: Harper and Row, 1988), chapter one.

[76]John Carter includes an entire chapter on rarity in his book, *Taste & Technique in Book Collecting* (London: Private Libraries Association, 1970), 137-70. See also Anthony Rota, "The Collecting of Twentieth-Century Literary Manuscripts," *Rare Books and Manuscripts Librarianship* 1 (April 1986), 45-47 for the market end of definitions generally applicable to rare books.

[77]See Deborah Cozort Day, "Appraisal Guidelines for Reprint Collections," *American Archivist* 48 (Winter 1985), 56-63.

only evaluating each item or collection on its own merits[78]; archivists will want to know what kinds of questions the analytical bibliographer seeks to answer so as to accommodate these into their own set of issues and concerns. The symbiotic relationship between archivist and analytical bibliographer should help ensure the adequate documentation of our society, a mission shared (if differently defined) by the two fields.

Conclusion: The Modern Archivist's Mission and Analytical Bibliography

The modern archivist has a very clear mission to identify, preserve, and make accessible the records of enduring or continuing value. Since the information that archivists seek to preserve in archives and manuscripts is not always found in these materials, it is logical that the archivist must seek to work with other disciplines that have responsibility for additional informational sources. Folklorists, oral historians, museum curators, *and* analytical bibliographers (and rare book custodians) all can play potentially important roles in documenting society, the major objective of the archival profession. Three possible means are suggested here for enhancing this relationship between archivists and analytical bibliographers: graduate education, documentation analysis and planning, and in-service training.

Graduate archival education is certainly an interdisciplinary affair. Not only are graduate archival programs found in history departments, applied or public history programs, library schools, and joint history-library science programs, but the content of archival education and archival work incorporates a wide variety of disciplines. The graduate archival education guidelines of the Society of American Archivists clearly reflect this and specifically note history, library and information science, public administration, management, preservation, and records management.[79] The Canadian counterpart of these guidelines, cited earlier, reflect a similar range emphasizing intellectual history, administrative history, records management, diplomatics, automated techniques, preservation, and other areas. There is little question, noting the general tendency of such guidelines and what has been discussed earlier in this

---

[78]See Helen W. Samuels, "Who Controls the Past," *American Archivist* 49 (Spring 1986), 109-24 and Larry Hackman and Joan Warnow-Blewett, "The Documentation Strategy Process: A Model and A Case Study," *ibid.* 50 (Winter 1987), 12-47.

[79]*American Archivist* 51 (Summer 1988), 380-89.

paper, that analytical bibliography can play an essential role in the educational preparation of an archivist and assist the archivist in managing the materials he or she will undoubtedly face during their career.

Since the archival profession is racing, it seems, to more aggressively ensure that society is being documented by bringing archivists and others together to formulate questions, develop strategies, and seek solutions, it is difficult to imagine that the analytical bibliographer should be left out of such cooperative ventures. The analytical bibliographer definitely brings a unique perspective of evidence, perhaps only matched by the museum curator's approach to artifacts, that would be an asset in the undertaking of larger documentation projects. For example, suppose that a group forms to document a specific urban area. That area's governments and their documentation will have a significant importance to understanding the nature of that region for present and future researchers. A major portion of that documentation will come in the form of published reports, proceedings, and studies. While the historian and archivist might first focus on the informational content of the publications, the analytical bibliographer will stretch these colleagues to consider the form of the information and perhaps suggest criteria that can be applied to ensure that information provided by the form will not be lost.

Finally, the archivist can seek to gain some additional in-service or continuing education by being aware of the major publications and journals in the field of analytical bibliography and rare book librarianship and the professional associations that support these fields. A regular reading of *Studies in Bibliography* (published annually) and the *Papers of the Bibliographical Society of America* (published quarterly) will help make archivists more aware of the tenets, practices, and applications of analytical bibliography and rare book librarianship. Some of the classic texts on analytical and forms of bibliography - such as by Stokes, Bowers, and Gaskell - should have a place on the archivist's basic bookshelf. Archivists might also wish to become more active in the Rare Books and Manuscripts Section of the Association of College and Research Libraries; this group appears to be the primary forum for dialogue between rare books custodians and scholars and archivists and manuscript curators. The 1989 program of this group, for example, had a theme of "Local History, Global Village: Regional Collecting, Regional Collections," with papers by historians, archivists, rare book librarians, and antiquarian booksellers. The publication of a bi-annual journal, *Rare Books and Manuscripts*, by the section is also worth perusing by archivists.

There are, obviously, differences in the fields of modern archives administration and analytical bibliography. But the similarities are more important, suggesting that greater efforts in cooperation ought to be undertaken.

THIRTEEN ARCHIVISTS CONFRONT A CHANGING WORLD: DOCUMENTATION STRATEGIES, THE REFORMULATION OF ARCHIVAL APPRAISAL, AND THE POSSIBILITIES OF MULTIDISCIPLINARY COOPERATION

Archival Appraisal: Present Practices and Limitations

The manuscript curator hurriedly scurries into her office and grabs the ringing telephone. An individual is moving and has some old family papers that the historical society might want and that need to be removed within the next week. The manuscript curator makes an appointment and a familiar chain of events is started. There will be some preliminary research about the family in question, rumination about the potential of the papers and how they fit into the historical society's collecting policy, a close examination of the papers, determination of whether the collection has an appropriate place in the historical society, and negotiation with the donor. The end result may be an acquisition with significant historical information.

At the same time that this is occurring, several miles away the local government's archivist-records manager is setting an appointment for the next agency to undergo a records survey, part of a long-term effort to compile a comprehensive survey of and retention schedule for the government's records. Setting the appointment also generates a familiar sequence of events for him. File cabinets, storage areas, and information systems are scrutinized, file clerks and administrators questioned, administrative histories compiled, local and state legislation examined, and consultation with the state archives concluded. Records inventory sheets are completed and records retention schedules developed and implemented. Some records will be destroyed, many will go to a records center for temporary storage, and a small portion will be transferred to the government archives. The end result of this process will be cost-savings to the government, increased efficiency in future information retrieval, and the preservation of records with important historical information.

These two scenarios are repeated daily throughout the nation and, for that matter the world, with some variation caused by institutional and cultural diversity. There is, of course, nothing ostensibly wrong with what is happening here; in fact, if things happened as smoothly as just described archivists and records managers would be a significantly more stress-free lot. Many records important for historical and other research use, as well as for ongoing administrative, legal, and fiscal purposes are identified and retained; the ultimate objective of archival appraisal is seemingly met. These efforts also allow for many of the time-honored and reliable archival appraisal techniques - such as sampling and records surveys - to be used and relied upon.

But, of course, there are some problems with what has just been described. One of the two occurrences is purely a reactive response. Both are done in isolation, the result of their own institutional acquisition policy or their own organization's records management program. Neither is the result of any significant preliminary analysis; that is, questions regarding what should be documented are not posed nor necessarily answered. Only existing records are examined, and there is little effort to consider missing documentation because there are few or no questions formulated to be answered. There is limited outside assistance involved because the archivists have primarily relied upon their own judgement. Although the records manager has a committee to approve final dispositions of records, the emphasis is probably more on aspects other than historical and research values. And, finally, there is a focus on past events. The records obviously document what has occurred, and there is minimal attention given to what is presently occurring in society.

Now there may be two reactions to what has just been described. The first is that it is a criticism of hypothetical events. However, these events represent faithfully how much of archival appraisal actually transpires; since I have worked both as a manuscript curator and a government records manager, I have also relied upon my own experience and knowledge in fabricating these scenarios.[1] The response might well be "so what!" "Why are these problems?" For this, some basic questions ought to be considered:

1.   How do archivists know they are documenting *what* should be documented? Do the total acquisitions of their archival and historical records repositories add up to the desired or needed documentation?

---

[1]For an introduction to archival appraisal consult the following: Maynard J. Brichford, *Archives & Manuscripts: Appraisal & Accessioning*, Basic Manual Series (Chicago: Society of American Archivists, 1977); Nancy E. Peace, ed., *Archival Choices: Managing the Historical Record in an Age of Abundance* (Lexington, Massachusetts: Lexington Books, 1984); and Julia Marks Young, comp., "Annotated Bibliography on Appraisal," *American Archivist* 48 (Spring 1985), 190-216.

2. How do archivists know they have the *best* documentation of what they want and need documented? Are there other better sources not in their repositories or under adequate control for consultation? Are there potentially better sources that are endangered?

3. How are archivists documenting their contemporary world for present and future research if archivists are primarily reactive *and* focused on older documentation? Are archivists trying systematically to document the present for the future, or are they relying too much on happenstance?

4. Are archivists really keeping pace with a fast-changing and increasingly complex society that is relying more and more on sophisticated information technology? Do their traditional appraisal approaches hold up in the late twentieth century?

Because of concerns such as these and recognition that there are some basic problems in archival appraisal, the archival profession has begun to chart a different course of action, generally referred to as "documentation strategies."[2] The

---

[2]The term "documentation strategy" was coined and initially defined at a session of the 1984 Society of American Archivists meeting that included papers presented by Helen W. Samuels, Larry J. Hackman, and Patricia Aronnson. The origins of the concept date from the early and mid-1970s efforts by some archivists to grapple with documenting social movements, minority issues, popular concerns, and other topics that were not well-represented in most archival and historical records repositories. Definition and development of the documentation strategy concept were bolstered by other influences, including the work from 1978 to 1983 of the Joint Committee on Archives of Science and Technology (JCAST), institutional collection analysis undertaken by a number of state repositories (especially Minnesota Historical Society, State Historical Society of Wisconsin, and the Michigan Historical Collections at the Bentley Historical Library), and the research fellowship program on modern documentation administered by the Bentley Historical Library since 1983.

The key writings on the documentation strategy approach include Helen W. Samuels, "Who Controls the Past," *American Archivist* 49 (Spring 1986), 109-24; Larry Hackman and Joan Warnow-Blewett, "The Documentation Strategy Process: A Model and a Case Study," *ibid.* 50 (Winter 1987), 12-47; and Philip N. Alexander and Helen W. Samuels, "The Roots of 128: A Hypothetical Documentation Strategy," *ibid.* 50 (Fall 1987), 518-31. Earlier influential writings that have been influential in the development of the concept include F. Gerald Ham, "The Archival Edge," *ibid.* 38 (January 1975), 5-13; Ham, "Archival Strategies for the Post-Custodial Era," *ibid.* 44 (Summer 1981), 207-16; Ham, "Archival Choices: Managing the Historical

documentation strategy, already mentioned several times in this book, was initially defined in the mid-1980s, although it evolved out of a decade or more of discussion within the archival community of the difficulties of documenting modern society.

The Archival Documentation Strategy

The archival documentation strategy is presently defined as a "plan formulated to assure the documentation of an ongoing issue, activity or geographical area . . . . The strategy is ordinarily designed, promoted, and in part implemented by an ongoing mechanism involving records creators, administrators (including archivists), and users. The documentation strategy is carried out through the mutual efforts of many institutions and individuals influencing both the creation of the records and the archival retention of a portion of them. The strategy is refined in response to changing conditions and viewpoints."[3]

A brief look at this approach's key features should indicate how it promises to resolve some of the major problems that archivists have had in identifying and selecting information with enduring value.[4] It should also open up possibilities for how non-archivists, such as librarians and historians, can participate in securing an adequate documentation of society. First, the approach involves a *group* of records creators, custodians, and users providing guidance for determining what needs to be documented, identifying what documentation should be preserved, and seeking the creation of new information for plugging up serious documentation gaps. Archivists play a vital role in the process, but they by no means conduct the process by themselves. A wide range of expertise is sought.

Record in an Age of Abundance," *ibid.* 47 (Winter 1984), 11-22 (also reprinted in the Peace volume); Clark A. Elliott, ed., *Understanding Progress as Process: Documentation of the History of Post-War Science and Technology in the United States; Final Report of the Joint Committee on Archives of Science and Technology* (Chicago: Society of American Archivists, 1983); and Hans Booms, "Society and the Formation of a Documentary Heritage: Issues in the Appraisal of Archival Sources," *Archivaria* 24 (Summer 1987), 69-107 (originally published in German in 1972).

[3]Samuels, "Who Controls the Past," 115.

[4]The relationship of the documentation strategy approach to archival appraisal is more fully treated in Richard J. Cox and Helen W. Samuels, "The Archivist's First Responsibility: A Research Agenda to Improve the Identification and Retention of Records of Enduring Value," *American Archivist* 51 (Winter/Spring 1988), 28-42.

Second, the process deliberately seeks to influence records creators to preserve their materials of archival value.[5] Existing archival and historical records repositories are already considerably strapped with too few resources and are not in a position to take on the voluminous documentation of the late twentieth-century. Expansion of the archival community may and probably will occur, but it is unlikely to be sufficient to handle all modern documentation.

Third, documentation strategies are designed to encourage study of the documentation of specific sectors of society. Studies of topics and functions examine all forms of evidence and therefore better support the selection and the management of modern records. A strategy incorporates (identifies and selects from) the documentation that should be saved from many records creators such as government regulatory agencies, the for-profit sector, citizens' lobby groups, professional associations, other organizations, and individuals and families. The strategy also often requires examination of all documentation, the records and manuscripts that archivists traditionally work with as well as printed materials, oral reminiscences, and artifacts.

Finally, the documentation strategy process most importantly seeks to ask the right questions before embarking on a survey of existing documentation, appraisal, and making acquisition decisions. These questions can be formulated through the combined knowledge of records creators, custodians, and users that provides a better understanding of society, its institutions, and its characteristics. In short, the documentation strategy provides a framework for inculcating a needed attitude within the archival community and the community of those who use historical materials; that attitude is one of knowing what of contemporary society is believed needed to be documented for present and future use. The strategy challenges archivists to reevaluate their existing appraisal system as incomplete, because while archival appraisal relies on approaches that are often reliable in

---

[5]This more active interest by records creators can occur in a variety of ways. Records creators can enter into agreements with archival and historical records repositories for the care of their archival materials. Such agreements need to include adequate financial and other support not traditionally provided with the donation of such materials. More important, records creators need to establish and support records management programs that include archival components. Finally, records creators need to place more emphasis on generating archival-quality (e.g., on alkaline paper or electronic formats with potential archival retention) records with readily recognizable archival value.

themselves, it often overlooks the broader mission of documenting society.

It should be understood that the documentation strategy approach is not intended to replace archival appraisal, but it instead adds another dimension to appraisal that has been heretofore underdeveloped. Archivists determine that records have historical value through a variety of means.[6] They occasionally resort to examining items with known value using criteria and techniques such as intrinsic value and sampling.[7] Collections are evaluated through the application of values such as evidential and informational analyses of specific types of records such as the National Archives study of the Federal Bureau of Investigation's case files, and through study of documentation by functional areas such as is now going on at the Massachusetts Institute of Technology in the area of colleges and universities.[8] Archivists also conduct appraisal through the lens of their own repositories by developing, using, and refining institutional collecting policies and plans, but also more recently through in-depth collection analysis that determines the strengths and weaknesses of existing holdings against informed perceptions about what their repositories should possess.[9] Archivists have also sought to develop regional and topical collection projects that plan for and take

[6]I am indebted to Helen W. Samuels, Massachusetts Institute of Technology, for the formulation of the appraisal hierarchy that I briefly describe here. We have used the hierarchy in the five documentation strategy seminars given in 1987-1989 and sponsored by the Society of American Archivists to explain the relationship of the documentation strategy approach to other archival appraisal techniques and theories.

[7]*Intrinsic Value in Archival Material*, Staff Information Paper 21 (Washington, D.C.: National Archives and Records Service, 1982); David R. Kepley, "Sampling in Archives: A Review," *American Archivist* 47 (Summer 1984), 237-42.

[8]John A. Fleckner, *Archives and Manuscripts: Surveys, Basic Manual Series* (Chicago: Society of American Archivists, 1977); Frank Boles and Julia Marks Young, "Exploring the Black Box: The Appraisal of University Administrative Records," *American Archivist* 48 (Spring 1985): 121-40; James Gregory Bradsher, "Researchers, Archivists, and the Access Challenge of the FBI Records in the National Archives," *Midwestern Archivist* 11, no. 2 (1986): 95-110; Susan D. Steinwall, "Appraisal and the FBI Files Case: For Whom Do Archivists Retain Records?" *American Archivist* 49 (Winter 1986), 52-63.

[9]Faye Phillips, "Developing Collecting Policies for Manuscript Collections," *American Archivist* 47 (Winter 1984), 30-42; Judith E. Endelman, "Looking Backward to Plan for the Future: Collection Analysis for Manuscript Repositories," *ibid.* 50 (Summer 1987), 340-55.

action to ensure the adequate documentation of specific past issues and events. The work of the Presidential Libraries in documenting various Presidencies and Presidential eras is the best-known (albeit controversial) example of this kind of effort. Documentation strategies, therefore, place on top of this appraisal scheme the broadest approach, one that incorporates an ongoing, multi-institutional cooperative documentation activity. What comes out of the strategy does not replace any of the other appraisal techniques except to affect how, where, and when they may be used. Documentation strategies provide the necessary context and coordination for the other appraisal activities.

It must also be stated that the documentation strategy mechanism or model is a relatively new concept that requires additional testing and refinement. However, three applications of the strategy that have been made will provide a better notion of what is involved in its use and its potential value for better ensuring the documentation of society, especially the possible role of other information and historical professionals.

The best developed use of the documentation strategy approach has come from the American Institute of Physics (AIP).[10] Thirty years ago the AIP established an *ad hoc* committee on the history and philosophy of physics concerned about what was occurring with the documentation of this field. Its initial focus was on the early segment of modern physics (1890-1940), but this attention soon changed to one concerned with the post World War Two period. The emphasis of AIP from the start was fostering a better-developed sense of history in the creators of physics documentation and promoting the preservation and use of the essential historical records. Therefore, the AIP does not collect, but determines what needs to be documented, identifies the documentation that needs to be saved, conducts documentation surveys and analysis, employs oral history to fill in documentation gaps, and uses micrographics to film inaccessible or endangered documentation. From the late 1960s to the present the AIP's History for the Center of Physics (formally created in 1965) has concentrated its energies on special projects analyzing the nature of national and international physics documentation guided by an ongoing advisory group of physics specialists, historians, archivists, and

---

[10]The AIP is discussed in Hackman and Warnow-Blewett, "The Documentation Strategy Process." See also Joan Warnow-Blewett, "Saving the Records of Science and Technology: The Role of a Discipline History Center," *Science & Technology Libraries* 7 (Spring 1987), 29-40.

other experts.[11] AIP's work has been successful enough that it has been used as a model for the creation of other discipline history centers in the areas of science and technology.[12]

A very different application of the documentation strategy approach has been the effort to apply it to a geographical region, in this case the six western most counties of New York.[13] Growing out of a major statewide assessment of archival and historical records programs,[14] the western New York effort was an attempt to determine more precisely how well the Empire State was being documented through existing archival appraisal and acquisition practices and to determine whether the documentation strategy model could be utilized for improving the documentation of regions within New York as well as the entire state. An advisory group of archivists, historians and researchers, librarians, and others was assembled to analyze the quality of documentation in western New York using a framework of fifteen topical areas covering the gamut of human activity and employing definitions of topical significance and documentation quality. The end result of this effort was the development of a tentative set of procedures for local documentation work and some assessment of the advantages and difficulties of conducting regional documentation analysis. There is little question that the process is a valuable one (even the brief effort in western New York increased the consciousness of historical records custodians and users about the challenges of adequately documenting the region), but there are still many questions about how to stimulate, support, and carry out such geographically-based documentation efforts.

The final example of a documentation endeavor was the work undertaken by the mid-1988 Evangelical Archives Conference. This conference was assembled to do a variety of things, including the development of a "framework" for

[11]For example, a recent project is focusing on multi-institutional collaborations in physics research.

[12]Such as the Center for the History of Electrical Engineering and the Charles Babbage Institute for the History of Information Processing.

[13]For a more detailed description of the project, refer to Richard J. Cox, "A Documentation Strategy Case Study: Western New York," *American Archivist* 52 (Spring 1989), 192-200.

[14]*Toward A Usable Past: Historical Records in the Empire State* (Albany: New York Historical Records Advisory Board, 1984).

documenting this aspect of religion in American society.[15] Despite the strong tradition of religious archives, the evangelical movement is not as strongly institutionalized as other aspects of religion and its theological underpinnings tend to encourage a future-looking rather than present or past perspective. The notable work that came out of their meeting demonstrates the powerful tool that the documentation analysis provides. The participants focused on developing a "strategy of documentation for the [evangelical] movement" since "it was not feasible for the 'gaps' in the documentation to be discussed until an overall framework was conceived." The framework encompasses the seven "activities or expressions" that the evangelical movement uses to carry out its work, namely denominations, fellowships, communities; education; human services; media; mission and ministries; political and social action groups; and professional organizations. Definitions of each of the areas were developed, along with efforts to ascertain the current status of their documentation, obstacles to their documentation, and mechanisms for documenting. Through this exercise a terribly elusive (at least for documentation) aspect of modern society was given workable parameters for recording its history.[16]

At least four common features are visible in the documentation applications briefly discussed. It is the sequence of events and planning aspects that make these efforts different from other archival appraisal work. They place in the forefront the definition of documentation needs, seeking an understanding of what is to be documented and how it can be documented. All three also involve, or plan to involve, records creators, custodians, and users. They are multi-institutional in scope; no one institution assumes all the responsibility for supporting the work or aims to be the main repository for documentation identified as needing to be preserved. Finally, these efforts at least equally emphasize the creation of institutional archival programs along with the more traditional

---

[15]For more information about this conference, refer to its report, *A Heritage At Risk: The Proceedings of the Evangelical Archives Conference* July 13-15, 1988 (Wheaton, Illinois: Billy Graham Center, Wheaton College, [1988]) and Richard J. Cox, "Evangelical Religious Institutions Consider Their Archival Needs: A Review of the 1988 Evangelical Archives Conference Proceedings," *Provenance* 7 (Spring 1989), 66-79.

[16]The difficulties of documenting religion are discussed in James M. O'Toole, "What's Different About Religious Archives?" *Midwestern Archivist* 9 no. 2 (1984), 91-101; O'Toole, "Things of the Spirit: Documenting Religion in New England," *American Archivist* 50 (Fall 1987), 500-17; and Robert Shuster, "Documenting the Spirit,"*ibid.* 45 (Spring 1982), 135-41.

acquisition done by existing archival and historical records repositories. All of these are essential features of the documentation strategy approach and indicate how standard archival appraisal may be undergoing enhancement if not reformulation.

Implications of the Archival Documentation Strategy

The documentation strategy should also be of interest to librarians and other information and historical professionals for a variety of reasons. Some of these reasons have already been mentioned in other essays in this volume on public historians, rare book librarians, and government document custodians. This kind of focus can be widely expanded to other disciplines.

All libraries, manuscript repositories, and their staffs are vitally concerned with selection issues. The emergence in recent years of a strong interest in collection development and collection management clearly reveals this concern. Stated needs for strong individual research collections or shared comprehensive holdings mark both the informational and cultural roles of libraries and associated manuscript repositories *and* the fact that there are limited resources to support these roles.[17] The documentation strategy approach is yet one more possible weapon for the arsenal of selection methodologies and models. Its multi-institutional, interdisciplinary basis should make a very comfortable fit for the library and related information fields. It certainly has potential for assisting in the selection and management of printed materials, such as government publications and reprint collections, that are often found in both libraries and manuscript and archival repositories.[18]

Since efforts to document society cannot be restricted only to archival sources, the librarian, rare book custodian and scholar, and manuscript curator need to be involved with

---

[17]Nancy E. Gwinn and Paul H. Mosher, "Coordinating Collection Development: The RLG Conspectus," *College & Research Libraries* 44 (March 1983), 128-40; Dan C. Hazen, "Collection Development, Collection Management, and Preservation," *Library Resources & Technical Services* 26 (January/March 1982), 6-10; Mosher, "Collection Development to Collection Management: Toward Stewardship of Library Resources," *Collection Management* 4 (1982), 41-48; Jutta Reed-Scott, "Collection Management Strategies for Archivists," *American Archivist* 47 (Winter 1984), 23-29; and Nina J. Root, "Decision Making for Collection Management," *Collection Management* 7 (Spring 1985), 93-101.

[18]Deborah Cozort Day, "Appraisal Guidelines for Reprint Collections," *American Archivist* 48 (Winter 1985), 56-63, and chapter ten in this volume.

documentation work. Not only do these individuals often deal with collections of mixed media - manuscript, printed, and even artifactual materials,[19] they bring different perspectives that may be absolutely essential to determining what must be saved in order to document society effectively. For example, the analytical bibliographer strongly argues that considerable evidence about society is conveyed not only in the texts of books but in their material characteristics.[20] This notion is also evident in the work of museum curators, anthropologists, and others who study material culture.[21] Such a perspective must be incorporated into the groups gathered to formulate and implement documentation strategies, if nothing else than to balance the archivist's customary focus on textual informational content. The remaking of archival appraisal also affects others outside of the archival profession.

Librarians, rare book custodians and scholars, and manuscript curators are also concerned with selection of materials for preservation. Until recently, however, the librarians and rare book custodians have thought of preserving "comprehensive" collections. Selection had mainly been thought of as a means to develop initial priorities for preservation actions, rather than as a process for making decisions to save one item and to destroy (either willfully or by neglect) another because of limited resources or other reasons.[22] The documentation strategy model provides another useful tool for

[19]Consider, for example, the potential of discovering rare imprints in archival collections and record groups and the growing similarities between published and archival materials. See Lise Hesselager, "Fringe or Grey Literature in the National Library: Or 'Papyrolatry' and the Growing Similarity Between the Materials in Libraries and Archives," *American Archivist* 47 (Summer 1984), 255-70 and Robert D. Armstrong, "The Beast in the Bathtub, and Other Archival Laments," *ibid.* 45 (Fall 1982), 375-82.

[20]See, for example, Roy Stokes, *Esdaile's Manual of Bibliography*, 5th rev. ed. (Metuchen, New Jersey: Scarecrow Press, 1981).

[21]See, for example, Michael J. Ettema, "History Museums and the Culture of Materialism," in *Past Meets Present: Essays About Historical Interpretation and Public Audiences*, ed. Jo Blatti (Washington, D.C.: Smithsonian Institution Press, 1987), 62-93; Jules David Prown, "Mind in Matter: An Introduction to Material Culture Theory and Method," in *Material Life in America, 1600-1860*, ed. Robert Blair St. George (Boston: Northeastern University Press, 1988), 17-37; and Thomas J. Schlereth, "Contemporary Collecting for Future Recollecting," *Museum Studies Journal* 113 (Spring 1984), 23-30.

[22]My ideas on this topic have been more fully discussed in chapter eleven in this volume. The relevant writings of library preservation selection have been discussed and cited in this essay.

preservation selection. Because it emphasizes the use of a wide diversity of expertise and forming the essential questions to be answered in documentation, individuals and institutions responsible for related information sources such as printed books and rare imprints will find some useful guidance for what materials should be given preservation attention by participating in the process.

One of the most recent noticeable trends among the institutions that comprise the state and local history field, notably history museums, is the concern about how to interpret the twentieth century for the public. New attention on common objects used in everyday life, instead of a preoccupation with items with aesthetic or intrinsically interesting characteristics, and the installation of exhibitions that attempt to explain all segments, even the painful or controversial ones, of society are reflections of the interest in interpreting the recent past.[23] Supporting this concern has been the rapid growth of material culture studies, resting on the premise that any human-made object is evidence of a mind operating at a particular time and, therefore, that an object can be studied, or "read", like textual manuscript and printed materials, for understanding the past.[24] These interests and activities have caused museum curators, researchers, and interpreters to reevaluate how they select artifacts for preservation and management. How many toasters from the 1960s need to be saved? Or, do any original toasters need to be saved because of the plethora of published and audio-visual advertisements and other documentation about the role and use of such common household appliances? Or, are there other objects more worthy of acquisition and preservation because they better show the kind and variety of activities carried out in typical 1960s kitchens?

Can any event, topic, or geographical area be documented adequately without careful, coordinated consideration of printed, manuscript, and artifactual information sources? Think about documenting a local neighborhood in a city. What can be gained if secondary historical research, or photographic

[23]See, for example, Harry Rubenstein, "Collecting for Tomorrow: Sweden's Contemporary Documentation Program," *Museum News* 63 (August 1985), 55-60; Thomas J. Schlereth, "Contemporary Collecting for Future Recollecting," *Museum Studies Journal* 113 (Spring 1984), 23-30; and, Edith Mayo, "Contemporary Collecting," *History News* 37 (October 1982), 8-11.

[24]For a convenient summary see Thomas J. Schlereth, *Material Culture Studies in America* (Nashville: American Associate for State and Local History, 1982).

documentation, or objects used by the neighborhood's residents, or records of the neighborhood associations, or papers of the families and individuals that live in this area, or the actual structures that make up the neighborhood are only collected and preserved? Yet, that kind of piecemeal acquisition of information sources is most often what archival and historical organizations do. These institutions neglect asking first *what* is wanted to be known about the neighborhood, as well as comparing the relative value of the wide diversity of information sources. The typical result is the preservation of important information, without knowing whether it is the best or even all of the information that is required.

The archival documentation strategy approach described in this paper may provide the best opportunity, at least at present, for ensuring not only that our society is adequately documented through the cooperation between historical societies, history museums, historical records repositories, and libraries. This approach provides a mechanism that potentially allows a wide variety of experts and interested individuals to gather together to consider the documentation of society. This essay has stressed historians, museum curators, archivists, and librarians, but it could be expanded to include folklorists, oral historians, ethnographers, and others seeking documentation that enables them to understand how society has developed and works.

Modern society is very complex, and there are enormous quantities of information already existing in and steadily being created by its inhabitants. Unless the historical and information professions act now, future generations will possibly have a confused sense of us and our world. The documentation strategy holds some promise for providing those generations a better portrait of ourselves and our worlds, especially if it is widely used not only by archivists but by librarians, historians, and museum curators. At the least, the strategy's results should be an improvement over the current grab-bag of surviving documentation that may or may not tell us and future generations about the origins of our society and its present nature.

FOURTEEN

ARCHIVISTS AND
INFORMATION POLICY IN
THE UNITED STATES:
LOOKING TOWARD THE
1990s

Introduction

Throughout the history of their profession, archivists have
faced innumerable challenges in carrying out their mission to
identify, preserve, manage, and make available for use records
of continuing or enduring value. It seems, however, that over
the past decade or so that these challenges have been
especially severe; declining resources, unfriendly national and
state legislative actions, and increasingly more sophisticated
electronic information technology, among other things, have all
hit hard archivists' ability to meet their mission. If nothing
else, the tensions of these years have jarred many archivists
out of a complacency in which they assumed that society
valued archival records and, hence, their work. Now they
understand not only that their repositories are under-funded
and under-utilized, but that the rectification of these conditions
is not merely dependent on shifting political and socio-economic
trends that they have little control over, but on their own
actions as well. There was a day when archivists were
primarily defined by the work that they performed in their
stacks and in their reference rooms. Now the idea of "activist"
archivists is not merely confined, as it once was, to their
personal political convictions and activities,[1] but is a concept
that is being used to characterize most of their work.
Archivists are devoting considerably larger portions of their
time to advocacy on behalf of their individual programs and
profession, attempting to divest themselves of an image of

---

[1]The first notion of the activist archivist was as follows: "Activist
archivists are those archivists who persistently seek to address major social
concerns of the archival profession and the public it serves and to improve
their own work places, their professional organizations, and the archival
profession in general. Activist archivists are advocates for a more
responsible, understanding, democratic profession, who believe these goals
are often best achieved through vocal or written expression at professional
and public meetings, and in the professional and general literature." Archie
Motley, "Out of the Hollinger Box: The Archivist as Advocate," *Midwestern
Archivist* 9, no. 2 (1984), 65.

loyal, but less than crucial, employees.[2] Archivists have an increasing sense of the need to make things happen, rather than waiting for events to engulf and sweep them along, defining their own profession and its potential success as they go.

Since the mid-1970s, and especially in the past decade, archivists have become especially energetic in their efforts to gain a more prominent societal profile. Much of that work has been inwardly directed, as archivists have worked to convince themselves of the need to be more active and have tried to position themselves and their institutions and professional associations to be able to support their increasingly more pro-active attitudes.[3] The notable achievements in the archival community in the 1980s reflect this internal bent. The preparation of a comprehensive goals and priorities statement for the archival profession is one of its major successes, although while it carries an agenda for major strengthening of the societal position of the archival community the statement's use and discussion has continued to be largely confined within the profession.[4] Efforts by the Society of American Archivists (SAA) to go beyond its own boundaries have been either limited or very recent. The establishment of a standing committee on public relations (1988) is, for example, too recent to be able to assess its potential benefits. Instead, much of the archival profession's emphases have been on very different matters, such as standards for individuals, functions,

[2]For a case study of the image of archivists, refer to Sidney J. Levy and Albert G. Robles, *The Image of Archivists: Resource Allocators' Perceptions* (Chicago: Society of American Archivists, 1984).

[3]The benchmark year for this new activity and attitude can be considered to be 1972, the year when the report of the Committee for the 1970's was released. This report laid out a very ambitious agenda for the Society of American Archivists, including the establishment of an executive office with professional staff and a major publication program. See Philip P. Mason, "The Society of American Archivists in the Seventies: Report of the Committee for the 1970's," *American Archivist* 35 (April 1972), 193-217.

[4]*Planning for the Archival Profession: A Report of the SAA Task Force on Goals and Priorities* (Chicago: Society of American Archivists, 1986) and *An Action Agenda for the Archival Profession: Institutionalizing the Planning Process; A Report to SAA Council by the Committee on Goals and Priorities* ([Chicago]: Society of American Archivists, August 31, 1988).

institutions, and educational programs.[5] Supporting, and in some cases leading to, these efforts has been an intensive decade-long period of self-assessment, reflected in the essays in this volume.[6] However, what still has not significantly changed is the archival community's societal profile. David Gracy, a former SAA president, recently wrote that the "society in which we live and which we serve is uncertain of the need for, value of, and use of archives."[7] While he urged a redefinition of archives to make them more relevant and understandable to

---

[5]Within the past few years the profession has adopted a program of individual certification of archivists, worked harder to develop and use descriptive standards, begun to more toward stronger standards for archival institutions, and initiated efforts to strengthen graduate archival education programs. Certification was adopted by SAA Council in 1987 and gotten underway two years later, leading to the creation of an Academy of Certified Archivists in fall 1989. The US MARC Archives and Manuscripts Control Format was introduced in 1983, transforming the manner in which archivists think about arrangement and description and leading to efforts to develop more stringent descriptive standards. The long-lived SAA Task Force on Institutional Evaluation produced in 1989 a work-book on assessing archival institutions and led to the establishment of a standing SAA Committee on Institutional Evaluation and Development; studying the adoption of standards for institutional accreditation is one of a number of charges to this new committee. In 1988 SAA Council adopted a more comprehensive set of guidelines for graduate archival education programs, and is now working with the American Library Association on accreditation of these programs. For readings on some of these developments, refer to William J. Maher, "Contexts for Understanding Professional Certification: Opening Pandora's Box?" *American Archivist* 51 (Fall 1988), 408-27; David Bearman, "Archives and Manuscript Control with Bibliographic Utilities: Opportunities and Challenges," *ibid.* 52 (Winter 1989), 26-39; Paul McCarthy, *Archives Assessment and Planning Workbook* (Chicago: Society of American Archivists, 1989); and Terry Eastwood, "Nurturing Archival Education in the University," *American Archivist* 51 (Summer 1988), 228-52.

[6]In 1982 through 1986 the National Historical Publications and Records Commission funded forty-two statewide projects to assess the condition of archival records and to plan for ways of improving their management and preservation. Many of these states developed plans that called for more energetic political advocacy, on both state and national arenas. See Lisa B. Weber, ed., *Documenting America: Assessing the Condition of Historical Records in the States* ([Albany]: National Association of State Archives and Records Administrators, [1984]); Edie Hedlin, "Archival Programs in the Southeast: A Preliminary Assessment," *Provenance* 11 (Spring 1984), 1-15; and Virginia Stewart, "Archives in the Midwest: Assessments and Prospects," *Midwestern Archivist* 10, no. 1 (1985), 5-16.

[7]"Archivists, You Are What People Think You Keep," *American Archivist* 52 (Winter 1989), 78.

society, it is also true that the archival community must move
more aggressively into the political realm.

What has been absent from the archival community's efforts
is a reinvigoration of a commitment to affect national, state,
and local legislation and information policies, which is the topic
of this concluding essay. Although archivists have from time
to time been successful in major national legislative initiatives,
such as the recent reconstitution of the National Archives as
an independent federal agency,[8] such successes have been few
and far between. More typical was the archival community's
response to the Family Educational and Privacy Rights Act
(Buckley Amendment). As one archivist noted, this act was
amended following a "storm of protest primarily from the
higher education community . . . . Apparently archivists were
not an effective part of the storm of protest. . . ."[9] Another
commentator had an even more devastating conclusion
concerning the role of archivists in information policy
formulation and enaction. Alice Robbin, studying how state
archives have tried to cope with personal privacy issues, had
the following to say:

> Very few archives had participated in the legislative process.
> . . . The telephone interviews [with state archivists]
> revealed two reasons for the lack of participation. First,
> there were structural problems within and outside the
> agency that translated into a lack of visibility and political
> clout. Second, archivists generally did not actively
> participate in the political process.[10]

This lack of participation in information policies is the missing
component of the more proactive modern archival community.
Archivists know themselves better than ever before. They are
also laying in place the standards that are needed for a solid
archival profession and are rapidly coming out of the stacks to
advocate for their institutions and profession. Archivists also
know what needs to occur for the essential improvements in
their work to happen. But some of their energy must be

[8]See Page Putnam Miller, "Archival Issues and Problems: The Central
Role of Advocacy," *Public Historian* 8 (Summer 1986), 60-73.

[9]Marjorie Rabe Barritt, "The Appraisal of Personally Identifiable
Student Records," *American Archivist* 49 (Summer 1986), 266.

[10]"State Archives and Issues of Personal Privacy: Policies and Practices,"
American Archivist 49 (Spring 1986), 171.

devoted to tracking, influencing, and initiating state and federal information policies that promote the identification, preservation, management, and use of archival records. The remainder of this essay explores the possibilities that archivists have in state and national information policies, a natural concluding point for this volume which has summarized, critiqued, and proposed actions that are necessary for the continued functioning and relevance of the American archival profession.

Defining Information Policy

The most difficult aspect in writing about archivists and information policy is trying to define what information policy actually is, how it is perceived, and what it should or could be. There are some useful definitions of information policy that can guide archivists in their important endeavors. Harold Borko has stated that "information policy generally refers to the rules, regulations, laws and procedures that govern the way information is used in society." In this definition he has captured the essence of information policy: a concern for the use of or access to information. Borko quickly showed the complexity of this simple definition when he wrote in the very next sentence that an information policy is not in a "vacuum", but is molded by governmental and leadership aspects.[11] The usefulness of Borko's definition is demonstrated in the recent major report on Florida's information policy which started out with the statement that the "state's information policy consists of a variety of laws and rules that govern how the state and local governments collect, use, store and disseminate information." Again the emphasis of this definition, and the report itself, is on access and use.[12]

There are a number of characteristics of information policy that make them sometimes difficult to monitor, enact, and regulate. Toni Carbo Bearman, drawing on the influential 1976 Rockefeller report on national information policy, stated a few years ago that it is useless to debate whether there is such a

---

[11]*Foundations of a National Information Policy*, Seminar on Library Automation and Information Networks 1988 (Taipei, Taiwan: June 9-10, 1988), 1.

[12]Joint Committee on Information Technology Resources, *Florida's Information Policy: Problems and Issues in the Information Age* ([Tallahassee]: Florida Legislature, April 1989), 1.

thing as national information policy since we have had such policies for nearly two centuries, starting with the Bill of Rights, and will continue to see such policies developed. The real issue is, instead, ensuring that these policies make sense and do what they are supposed to do.[13] It is easy to see in her comments a shift from the notion of one all encompassing information policy to the more complex, but realistic concept of a plurality of information policies. Another individual clearly showed one of the most disturbing aspects of information policy, its changeability due to technology:

> Technology has rendered former policies governing information obsolete. These former policies were based on assumptions about information transfer and use in a predominantly print culture. Our culture is now no longer predominantly print. . . . the influence of electronic communication devices and computers has altered the base upon which previous policies were formulated. It is also this rapid introduction of new technology that is responsible for the piecemeal character of information policy . . . . a policy is made in response to a new technology. Soon after implementation of the policy a new technological application is invented that requires modification of the existing policy or promulgation of another policy to cover this new aspect. Furthermore, with change occurring so rapidly, it is difficult to predict the characteristics of new changes that will require new policy.[14]

Others have also shown that information policy does not mean the same thing to different groups. Government agencies, private sector groups, and professional associations have different agendas when they consider information policies.[15] Robert Lee Chartrand, one of the leading authorities in this area, has suggested (with others) that we are really considering not a single information policy but many information policies, clustered about the way we need to govern information and its

[13]"National Information Policy: An Insider's View," *Library Trends* 35 (Summer 1986), 105-18.

[14]Robert Burger, "The Analysis of Information Policy," *Library Trends* 35 (Summer 1986), 180-81.

[15]Kaser, *Information Policy and Networking*, Seminar on Library Automation and Information Networks 1988, (Taipei, Taiwan: June 9-10, 1988), 1-2.

effect on society. Information policies take into account "the vital and often interrelated facets of information communications, information technology, information economics, information privacy, information systems, information confidentiality, information science, information networks, and information management."[16] Or, as Forest Woody Horton, Jr., has more humorously articulated this concern, "national information policy is much like the octopus and chameleon. It takes on the background coloration and composition of its environmental habitat."[17]

Despite the difficulty of absolutely defining information policy (or policies), there is little question that whatever it is, it is needed. Horton noted that information policy is necessary because the "core concern of today's concerned citizens and various groups of information professionals is that national and federal programs, laws, and policies too often consciously or inadvertently overlook the question of how the public will be affected by the new laws, programs, or policies."[18] Borko suggested four basic objectives that provide a foundation for a national information policy, including the necessity of information for decision making, accessible information, the wide distribution of information about government operations so that the citizenry can oversee such government, and the essentiality of information to society's progress in science and technology as well as the arts and culture.[19] Access and privacy to information, threatened by increasing use of electronic information technology, seem most often to emerge from a multiplicity of issues as the core of interest in what constitutes an information policy.[20] Sandy Morton captured at least one reason for this when she wrote the following:

[16]"Public Laws and Public Access," *Information Society* 5 (1987), 7-18.

[17]"Information Policy: The National Information Policy Chameleon," *Information Management Review* 3, no. 2 (1987), 79-84.

[18]"Information Policy," 79-80.

[19]*Foundations*, 4.

[20]Adrian T. Higgins, *Federal Information Policies: Their Implementation and Implications for Information Access* (Washington, D.C.: Library of Congress, 1986). See also the following year's forum, Douglas Price, *Federal Information Policies: Views of a Concerned Community* (Washington, D.C.: Library of Congress, 1987). See also the special issue of *Library Trends* 35 (Summer 1986) on "Privacy, Secrecy, and National Information Policy."

The Information Age has brought with it boundless promise. Despite its best intentions, however, it seems as if the U.S. government has been unable to come to terms with this new age.

The trends have become: The U.S. government has resorted to tactics such as reclassifying documents to restrict access and "privatization" of federal agencies that are information-rich sources for librarians, businesspeople, and the people.[21]

Not surprisingly, therefore, numerous publications like *Less Access to Less Information By and About the U.S. Government: A 1981-1987 Chronology* (and it's updates) and the *Report of the Commission on Freedom and Equality of Access to Information*[22] have appeared in recent years and have become a cornerstone of the literature on national information policies.

Besides access, information as a valuable resource or commodity has emerged as a cornerstone of the concept of information policies.[23] This is most clearly seen on the federal level. Until the Office of Management and Budget (OMB) Circular A-130, "Management of Federal Information Resources," appeared in 1985, it could be argued that there was little basis for coherent national information policies. OMB's circular grew directly out of responsibilities assigned to it, through the Paperwork Reduction Act of 1980, to develop a centralized and coordinated federal information policy. This circular partly rectifies this problem by establishing a framework for subsequent information policies and providing some foundation for a definition of what an information policy is about. It includes certain basic assumptions, such as government information being a valuable resource that also requires reasonable access while protecting individual privacy. The circular also identifies crucial information management policies, including the Privacy Act and the Freedom of

---

[21]"Viewpoint: Sensitive, but Unclassified Government Information: The Debate Continues," *Information Management Review* 3 (Spring 1988),61.

[22]The first publication was released by the American Library Association Washington Office in February 1988. The other report was commissioned by the American Library Association and issued to its Council in January 1986.

[23]See Cees J. Hamelink, *The Technology Gamble; Informatics and Public Policy: A Study of Technology Choice* (Norwood, New Jersey: Ablex Publishing Corporation, 1988) for an international perspective on this issue.

Information Act. Finally, the circular advocates that information technology shall be used wherever and whenever possible to manage government information effectively and efficiently. Still, the circular has not been received with unanimous acclaim, some fearing the loss of access to certain government information.[24]

Why Archivists Should Be Interested in Information Policies

Why should archivists be interested in information policies given their variety of interpretations and often controversial nature? The most obvious, and traditional (for archivists at least), reason is that many archival and historical records repositories exist to document various public policies, including those concerning information. Government archives - federal, state, and local - come readily to mind as repositories that serve this and other purposes.[25] More controversial is the quasi-public system of Presidential Libraries, institutions specifically designed to document federal policy administration by administration.[26] Outside of the government realm, there are also many special subject repositories that have a specific or partial focus on public policy related matters. Even repositories that seek to document geographically-defined areas, like state and local historical societies, get involved in broader issues by seeking to acquire the papers of public officials with national and local significance or serving as the official repositories of local government records. Archivists have also gone beyond the boundaries of their institutions to work with records creators, subject specialists, and researchers in order to ensure the more effective documentation of broad public policy issues and concerns. Many of these public policy issues also concern what we can term information policies. The health

[24]For additional information and views about this important policy, refer to J. Timothy Sprehe, "OMB Circular No. A-130, The Management of Federal Information Resource: Its Origins and Impact," *Government Information Quarterly* 4, no. 2 (1987), 189-96, and Peter Hernon, "The Management of United States Government Information Resources: An Assessment of OMB Circular A-130," *ibid.* 3, no. 3 (1986), 279-90.

[25]See, for example, Frank B. Evans and Harold T. Pinkett, eds., *Research in the Administration of Public Policy* (Washington, D.C.: Howard University Press, 1975).

[26]Cynthia J. Wolff, "Necessary Monuments: The Making of the Presidential Library System," *Government Publications Review* 16 (1989), 47-62.

care system in this country is one example of the relationship between archivists (and related professionals like medical records librarians), public policy, and information policy. The discovered link between women using diethylstilbestrol (DES) and vaginal cancer in their female children required the use of patient and hospital administrative records over a fifteen to twenty year period. Managing and preserving such records extends through professional, public policy, and information policy concerns.[27]

Archivists still obviously need to do more than considering how to document information and other public policies. Since one of the driving forces for information policy development and adherence in the past several decades has been the increasing use of technology to store, manipulate, and access information, there should be little question that the archivist has a big stake in information policies. Richard Kesner, for example, has eloquently argued that if archivists do not become more comfortable with electronic information technology they will be "relegated to the antiquarian curatorial role" that archivists have tried to rid themselves of, both in practice and image. Kesner's focus has been on the automation of the office and the organization or institution, but it is relatively easy to extend his concerns to the broader, somewhat more elusive, realm of information policies. Kesner wrote, for example, that "EDP and telecommunications products are altering the way people create, distribute, file, and retrieve information."[28] Since an increasing portion of all recorded information is in electronic form, the ways that archivists must deal with information are being altered. Some of these alterations are, again, internal to the archival profession itself, relating to basic archival principles and practices.[29] Others concern a more proactive posture by

[27]Joan Krizack, "Understanding the Nature of Hospitals and Their Relation to the U.S. Health Care System: The First Step in Documenting Hospitals," unpublished paper, September 1988.

[28]"Automated Information Management: Is There a Role for the Archivist in the Office of the Future?" *Archivaria* 19 (Winter 1984-85), 163, 165. See also his *Automation for Archivists and Records Managers* (Chicago: American Library Association, 1984) and *Information Systems: A Strategic Approach to Planning and Implementation* (Chicago: American Library Association, 1988).

[29]Many of these concerns were considered at the Archival Administration in the Electronic Age: An Advanced Institute for Government Archivists held June 4-16, 1989 at the University of Pittsburgh School of Library and Information Science. A few examples of the potential changes

archivists that build into electronic information systems the capability to identify and preserve in a usable fashion information with a long-term value.[30]   To the extent that information policies affect information technology, then, archivists must be concerned with policy formulation and implementation.

The primary motivation for archivists being involved in or concerned with information policies is, of course, their concern or conviction that the historical document is vital to the understanding of present society and that society's future. This is a fundamental purpose of the archival community world-wide.[31]   Since information policies affect the allocation of resources to public and private archival programs, access to archival records held in public and to a less degree private repositories, and other issues vital to the archival mission, archivists must take a more active role in the formation of information policies.   Frank Evans recently made an effort to characterize national historical records policies throughout the world.   Among other things he concluded that such national policies focus on government records, and that these policies are also shaped by national identity and pride, threats to national security, and other political, economic, and social policies and systems.   Interestingly, Evans also concluded that "public" perceptions of the value of historical records is a factor in the nature and success of national archival programs and

will illustrate this point.   The nature of electronic information systems potentially moves the archives from an institution concerned with older information to a repository that is also supervising the location and use of current information; the alternative is the possible loss of great quantities of documentation of continuing value for the governments and various publics.   This technology also challenges the archival definition of a record and makes largely meaningless certain basic archival principles such as original order, record series, and provenance.

[30]For example, archivists have traditionally received records after their creation; the federal government operates, for example, on a thirty year rule of transferal of archival materials to the National Archives.   Information stored in electronic form will be lost long before thirty years are up primarily due to the rapidly changing nature of both the hard-ware and software.   Archivists will have to intervene in the creation of information systems to ensure that archival information is identified and preserved in an accessible form.

[31]See Hugh A. Taylor, "The Collective Memory: Archives and Libraries As Heritage," *Archivaria* 15 (Winter 1982-83), 118-30.

policies.[32] The implication is that without such basic policies, any number of political, social, economic, and technological interests could undermine the archivist's unique role in and for society, the preservation of the documentary heritage. This is clearly evident on a more local level in the recent report on Florida information policy. While the report acknowledged that the "centerpiece of the state's information policy" is the state's Public Records Law, it also noted that "there is no evidence that the applications and systems being developed by agencies and local governments are explicitly considering archival and dissemination issues . . . ."[33]

There are other reasons for archivists to be concerned with information policies. Any piece of legislation or executive order or study commissioned by a state or federal agency and leading to the formulation of information policies could threaten the preservation of federal, state, and local archival records. The Paperwork Reduction Act of 1980 (P.L. 96-511) is but one example of why archivists should be concerned. On the one hand the act sought to manage better the records of the national government. On the other hand, however, the act "authorized OMB to oversee virtually all Federal information-related activities . . . , to develop government information management policies, and to reduce the paperwork burdens imposed on the public by government information collection."[34] What is the role of the National Archives? How does OMB relate to the National Archives? Were archivists involved in the formulation of the public law? These questions become even more relevant with the National Archives' loss of the records management function with its achievement of administrative independence in 1984.[35] The answers to these and other questions do not appear to be flattering ones to the American archival community.

[32]Frank B. Evans, "National Archival Policies Abroad For Historical Records," paper presented to the Society of American Archivists, September 4, 1987.

[33]*Florida's Information Policy*, 2, 21.

[34]David Plocher, "Discussion Forum: Institutional Elements in OMB's Control of Government Information," *Government Information Quarterly* 5, no. 4 (1988), 318.

[35]Linda Vee Pruitt, "Archives and Records Management in the Federal Government: The Post-GSA Context," *Provenance* 3 (Fall 1985), 87-93.

Archivists and Information Policy: A Retrospective View

The track record of archivists' involvement in the development of information policies in this country has not been, to date, a very good one. At the beginning of the establishment of the archival profession and archival institutions, there was a heavy emphasis on legislation that supported these programs and the archival mission. When the Society of American Archivists was founded in 1936, one of its preeminent concerns was the promotion of uniform state archival legislation as the "most direct course to a general improvement in the administration of state and local archives."[36] One pioneer state archivist emphatically stated that "as soon as the [state] archivist has been appointed, work should begin on drafting legislation creating the archives department."[37] Although this was the result of thirty years of creating state archives throughout the nation and the long, arduous campaign to establish the National Archives,[38] this professional preoccupation was a short-lived emphasis. This short-life has certainly been borne out in the past decade of intense self-scrutiny by archivists of their institutions and their profession. H.G. Jones' indictment of the general lack of state leadership was accompanied by a depiction of archival programs caught in a cycle of poverty.[39] The intensification of change in information technology and information policies have only made these weaknesses look worse.

Archivists have not been disinterested in information policies, although their level of interest is perhaps not as high as it should be. An examination of the last fifteen years of the

[36]Albert R. Newsome, "Uniform State Archival Legislation," *American Archivist* 2 (January 1939), 2.

[37]Thornton W. Mitchell, ed., *Norton on Archives: The Writings of Margaret Cross Norton on Archival & Records Management* (Carbondale: Southern Illinois University Press, 1975), 45.

[38]For the context of these early years, read Victor Gondos, Jr., *J. Franklin Jameson and the Birth of the National Archives 1906-1926* (Philadelphia: University of Pennsylvania Press, 1981); William F. Birdsall, "The American Archivists' Search for Professional Identity, 1909-1936," Ph.D. dissertation, University of Wisconsin-Madison, 1973; and Ernst Posner, *American State Archives* (Chicago: University of Chicago Press, 1964).

[39]Jones, "The Pink Elephant Revisited," *American Archivist* 43 (Fall 1980), 473-83 and Weber, ed., *Documenting America*, 8.

premier archival journal, *The American Archivist*, reveals a diversity of statements, analyses, and case studies of topics closely identified with information policies. Access, the core topic of information policies, looms as a major topic in the pages of this journal. Studies on freedom of information, privacy, and copyright legislation are staples of the archival literature.[40] Other related issues are also present, including the ownership of public records, state archives legislation, and appraisal of legally restricted records.[41] What is most noticeably lacking, however, is a consistent attention by archivists on developing trends, represented by major reports and studies, in national information policies. From the pivotal Rockefeller Report in 1976 until the present, archivists have accumulated a spotty record in keeping up with such reports and their implications for information professionals such as themselves.[42] When archivists have paid attention to such

[40]Karyl Winn, "Common Law Copyright and the Archivist," *American Archivist* 37 (July 1974), 375-86; Alan Reitman, "Freedom of Information and Privacy: The Civil Libertarian's Dilemma," *ibid.* 38 (October 1975), 501-08; Trudy Huskamp Peterson, "After Five Years: An Assessment of the Amended U.S. Freedom of Information Act," *ibid.* 43 (Spring 1980), 161-68; Michael J. Crawford, "Copyright, Unpublished Manuscript Records, and the Archivist," *ibid.* 46 (Spring 1983), 135-47; Raymond H. Geselbracht, "The Origins of Restriction on Access to Personal Papers at the Library of Congress and the National Archives," *ibid.* 49 (Spring 1986), 142-62; Robbin, "State Archives and Issues of Personal Privacy"; and Roland M. Baumann, "The Administration of Access to Confidential Records in State Archives: Common Practices and the Need for a Model Law," *ibid.* 49 (Fall 1986), 349-69.

[41]J. Frank Cook, "Private Papers of Public Officials," *American Archivist* 38 (July 1975), 299-324; Walter Robertson, Jr., "NARS: The Politics of Placement," *ibid.* 39 (October 1976), 485-92; George W. Bain, "State Archival Law: A Content Analysis," *ibid.* 46 (Spring 1983), 158-74; Susan D. Steinwall, "Appraisal and the FBI Files Case: For Whom Do Archivists Retain Records?" *ibid.* 49 (Winter 1986), 52-63; and Barritt, "Appraisal of Personally Identifiable Student Records."

[42]Consider the following reports that did _not_ receive mention in the pages of the *American Archivist*: U.S. Domestic Council Committee on the Right of Privacy, *National Information Policy: Report to the President of the United States* (Washington, D.C.: National Commission on Libraries and Information Science, 1976); U.S. Office of Technology Assessment, *Computer-Based National Information Systems: Technology and Public Policy Issues* (Washington, D.C.: U.S. Government Printing Office, 1981); U.S. Congress, House, Committee on Science and Technology, Subcommittee on Science, Research, and Technology, *Information and Telecommunications: An Overview of Issues, Technologies, and Applications* (Washington, D.C.: Congressional Research Service, Library of Congress, 1981); U.S. Congress,

reports and studies, it has usually led to some lament about the lack of attention by the authors of these studies to archival interests and concerns.[43]

The omission of archivists in keeping current with information policies trends and issues may be a result of a form of professional myopia that has been criticized before.[44] The lack of participation by archivists in information policies may be also due to their close connection with the historical profession. The American archival profession emerged from the American Historical Association, until recently was primarily educated by and as historians, and has remained generally very active in professional historical associations.[45] Until the emergence of "public history" in the 1970s, however, historians (as a profession at least) seemed to have little interest in public policy or information policy, and there is no consensus in that field that this is what public history is about. It is also a manifestation of a malaise afflicting the archival community that has restrained them from having a more active role in the formulation of essential information policies. Larry Hackman, in reviewing the 1985 report of the Committee on the Records of Government, stated that the report "points out perceptively that archivists have largely failed to document that good records and archives programs contribute to better policy and better government programs overall."[46]

Office of Technology Assessment, *Information Technology R&D: Critical Trends and Issues* (Washington, D.C.: Government Printing Office, February 1985); and U.S. Congress, Office of Technology Assessment, *Intellectual Property Rights in An Age of Electronics and Information* (Washington, D.C.: Government Printing Office, April 1986).

[43]For example, Larry J. Hackman said the following about Carol M. Barker and Matthew H. Fox, *Classified Files: The Yellowing Pages; A Report on Scholars' Access to Government Documents* (New York: The Twentieth Century Fund, 1972): "Nowhere in the report is there acknowledgement that government archivists have frequently convinced former government officials to preserve records that might otherwise be destroyed and make them available with minimum restriction"; *American Archivist* 36 (April 1973), 238.

[44]Margaret S. Child, "Reflections on Cooperation Among Professions," *American Archivist* 46 (Summer 1983), 286-92.

[45]See Mattie U. Russell, "The Influence of Historians on the Archival Profession in the United States," *American Archivist* 46 (Summer 1983), 277-85.

[46]*American Archivist* 49 (Spring 1986), 189.

A glance at some of the formative documents in information policies shows an overwhelming lack of participation by archivists in the process, while government officials, lawyers, journalists, business leaders, information scientists, and others are all well-represented. The effort by the National Telecommunications and Information Administration of the U.S. Department of Commerce a decade ago to define information policy by identifying the major issues in such policy is one example of this problem. Issues examined included the dissemination of information, access to information, information privacy, the functioning of information markets, property rights and subsidies in the creation of information, and managing information. It is not hard to see that archivists would be interested in such topics. However, not only were no archivists represented in this effort, but there was little from the archival perspective included here. When archivists, archives, or archival institutions are mentioned it is in relation to their involvement with records management functions, not the identification, preservation, and administration of records of enduring value.[47] Another example is the Commission on Freedom and Equality of Access to Information, established in 1983 and issuing a report in 1986, that consisted of a "distinguished group of information policy experts." This group was chaired by a former administrator of the National Archives, although he was clearly outnumbered by librarians, journalists, legal scholars and lawyers, publishers, political scientists, and others.[48]

Archivists and Information Policy: A Prospective View

What are the crucial aspects of information policy that archivists ought to be concerned with and involved in? As was noted above, there are a number of areas, primarily access and appraisal, that archivists have written about fairly extensively, although they often have not identified these issues and concerns as part of an information policy. Access has been a focus of the archival community for at least the past several decades. In this matter government records have primarily been given attention. Most frequently archivists have examined the matter of the right to privacy against the right to know.

---

[47]Issues in Information Policy.

[48]*Report of the Commission on Freedom and Equality of Access to Information.*

More recently archivists have examined in greater detail more specific aspects of privacy and access, such as the problem with expungements in the name of privacy from records maintained as archival. "Under current expungement procedures, historically valuable information is legally destroyed. . . . The easiest solution . . . would be to have Congress change the Federal Records Act to provide that once records have been appraised as having enduring value, they be considered archival, and thus not subject to expungement."[49] If any consensus emerges from the archival studies and literature, it is that access is a ticklish issue, complicating already complicated problems of dealing effectively with immense quantities of information and increasingly sophisticated information technology that make preservation and management more difficult than before.

Appraisal, or in a broader sense - the effective documentation of society, has also emerged as a issue in the modern electronic information age. It has already been mentioned that archivists have become increasingly concerned with their ability to preserve the historical record in a more fragile electronic form. This concern has been further exacerbated by the increasing challenges of the archival community regarding their ability to appraise adequately and in a timely enough manner records in any format. In a highly publicized case, a suit was successfully brought against the National Archives questioning the manner in which records of the Federal Bureau of Investigation were being appraised.[50] More recently another case has been brought against the National Archives concerning its handling of automated records in the White House that relate to the Iran-Contra affair. It is clear that although the theory of archival appraisal has improved through the years, that public policy that allows the theory to be effectively applied is not sufficient. In both court cases mentioned here, the main problem was that the National Archives lacked, or contended that it lacked, sufficient authority to define a public record and to carry out its examination of that record and, as well, did not possess the resources in any event had it had the necessary authority.

Advocacy, the effort to effect public policy in conformity with the mission and interests of the archival community, has also

---

[49]James Gregory Bradsher, "Privacy Act Expungements: A Reconsideration," *Provenance* 6 (Spring 1988), 21.

[50]Steinwall, "Appraisal and the FBI Files Case."

emerged as an issue in the archival profession. Most recently this was reflected in the profession's successful effort to liberate the National Archives from the General Services Administration and recreate it as an independent federal agency. One commentator on this movement optimistically noted that a logical outgrowth of this effort is a renewed interest by archivists and historians in federal information policies.[51] But it is difficult to find sufficient life here yet. None of the national archival and records management professional associations possess at this point a clear agenda for the development of information policies necessary to support the archival mission. When they have developed or been given agendas, such as with the Report on the Records of Government, they have not followed through.[52] When archivists have had the opportunity to develop agendas that could influence national, state, and local information policies, they have sometimes fumbled the opportunity.[53] A few states, most notably New York, have been especially energetic in attempting to put the state archives in a position suitable to affecting state and national information policies.[54] New York's state

[51]Miller, "Archival Issues and Problems."

[52]See Anna Nelson's comments in "The 1985 Report of the Committee on the Records of Government: An Assessment," *Government Information Quarterly* 4, no. 2 (1987), 143-50.

[53]Two recent examples come to mind. One was the effort by the American Association for State and Local History to support a program of assistance for local governments wishing to improve the management of their records. This effort brought together an interesting group of archivists, historians, local officials, local government association leaders, and records managers. Rather than develop a national agenda, however, the project ultimately produced some useful technical publications. This certainly represents one lost opportunity. Another similar loss is the discussion a few years ago by a number of archival and historical professional associations to promote federal legislation that would create a trust fund for the American documentary heritage. Disagreements between the potential architects of the trust doomed it to never getting off the drawing board.

[54]New York has built an impressive array of legislation and issued a number of important reports on archival issues in the last decade. The cornerstone of these efforts was the statewide historical records assessment report, *Toward A Usable Past*, issued by the New York State Historical Records Advisory Board in 1984. See also the subsequent reports on preservation issues, *Our Memory At Risk*, issued by the New York Document Conservation Advisory Council in 1987; a report on local government records, *The Quiet Revolution*, produced in late 1988; and *A*

archivist, Larry J. Hackman, has also given the archival profession its first clear articulation of what a national archival policy could look like, and this proposal is worth a more detailed examination here.

Hackman has long been one of the leaders in the archival profession in advocating a stronger national and state public policy role for archivists. As Director of the Records Program of the National Historical Publications and Records Commission he laid the foundation for the state historical records assessment and reporting projects. As Archivist for the State of New York since 1981, he has largely directed his energies to gaining a more prominent policy role for his institution in state government that ensures the preservation of New York documentary resources. Hackman has also become more vocal in his opinion that one of the major obstacles to the satisfactory documentation of society is the lack of a clear national policy on historical records.[55] He has urged a "vigorous discussion on the role of government in historical records affairs" that leads to a "sound base for a true national historical records program and informed discussion of the appropriate role of state governments as well."[56] To facilitate this discussion, Hackman drafted an outline of what such a policy could like.

The advantages of such a policy, according to Hackman, would be many.[57] It would encourage better coordination among federal programs concerned with archival records,

Strategic Plan for Managing and Preserving Electronic Records in New York State Government: Final Report of the Special Media Records Project (Albany: New York State Archives and Records Administration, August 1988). The potential long-term benefits of these efforts to influence and re-direct public policy on behalf of an archival agenda are partly evident in legislation that has been passed to develop re-grant programs for historical records programs and local governments. For a description of how all these pieces are meant to fit together see Larry J. Hackman, "From Assessment to Action: Toward a Usable Past in the Empire State," *Public Historian* 7 (Summer 1985), 23-34.

[55]For a full statement of how such policy fits into the overall needs of the archival profession, see his "A Perspective on American Archives," *Public Historian* 8 (Summer 1986), 10-28 and "Toward the Year 2000," *ibid.*, 92-98.

[56]"Toward the Year 2000," 97.

[57]His proposal is in "The United States Needs a National Historical Records Policy!" *History News* 43 (March/April 1988), 32-37.

ensure access to such records, foster research and development that is necessary to support such continued access, promote the understanding of historical records as a "public good", and provide an opportunity for increased public support of historical records programs and issues. Although Hackman does not explicitly discuss this, the enacting of such a policy would help the archival community to compete with and to better inform many of the other information policies that have an impact on the future historical record, but without sufficient input from the guardians of this record. If information policies are, as Horton suggests, like the octopus or chameleon, there is no archival coloration or composition because the archival community is not part of the present information policy environment. Hackman's proposal has provided one way to change this, although the vigorous discussion that he sought has not occurred.

There are possibilities, however, for seeing that this discussion does eventually occur. A recent report by the National Academy of Public Administration (NAPA) on behalf of the National Archives on the impact of electronic recordkeeping on federal archival records is an encouraging sign. The first recommendation was for the National Archives to "lead and develop a systematic, long-term strategic plan for electronic records." This plan would need to be developed "in collaboration with the Office of Management and Budget (OMB), the General Services Administration (GSA), and the National Institute of Standards and Technology (NIST) (formerly the National Bureau of Standards)." These bodies have been clearly crucial in the past development of information policies, and NAPA has identified the need for the National Archives to become a more vital player in this arena. Another recommendation in this report noted that "NARA should work with OMB to determine appropriate federal requirements for the management of all records that result from federally mandated and funded programs; such requirements should include criteria for the management of records generated by new technologies."[58] That the National

---

[58]National Academy of Public Administration, *The Effects of Electronic Recordkeeping on the Historical Record of the U.S. Government: A Report for the National Archives and Records Administration*, Contract NAXXOP8800009 ([Washington, D.C.: NAPA, January 1989), 4-5. Other related recommendations include the building of recordkeeping rules and procedures into electronic information systems, getting NARA "involved in federal and private sector standard setting activities", and urging NARA to "work with OMB and the appropriate congressional committees to pursue

Archives is, at least, considering a more proactive stance in the development and implementation of information policies is a hopeful sign. If the National Archives can link itself with the state archival institutions committed to an investment in state and national information policies,[59] then a new era for the archival community might be at hand.

Conclusion: Recommendations

It might seem presumptuous, even foolish, for yet another individual to suggest what the archival profession must do in the area of information policies, given the general lack of success that has already occurred here. There seems to be an urgency in this area, however, that compels one to add his voice in the hopes that there will soon be a chorus that leads to action. Kathleen M. Heim started off her call for librarians' greater involvement in information policies with the following statement: "Librarians and information scientists will fail to maintain credibility and competency in the next decade unless they understand and influence the complex factors that comprise the contemporary information infrastructure."[60] There are some who worry that archivists may already have lost so much ground to the rapidly changing information technology and the ability to influence that technology's design and use that the archivist's credibility and competency is questionable. On the other hand, the archival community brings such a unique perspective to the myriad views of the information designers, vendors, and users that this community may, with adjustments in basic archival principles and methods, have a voice that needs to be heard.[61] The recommendations below are

the legislative avenues towards better management of electronic records."

[59]The interest by state archives in these concerns is evident in the recent participation of sixteen of these institutions in the first of two two-week institutes on archival administration in the electronic age held in June 1989 at the University of Pittsburgh School of Library and Information Science. The first of these institutes focused on a review of electronic information technology and strategic planning.

[60]"National Information Policy and A Mandate for Oversight by the Information Professions," *Government Publications Review* 13, no. 1 (1986), 21.

[61]This was partially borne out in the two-week advanced institute for government archivists held in June 1989 at the University of Pittsburgh School of Library and Information Science. This institute focused on

concerned with assisting the archival profession to prepare for this new dynamic role and need to be kept in mind as the profession works in the 1990s and prepares for the new century.

Refocus the national professional archival associations. How should the national archival profession deal with information issues and the formulation of information policies? There is no disagreement that the archival profession has a national voice through its main professional association, the Society of American Archivists, and other associations such as the National Association of Government Archives and Records Administrators. Other information professional associations have successfully worked in this arena. The Special Libraries Association, to name one example, has been particularly energetic in information policies. Its involvement started in 1941 when it set up an Washington D.C. liaison and was continued in 1985 when SLA's headquarters itself was moved to the nation's capital. Over the past decade the Association has become more vocal on information policy-related matters; as one SLA leader noted, the 1985 headquarters relocation "recognized that SLA had to take an active role as an educator in attempting to shape policies in ways that are productive and useful to the profession's future."[62] At present, there are no professional archival associations with either a national information policy agenda or visibility on Capitol Hill. These associations, together or individually, must adopt - with sufficient fanfare and noise - such an agenda as well as reevaluate how they carry forth these agendas. The archival profession may be small, but its mission is overwhelmingly important and deserves more promotion as well as more attention.

Stress changes in the information technology systems. The traditional view of the archival profession has been to analyze

strategic planning for state government archives in the electronic information age. Although there was at first some uneasiness with the thought of generally humanities-trained state archivists dealing with the complexities of the information technologies, the outlook changed to recognizing that the archivists bring a unique and necessary perspective and that there are opportunities for influencing both information policies and the actual systems designs.

[62]Donna Scheeder, "The SLA Government Relations Program," *Special Libraries* 79 (Summer 1988), 186. See also Sandy I. Morton, "SLA Responds to U.S. Government Information Issues in the '80s," *ibid.*, 189-93.

records long after they were created. As David Gracy has rightly pointed out, archivists have too strongly stressed archives as "non-current" records.[63] While Gracy draws attention to this because of the problems it causes to the public perception of the archivist's mission in society, it is also true that archival records in electronic form cannot be effectively saved *after* their creation. To try to do so inflicts virtually insurmountable problems on the archivist's efforts to identify and preserve in an accessible format such records. Concepts, practices, and procedures developed for paper-based information systems simply do not hold up with electronic records. Overcoming this problem suggests two related actions needed to be taken by the archival community. One, archivists must play a greater role in the development of information policies that can regulate what technologies are used and how they are used; this approach has been the main focus of this essay. Although information policies are intended to govern information in all forms, it is also true that the stress on policies has mainly occurred in the past two decades when the growing use of electronic technology has threatened to make the curtailment of access to or violation of individual privacy through large portions of that information easier to achieve. Two, archivists must move directly to influence information technology standards, at least those set by standards organizations, so that systems can be used to identify, preserve, and make available for use the portion of information that has archival value. If archivists make this effort, there is sufficient opportunity for success that may eliminate many of the problems that archivists now encounter when dealing with electronic records.[64]

Transform archival education. The education of archivists has been traditionally divided between courses and programs offered in history departments and library and information science schools. This is not the problem. The main problem continues to be a reliance on a three course format that includes a strong emphasis on the practicum or field work. This reveals a continuing sense that archivists are archivists

[63]"Archivists, You Are What People Think You Keep."

[64]Charles M. Dollar and Thomas E. Weir, Jr., "Archival Administration, Records Management, and Computer Data Exchange Standards: An Intersection of Practices," unpublished paper, 1989, and John McDonald, "Data and Document Interchange Standards: A View from the National Archives of Canada," paper given at the 1987 Society of American Archivists meeting.

by virtue of what they do, not what they know. The content of archival education must be made equal in quality to that taught in other university graduate programs. The focus in these educational programs must change from a concentration on what they do *in* the stacks to a more balanced view of what must go on outside of the stacks and, indeed, outside of the walls of the archival repositories. The archivist must be able to not only serve as a custodian of the documentary heritage but be able to shape it as well. Shaping it requires that archivists not only know how information systems function, but how these systems are used and regulated by information policies. Archival education must accommodate this, and this might require a significant transformation of who teaches, what they teach, and where they teach.

Establish more opportunities for research and development in archival administration. The archival profession still lacks a suitable foundation for support of research and development. The summer fellowship program of Bentley Historical Library at the University of Michigan has had tremendous impact on archival knowledge since its inception in 1983, but it remains the only real research program in the profession. The lack of sufficient graduate programs and the ineffectiveness of the one existing clearinghouse of archival literature located at the National Archives only makes this area a more difficult one for the archival community. Furthermore, and most important for the purpose of this essay, the absence of a mechanism for archival research and development weakens the archival community's prospects for initiating and sustaining national archival policies. Archivists need a way of gathering information quickly and efficiently to support whatever national agendas might be. The lack of exposure that archivists have to current trends in information technology and the politics of information use and access does not put this profession in an enviable position as it looks forward to the twenty-first century. The future of the historical record may depend on what decisions archivists make to rectify this and the kinds of problems considered in this essay and, indeed, this volume.

FIFTEEN

BIBLIOGRAPHICAL ESSAY:
ESSENTIAL WRITINGS ON
THE ARCHIVAL PROFESSION
IN THE UNITED STATES IN
THE 1980s

The emphasis of this book has been on the recent development, primarily during the past decade, of the archival profession in the United States. Through its various essays a number of ideas, conclusions, and recommendations have been made concerning this profession and its mission. While these ideas, conclusions, and recommendations are solely my responsibility, they have not been formed in a vacuum nor are they without their detractors or fundamentally different perspectives. This is especially evident in the many other writings on the archival profession that have appeared over the last decade or so, a number of which have stressed changes to the archival profession and its work. The purposes of this brief essay are to cite these writings and to suggest additional readings for individuals interested in knowing more about recent trends and events in the American archival profession. Some of these essays support the themes presented in this book, while others present countervailing views; all are, however, important for understanding what has happened to the archival profession in recent years, as well as suggestive of future trends.

Archival Self-Assessment and Planning

If anything characterizes this past decade, it is the fact that it has been a time of extreme self-analysis by the American archival profession. The most important effort in this regard was the series of state assessments of historical records and historical records programs undertaken by the state historical records advisory boards with funding provided by the National Historical Publications and Records Commission. The early phase of these reports has been summarized and evaluated in *Documenting America: Assessing the Condition of Historical Records in the States* ([Albany], [1984]). Although these reports have not been utilized to everyone's liking, at least two other interesting efforts of regional evaluation based on them appeared -- Edie Hedlin, "Archival Programs in the Southeast: A Preliminary Assessment," *Provenance* 11 (Spring 1984), 1-15, and Virginia Stewart, "Archives in the Midwest: Assessments and Prospects," *Midwestern Archivist* 10, no. 1 (1985), 5-16. For a different view of the value of conducting such intensive self-study and analysis, Larry J. Hackman, "From Assessment to Action: Toward a Usable Past in the Empire State," *Public Historian* 7 (Summer 1985), 23-34 is worth reading, showing how one state intended to use their assessment report for additional planning and action.

Although these state assessments provide immense detail about the condition of historical records in the United States, there are other studies that supplement the information found in them. The most noteworthy of these studies are *Committee on the Records of Government: Report* (Washington, D.C., March 1985); [Howard P. Lowell], *Preservation Needs in State Archives* (Albany, 1986); and Charles Phillips and Patricia Hogan, *A Culture At Risk: Who Cares for America's Heritage?* (Nashville, 1984). That these reports and the state assessment reports have not been used more frequently and creatively for the benefit of preserving America's historical records is an unfortunate circumstance. Membership and institutional surveys have also supplemented these reports. The Society of American Archivists (SAA) has prepared some detailed profiles of its members. At the time of writing this book, SAA was preparing a final report on a 1989 membership survey. Previous to this, the most recent analysis was David Bearman, "1982 Survey of the Archival Profession," *American Archivist* 46 (Spring 1983), 233-39.

The past decade has also been a time of significant efforts by the archival profession to conduct national planning. Archivists in both Canada and the United States have produced detailed national plans that should be read by anyone interested in recent developments in the archival community. The United States plan is *Planning for the Archival Profession: A Report of the Society of American Archivists Task Force on Goals and Priorities* (Chicago, 1986). The Canadian report is *Canadian Archives: Report to the Social Sciences and Humanities Research Council of Canada by the Consultative Group on Canadian Archives* (Ottawa, 1980); for an important commentary on this report refer to Terry Eastwood, "Attempts at National Planning for Archives in Canada, 1975-1985," *Public Historian* 8 (Summer 1986), 74-91.

Planning extends back farther than the past decade, but even now there has not emerged much of an interest in these earlier efforts. The work of the Society of American Archivists' Committee for the Seventies laid a foundation for many subsequent activities and has been briefly recounted by Philip P. Mason, "Archives in the Seventies: Promises and Fulfillment," *American Archivist* 44 (Summer 1981), 199-206. Ernst Posner's early 1960s evaluation of state archival institutions has been analyzed by H. G. Jones, "The Pink Elephant Revisited," *American Archivist* 43 (Fall 1980), 473-83.

And many of the participants in the 1977 Conference on Setting Priorities for Historical Records were to emerge as advocates for national archival planning; see Mary Lynn McCree and Timothy Walch, eds., "Setting Priorities for Historical Records: A Conference Report," *American Archivist* 40 (July 1977), 291-347.

The SAA Goals and Priorities Task Force has now become a standing committee within that association, endeavoring to continue discussion about a national professional agenda. The more important products of its recent work are three research agendas - Richard J. Cox and Helen W. Samuels, "The Archivist's First Responsibility: A Research Agenda to Improve the Identification and Retention of Records of Enduring Value," *American Archivist* 51 (Winter/Spring 1988), 28-42; Paul McCarthy, "The Management of Archives: A Research Agenda," pp. 52-69; and Lawrence Dowler, "The Role of Use in Defining Archival Practice and Principles: A Research Agenda for the Availability and Use of Records," pp. 74-86. The Goals and Priorities Report also now has an update, *An Action Agenda for the Archival Profession: Institutionalizing the Planning Process; A Report to SAA Council* (Chicago, August 31, 1988). The GAP report's implications for the local archival repository have been discussed by Gregory S. Hunter, "Filling the GAP: Planning on the Local and Individual Levels," *American Archivist* 50 (Winter 1987), 110-15.

Out of such studies and self-scrutiny have come some articles that question basic assumptions about the archival profession. Some of the articles in this volume are certainly of this ilk. For others see Peter J. Wosh, "Creating a SemiProfessional Profession: Archivists View Themselves," *Georgia Archive* 10 (Fall 1982), 1-13, an essay that questions whether archivists constitute a profession or not, and Larry J. Hackman, "A Perspective on American Archives," *Public Historian* 8 (Summer 1986), 10-28, and "Toward the Year 2000," 92-98, that recommends a number of needed changes to archival institutions and practice.

The Historical Background of Recent Archival Developments

A number of important studies on the historical development of the American archival profession have also recently appeared, in some ways complementing the recent self-assessments and planning efforts. These studies provide significant clues concerning the present condition of the archival profession and the records the profession cares for. Richard C. Berner's characterization of public records and

historical manuscripts traditions is an extremely valuable way
for understanding present archival issues and concerns. The
main limitation of his *Archival Theory and Practice in the
United States: A Historical Analysis* (Seattle, 1983) is its focus
on archival arrangement and description. Other important
studies include Donald R. McCoy, *The National Archives:
America's Ministry of Documents 1934-1968* (Chapel Hill, 1978);
Burl Noggle, *Working With History: The Historical Records
Survey in Louisiana and the Nation, 1936-1942* (Baton Rouge,
1981); Victor Gondos, Jr., *J. Franklin Jameson and the Birth
of the National Archives, 1906-1926* (Philadelphia, 1981); and
Timothy Walch, ed., *Guardian of Heritage: Essays on the
History of the National Archives* (Washington, D.C., 1985).
The only substantive treatment of the development of the
Society of American Archivists is J. Frank Cook, "The Blessings
of Providence on an Association of Archivists," *American
Archivist* 46 (Fall 1983), 374-99. There are also a number of
useful biographical studies of archival leaders appearing; typical
of this genre are Rodney A. Ross, "Waldo Gifford Leland:
Archivist by Association," *American Archivist* 46 (Summer
1983), 264-76, and Jane F. Smith, "Theodore R. Schellenberg:
Americanizer and Popularizer," *American Archivist* 44 (Fall
1981), 313-26.

The Re-Emergence of Archival Advocacy

A recognition of the need for a more aggressive advocacy on
behalf of the documentary heritage is another distinct
characteristic of recent trends in the archival profession. The
successful movement to gain independence for the National
Archives has been chronicled and evaluated by Page Putnam
Miller, "Archival Issues and Problems: The Central Role of
Advocacy," *Public Historian* 8 (Summer 1986), 60-73 and
Charlene N. Bickford, *The Coalition to Save Our Documentary
Heritage: An Important Lesson in Archival Advocacy* (n.p.,
1983). This effort has spawned a number of other proposals
for more strenuous advocacy, such as Larry J. Hackman, "The
United States Needs a National Historical Records Policy!"
History News 43 (March/April 1988), 32-37. There are a small
number of other more specific analyses of areas requiring
advocacy, including Alice Robbin, "State Archives and Issues of
Personal Privacy: Policies and Practices," *American Archivist* 49
(Spring 1986), 163-75; Roland M. Baumann, "The
Administration of Access to Confidential Records in State
Archives: Common Practices and the Need for a Model Law,"
American Archivist 49 (Fall 1986), 349-69; and James Gregory
Bradsher, "Privacy Act Expungements: A Reconsideration,"

Provenance 6 (Spring 1988), 1-25.

Archival Standards and Knowledge: The New Frontier

Standards and guidelines for archival institutions and programs are other examples of the new sense of archival professionalism that have emerged over the past decade. Most important in this regard has been the products of SAA's Task Force on Institutional Evaluation: *Evaluation of Archival Institutions: Services, Principles, and Guide to Self-Study* (Chicago, 1982); Paul Conway, "Perspectives on Archival Resources: The 1985 Census of Archival Institutions," *American Archivist* 50 (Spring 1987), 174-91; and Paul H. McCarthy, ed., *Archives Assessment and Planning Workbook* (Chicago, 1989). But other examples of this new interest also abound, including National Association of Government Archives and Records Administrators (NAGARA) brochures like *Policy Statement Regarding the Preservation and Disposition of the Official Records of Governors* (n.p., 1981) and *Principles of Management of Local Government Records* (n.p., 1982); *Program Reporting Guidelines for Government Records Programs* (n.p., n.d.); and [Richard J. Cox and Judy Hohmann], *Strengthening New York's Historical Records Programs: A Self-Study Guide* (Albany, 1988).

Driving the move to standardization have been a number of influences, not the least of which is interest in redefining the very essence of archival work and the values of archival records. Hugh Taylor, "The Collective Memory: Archives and Libraries as Heritage," *Archivaria* 15 (Winter 1982-83), 118-30 and Terry Cook, "From Information to Knowledge: An Intellectual Paradigm for Archives," *Archivaria* 19 (Winter 1984-85), 28-49 are outstanding examples of such thinking. Perhaps the most influential writings have been F. Gerald Ham's triptych of essays, "The Archival Edge," *American Archivist* 38 (January 1975), 5-13; "Archival Strategies for the Post-Custodial Era," *American Archivist* 44 (Summer 1981), 207-16; and "Archival Choices: Managing the Historical Record in an Age of Abundance," *American Archivist* 47 (Winter 1984), 11-22.

One of the most significant trends in the recent archival profession has been its re-awakened concern for archival knowledge, principles, and theory. The earliest concern was the archivists' supposed lack of interest in conducting research, as described by David Mycue, "The Archivist as Scholar: A Case for Research by Archivists," *Georgia Archive* 7 (Fall 1979), 10-16. The seminal writing in this area was Frank G. Burke's "The Future Course of Archival Theory in the United States,"

American Archivist 44 (Winter 1981), 40-46. Burke's essay has generated considerable response through the years, including Lester J. Cappon, "What, Then, Is There to Theorize About?" *American Archivist* 45 (Winter 1982), 19-25; Gregg D. Kimball, "The Burke-Cappon Debate: Some Further Criticisms and Considerations for Archival Theory," *American Archivist* 48 (Fall 1985), 369-76; and John W. Roberts, "Archival Theory: Much Ado About Shelving," *American Archivist* 50 (Winter 1987), 66-74. In addition to the essays that consider the nature or existence of archival theory, there have also been some efforts to define specific theoretical segments of archival principles and practice, such as James M. O'Toole, "On the Idea of Permanence," *American Archivist* 52 (Winter 1989), 10-25, although much more is needed to be done here. Affecting to some extent the development of archival knowledge have been inadequate mechanisms for access to the archival literature; see Victoria Irons Walch, *Information Resources for Archivists and Records Administrators: A Report and Recommendations* (Albany, 1987); Malvina B. Bechor, "Bibliographic Access to Archival Literature," *American Archivist* 50 (Spring 1987), 243-47; and David Moltke-Hansen, "Reflections on the Problems of Access to Archival Literature," *American Archivist* 47 (Summer 1984), 293-95.

The area of basic archival knowledge that has received the greatest attention in recent years has been appraisal. In the early part of the 1980s, the documentation of science and technology was the recipient of much of this attention, as seen in the work of the Joint Committee for the Archives of Science and Technology and subsequent efforts: Clark A. Elliott, ed., *Understanding Progress as Process: Documentation of the History of Post-War Science and Technology in the United States* (n.p., 1983) and Joan K. Haas, Helen W. Samuels, and Barbara Trippel Simmons, *Appraising the Records of Modern Science and Technology: A Guide* (Cambridge, 1985). Growing out of such efforts has come some suggestions for the reformulation of basic archival appraisal principles and practices, such as Helen W. Samuels, "Who Controls the Past," *American Archivist* 49 (Spring 1986), 109-24, and Larry J. Hackman and Joan Warnow-Blewett, "The Documentation Strategy Process: A Model and A Case Study," *American Archivist* 50 (Winter 1987), 12-47. Demonstrating that appraisal is the topic of such new attention is its treatment in a separate collection of essays, Nancy Peace, ed., *Archival Choices: Managing the Historical Record in An Age of Abundance* (Lexington, 1984) and a special issue (Spring 1985) of the *American Archivist*. Other important essays on archival appraisal include Leonard Rapport, "No Grandfather Clause:

Reappraising Accessioned Records," *American Archivist* 44 (Spring 1981), 143-50; Rapport, "In the Valley of Decision: What to Do About the Multitude of Files of Quasi Cases," *American Archivist* 48 (Spring 1985), 173-89; Michael A. Lutzker, "Max Weber and the Analysis of Modern Bureaucratic Organizations: Notes Toward a Theory of Appraisal," *American Archivist* 45 (Spring 1982), 119-30; Fredric Miller, "Documenting Modern Cities: The Philadelphia Model," *Public Historian* 5 (Spring 1983), 75-86; and David J. Klaassen, "Achieving Balanced Documentation: Social Services from a Consumer Perspective," *Midwestern Archivist* 11, no. 2 (1986), 111-24.

Other than appraisal, the issue of who uses, and how they use, archival materials is the concern that has captivated archivists in recent years. Paul Conway has led the way in this important topic, with two stimulating essays, "Facts and Frameworks: An Approach to Studying the Users of Archives," *American Archivist* 49 (Fall 1986), 393-407 and "Research in Presidential Libraries: A User Survey," *Midwestern Archivist* 11, no. 1 (1986), 35-56. The debates about who should use archives is captured well in Elsie T. Freeman, "In the Eye of the Beholder: Archives Administration from the User's Point of View," *American Archivist* 27 (Spring 1984), 111-23; William L. Joyce, "Archivists and Research Use," *American Archivist* 47 (Spring 1984), 124-33; Mary Jo Pugh, "The Illusion of Omniscience: Subject Access and the Reference Archivist," *American Archivist* 45 (Winter 1982), 33-44; Fredric Miller, "Use, Appraisal, and Research: A Case Study of Social History," *American Archivist* 49 (Fall 1986), 371-92; and Bruce W. Dearstyne, "What Is the Use of Archives? A Challenge for the Profession," *American Archivist* 50 (Winter 1987), 76-87.

Building for the Future: Archival Education and Training

The appropriate education and training of archivists has been a consistent topic in the archival literature for half a century. The most recent writings on this topic have represented a shift, however, from debates about placement to content. There are a number of important writings on this topic. Jacqueline Goggin, "'That We Shall Truly Deserve the Title of Profession': The Training and Education of Archivists, 1930-1960," *American Archivist* 47 (Summer 1984), 243-54 and Richard C. Berner, "Archival Education and Training in the United States, 1937 to Present," *Journal of Education for Librarianship* 22 (Summer/Fall 1981), 3-19 provide the best recent historical analysis of archival education. Terry Eastwood, "Nurturing Archival Education in the University,"

American Archivist 51 (Summer 1988), 228-52 is certainly the finest statement relative to the content of graduate archival education, setting forth what is likely to be the direction for American graduate programs for at least the next decade. Lawrence J. McCrank, in "Public Historians in the Information Profession: Problems in Education and Credentials," *Public Historian* 7 (Summer 1985), 7-22 and "Prospects for Integrating Historical and Information Studies in Archival Education," *American Archivist* 42 (October 1979), 443-55, has provided an interesting perspective on the integration of archival education into the education of other information professionals. Paul Conway, "Archival Education and the Need for Full-Time Faculty," *American Archivist* 51 (Summer 1988), 254-65 is an argument for a dramatic change from the archival profession's traditional reliance on adjunct, part-time faculty. There have been, as well, a few efforts to propose specific ways of teaching archival administration, including Francis X. Blouin, Jr., "The Relevance of the Case Method to Archival Education and Training," *American Archivist* 41 (January 1978), 37-44; Janice E. Ruth, "Educating the Reference Archivist," *American Archivist* 51 (Summer 1988), 266-76; Susan E. Davis, "Development of Managerial Training for Archivists," *American Archivist* 51 (Summer 1988), 278-85; and Lisa Weber, "Educating Archivists for Automation," *Library Trends* 36 (Winter 1988), 501-18.

Future Challenges: Electronic Information Technology and the Changing Information Professions

Perhaps no issue has caused greater concern than the increasing use of electronic information technology and its implications for the identification and preservation of the archival record. This issue has produced a wide variety of responses from archivists, including Richard M. Kesner, "Computers, Archival Administration, and the Challenges of the 1980s," *Georgia Archive* 9 (Fall 1981), 1-18; Kesner, "Automated Information Management: Is There a Role for the Archivist in the Office of the Future?" *Archivaria* 19 (Winter 1984/85), 162-72; Hugh Taylor, "Information Ecology and Archives of the 1980s," *Archivaria* 18 (Summer 1984), 25-37; John A. Vernon, "Technology's Effect on the Role of the Archivist," *Provenance* 3 (Spring 1985), 1-12; Trudy Huskamp Peterson, "Archival Principles and Records of the New Technology," *American Archivist* 47 (Fall 1984), 383-93; John C. Mallinson, "Preserving Machine-Readable Archival Records for the Millenia," *Archivaria* 22 (Summer 1986), 147-52, and Sue Gavrel's reply, 153-55. In addition to his two articles listed above, Kesner has

above, Kesner has written two important books that try to support archivists using and coping with the electronic information systems, *Automation for Archivists and Records Managers: Planning and Implementation Strategies* (Chicago, 1984) and *Information Systems: a Strategic Approach to Planning and Implementation* (Chicago, 1988). The quarterly newsletter produced by *Archives and Museum Informatics* is a good source for tracking relevant studies and publications in this area.

The relationships between the archival profession and historical and information professions has continued to be a major topic of concern in the past decade. George Bolotenko's testy "Archivists and Historians: Keepers of the Well," *Archivaria* 16 (Summer 1983), 5-25, resulted in a number of equally agitated responses in the pages of volumes 17 through 20 of this Canadian journal. Whether this essay and its responses improved anything in the profession is a matter of debate, but these articles have not been alone in testing these waters. David A. Clary, "Trouble is My Business: A Private View of 'Public' History," *American Archivist* 44 (Spring 1981), 105-12, took on the public history movement, which was also the subject of a collection of essays in Bruce W. Dearstyne, ed., "Archives and Public History: Issues, Problems, and Prospects," *Public Historian* 8 (Summer 1986), 6-98. Mattie U. Russell, "The Influence of Historians on the Archival Profession in the United States," *American Archivist* 46 (Summer 1983), 277-85, made a strong case for the continuing association of the historical and archival professions. The books - Robert L. Clark, Jr., *Archive-Library Relations* (New York, 1976) and Lawrence J. McCrank, ed., *Archives and Library Administration: Divergent Traditions and Common Concerns* (New York, 1986) - on the similarities and differences between the library and archives fields are also books worth examining.

While there have been a number of essays exploring the relationship between archives administration and records management over the past two decades, the best manner of approaching this issue is through the nature of local government records programs. Local government archival records are one aspect of the records world that have continued to challenge the archival community. Although there has been substantial progress in specific states and localities, the overall care and condition of local government records seems not to have exhibited significant improvement. Some essays and volumes worth reading are H. G. Jones, *Local Government Records: An Introduction to Their Management, Preservation, and Use* (Nashville, 1980); Bruce W. Dearstyne, *The Management of Local Government Records: A Guide for Local*

North Carolina's Local Records Program at Age Twenty-five,"
American Archivist 49 (Winter 1986), 41-51; Richard J. Cox,
"The Need for Comprehensive Records Programs in Local
Governments: Learning by Mistakes in Baltimore, 1947-1982,"
Provenance 1 (Fall 1983), 14-34; John Daly, "State Archives and
Metropolitan Records: The Case of Chicago," *American Archivist*
51 (Fall 1988), 470-74; and Robert W. Arnold, III, "The Albany
Answer: Pragmatic and Tactical Considerations in Local
Records Legislative Efforts," *American Archivist* 51 (Fall 1988),
475-79. Indicative of renewed state efforts to improve the
management of local public records is the report, *The Quiet
Revolution: Managing New York's Local Government Records
in the Information Age* (Albany, December 1, 1987).

*Archives and the Future: Cooperative Ventures and Archival
Advocacy*

For generations the work of the archivist has been defined
largely by his or her institutional parameters. This outlook
has minimized the possibility of cooperation, but cooperation
has nevertheless emerged in the past decade as a major issue.
Frank G. Burke's "Archival Cooperation," *American Archivist* 46
(Summer 1983), 293-305, remains the fullest treatment of this
topic and the best starting point for further reading. Other
important writings on archival cooperation are John A.
Fleckner, "Cooperation as a Strategy for Archival Institutions,"
American Archivist 39 (October 1976), 447-59; Avra Michelson,
"Description and Reference in the Age of Automation,"
American Archivist 50 (Spring 1987), 192-208; Max J. Evans,
"The Visible Hand: Creating a Practical Mechanism for
Cooperative Appraisal," *Midwestern Archivist* 11, no. 1 (1986),
7-13; and Margaret S. Child, "Reflections on Cooperation
Among Professions," *American Archivist* 46 (Summer 1983),
286-92. The essays by Michelson and Evans stress the need
for cooperation in developing a national data base of archival
holdings, while the other essays are broader in scope. Also
important for an understanding of concepts of archival
cooperation is the special issue of the *Midwestern Archivist* 6,
no. 2 (1982), 91-240, on archival networks, the earliest effort at
multi-institutional cooperation in the archival profession. There
also needs to be some effort to assess how the many regional,
state, and local archival associations relate to the national
groups and what kinds of cooperation they can stimulate. The
only effort to look at this area is Patrick M. Quinn, "Regional
Archival Organizations and the Society of American Archivists,"
American Archivist 46 (Fall 1983), 433-40.

Archivists have also become extremely concerned about their

image both within and without their institutions, understanding that this image affects their support for and success in meeting their mission. David B. Gracy, II, has been the foremost proponent of transforming the archival image, writing a series of interesting essays including "Our Future Is Now," *American Archivist* 48 (Winter 1985), 12-21, and "What's Your Totem? Archival Images in the Public Mind," *Midwestern Archivist* 10, no. 1 (1985), 17-23. Under Gracy's SAA presidency, that association produced the first systematic analysis of the archival image, Sidney J. Levy and Albert G. Robles, *The Image of Archivists: Resource Allocators' Perceptions* (Chicago, 1984). Perhaps partly tied to this interest in image is the archival community's recent adoption of an individual certification program. Only one major essay has thus far appeared on this topic, and it has a skeptical outlook; see William J. Maher, "Contexts for Understanding Certification: Opening Pandora's Box?" *American Archivist* 51 (Fall 1988), 408-27.

One topic relating to the archival profession's advocacy and image deserving fuller attention is the activity and impact of the federal funding agencies, such as the National Historical Publications and Records Commission and the National Endowment for the Humanities, on archival practice. There have been some friendly, cursory efforts to do this, such as in Jeffrey Field, "The Impact of Federal Funding on Archival Management in the United States," *Midwestern Archivist* 7, no. 2 (1982), 77-86; Larry J. Hackman, "The Historical Records Program: The States and the Nation," *American Archivist* 43 (Winter 1980), 17-32; and F. Gerald Ham, "NHPRC's Records Program and the Development of Statewide Archival Planning," *American Archivist* 43 (Winter 1980), 33-42. What is needed are objective studies measuring the impact of such funding on archival administration completed by individuals outside of the archival profession with no vested interest in this community.

Further stimulating the development of archival standards, cooperation, and the general archival profession has been the adoption of the US MARC Archives and Manuscripts Control Format for description. Writings on the origins, uses, and implications of this format include Richard Lytle, "An Analysis of the Work of the National Information Systems Task Force," *American Archivist* 47 (Fall 1984), 357-65; David Bearman, *Toward National Information Systems for Archives and Manuscripts Repositories: The National Information Systems Task Force* (Chicago, 1987); and Nancy Sahli, "National Information Systems and Strategies for Research Use," *Midwestern Archivist* 9, no. 1 (1984), 5-13.

INDEX

ACADEMIC libraries, *see* Libraries

Access, Archival, *see* Archives

Accreditation, Archival, *see* Archivists

Adams, Herbert Baxter, 69, 204

Adams, Thomas R., 266*ff.*, 275*ff.*

Advocacy, Archival, *see* Archivists

Alabama, *x*, 189*ff.*

Alabama Department of Archives and History, 189*ff.*

Albany, New York, 337

Aldredge, Everett, 146

Almagno, R. Stephen, *xvi*

American Archivist, xi, xiii, 65, 139*ff.*, 168*ff.*, 172*ff.*, 178, 205, 265*ff.*, 317

American Association for State and Local History, 4, 6, 8, 33, 35*ff.*, 44, 58, 68, 70, 75*ff.*, 90*ff.*, 161, 211

American Bar Association, 30, 34

American Council of Learned Societies, 4

American Historical Association, 18, 22, 70, 83*ff.*, 318

American Institute of Physics, 297*ff.*

American Library Association, *xiii,* 39, 103, 127, 149, 161, 183, 311

    Committee on Accreditation, 153*ff.*

    Library History Round Table, 198

American Medical Association, 30, 34

American State Archives, 53*ff.*, 71

Ames, Herman V., 84

Analytical bibliography, 261*ff.*

Andrew Mellon Foundation, 4, 13, 92, 126*ff.*, 178, 199

Anglo-American Cataloguing Rules, 271

Anthropologists, 301

Applied history, *see* Public history

Appraisal, Archival, *see* Archives, Documentation strategies

Archivaria, 65, 174

Archive-Library Relations, 221

Archives, xii

Archives

access, 311, 319*ff.*

accreditation, *xi,* 35

administration, 109*ff.*, 330

ancient world, 3

appraisal, *xiii,* 41*ff.*, 73*ff.*, 107*ff.*, 212*ff.*, 227*ff.*, 240*ff.*, 243*ff.*, 251*ff.*, 263*ff.*, 276, 285*ff.*, 291*ff.*, 319*ff.*, 330, 333*ff.*

arrangement and description, 108*ff.*, 232*ff.*, 270*ff.*, 331

automated systems, 236*ff.*

business, 173, 211

cartographic, 280

colleges and universities, 296

colonial America, 3

cooperation, 20, 227*ff.*, 337*ff.*

federal government, 7, 14, 210*ff.*, 213, 312

history, 110, 182*ff.*, 330*ff.*

institutional evaluation and planning, 188*ff.*, 199*ff.*, 330

literary, 286

local government, *xii,* 5, 47, 69*ff.*, 167, 312, 336*ff.*

medieval Europe, 3

municipal, 76*ff.*, 312

national planning, 4*ff.*, 23*ff.*, 53*ff.*, 74*ff.*, 164, 187

Native American, 173

preservation *xiii,* 2*ff.*, 14*ff.*, 17*ff.*, 75, 106, 109, 243*ff.*, 281*ff.*, 301*ff.*

privacy issues, 307, 319*ff.*,331

publishers', 285*ff.*

reference, 108*ff.*

religious, 298*ff.*

Renaissance, 3

standards, *xi,* 10, 19, 41, 187, 326, 332*ff.*

state government, 5, 15, 65, 135, 170, 190*ff.*, 213, 221, 226*ff.*, 245, 282, 307, 312,

329, 331
state planning, 4*ff.*, 62*ff.*, 338
use, 210, 257, 330, 334
value of, 2, 43, 207*ff.*, 229,
    252*ff.*, 281, 287
see also Canada, Clay tablets,
Committee on the Records of
Government, Diplomatics,
Electronic records, Historical
societies, National Archives,
Presidential libraries
Archives Research Information
Center, 162
Archivists, 7*ff.*
advocacy, 187, 211, 219,
    304*ff.*, 320*ff.*, 331*ff.*,
    337*ff.*
altruism, 35*ff.*
certification, *xi*, 16, 19, 36,
    46*ff.*, 99, 103*ff.*, 110,
    114, 119, 122, 125,
    186*ff.*, 338
competencies, 125
continuing education, 138*ff.*
culture, 34*ff.*
education, *xi, xii,* 10*ff.*, 31,
    45*ff.*, 59*ff.*, 73, 98*ff.*,
    113*ff.*, 176*ff.*, 180,
    185, 187*ff.*, 192*ff.*,
    198*ff.*, 215*ff.*, 220,
    240, 260, 288*ff.*,
    326*ff.*, 334*ff.*
employers, 134*ff.*
history, 182*ff.*
image, 23*ff.*, 32*ff.*, 36, 42, 51,
    102, 176, 179*ff.*, 186,
    206*ff.*, 304*ff.*, 337*ff.*
in-service training, 138*ff.*
leadership, *xii,* 72*ff.*, 90*ff.*,
    176, 178*ff.*
organization, 33*ff.*
power, 37, 51*ff.*, 206
practicum, 105, 127*ff.*, 129,
    192, 326*ff.*
professionals, *xi,* 30*ff.*, 55,
    206, 274*ff.*, 330
publications, 65*ff.*, 122*ff.*,
    159, 164*ff.*, 333
recruitment, 104, 130*ff.*
regional associations, 63*ff.*
research, *xii,* 10 *ff.*, 105*ff.*,
    122*ff.*, 177*ff.*, 195*ff.*,
    217*ff.*, 327
specialization, 146*ff.*
theory, 11*ff.*, 30*ff.*, 60, 101,
    105*ff.* 122*ff.*, 125*ff.*, 129*ff.*,

176*ff.*, 193*ff.*, 212, 217,
220, 221, 267, 332*ff.*
    see also Archives,
    Canada, International
    Council on Archives,
    National Association of
    Government Archives and
    Records Administrators,
    National Historical
    Publications and Records
    Commission, Society of
    American Archivists, US
    MARC Archives and
    Manuscripts Control
    Format
Arkansas, 84
Arnold, Robert W., III, 337
Arrangement and description, *see*
    Archives
Arts, *see* museums
Assessment reports, 4*ff.*, 44, 54,
    70, 76, 94*ff.*, 189, 328*ff.*
Association des archivistes du
    Quebec, *xii*
Association of Records Managers
    and Administrators, 33,
    44, 58, 70, 91
Athens, Georgia, 84
Atkinson, Ross, 250, 256, 266
Augusta, Georgia, 84
Autograph collectors, 14

BABYLONIANS, 273
Baker, David, 149
Baltimore,*viii,* 82*ff.*
Bardwick, Judith, 49
Basic Manual Series, 173
    see also Society of
    American Archivists
Baumann, Roland M., 331
Bearman, David, *xiv,* 329, 338
Bearman, Toni Carbo, *xiv,* 308
Belchor, Malvina B., 333
Bell, Lionel, 147*ff.*
Bemis, Samuel Flagg, 146
Bennett, William, 17, 21
Bentley Historical Library, *x, xii,*
    13, 178, 199, 217, 327
Berger, Sidney, 275
Berner, Richard, 12, 119, 139,
    155, 330*ff.*, 334
Bickford, Charlene N., 331
Bierbaum, Esther Green, 142
Bill of Rights, 309
Binberg, Herbert R., 275
Bishop, Christine, *xiv*

Blegen, Theodore C., 22, 167
Blouin, Francis, 121*ff.*, 270, 335
Boissonnas, Christian, 38
Bolotenko, George, 336
Booms, Hans, 263
Boorstin, Daniel, 17, 287
Borko, Harold, 308, 310
Boston, 81*ff.*
Bowers, Fredson, 283, 289
Bradsher, James Gregory, 331
Bridges, Ed, *xiv*
Brittle books, 244
Brooklyn, New York, 84
Brooks, Philip C., 169
Buchen, Philip W., 7
Buck, Solon, 121
Buckley Amendment, 307
Bureau of Labor Statistics, 132
Burke, Frank, 11*ff.*, 51, 126,
    129, 176*ff.*, 193*ff.*, 217,
    332*ff.*, 337
Business archives, *see* Archives

CALIFANO, Joseph A., 7
California, 95, 131
Canada,
    archival education, 113*ff.*,
        126, 288
    archival planning, 329
    library education, 143*ff.*, 159
Cantelon, Philip, 210
Cappon, Lester J., 172, 333
Carter, John, 264
Cartographic archives, *see*
    Archives
Certification, *see* Archivists
Chartrand, Robert Lee, 309
Cheney, Lynne V., 17
Chicago, 81*ff.*, 337
Child, Margaret, 239, 337
Christianson, Elin B., 148
Civil War, *viii*
Clark, Robert, 221, 336
Clary, David A., 205, 336
Clay tablets, 3, 273
Cleveland, 81
Coalition for the Preservation of
    Architectural Records, 57
Collection development and
    management, *see* Librarians
College and university archives,
    see Archives
Colson, John C., 269
Commager, Henry Steele, 1
Commission on Freedom and
    Equality of Access, 311, 319

Committee on the Records of
    Government, 4, 7, 13, 58,
    318, 321, 329
Competencies, *see* Librarians
Conant Report, 39, 125
Conference of Archivists, 22, 158
Conference on Setting Priorities
    for Historical Records, 54,
    330
Conway, Paul, *xiv*, 332, 334, 335
Conzen, Kathleen Neils, 69
Cook, J. Frank, 331
Cook, Terry, 332
Cooperation, archival, *see*
    Archives
Copyright, 317
Corporate culture, 49*ff.*
Council on Library Resources, 4,
    247
Cox, Lynn, *xiii*, *xiv*
Craft of Public History, 203*ff.*
Critical bibliography, *see*
    Analytical bibliography

DALLAS, 81
Daly, John, 337
Danisiewicz, Thomas J., 37
Davis, Susan E., 335
Deal, Terrence, 49*ff.*
Dearstyne, Bruce, *xi*, *xii*, 76,
    334, 336
Detlefsen, Ellen Gay, *xiv*
Detroit, 81
de Valinger, Leon, 85*ff.*
Diplomatics, 279*ff.*
*Directory of Archives and
    Manuscripts Repositories
    in the United States*, 86
Divinity, 28
Documentation strategies, 20,
    107*ff.*, 214*ff.*, 228, 230*ff.*,
    254*ff.*, 287, 293*ff.*, 333
    See also Archives
Documenting America, *xii*, 5*ff.*,
    328
Dowler, Larry, 330
Duncan, Grace, *xiv*

EASTWOOD, Terry, 45, 122,
    126, 329, 334*ff.*
Education, Archival, *see*
    Archivists
Eisenstein, Elizabeth, 270
Electronic records, 14, 245, 323,
    335
Elliott, Clark A., 333

Ericson, Tim, *xiv*
Ethnographers, 303
Etzioni, Amitai, 37
Europe, 139, 147, 167*ff.*, 198*ff.*, 269
Evaluation of Archival Institutions, 199*ff.*
Evangelical Archives Conference, 298*ff.*
Evans, Frank B., 216*ff.*, 314*ff.*
Evans, Max J., 179, 238, 337

FAMILY Educational and Privacy Rights Act, 307
Federal archives, *see* Archives
Federal Bureau of Investigation, 296, 320
Federal Records Act, 320
Field, Jeffrey, 338
Fleckner, John A., 337
Flexner, Abraham, 25*ff.*
Florida, 142, 282, 308, 315
Floyd County, Georgia, 96
Folklore, 288, 303
Forgeries, 281
Forsyth, Patrick B., 37
Fort Worth, Texas, 81
Freedom of Information Act, 311*ff.*
Freeman, Elsie T., 334
Fry, Bernard, 233*ff.*

GASKELL, Philip, 286, 289
Gavrel, Sue, 335
Geary, James, 155
General Services Administration, 138, 186, 321, 323
George, Gerald, 8
Georgia, 96
Goggin, Jacqueline, 188, 334
Gondos, Victor, Jr., 331
Gould, Donald P., 149*ff.*
Government Printing Office, 223, 225*ff.*
Government publications, *xiii*, 221*ff.*, 270
Gracy, David B., 9*ff.*, 23, 102, 179, 209, 306, 326, 338
Great Britain, 143, 216, 277*ff.*
Green, Constance McLaughlin, 69
Griffith, Ernest S., 89

HAAS, Joan K., 333
Haas, Warren J., 248
Hackman, Larry J., *xiv*, 256, 318, 322*ff.*, 328*ff.*, 330, 331, 333, 338
Ham, F. Gerald, 231, 332, 338
Hawkings, Stephen, *vii*
Hazen, Dan, 250
Health care, 312*ff.*
Hedlin, Edie, 328
Heim, Kathleen M., 324
Helmuth, Ruth, 126
Hernon, Peter, 128
Historians, 1*ff.*, 9, 69, 215
    relationship with archivists, 11*ff.*, 14, 33, 99*ff.*, 102, 107*ff.*, 151*ff.*, 158, 166, 172, 174, 196*ff.*, 201, 221, 300*ff.*, 318, 336
    urban research, 87*ff.*
    see also American Historical Association, Local history, Organization of American Historians, Public history
Historical editing, 203, 218, 276*ff.*, 283*ff.*
Historical records, *see* archives
Historical Records Survey, 70*ff.*, 85, 169, 331
Historical societies, 6, 8*ff.*, 87*ff.*, 154, 168, 170*ff.*, 182*ff.*, 203, 302*ff.*, 312
Historical Society of Pennsylvania, 84
Historic preservation, 218
Hitler, Adolf, 281
Hogan, Patricia, 329
Holmes, Oliver Wendell, 169
Honolulu, 81
Horton, Forest Woody, Jr., 310, 323
Houston, Texas, 81
Hunter, Gregory S., 330
IMAGE, archival, *see* Archivists
Indianapolis, Indiana, 81
Indiana University School of Library and Information Science, 130
Information, 40, 244
Information Age, 188, 197
Information policies, *xiv*, 13, 18, 43, 304*ff.*
Information professions, 106, 205
Information resource management, 106
Information science, 41, 218
Information technology, 2, 7, 214, 270, 272*ff.*, 304*ff.*,

313*ff.*, 326, 335
International City Management
　　Association, 80, 91
International Council on
　　Archives, 198
International Institute of
　　Municipal Clerks, 80, 91, 93
International Standard
　　Bibliographic Description,
　　271
Iran-Contra affair, 320

JAMESON, J. Franklin, 89, 221,
　　331
Johnson, G. Wesley, Jr., 202*ff.*
Joint Committee on the Archives
　　of Science and Technology,
　　57, 217, 333
Joint Committee on the
　　Management, Preservation,
　　and Use of Local
　　Government Records, 75*ff.*,
　　90*ff.*
Jones, H. G., 87, 90, 110*ff.*, 154,
　　170*ff.*, 316, 329, 336*ff.*
*Journal of Library
　　Administration*, *xiii*, *xiv*, 174
*Journal of the American Society
　　for Information Science*,
　　xiv
Joyce, William L., 334

KAMMEN, Michael, 9
Kansas, 142
Kennedy, Allen, 49*ff.*
Kentucky, 96
Kesner, Richard, 313, 335*ff.*
Kimball, Gregg D., 333
Kimmel, Margaret Mary, *xiv*
King Report, 123, 125
Klaassen, David J., 334
Knowledge, professional, 26, 30*ff.*
Koenig, Michael, 137
Kyvig, David E., 204

LAW, 28*ff.*, 32
Leland, Waldo G., 22, 158,
　　167*ff.*, 331
Lerner, Gerda, 1
Levy, Sidney J., 338
Librarians
　　collection development and
　　　　management, 227*ff.*,
　　　　248*ff.*, 254, 300*ff.*
　　competencies, 123*ff.*, 149*ff.*
　　continuing education, 140*ff.*

education, 39, 115*ff.*,
　　273*ff.*
employers, 136*ff.*
faculty, 156*ff.*
image, 39
in-service training, 140*ff.*
knowledge, 123*ff.*
paraprofessionals, 150
personality traits, 133*ff.*
practice vs. theory, 127*ff.*,
　　141*ff.*
preservation, 243*ff.*, 301*ff.*
profession, 37*ff.*, 274*ff.*
recruitment, 130*ff.*
relationship with
　　archivists, *xiii*,
　　11*ff.*, 33, 41,
　　102*ff.*, 107*ff.*,
　　151*ff.*, 158, 174,
　　201, 203, 217,
　　221*ff.*, 243*ff.*,
　　261*ff.*, 300*ff.*, 336
subject specializations,
　　148*ff.*
See also American
Library Association,
Analytical bibliography,
Anglo-American
Cataloguing Rules, Brittle
books, Conant Report,
Council on Library
Resources, Information
professions, Information
science, Rare books.
Libraries
　　academic, 144
　　history of, 182
　　public, 142, 154
　　rural, 142
Libraries & Culture, *xiii*, *xiv*
*Library Education and Personnel
　　Utilization*, 149*ff.*
Library of Congress, 111
Literary archives, *see* Archives
Livingston, Marcy, *xiv*
Local government archives, *see*
　　Archives
Local Government Records, 87
Local history, 69*ff.*, 224
Long Island, 84
Los Angeles, 81
Louisiana, 331
Lowell, Howard P., 329
Lutzker, Michael A., 334
Lytle, Richard, 338

McALLISTER, Desretta V., 138
McCarthy, Paul, 147, 330, 332
McCoy, Donald, 331
McCrank, Lawrence, 148, 205,
    273*ff.*, 335, 336
McCree, Mary Lynn, 330
Machine-readable records, *see*
    electronic records
Maher, William J., 338
Mallinson, John C., 335
Maryland Historical Society, *viii*
Mason, Philip P., 329
Massachusetts, 143
Massachusetts Institute of
    Technology, 296
Medicine, 28*ff.*, 32
Megatrends, 1
Memphis, 81
Metzger, Philip A., 160
Michelson, Avra, *xiv*, 337
Middle East, 269
Midwest Archives Conference,
    xiv, *xvii*
Midwestern Archivist, *xii*, *xiv*, 65,
    174
Miller, Fredric, 334
Miller, Page Putnam, 331
Minnesota, 95
Mississippi, 95
Modern Archives, 61
Modern Archives Institute, 118
Moltke-Hansen, David, 333
Monasteries, 3
Morison, Samuel Eliot, 17
Morton, Sandy, 310*ff.*
Munby, A. N. L., 278
Municipal archives, *see* Archives
Munro, William B., 79
Museums, 6, 108, 142, 154, 203,
    218, 245*ff.*, 288, 301*ff.*
Mycue, David, 332

NATIONAL Academy of Public
    Administration, 323
National Archives, 4, 14, 16, 18,
    22, 33, 44, 60*ff.*, 65, 89*ff.*,
    111, 118, 138*ff.*, 145, 162,
    168*ff.*, 175, 185*ff.*, 202, 211,
    221, 235, 239*ff.*, 252, 296,
    307, 315*ff.*, 319*ff.*, 321,
    323*ff.*, 327, 331
National Association of County
    Recorders and Clerks, 91
National Association of
    Government Archives and
    Records Administrators, 4*ff.*,

33, 35, 44, 58, 70, 75, 91,
    94, 104, 161, 175*ff.*,
    178*ff.*, 219*ff.*, 325, 332
National Association of State
    Archives and Records
    Administrators, *see*
    National Association of
    Government Archives and
    Records Administrators
National Center for State Courts,
    91
National Conservation Advisory
    Council, 247
National Coordinating Committee
    for the Promotion of
    History, 18
National Council on Public
    History, 161, 203*ff.*, 211,
    219*ff.*
National Endowment for the
    Humanities, 17, 178, 199,
    338
National Historical Publications
    and Records Commission,
    x, 4*ff.*, 17, 44, 55, 62*ff.*,
    67, 70, 75*ff.*, 86*ff.*, 90*ff.*,
    126*ff.*, 173, 175, 178, 189,
    241, 322, 328, 338
National Information Center for
    Local Government
    Records, 92*ff.*
National Information Systems
    Task Force, 57, 237, 338
National Institute of Standards
    and Technology, 323
National Library Week, 39
National Telecommunications
    and Information
    Administration, 319
Native American archives, *see*
    Archives
Nelson, Anna, 13
New England, 82
Newsome, A. R., 22
New York, 96, 298, 321*ff.*, 329,
    332, 337
New York City, 82*ff.*, 84
New York State Archives, 195
New York State Historical
    Records Advisory Board,
    2
Noggle, Burl, 331
Norton, Margaret C., 167

OFFICE of Management and
    Budget, 311, 315, 323

Oral history, 203, 288, 303
Organization of American
    Historians, *xi*, 1
O'Toole, James M., *xiv*, 281, 333
Owen, Thomas, 190

*PAPERS of the Bibliographical
    Society of America*, 289
Paperwork Reduction Act, 311,
    315
Paris, Marion, 137
Peace, Nancy, 333
Peterson, Trudy Huskamp, 46,
    335
Philadelphia, 82*ff.*, 84, 334
Phillips, Charles, 329
Phillips, U. B., 84
Phoenix, Arizona, 81
Physics, 297
Pittsburgh, 81
Planning, archival, *see* Archives
*Planning for the Archival
    Profession*, 7*ff.*, 55, 329
Plateauing Trap, 49
Posner, Ernst, 53*ff.*, 71, 85, 139,
    170*ff.*, 329
Practicum, archival, *see*
    Archivists
Preservation, *see* Archives
Presidential Libraries, 297, 312
Privacy Act, 311
Professionalism, 10, 16, 22*ff.*
    sociological models, 25*ff.*
Professions
    altruism, 27
    cohesion, 26
    community sanction, 26, 28
    culture, 27
    deprofessionalization, 42*ff.*
    education, 184
    formation, 27*ff.*, 36
    history, 183*ff.*
    knowledge, 26, 215*ff.*
    power, 28, 37, 184
    see also archivists, divinity,
        law, librarians, medicine,
Prologue, 174
Provenance, *xii*, *xiv*, 65, 174
Ptolemy, *vii*
Public administration, 218
Public Archives Commission, 70,
    83*ff.*, 167
Public Historian, *xii*, *xiii*, *xiv*,
    174, 202*ff.*, 210
Public history, *xiii*, 11, 13*ff.*, 111,
    154, 158, 191, 201*ff.*, 318,
335, 336
    see also National Council
        on Public History
Public libraries, *see* Libraries
Publishers' archives, *see* Archives
Pugh, Mary Jo, 334

QUINN, Patrick M., 337

RAPPORT, Leonard, 333*ff.*
Rare books, 261*ff.*
Rare Books and Manuscripts,
    xiii, 289
Rare Books and Manuscripts
    Section, Association of
    College and Research
    Libraries, 289
Record group, 235, 238, 281
Records management, 7, 146*ff.*,
    203, 205, 215, 218, 238*ff.*,
    321, 336
    municipal, 77*ff.*
    relations with archivists,
        13, 33, 41, 74*ff.*,
        102, 213
    see also Association of
        Records Managers and
        Administrators,
        Information resource
        management
Reference, archival, *see* Archives
Religious archives, *see* Archives
Renaissance, 276
Replevin, 14, 278
Reprint collections, 287
Research, professional, 26
    see also Archivists
Research Libraries Group, 241
    Conspectus program, 249,
        258
    Cooperative Preservation
        Microfilming Project,
        248*ff.*
Reston, James, 21
Richardson, Elliot, 7
Richardson, John, 128
Robbin, Alice, 307, 331
Roberts, John W., 333
Robles, Albert G., 338
Rockefeller Report, 308, 317
Rome, Georgia, 96
Ross, Rodney A., 331
Ruddell, Richard, 85
Rundell, Walter, *ix*, 170
Rural libraries, *see* Libraries
Russell, Mattie U., 336

Ruth, Janice E., 335

SAGAN, Carl, *vii*
Sahli, Nancy, 338
St. Augustine, 84
Samuels, Helen, 256, 330, 333
San Antonio, Texas, 81
San Diego, California, 81
Sanford, Corinne, *xiv*
San Francisco, California, 81
Schellenberg, T. R., 60*ff.*, 166,
    169, 229, 235, 252*ff.*, 331
Schlesinger, Arthur M., 88
Schulz, Constance, 135
Scriptoriums, 3
Sellberg, Roxanne, 137
Shera, Jesse, 182
Shi, David E., 9
Simmons, Barbara Trippel, 333
Smith, Jane F., 331
Social Science Research Council,
    4
Society of American Archivists,
    ix, *xiii*, *xiv*, 4, 7*ff.*, 22*ff.*, 31,
    33, 35, 44, 70, 117*ff.*, 146,
    165, 183, 185, 194*ff.*, 201*ff.*,
    209, 211, 219*ff.*, 229, 264*ff.*,
    316, 325, 331
    Archival History Round
        Table, 197*ff.*
    Archives and Society Task
        Force, 24, 43, 102,
        209
    Committee for the Seventies,
        53*ff.*, 102*ff.*, 165, 172,
        329
    Committee on Education and
    Professional Development, *x*,
        101, 122, 219
    Committee on Goals and
        Priorities, 18, 23*ff.*,
        57*ff.*, 70, 94, 161,
        219, 305*ff.*
    Committee on Public
        Relations, 305
    education, 98*ff.*, 122, 140*ff.*,
        145, 152, 156, 161,
        192, 288
    Goals and Priorities Task
        Force, *x*, *xii*, 53*ff.*,
        177*ff.*, 200, 209, 330
    membership, 10, 329
    municipal records, 85*ff.*, 91
    publications program, 168*ff.*,
        178*ff.*
    Task Force on Institutional

Evaluation, 199*ff.*, 332
    see also Joint Committee
        on the Archives of
        Science and Technology,
        Joint Committee on the
        Management,
        Preservation, and Use of
        Local Government
        Records, National
        Information Systems
        Task Force
Society of Georgia Archivists, *xii*,
    xiv
Special Libraries Association,
    325
Standards, archival, see Archives
    State government
        archives, see Archives
State Historical Records Advisory
        Boards, 62*ff.*, 66*ff.*
    New York, 63
State University of New York at
        Albany, 177
Stewart, Virginia, 51, 328
Stokes, Roy, 289
Studies in Bibliography, 289
Susman, Warren I., 52
Syracuse, New York, 84
Szladits, Lola L., 277

TANSELLE, G. Thomas, 266,
    276*ff.*, 280, 283*ff.*
Taylor, Hugh, 332, 335
Technology, see Information
        technology
Theory, professional, 26
    see also archivists,
        librarians
Toffler, Alvin, 1
Trevor, Karl, 130
Trust for Our Documentary
        Heritage, 17*ff.*
Turner, Frederick Jackson, 88

UNESCO, 158
U. S. Department of Commerce,
    319
US MARC Archives and
Manuscripts Control Format,
    237*ff.*, 241, 258, 271, 338
University of British Columbia,
    45, 177, 180, 192
University of Maryland, *ix*, 180
University of Michigan, see
        Bentley Historical Library
University of Pittsburgh, *xiii*,

xiv, 177
University of Sheffield, 152
University of Texas, 177

VAN House, Nancy, 131*ff.*
Vernon, John A., 335

WALCH, Timothy, 330, 331
Walch, Victoria Irons, 333
Warner, Robert, 178, 216*ff.*
Warner, Sam Bass, 79, 89
Warnow-Blewett, Joan, 256, 333
Washington, D. C., *xiv*
Weber, Lisa, *xiii*, 335
Weber, Max, 334
Weldon, Edward, 205
Western Washington University, 192
White, Herbert S., 127, 137
Whitehill, Walter Muir, 170*ff.*
Williams, Lisa, 250
Williamsburg, Virginia, *ix*
Williamson Report, 127
Woodward, David, 280
Wosh, Peter J., 330
Wright, Louis B., 273

YALE University, 247*ff.*
Young, Julia Marks, *xiv*

ZINN, Howard, 40